D1171205

THE KING'S GREAT MATTER

The King's Great Matter

A Study of Anglo-Papal Relations 1527-1534

Geoffrey de C. Parmiter

He does not die that can bequeath
Some influence to the land he knows.
Belloc, Duncton Hill.

Al Rey la hacienda y la vida
se ha de dar; pero el honor
es patrimonio del alma,
y el alma sólo es de Dios.
Calderón, El Alcalde de Zalamea, i, 18.

LONGMANS

LONGMANS, GREEN AND CO LTD
48 Grosvenor Street, London W.1.
*Associated companies branches and representatives
throughout the world*

*Printed in Great Britain
by T and A Constable Ltd, Hopetoun Street
Printers to the University of Edinburgh*

FILIAE CARISSIMAE SUAE
ANN
IAM FILIAE QUOQUE
SANCTI AUGUSTINI
HOC OPUS
AUCTOR

CONTENTS

PREFACE

It may be thought that the publication of yet another book about Henry VIII requires some explanation, or even apology; but in view of the perennial and widespread interest in the Tudors, I do not propose to do either. The present volume is concerned only with the so-called 'divorce' of Henry VIII from his first wife, Catherine of Aragon. This, it is true, is a well worn theme, but in studying the matter afresh I have tried to bring to this complex and difficult subject a greater clarity of exposition than it has yet received.

The events with which this study is concerned were of crucial importance to England and Englishmen. The tortuous manoeuvres of Henry VIII to obtain the annulment of his marriage to Catherine of Aragon produced a set of circumstances that ensnared men of the greatest eminence, such as Thomas More and John Fisher, and brought them to their deaths; and it was those circumstances that provided the foundation for several modern institutions. It was in the early sixteenth century that modern England first began to emerge, and it is this characteristic that furnishes the Tudors with their undying interest for present day Englishmen. The fall of Wolsey marked the end of an age imbued with medieval thought; new and pregnant ideas appeared with the emergence of Thomas Cromwell, and for good or ill those ideas controlled the early shaping of the England that we know today. Although Cromwell eventually suffered the fate of those whom his early legislation had brought to the scaffold, the work that he did had an influence which long outlived him. I do not, therefore, need to apologize for another study of a subject that must always retain its interest.

In the course of this book I have quoted frequently and extensively from contemporary documents, and in doing so I have adopted a compromise. When quotations occur in the text I have modernized the spelling and punctuation. I have done this partly for the convenience of the reader, as it is disconcerting to come suddenly upon a passage with antique spelling, and partly for the sake of uniformity, as not all the quotations are from English documents; some are translated from Latin, French, Italian or Spanish originals. But when a quotation occurs in a footnote I have, in many cases, reproduced the original form of the document quoted; this, I hope, will do something to preserve a little of the flavour of the original.

Preface

I have not thought that any useful purpose would be served by including a bibliography, since reference can easily be made to such works as Conyers Read, *Bibliography of British History; Tudor Period 1485-1603* (Oxford, second edition, 1959).

Geoffrey de C. Parmiter
London

LIST OF ABBREVIATIONS

[*References to works marked with an asterisk are to the number of the document in the work cited, unless a page number is given. In all other cases the reference is to the page number.]

B.M. British Museum.

B.I.H.R. Bulletin of the Institute of Historical Research.

BURNET The History of the Reformation of the Church of England. In Two Parts. . . . By Gilbert Burnet. Second edition, London, 1681. [References to documents are to the pages of the section headed 'Collection of Records' (Coll. of Rec.) in each volume.]

CAVENDISH, *Wolsey* The Life and Death of Cardinal Wolsey. By George Cavendish. Ed. by Richard S. Sylvester. E.E.T.S., 1959.

*DENZINGER Enchiridion Symbolorum Definitionum et Declarationum de rebus Fidei et Morum. Auctore Henrico Denzinger. Editio xxxi, 1960.

D.N.B. The Dictionary of National Biography, from the earliest times to 1900. 21 vols., Oxford, 1885-1900.

E.E.T.S. Early English Text Society.

E.H.R. English Historical Review.

EHSES Römische Dokumente zur Geschichte der Ehescheidung Heinrichs VIII von England, 1527-1534. By Stephan Ehses. Paderborn, 1893.

FOXE, *Acts and Monuments* The Acts and Monuments of John Foxe: a new and complete edition: with a preliminary dissertation by George Townsend. Ed. by S. R. Cattley. 8 vols., London, 1837-41.

G. & H. Documents illustrative of English Church History, compiled from original sources. By Henry Gee and William John Hardy. London, 1896.

HALL, *Chronicle* Henry VIII, by Edward Hall. With an introduction by Charles Whibley. 2 vols., London, 1904.

Harl. Misc. The Harleian Miscellany: or, a Collection of Scarce, Curious, and Entertaining Pamphlets and Tracts, As well in Manuscript as in Print, found in the late Earl of Oxford's Library. 8 vols., London, 1744-46.

HARPSFIELD The Life and Death of Sir Thomas More, knight, sometymes Lord high Chancellor of England, written in the tyme of Queene Marie by Nicholas Harpsfield, L.D. Ed. by E. V. Hitchcock, with introduction by R. W. Chambers. E.E.T.S., 1932.

L. & P. Calendar of Letters and Papers, Foreign and Domestic, Henry VIII. Ed. by J. S. Brewer (vols. 1-4), James Gairdner (vols. 5-13; with R. H. Brodie, vols. 14-21); 21 vols. in 33 parts. London, 1862-1910. Second ed. of vol. 1, in 3 parts, by R. H. Brodie, London, 1929-1932.

LE GRAND Histoire du divorce de Henri VIII, Roy d'Angleterre, et de Cathérine d'Aragon. By Joachim le Grand. 3 Vols., Paris, 1688.

Life of Fisher The Life of Fisher. Transcribed from MS. Harleian 6382 by the Rev. Ronald Bayne, M.A. E.E.T.S., 1921 [attributed to Richard Hall].

MANSI Sacrorum Conciliorum nova et amplissima collectio. Ed. by J. D. Mansi. 31 vols., Florence-Venice, 1759-1798.

NICHOLS, *Narratives* Narratives of the Days of the Reformation, chiefly from the manuscripts of John Foxe the martyrologist, with two contemporary biographies of Archbishop Cranmer. Edited by J. G. Nichols. Camden Society, vol. 77, 1859.

POCOCK Records of the Reformation. The Divorce, 1527-1533. Collected and arranged by Nicholas Pocock. 2 vols., Oxford, 1870.

POCOCK-BURNET History of the Reformation of the Church of England. By Gilbert Burnet. Ed. by Nicholas Pocock. 7 vols., Oxford, 1865.

P.R.O. Public Record Office, London.

ROGERS The Correspondence of Sir Thomas More. Ed. by E. F. Rogers. Princeton, 1947.

ROPER The Lyfe of Sir Thomas Moore, knighte, written by William Roper, Esquire, whiche maried Margreat, daughter of the sayed Thomas Moore. Ed. by E. V. Hitchcock, E.E.T.S., 1935.

RYMER, *Foedera* Foedera, conventiones, leterae, et cujuscunque generis acta publica, inter reges Angliae et alios quovis imperatores, reges, pontifices, principes vel communitates ab . . . anno 1101, ad nostra usque tempora, habita aut tractata; ex autographis . . . fideliter exscripta . . . Ed. T. Rymer (vols. 1-15) and R. Sanderson (vols. 16-20). 20 vols., London, 1704-35.

Span. Cal. Letters, Despatches, and State Papers relating to the negotiations between England and Spain, preserved in the archives at Vienna, Brussels, Simancas, and elsewhere. London, 1862- . (The 'Spanish Calendar').

S. T. C. A Short-Title Catalogue of Books printed in England, Scotland and Ireland, and of English books printed abroad, 1475-1640. Compiled by A. W. Pollard, G. R. Redgrave, and others. London, 1926.

STAPLETON The Life and Illustrious Martyrdom of Sir Thomas More, Formerly Lord Chancellor of England (Part III of 'Tres Thomae,' printed at Douai, 1588). By Thomas Stapleton, S.T.D. Translated, for the first time, into English, by Philip E. Hallett. London, 1928.

State Papers State Papers during the reign of Henry the Eighth. 11 vols., London (Record Commissioners), 1830-52.

TIERNEY-DODD The Church History of England from 1500 to the year 1688, chiefly with regard to Catholics. By Charles Dodd [pseudonym for Hugh Tootel]; ed. by M. A. Tierney. 5 vols., London, 1839-43.

T.R.P. Tudor Royal Proclamations. Vol. 1. The Early Tudors (1485-1553). Ed. by Paul F. Karkin. Yale, 1964.

Ven. Cal. State Papers and Manuscripts relating to English affairs, existing in the archives and collections of Venice, and in other libraries of northern Italy. London, 1864- . (The 'Venetian Calendar').

WILKINS, *Concilia* Concilia Magna Britanniae et Hiberniae [1446-1717]. Ed. by D. Wilkins. 4 vols., London, 1737.

WRIGHT, *Chapters* Three Chapters of Letters relating to the Suppression of Monasteries. Ed. by Thomas Wright. Camden Society, 1843.

I

Introduction

I

Henry VIII succeeded his father on 22 April 1509. Less than two months later he married Catherine of Aragon, but within a few years the inability of his wife to bear him a son began to trouble him. He had a deep and passionate desire for a male heir, a desire which, in an age before any woman had sat on the English throne, was natural and comprehensible. There was no precedent for a queen regnant[1] and, to the minds of many men, the prospect of a reigning queen seemed to threaten the country with civil war or foreign domination at the hands of a foreign prince as consort. Yet Henry had no son to succeed him. Catherine had borne him several sons, but either they were stillborn or they died soon after birth; she appeared to be incapable of producing a sturdy heir and by 1514 her position was not an easy one.[2] In 1516, however, the princess Mary was born and she seemed to be a vigorous child; the event revived Henry's hopes and led to an improvement in his relations with Catherine. He is reported to have said, 'We are both young; if it was a daughter this time, by the grace of God the sons will follow'.[3] But sons did not follow, and by 1525 it was plain that Catherine would have no more children. Henry could now satisfy his desire for a male heir only by marrying some other woman, but so long as Catherine

[1] If the case of the empress Matilda (1102-67), the daughter of Henry I who married Henry V of Germany, could have been regarded in the sixteenth century as a precedent for a queen regnant, it was not one that would have given any encouragement to follow it.

[2] Vetor Lippomano to —, 1 Sept. 1514 (*Ven. Cal.*, ii, 479): 'It was also said that the King of England meant to repudiate his present wife, the daughter of the King of Spain and his brother's widow, because he is unable to have children by her, and intends to marry a daughter of the French Duke of Bourbon.' A. F. Pollard (*Wolsey*, pp. 19, 283) suggested that an actual project for a divorce was mooted in August 1514, but the references he cited do not appear to support this suggestion; it seems that, at most, there was merely a rumour; cf. Mattingly, *Catherine of Aragon*, 320, 321.

[3] Sebastian Guistiniani to the Council of Ten, 24 Feb. 1516 (*Ven. Cal.*, ii, 691).

remained alive he was unable to do so. Wolsey's foreign policy was now directed towards curbing the overweening power of Charles V, the nephew of Henry's wife, who ruled great dominions in Spain and the Netherlands and was emperor as well. For this purpose he set about forming an alliance with France, and it would have been convenient for him if Henry had been a bachelor so that a marriage with a French consort could have been promoted to cement the alliance. So, for their different reasons, both Henry and Wolsey were anxious that the king should be enabled to marry again.

To what extent the idea of bringing his marriage to an end arose independently in Henry's mind, and to what extent Wolsey was responsible, we shall probably never be able to determine. Indeed, it was suggested that the idea originated in France. In February 1527 an embassy headed by Gabriel de Grammont, bishop of Tarbes, arrived in England in response to Wolsey's moves to promote an alliance with France by which the power of Charles V might be reduced. By the treaty of Madrid, signed on 14 January 1526, after the disaster at Pavia, Francis I, the king of France, had engaged himself to marry, as his second wife, the sister of Charles V, the infanta Eleanor. The prospect of such a marriage was most unwelcome to Wolsey, now actively pursuing his new policies, and the cardinal had readily assured Francis that he was not bound by the treaty of Madrid and that he would do better to marry the English princess Mary. Francis, however, was anxious to secure the release of his sons, who were the prisoners of Charles V, and he would do nothing that might render their liberty more difficult to obtain; Wolsey's suggestion, therefore, was not then taken up. But the harsh conditions upon which Charles V was insisting turned Francis's mind towards England, and the French ambassadors came to arrange an offensive alliance. The negotiations were protracted, but three treaties were eventually signed on 30 April. Soon afterwards the bishop of Tarbes was again in England and on 29 May a further treaty was signed, for the maintenance of an army in Italy.

In July Wolsey set out for France as Henry's ambassador to continue negotiations with the French king at Amiens. While on his way, and before he left England, he told the bishop of Rochester, John Fisher, 'taking an oath of him to keep it close and secret', that Henry's anxiety about the validity of his marriage had been aroused by the French ambassadors. While discussing the proposal that Francis I should marry the English princess Mary, Wolsey said, they had raised the question of her legitimacy. They pointed out, Fisher was told, that her mother, at the time of her marriage to Henry, was the widow of Henry's dead brother, Arthur, and they questioned whether it were lawful for a man to marry the widow of his deceased brother; whereupon Wolsey showed them the bull of dispensation, and further discussion had been postponed until the cardinal's arrival in France.[1]

A different explanation was given by Henry himself, but this version was not made public until November 1528.[2] According to Henry, his doubts originated with his own meditations upon a text in the book of Leviticus,[3] which he read as a declaration that marriage with a brother's wife was sinful and that such a marriage would be childless. This is the story which Wolsey gave to Casale in December 1527.[4]

A third version comes from the pen of Reginald Pole. Pole was a near kinsman of Henry, being related to him through the king's mother as well as through his father. After the marriage suit had come to an end and when the breach with Rome was an accomplished fact, Pole wrote to plead the cause of Christian unity, and in his discourse he recalled the origin of the divorce.[5] Addressing Henry, he wrote:

At your age of life, and with all your experience of the world, you were enslaved by your passion for a girl. But she would not give you your will unless you rejected your wife, whose place she longed to take. The modest woman would not be your mistress; no, but she would be your wife. She had learned, I think, if from nothing else, at least from the example of her own sister, how soon you got tired of your mistresses; and she resolved to surpass her sister in retaining you as her lover. . . . Now what sort of person is it whom you have put in the place of your divorced wife? Is she not the sister of her

[1] See p. 17.
[2] See p. 72.
[3] Lev. xx, 21.
[4] See p. 18, note 1, and p. 31.
[5] The word 'divorce' is used throughout this work as a term of convenience, since the king's great matter is now universally referred to as 'the divorce'. It should be emphasized, however, that what Henry was seeking was not a divorce as that term is now understood (i.e. the dissolution of a valid marriage bond) but a declaration that his marriage was void, or, in other words, that he had never been married at all. Such a declaration, known nowadays as a decree of nullity, was termed by the canonists *divortium a vinculo matrimonii* and could only be obtained from an ecclesiastical court on the ground of some canonical impediment existing *before* marriage. The effect was to declare the marriage void *ab initio*.

whom you first violated, and for a long time after kept as your concubine?[1] She certainly is. How is it, then, that you now tell us of the horror you have of illicit marriage? Are you ignorant of the law which certainly no less prohibits marriage with a sister of one with whom *you* have become one flesh, than with one with whom your brother was one flesh? If the one kind of marriage is detestable, so is the other. Were you ignorant of this law? Nay, you knew it better than others. How do I prove that? Because, at the very time you were rejecting the dispensation of the pope to marry your brother's widow, you were doing your very utmost[2] to get leave from the pope to marry the sister of your former concubine.[3]

Pole roundly asserted that it was Anne Boleyn who had first put forward the idea that Henry's marriage with Catherine should be declared null and void.

She herself sent her chaplains, grave theologians, as pledges how ready her will was, not only to declare to you that it was lawful to put her away, but to say that you were sinning mortally to keep her as your wife even for a single moment, and to denounce it as a high crime against God unless you straightway repudiated her. This was the first origin of the whole lying affair.[4]

Queen Catherine herself laid the blame at Wolsey's door,[5] and Charles

---

[1] 'Quam tu et violasti primum et diu postea concubinae loco apud te habuisti?'
[2] 'Magni vi contendebas'.
[3] *Pro Ecclesiasticae Unitatis Defensione*, lib. III, fol. lxxvi, lxxvii; the translation given above is taken from Bridgett, *Life of Blessed John Fisher*, 148. Pole's work was published in Rome in 1536 (and subsequently in Ingoldtsadt in 1587) in answer to Richard Sampson's *Oratio quae docet hortatur admonet omnes potissimum Anglos regiae dignitati cum primis ut obediant, &c.* (London, 1533), an attack on papal jurisdiction.
[4] *Pro Ecclesiasticae Unitatis Defensione*, lib. III, fol. lxxvi; the translation is that of Mgr P. Hughes (cf. *Reformation in England*, i, 159).
[5] On 24 Oct. 1528, Catherine told Campeggio that Wolsey had 'blown this coal' between herself and the king; see p. 68, *post*, note 1. According to Edward Hall's account, the queen, in the course of her speech before the legates for the marriage suit said: 'But of thys trouble I onely may thanke you my lorde Cardinal of Yorke, for because I have wondered at your hygh pride and vainglory, and abhorre your volupteous life, and abhominable Lechery, . . . therfore of malice you have kindled thys fyre, and set thys matter a broche, and in especial for the great malice that you beare to my nephew the Emperour, whom I perfectly know you hate worse then a Scorpion, because he would not satisfie your ambicion, and make you Pope by force . . .' (Hall, *Chronicle*, ii, 148). Cavendish does not include such a statement in his account of the queen's speech (Cavendish, *Wolsey*, 80-2). Wolsey himself stated that the queen, as early as 1527, declared that the divorce proposal was due to his 'procurement and setting forth' (Wolsey to Henry VIII, 5 July 1527; *State Papers*, i, 196, at p. 200; *L. & P.*, iv, 3231).

V and the imperial and French ambassadors were of the same opinion. Similar views were expressed by Polydore Vergil and William Tyndale.[1] Neither Polydore Vergil nor Tyndale was well disposed towards Wolsey, but Tyndale, who wrote in 1530, professed to be reporting the common talk. It is not unreasonable, therefore, to suppose that Wolsey's contemporaries, for the most part, believed that he was the contriver of the divorce. Writing in the reign of queen Mary, Nicholas Harpsfield stated that 'the beginning then of all this broil . . . proceeded from cardinal Wolsey, who first by himself, or by John Longland, bishop of Lincoln and the king's confessor, put this scruple and doubt in his mind'.[2]

2

On 14 November 1501 Catherine of Aragon, the youngest daughter of Ferdinand and Isabella of Spain, was married in St Paul's to prince Arthur, the eldest son of Henry VII. Unhappily, prince Arthur was a sickly youth and died at Ludlow on 2 April 1502, to the great grief of his parents. For political reasons, Spain was most anxious to bring about a new marriage tie with England, and though Ferdinand, in a letter dated 10 May, instructed Estrada, his ambassador in England, to demand the return of Catherine together with the portion of the dowry already paid and the marriage portion due to her, yet, by another letter also dated 10 May, he instructed Estrada to arrange a marriage between Catherine and

---

[1] Polydore Vergil, *Anglica Historia* (ed. 1570), 685; Tyndale, *Practice of Prelates* in *Works of the English and Scottish Reformers*, ed. Russell, ii, 463.
[2] Harpsfield, *A on the Treatise Pretended Divorce between King Henry VIII and Katherine of Aragon* (Camden Society 1878), 175. The work was written in 1556. Richard Hall expressed a similar opinion: 'Now what the cause was of this the Cardinalls vniust and malicious grudge against this noble Queene [Catherine], it shall not be impertinent to our purpose . . . to ope vnto you. . . . These and such other things lying hott boylinge in the Cardinalls stomache against the Emperour, he conceived at last such malice against him . . . [that he] fought by all the meanes he coulde to annoy and displease his freindes and kindred for his sake. Amonge which the vertuous ladie Queene Catherin his Aunte was one, whom for her nephewes sake he agreeved and hurt many waies, but specially by raysinge this secrett matter of discorde between the kinge and her' (*Life of Fisher*, 49, 50). The account of Nicholas Sander in *De Origine ac Progressu schismatis Anglicanis liber* (Cologne 1585) is inaccurate and improbable.

Henry, the new prince of Wales.[1] The demand for the payment of Catherine's portion is significant as it may well have been made on the assumption that her marriage with Arthur was complete in every respect. In July Isabella wrote to Estrada to urge him to hasten the negotiations for the new marriage, and she stated that the balance of the dowry would be paid when that marriage had been consummated.[2]

The negotiations, however, were lengthy and it was not until 23 June 1503 that a new marriage treaty was signed. Catherine and Henry were solemnly betrothed on 25 June in the house of the bishop of Salisbury.

The marriage treaty required that a papal dispensation be obtained because Catherine, by her marriage with Arthur, had contracted the impediment of affinity, and that marriage, it was stated, had been consummated. In August Ferdinand protested that it was well known in England that Catherine was a virgin,[3] but it seems that, despite this, the marriage treaty was ratified without any amendment.[4] Before the treaty was ratified, the pope, Alexander VI, died on 18 August 1503; his successor, Pius III, died soon afterwards, on 18 October, and no dispensation had been obtained. Henry's agents made strenuous efforts to obtain the dispensation from Julius II, the successor of Pius III. There appear to have been considerable delays and on 6 July 1504 the pope himself wrote to Henry VII explaining that the delay was due to his desire to give the matter mature consideration, and he added that he would send the necessary bull to England by the dean of St Paul's,

---

[1] See *Span. Cal.*, i, 317, 318.
[2] Queen Isabella to Ferdinand, duke of Estrada, 12 July 1502 (*Span. Cal.*, i, 327): 'Let it likewise be stipulated that we shall pay the rest of the dowry when the marriage is consummated, so please God'.
[3] Ferdinand to de Rojas, ambassador in Rome, 23 Aug. 1503 (Pocock, ii, 426; *Span. Cal.*, i, 370): 'In the clause of the treaty which mentions the dispensation of the pope, it is stated that the Princess Katherine consummated her marriage with Prince Arthur. The fact, however, is, that although they were wedded, Prince Arthur and the Princess Katherine never consummated the marriage. It is well known in England that the Princess is still a virgin. But as the English are much disposed to cavil, it has seemed to be more prudent to provide for the case as though the marriage had been consummated, and the dispensation of the Pope must be in perfect keeping with the said clause of the treaty. The right of succession depends on the undoubted legitimacy of the marriage.' (The quotation is from the calendar; the original letter is in Spanish.)
[4] The treaty was ratified by Isabella on 30 Sept. 1503, and by Henry VII on 3 Mar. 1504; cf. *Span. Cal.*, i, 378, 379, 393.

Robert Sherborne, who was then in Rome.[1] In August the Spanish ambassador, Estrada, while complaining at the delay, stated that a dispensation had arrived; the precise nature of the document referred to is open to doubt because Estrada went on to say that he would have to await the arrival of the bulls which were being brought by Sherborne who was unlikely to reach England before the middle of October.[2]

Sherborne did not arrive until November and he did not bring the bulls with him. Henry complained to the pope,[3] but it was not until 17 March 1505 that the bishop of Worcester, Silvestro de Gigli, informed Henry VII that the pope had instructed him to bring to England the original bull of the dispensation for the marriage. He went on to say that it had grieved the pope to learn that copies of the bull which, under a pledge of secrecy, had been sent to Spain for the consolation of queen Isabella who was then on her death-bed, had been sent from Spain to England.[4] However, in a document dated 27 June 1505, the prince of Wales, Henry, made a secret protest against the validity of the contract for his marriage with Catherine, because it was entered into when he was under age.[5] Henry VII was beginning to question the wisdom of a Spanish alliance, and delays began to multiply. The result caused Catherine, who was in England, much personal distress. Her position was an ambiguous one, for although she was formally betrothed she was not yet married, and she lacked money, clothing and advisers. However, Henry VII died on 22 April 1509, and, on the advice of his ministers, the new king married Catherine on 11 June.

[1] Pope Julius II to Henry VII, 6 July 1504 (*Span. Cal.*, i, 396). There is a bull of dispensation dated 26 Dec. 1503 (Burnet, i, Coll. of Rec., p. 9; Burnet states that 'upon this bull they [i.e. Henry and Catherine] were married') but, in view of the pope's letter of 6 July 1504, it cannot have been effective even if it is authentic.
[2] Estrada to Isabella, 10 Aug. 1504 (*Span. Cal.*, i, 398). The dispensation to which Estrada referred may have been the copy of the original which had been sent to Spain and thence to England.
[3] Henry VII to Pope Julius II, 28 Nov. 1504 (Pocock, ii, 429; *Span. Cal.*, i, 414).
[4] Bishop of Worcester to Henry VII, 17 Mar. 1505 (*Span. Cal.*, i, 426). Isabella died on 26 Nov. 1504. On 24 Nov. Ferdinand wrote to Henry VII that he was sending the dispensation of the pope respecting the marriage of Catherine and Henry, prince of Wales (Ferdinand to Henry VII, 24 Nov. 1504; *Span. Cal.*, i, 407).
[5] The protest, in Latin, is printed in full in Burnet, i, Coll. of Rec., p. 10. The date of the protest was the eve of Henry's fifteenth birthday; he was born on 28 June 1491, and Catherine on 15 Dec. 1485. The object of the document was to maintain freedom of action until the dowry should be sent from Spain; cf. Henry's Protestation as calendared (*Span. Cal.*, i, 435), and de Puebla to Almazan, 7 Sept. 1507 (*Span. Cal.*, i, 545).

Catherine was delivered of a stillborn daughter in 1510;[1] a son, Henry, was born prematurely on 1 January 1511, but he died on 22 February.[2] In September 1513 the Venetian ambassador reported the birth of another son,[3] but this child was either stillborn or died immediately after birth. In July 1514 Henry wrote to Margaret of Savoy announcing that his wife was pregnant;[4] a son was prematurely born in December 1514, but was dead at birth.[5] On 18 February 1516 the princess Mary was born and, of all Catherine's children, she was the only one to survive.[6] At the end of July 1517 the queen was unwell and there were rumours that she was again pregnant,[7] but no more is heard of the matter, and it is likely that she had a miscarriage. In July 1518 Henry, who was at Woodstock, wrote to Wolsey that the queen was pregnant once more, and he said that on account of her condition he was loth to move to London because 'about this time is partly of her dangerous times', and because of that I would remove her as little as I may now'.[8] Henry's precautions, however, were of no avail; the child was stillborn

[1] The date is uncertain. On 1 Nov. 1509 Henry wrote to Ferdinand to tell him that Catherine was pregnant (*Span. Cal.*, ii, 23). On 27 Mar. 1510, Catherine wrote to Ferdinand and said that 'some days before' she had been delivered of a stillborn daughter (*Span. Cal.*, ii, 43). The *D.N.B.* gives the date as 31 Jan. 1510.
[2] Reading in the Senate of letters from Venetian ambassador in London, 20 Feb. 1511 (*Ven. Cal.*, i, 95); Doge and Senate to ambassador Donato at papal court, 5 Mar. 1511 (*Ven. Cal.*, i, 96); *L. & P.*, i, 1491, 1495, 1513; Hall, *Chronicle*, i, 22-7.
[3] Receipt of letters of news, 8 Oct. 1513 (*Ven. Cal.*, ii, 329); cf. Bannisius to Carpi, 8 Oct. 1513 (*Ven. Cal.*, ii, 331).
[4] Henry VIII to Margaret of Savoy, 13 July 1514 (*L. & P.*, i, 3074).
[5] Badoer to the State, 8 Jan. 1515 (*Ven. Cal.*, ii, 555). Badoer, the Venetian ambassador, wrote that the queen had been delivered, in the eighth month of her pregnancy, of a stillborn male child, to the great grief of the whole court. At this time Henry was extremely indignant at his betrayal by the Spanish king, and vented his ill humour on queen Catherine whom he taunted with her father's bad faith. Peter Martyr attributed the premature birth of the child to Henry's ill usage of Catherine (*Ep.*, p. 545).
[6] *L. & P.*, ii, 1505, 1573. That the risks of her pregnancy might not be increased, Catherine was not told of the death of her father on 23 Jan. (*L. & P.*, ii, 1563, 1610). It was after this birth that Henry was reported to have said, 'We are both young; if it was a daughter this time, by the grace of God the sons will follow' (*Ven. Cal.*, ii, 691). Catherine was then thirty, and Henry twenty-four.
[7] Francesco Chieregato to the marquis of Mantua, 1 Aug. 1517 (*Ven. Cal.*, ii, 942).
[8] *State Papers*, i, 1; Henry also wrote, in the same letter, 'My Lord I wrytt thys unto [*sic*; ? 'you' omitted] nott as a ensuryd thyng, but as a thyng wherin I have grette hoppe and lyklyodes'.

on 10 November. This was Catherine's last child, as things turned out. Henry had not yet abandoned hope of a male child, and in 1519 he undertook to lead a crusade against the Turks should he have an heir.[1] By 1525, however, when Catherine was forty years old, it was plain to Henry that she could not give him the son he wanted.[2] It was probably not long after the realization that Catherine could not produce a male heir, perhaps, in 1526, that Henry was first attracted to Anne Boleyn. Anne's elder sister, Mary, had been Henry's mistress,[3] probably between 1522 and 1525, but there is nothing to suggest that Henry was attracted to Anne at the end of this period.[4] Neither do the surviving letters of Henry to Anne enable us to reach a conclusion, as the earlier ones cannot be dated with certainty.[5]

The secret of the fascination which Anne Boleyn had for Henry puzzled the king's contemporaries and has remained a puzzle ever since; but there can be no doubt that Henry was ardently in love with her. If

---

[1] Henry VIII to Leo X, Aug. 1519 (*L. & P.*, iii, 432). In 1519, also, Henry had an illegitimate son (named Henry Fitzroy) by Elizabeth Blount. The boy was created duke of Richmond in 1525.

[2] At the legatine court Henry said, as reported by Cavendish: 'ffor all suche issue males as I haue receyved of the quene died incontynent after they ware borne, so that I dought the punysshement of god in that behalf, Thus, beyng trobled in waves of a scripulos conscience, And partly in dispayer of any Issue male by hir, it drave me at last to consider the state of this Realme, And the Daynger it stode in for lake of Issue male, to succed me in this Emperyall dignyte' (Cavendish, *Wolsey*, 83; a comma has been substituted for the virgula (/) employed by Cavendish, whose punctuation is very erratic); cf. Hall, *Chronicle*, ii, 151.

[3] Elizabeth Blount, sister of lord Mountjoy who was the friend of Erasmus, had previously been Henry's mistress. Cf. note 1, above.

[4] Anne Boleyn's father was created viscount Rochford on 16 June 1525, and James Gairdner (in *D.N.B.*) suggested that this was because Henry had begun to be attracted to Anne; but the influence may equally well have been that of Mary Boleyn.

[5] For the king's famous love letters, see *L. & P.*, iv, 3218-20, 3325-26, 3990, 4383, 4403, 4410, 4477, 4537, 4539, 4597, 4648, 4742, 4894. They are printed in *Harl. Misc.*, ii, 51-61 (reprinted from Hearne's edition of the letters in 1714), in Crapelet, *Lettres de Henri VIII à Anne Boleyn* (Paris 1826; 2nd. ed. 1835), and in Byrne, *Letters of King Henry VIII* (London 1936), 54-85. The originals are in the Vatican Library. July 1527 has been conjectured as the date of the earliest letter. The French ambassador, the pope and others believed that Henry began to cohabit with Anne Boleyn in 1529. Against this belief must be set the fact that Anne did not have a child until 1533; thereafter she seems to have had a miscarriage almost every year. Ortiz, it is true, wrote from Rome (*L. & P.*, v, 594) that Anne had a miscarriage in 1531, but the report cannot be relied upon.

the description furnished by a Venetian gentleman in 1532 is trustworthy, her personal appearance does little to solve the puzzle: 'Madame Anne is not one of the handsomest women in the world; she is of middling stature, swarthy complexion, long neck, wide mouth, bosom not much raised, and in fact has nothing but the English king's great appetite, and her eyes, which are black and beautiful'.[1] It was said that there was a defect on one of her nails, which she tried to hide behind her other fingers.[2] She was distinguished neither for beauty nor for intellect, and her virtue did not even command the respect of her own contemporaries.

[1] Summary of the interview between the kings of England and France, 31 Oct. 1532 (*Ven. Cal.*, iv, 824). According to Cavendish, Wolsey alluded to Anne Boleyn as 'the nyght crowe' (Cavendish, *Wolsey*, 137).

[2] *L. & P.*, iv, Intro., p. ccxxxvii. It was for this reason that Nicholas Sander, in *De Origine ac Progressu Schismatis Anglicani liber*, credited Anne with six fingers. His description of Anne is scarcely flattering (Lewis's trans., p. 25): 'Anne Boleyn was rather tall of stature, with black hair, and an oval face of a sallow complexion as if troubled with jaundice. She had a projecting tooth under the upper lip, and on her right hand six fingers. There was a large wen under her chin, and therefore to hide its ugliness she wore a high dress covering her throat.' It will be noticed that Sander and the Venetian gentleman are not in agreement as to her height.

II

Divided Counsel

I

Whatever may be the truth about the origins of Henry's wish to be freed from the bonds of his marriage with Catherine, the first definite step towards its fulfilment was taken in the spring of 1527. The scheme at first devised was a simple one. Henry was complaining that his marriage with Catherine was placing an insupportable burden upon his conscience, and he wished for relief. In these circumstances it might be thought that the most appropriate procedure for Henry to adopt was to present a petition in the ecclesiastical court praying that his marriage might be declared null and void. Such a procedure would have involved Henry as the initiator of an unpleasant business and would have had the further disadvantage that Catherine would be the respondent to the petition and would thereby be enabled to take an active and vigorous part in her own defence, with a recognized right of appeal to the pope. The scheme propounded was so contrived that these disadvantages were largely eliminated. It was resolved that the question should be decided in England by Wolsey, as legate, but, in order to relieve Henry of the need to initiate the proceedings, it was proposed that the legate should summon the king to answer the charge that he was living in open sin with his brother's widow.

It is noteworthy that this procedure assumed the invalidity of Henry's marriage to Catherine which was the very question in issue. Wolsey's scheme placed substantial practical difficulties in Catherine's way should she wish to take part and defend her marriage. She was, of course, entitled to be joined as an intervening party because her rights and status would be affected by any judgment of Wolsey's court, but Wolsey and those concerned with him were of the opinion (rightly, as matters turned out) that she would not exercise her right. Great efforts were made to keep Catherine in ignorance of what was afoot,[1] and Wolsey calculated

[1] Catherine was 'full of apprehension', according to the Spanish ambassador, writing on 18 May (*Span. Cal.*, iii, pt. 2, pp. 193, 207), but it was not until 22

that, even should Catherine learn the real nature of the proceedings, she would realize that it would be necessary to submit to the jurisdiction of the court in order to make an application to be joined as a party, and once she had submitted she would be at the mercy of Wolsey and the king; and great doubt surrounded the question whether and to what extent an appeal lay from Wolsey's general jurisdiction as legate *a latere*.

With his customary dispatch in the discharge of business, Wolsey had everything prepared with great expedition. In April Dr Richard Wolman had gone to Winchester to examine Richard Fox, the aged bishop of Winchester who had looked with disfavour on the marriage when it was first proposed.[1] On 17 May 1527 the court arranged by Wolsey assembled secretly at his house in Westminster. There were present William Warham,[2] the archbishop of Canterbury who had opposed Catherine's marriage seventeen years before, Stephen Gardiner who was then Wolsey's secretary, William Clayborough as registrar of the court, and three doctors of law, John Allen, William Benet and John Cocks, as *testes*. After the administration of oaths to those taking part, the proceedings opened with the reading of Wolsey's requisition to the king requiring him to answer the charge that he was living in open sin with Catherine, and the proposal that an assessor be appointed to examine the cause. The king, who was sitting in court at the right hand of the cardinal, acceded to this proposal and Warham was appointed assessor. Then Wolsey, after protesting his loyalty, demanded the king's answer to the charge which was read out; to that the king made answer, reading his reply from a prepared document. The court then adjourned.

[1] The examination took place on 5 and 6 April; see *L. & P.*, iv, p. 2588, where the record of the examination is calendared.

[2] It appears from Wolsey's letter to Henry of 5 July 1527 (*State Papers*, i, 200), that Warham fully believed Wolsey's story about the doubts said to have been raised by the bishop of Tarbes, and was induced to believe that Henry only wished to discover what was the truth about the matter; it was, apparently, this belief of the archbishop that enabled Wolsey to persuade him to take part in this secret trial.

June that Henry told her of his conscientious scruples; when she burst into tears Henry had to pacify her by the assurance that the object of the proceedings was merely to remove the doubts as to Mary's legitimacy which had been raised by the bishop of Tarbes (*Span. Cal.*, iii, pt. 2, p. 276). For an indication of the precautions taken to keep Catherine in ignorance of what was afoot, see Wolsey's letter to Henry, 5 July 1527 (*State Papers*, i, 196). An interesting precedent for these proceedings was furnished by the case of the duke of Suffolk; cf. *L. & P.*, iv, 5859.

The court sat again on 20 May when the king's proctor, John Bell, appeared and put in a justification on Henry's behalf; after a further adjournment he produced a copy of the bull of Julius II granting the dispensation for the marriage. Wolman, who had been appointed promotor of the suit, asked for a decree requiring publication of the bull, and that was granted. After another adjournment the court sat again on 31 May when Wolman produced a set of objections to the marriage, a copy of which was ordered to be given to Bell.[1] The court then adjourned once more. It may be presumed that the next stage in the proceedings would have been a judgment of the court but, as it turned out, Wolsey's scheme was overtaken by events and the court never sat again.

While the preparations for the secret court were going forward, Wolsey had been sounding the bishops for their opinions as to the lawfulness of the king's marriage. Fortunately, the opinion of the bishop of Rochester, John Fisher, has been preserved. He said that such printed authorities ('dumb masters' he called them) as he had been able to consult differed among themselves, but he himself could see no sound reason to think that the marriage was prohibited by divine law. Where matters were not clear it was for the pope to decide; and in this case the pope had decided by granting a dispensation, and Fisher had no doubt that in doing so he had acted within his power.[2]

Meanwhile there had occurred in Italy a disaster which was to have a considerable influence on the course of the king's great matter. On 6 May 1527, before Wolsey's court had assembled but unknown to those taking part, the soldiers of Charles V's armies in Italy had mutinied and captured Rome, and during the remainder of the month the city was pillaged and plundered and was the scene of every kind of outrage. Many cardinals and bishops were held as hostages by the mutinous soldiers and the pope only saved himself from a similar fate by hasty flight to the castle of St Angelo, where he remained, a prisoner, for seven months.

The news of these events, when it reached him, caused Wolsey no little apprehension. In sending the latest intelligence to the king, he wrote, 'if the pope's holiness fortune either to be slain or taken, as God forbid, it shall not a little hinder your grace's affairs, which I have now in hand, wherein such good and substantial order and process hath hitherto

[1] The proceedings are calendared at *L. & P.*, iv, 3140.
[2] Fiddes, *Life of Cardinal Wolsey* (London 1724), 185; bishop of Rochester to Wolsey, June 1527 (*L. & P.*, iv, 3148). cf. *State Papers*, i, 189.

been made and used, as the like, I suppose, hath not been seen in any time heretofore'.[1] In the face of this disquieting news, Wolsey changed his plan. The original plan, it is true, had one weakness, but with skill that might have been obviated. The queen might deny the jurisdiction of Wolsey's court, but there were formidable difficulties in her way should she attempt to obtain from the pope a declaration of Wolsey's lack of jurisdiction. The risks of the original plan miscarrying were therefore not great. But the fact, now established, that the pope was in the power of the imperial troops gave a very different appearance to the situation. To guard against the possibility of Catherine's assertion that he had no jurisdiction to try the case, Wolsey realized that it would be necessary to obtain papal confirmation of the judgment of his court.[2] But how could he hope to obtain from the pope, then a prisoner of the emperor's armies, confirmation of a judgment adverse to the emperor's aunt?

It could now be plausibly argued that the liberty of the church was in grave danger, and to meet the new situation Wolsey proposed that, for the period of his captivity, the pope should delegate all his powers to some cardinal not subject to imperial influence. Wolsey himself was to be that cardinal, so that, armed with the fulness of papal power, he would be able to give a judgment that did not require papal confirmation; thus he himself would be able to give the king the relief that he sought and then reap the reward of his master's gratitude. Moreover, with the emperor now dominating large parts of Europe, and Italy in particular, Wolsey was anxious to concert some continental arrangement that would reduce the danger from Charles V.

Accordingly, Wolsey was appointed plenipotentiary for concluding a league of peace between Henry, the emperor, Francis I of France, and the Venetians. He was also appointed the king's lieutenant and plenipotentiary in France, consequent upon the captivity of the pope. There was a third commission empowering him to treat for the projected marriage of the princess Mary with one of the French princes, and a general commission to arrange an offensive league against the emperor.[3] The cardinal was also provided with 'A memorial of such things as the

[1] Wolsey to Henry VIII, 2 June 1527 (*State Papers*, i, 189; *L. &. P.*, iv, 3147). This letter was written two days after the last session of Wolsey's secret court.
[2] Wolsey to Henry VIII, 29 July 1527 (*State Papers*, i, 230; *L. & P.*, iv, 3311).
[3] Of these commissions, the first four were signed on 18 June 1527; for the text of the second and third, see Rymer, *Foedera*, xiv, 198, 207. The fifth commission was signed on 20 June; cf. *L. & P.*, iv, 3186(5).

king's most trusty counsellor, the Lord Legate, shall, on the king's behalf, treat and conclude with the French King'. In this document Wolsey was instructed, first, that if the French king should agree to it, 'the determination of the alternative for the marriage of my lady princess [Mary], to be in to the person of the duke of Orleans', the dowry and necessary securities being committed to Wolsey's discretion. Second, if the French king should not assent, 'the said alternative to be resolved in neutrum' with the provisions mentioned in the treaty *arctioris conjunctionis*. Third, 'to amplify and extend the peace perpetual', and to convert the provision for carrying on war in Flanders, according to the defensive league, into a contribution for the defence of Italy. Fourth, to determine Calais as the place of personal meeting between the kings of France and England, and to arrange the order of the meeting. Fifth, to conclude a league with the pope, France and the Venetians 'for defence of Italy, and reintegration of the state of the pope's holiness, and the church, in to the pristine manner', with a pension for Henry of 30,000 ducats or more. Sixth, to treat for universal or particular peace between all Christian princes. Seventh, to fix the limit beyond which the king would not go in the offers to be made to the emperor for the redemption of the French king's children. Eighth, to concert measures with the French king to prevent the calling of a general council by the emperor or at his dictation, and to prevent the deprivation of the pope, the election of a new pope, or the translation of the holy see to Spain, Germany or elsewhere. The memorial concluded with a statement that, since Wolsey had conferred with the king 'in and upon the premisses' and knew the king's mind thereon, and because it was impossible to give precise instructions about everything, such matters were left to his discretion.[1]

Shortly before he left England, Wolsey received a message from the king, by the hand of Dr Wolman, which considerably troubled his mind. It seemed to Wolsey that Henry, as the result of a message brought to him by Dr Sampson[2] from the cardinal, now believed him to be wavering

[1] *State Papers*, i, 191-3; *L. & P.*, iv, 31 86(6). The memorial, which is signed at the beginning and the end by the king, is undated; it was probably signed on 18 June, when Wolsey's commissions were signed (see p. 14, note 3). The memorial is in the handwriting of Dr Stephen Gardiner, now appointed the king's secretary, who with Dr John Allen, accompanied Wolsey to France. At the date of the memorial, princess Mary was in her twelfth year and Henry, duke of Orleans, in his ninth.
[2] Richard Sampson was archdeacon of Suffolk, dean of Windsor and dean of the chapel.

15

and in doubt about the king's 'secret matter', and he hastened to write to Henry with assurances that this was not so; he had no more doubts now, he said, than he had before the matter came to the queen's knowledge.[1] He explained that what he had said to Dr Sampson was that, assuming Catherine's marriage with Arthur never to have been consummated, as the queen asserted, so that no affinity thereby arose, yet, because she had been 'married *in facie ecclesiae*, and contracted *per verba de presenti*, there did arise *impedimentum publicae honestatis*, which is no less *impedimentum ad dirimendum matrimonium*, than affinity, whereof the bull maketh no express mention'.[2] Wolsey added that the queen seemed very stiff and obstinate in the matter, and therefore he advised Henry that 'till it were known what should succeed of the pope, and to what point the French king might be brought, your grace should handle her both gently and doulcely'.[3]

After pondering his varied instructions during his journey to France, Wolsey had determined the manner in which he would deal with the king's personal problem. Writing to Henry soon after his arrival in France, and before he had met the French king, he set out his scheme. He was of the opinion, he said, that either the pope's consent must be had, to circumvent the queen should she deny his jurisdiction, or the cardinals must approve. But to obtain the pope's consent it was first necessary to secure his liberation, and if that could be achieved the pope, doubtless, could be induced to conclude everything to Henry's satisfaction; but if the pope could not be freed, then it would be necessary for the cardinals to meet at Avignon and, under Wolsey's guidance, com-

---

[1] See p. 11, note 1.

[2] When two parties to a marriage had been formally contracted, either by betrothal in the strict sense (*sponsalia per verba de futuro*) or by the marriage ceremony (*matrimonium ratum* or *sponsalia per verba de presenti*) there was created a diriment impediment (*impedimentum ad dirimendum matrimonium*) which invalidated a marriage subsequently contracted by either party with a near relative of the other. The particular impediment thus arising was known as *publica honestas* and, unlike the diriment impediment of affinity, it arose irrespective of consummation. Thus Wolsey is here saying that even if Catherine's marriage to Arthur was not consummated (*matrimonium ratum sed non consummatum*), so that the impediment of affinity did not arise, she was still prevented from marrying Henry by the impediment of *publica honestas*. The impediment was often referred to by the old canonists as *quasi-affinitas*.

[3] Wolsey to Henry VIII, 1 July 1527 (*State Papers*, i, 194, 195; *L. & P.*, iv, 3217).

mission Wolsey to act as the pope's vicar and enable him to bring the king's secret matter to a successful conclusion.[1]

Wolsey set out for France on 3 July 1527, and among those who accompanied him was Sir Thomas More, then chancellor of the duchy of Lancaster. The cardinal's progress proved to be the most splendid of all the splendid pageants contrived by him on such occasions.[2] Before taking ship, Wolsey stopped at Rochester and conferred with bishop Fisher. Fisher was a staunch friend of the queen, and Wolsey was anxious to discover how much the bishop knew about the affair. Having learned that a messenger from the queen had told Fisher that there were certain matters between herself and the king upon which she desired his advice, Wolsey inquired whether the bishop had any idea of what those matters might be. Fisher answered that he had no certain knowledge, but from rumours that he had heard he conjectured that they concerned a proposal for a divorce. Thereupon Wolsey told him that the king contemplated no such thing and had been most anxious to keep the matter as secret as possible. Nevertheless, he had the king's authority to disclose the facts to Fisher under an oath of secrecy, which the bishop readily took. The matter had arisen, so Wolsey told Fisher, because the bishop of Tarbes, during the discussions for a matrimonial treaty with France, had raised a doubt about the legitimacy of the princess Mary, and this had caused the king to seek the opinions of certain men learned in the law concerning the dispensing power of the pope.[3] Some hint of what was afoot had reached the queen's ears and she had expostulated with the king in a very disagreeable manner and complained that the proposed divorce was due to Wolsey's instigation and procurement. Fisher appears to have accepted this explanation, and blamed the queen for her im-

[1] Wolsey to Henry VIII, 29 July 1527 (*State Papers*, i, 230; *L. & P.*, iv, 3311); and cf. *L. & P.*, iv, 3401 (articles proposed by Wolsey for the government of the church during the pope's captivity, and a draft appointment of Wolsey as the pope's vicar during his captivity, with full powers of dispensation, etc.).

[2] For a description of the splendour of this embassy, written by George Cavendish who was in Wolsey's service, see Cavendish, *Wolsey*, 44 et seq.

[3] At this point in Wolsey's letter to the king, in which he described his interview with Fisher, he wrote: 'And thus declaring the hol matier unto him at lenght, as was divised with Your Highnes at Yorke Place, . . .' (*State Papers*, i, 200). From this it appears that the story of the doubts raised by the bishop of Tarbes concerning Mary's legitimacy had been previously concerted by the king and Wolsey; cf. p. 2.

17

petuous behaviour. He said that he would speak to her, but Wolsey contrived to dissuade him from such a course.[1]

When Wolsey set out upon this embassy, it had been his intention that when the matrimonial question had been satisfactorily settled and the king released from his marriage with Catherine, Henry should marry Renée, the daughter of Louis XII.[2] Such a marriage would

[1] Wolsey to Henry VIII, 5 July 1527 (*State Papers*, i, 197-201). It is not easy to accept the truth of the story told by Wolsey to Fisher. In the first place, when writing to Henry from Amiens on 16 Aug. 1527 (*State Papers*, i, 256), only a little over a month after his statement to Fisher, Wolsey said that he did not propose to discuss the king's 'secret matter' with Francis I until he should be at the point of departure, 'handeling the same after suche a clowdy and dark sorte, that he shal not knowe Your Graces utter determynacion and intent in that behalf' (ibid. 260). If the question of the validity of the marriage had arisen with the French ambassadors, it is hard to understand why Wolsey, who was about to discuss the matter, should have adopted such an approach. In reply to this letter, Henry's secretary, William Knight, wrote on 19 Aug. that the king had commanded him 'to yeve unto yow his moste herti thankes, for abydyng a tyme convenyent, bifore that ye discovre any parte of the saide secret unto the French King' (ibid. 261). This suggests that the origin of Henry's doubts was other than that disclosed to Fisher. Again, five months later, on 5 Dec. 1527, Wolsey wrote to Sir Gregory Casale, Henry's resident agent in Rome, to give him instructions with regard to the marriage suit. In this letter he gave a very different account of the origin of Henry's doubts. There is no mention of French suspicions; instead, Casale was told that Henry's doubts arose from his own consideration of the scriptures. Partly by his own study and partly by the opinions of many divines and other learned men of all sorts, Henry found that he could no longer, with a good conscience, continue in his marriage, because he had God and the quiet and salvation of his own soul chiefly before his eyes. He had consulted the most learned divines and canonists, and many of them were of opinion that the pope could not dispense in the case of first degree affinity, while the remainder considered that in such a case the pope could only dispense upon very weighty reasons and no such reasons were to be found in the bull of dispensation (this letter, which is in Latin, is printed in full in Burnet, i, Coll. of Rec., p. 12, Pocock-Burnet, iv, 19-23, and in Pocock, ii, 19; see p. 31). The story that Henry's doubts originated with the French ambassadors was, apparently, put forward only to the bishop of Rochester, under an oath of secrecy, and to no one else. On the other hand, we know from the letters of Turenne, who was one of the French ambassadors, that the French, far from questioning the legitimacy of Mary's birth, were very favourably disposed towards a marriage between her and Francis I (cf. *L. & P.*, iv, pt. 3, App. 104-108).
[2] So Guicciardini; it was also du Bellay's opinion; see Le Grand, iii, 166. cf. Shakespeare, *King Henry VIII*, act iii, scene 2:

> 'It shall be to the duchess of Alençon,
> The French king's sister: he shall marry her.—
> Anne Bullen? No; I'll no Anne Bullens for him:
> There's more in it than fair visage.—Bullen!'

greatly strengthen Wolsey's foreign policy, which was now based on a French alliance directed against the emperor, and would provide a solid basis for his own personal schemes. Henry, however, was by now determined to marry Anne Boleyn. Although Wolsey was aware of a relationship between the king and Anne Boleyn, it seems clear that at this time he supposed that she would remain Henry's mistress, as other women before her had done. Had Wolsey suspected the possibility of marriage, the prospect would have been most unwelcome to him. Anne's relations were the core of the anticlericals whom Wolsey had hitherto managed to hold in check,[1] but should Anne become the king's wife, the cardinal's last prop seemed likely to be withdrawn. Wolsey's personal position was already precarious; taxation at home and failure abroad had alienated much sympathy from the cardinal whom the people held to be responsible. Having incurred the hostility of almost all sections of the population,[2] his only support was now the king. With Anne Boleyn married to the king, Wolsey's downfall seemed assured.

[1] Anne Boleyn's father, her cousin Sir William Fitzwilliam, and Sir Francis Bryan and other relatives, were biding their time to attack the cardinal and the church. Chapuys, the imperial ambassador, reported that 'the lady [Anne Boleyn] and her father . . . are more Lutheran than Luther himself', and that 'he and his daughter are considered as true apostles of the new sect' (Chapuys to Charles V, 22 Mar. 1531; *L. & P.*, v, 148; and Chapuys to Charles V, 6 Mar. 1532; *L. & P.*, v, 850).

[2] The Spanish despatches contain much evidence of Wolsey's unpopularity at this time; cf. *Span. Cal.*, iii, pt. 2, 69 (pp. 190-3), 75 (pp. 207, 209), 113 (pp. 274-5). For example, on 18 Mar. 1527, Mendoza, in a long despatch to the emperor, wrote that 'disaffection to the king and hatred to the legate [Wolsey] are visible everywhere. . . . The cause [i.e. their proposal to make the duke of Richmond king of Ireland] has aroused such ill-will that were only a leader to present himself and head the malcontents, the king would soon be obliged to change his councillors' (Está la cosa tan preñada de malas voluntades que si ubiere uno que guiare la dança, creen que se mudaria todo el Consejo de Rey de Inglatierra) (*Span. Cal.*, iii, pt. 2, pp. 109, 110). On 23 Feb. 1528, du Bellay wrote to Montmorenci, 'Quant à Monsieur le Legat, vous ne debvez doubter qu'il n' aille de bon pied, & ce qui le mect en grand soucy, est que ceulx qui le verroyent voulentiers trebucher, sont bien aises que le peuple crie le meutre, & vouldroient aulcuns que tout allast mal, afin qu'ils peussent dire sont des fruicts de Monsieur le Legat' (Le Grand, iii, 85). cf. *L. & P.*, iv, 3304).

It is Wolsey speaking to Cromwell. The mistake in the name of the bride intended for the king was derived from Polydore Vergil, and has often been repeated by later writers; in reality, Margaret, duchess of Alençon, had married Henry, king of Navarre, in the previous January. Renée married Hercule d'Este, duke of Ferrara, in 1528.

Wolsey left England believing that he enjoyed the full confidence of the king and that he had the exclusive management of the king's great matter. While he was in France, however, he made the disquieting and painful discovery of the king's real matrimonial intentions, and he became aware that the king was deceiving him.[1] Early in August Wolsey learned from Hacket, the king's agent in the Netherlands, that it had come to the knowledge of Margaret of Savoy[2] that Henry intended to be divorced. Wolsey concluded that the emperor had knowledge of the matter and would do all he could at Rome to prevent it. He therefore proposed to use the services of Ghinucci, the bishop of Worcester, and of Gambara, the nuncio, and Sir Gregory Casale; they were to try and find some means of access to the pope in the castle of St Angelo and obtain for Wolsey general powers to act as the pope's vicar during the captivity of his holiness, but without disclosing to the pope the manner in which such powers were to be used; a special clause was to be inserted in the papal commission to be granted to Wolsey providing that no appeal might lie to the pope from any decision of his.[3]

Wolsey had concluded all his ostensible business by the middle of August. On 16 August, at the end of a letter to Henry, he wrote:

So that now, sir, there is little or nothing more to be capitulated or treated with the French king, unless it be the opening of your secret matter; the disclosing whereof I purpose to defer till I shall be at the point of my departing: handling the same after such a cloudy and dark sort, that he shall not know your grace's utter determination and intent in that behalf, till your highness shall see, to what effect the same will be brought.[4]

Wolsey remained in France for another month, and his time was, presumably, occupied with the promotion of the match with Renée; although his utterances were, doubtless, of the cloudy and dark sort, he told the French king's mother, Louisa of Savoy, that if she lived to be

[1] On 31 July Sir William Fitzwilliam (a cousin of Anne Boleyn) wrote to Wolsey and told him that the king was entertaining the duke of Norfolk and his wife, the duke of Suffolk, the marquis of Exeter, the earls of Oxford, Essex and Rutland, viscounts Fitzwalter and Rochford, and others; all these were hostile to Wolsey (*L. & P.*, iv, 3318).
[2] Margaret of Savoy was archduchess of Austria and regent of the Netherlands.
[3] Wolsey to Henry VIII, 11 Aug. 1527 (*State Papers*, i, 254; *L. & P.*, iv, 3340); Wolsey to Henry VIII, 5 Sept. 1527 (*State Papers*, i, 267; *L. & P.*, iv, 3400).
[4] *State Papers*, i, 260.

one year older she would see a perpetual union brought about between England and France.[1]

Because he knew that Wolsey would be hostile to his marriage with Anne Boleyn, Henry did not adopt the cardinal's suggestion that Ghinucci, Gambara and Casale should be sent to the pope. Instead, without informing Wolsey, he despatched his secretary, Dr William Knight, with instructions upon two matters. The first was to obtain from the pope a dispensation to enable him to marry a second wife while his marriage with Catherine was still subsisting, with the provision that the issue of both marriages should be legitimate; such a 'licence for bigamy' would have suited Henry well. Secondly, Knight was to obtain from the pope a dispensation to enable the king, in the event of his marriage with Catherine being declared void, to marry a woman with whom he had contracted an affinity of the first degree.[2]

Wolsey got wind of Knight's mission, and although he was unaware of the precise details of the instructions given to Knight, he learned of the proposal to obtain a licence for bigamy. On 5 September he wrote to Henry from Compiègne to dissuade him from sending Knight to Rome. He said that the bishop of Worcester, Ghinucci, was a more suitable negotiator with the pope, as he was more experienced and would have less difficulty in obtaining access to his holiness. Wolsey proposed

that the going of Mr Secretary [Knight] to the pope be put over and suspended; and that the sending of my lord of Worcester, which hath been privy to your secret matter, shall be more convenable for the obtaining of your grace's desire, and of the general faculty to me *omnia faciendi et exequendi durante captivitate Summi Pontificis*, which shall as highly make to your grace's purpose, if the same may be attained, as your highness can devise or wish, without disclosing any particularity of the said secret matter to the said pope's holiness, and, by mean thereof, I may delegate such judges, as percase the queen will not refuse or appeal from.[3]

[1] Le Grand, iii, 186. In the following year Wolsey told du Bellay that he had made this statement with the divorce in view (ibid.).

[2] Through his relations with Anne's sister, Henry had contracted affinity in the first degree with Anne. Save that it was illicit, this was precisely the same affinity which he later asserted that Catherine, by her marriage with Arthur, had contracted with him. This sheds an interesting light on the king's later scruples. Henry was thus proposing to contract a second marriage which would, on the Leviticus text, be as sinful as that with Catherine, and he was invoking the papal power of dispensation to enable him to do so. This was one of the points touched on by Reginald Pole; see p. 4.

[3] Wolsey to Henry VIII, 5 Sept. 1527 (*State Papers*, i, 271; *L. & P.*, iv, 3400).

Knight arrived at Compiègne on 10 September and delivered the king's letters to Wolsey.[1] The king thanked the cardinal for his diligent service which should not be forgotten. Since no one had been sent to the pope since his captivity the king thought, lest the queen should anticipate him in his great matter, that Knight should go to Rome, and he requested Wolsey to give the necessary instructions.[2] He did not disclose to Wolsey, however, that he himself had already given Knight explicit instructions. Two days later Knight reported to Henry that a fortnight previously Wolsey had sent Sir Gregory Casale, Robert Jerningham and Haccombe, with Gambara, to Lautrec, then commanding the French army that was to liberate the pope; they were to obtain the protestation desired by the king, and a general commission for Wolsey from the pope. Wolsey had instructed him to go to Venice, dissembling his purpose until he could proceed. Casale and Gambara would let him know whether access could be had to the pope; if so, 'I shall set forth the protestation; but as touching the general commission, inasmuch as he purposeth to commune with your highness first upon the same, I shall nothing attempt for the obtaining thereof, till I be advertised from his lordship'.[3]

Since his letter to Henry asking that Knight's 'going to the pope be put over and suspended', Wolsey had been expecting a messenger from England with orders for Knight's recall, and he asked Knight to await the messenger's arrival; to avoid the cardinal's suspicion, Knight agreed to remain at Compiègne. When, however, the messenger, Christopher Mores, arrived, Wolsey found that he carried no such orders. It was now plain to him that the conduct of the king's great matter was being taken out of his hands, and it seems probable that it was at this time that he first suspected that it was Anne Boleyn whom the king intended to marry. On 13 September Knight and Wolsey both wrote to Henry. Knight acknowledged the receipt, by Christopher Mores, of the king's letters 'concerning your secret affair, which is to me only committed'. He went on to write:

And where at my coming hither my lord legate [Wolsey] supposed to have so

---

[1] Knight to Henry VIII, 12 Sept. 1527 (*State Papers*, vii, 1; *L. & P.*, iv, 3420).
[2] Henry VIII to Wolsey, [11 Sept.], 1527 (*L. & P.*, iv, 3419). The date '11 Sept.' is wrongly ascribed to this letter in the calendar; there is no date in the only copy preserved.
[3] Knight to Henry VIII, 12 Sept. 1527 (*State Papers*, vii, 1; *L. & P.*, iv, 3420).

fully contented your highness, that by the coming of Christopher Mores I should have been by your grace countermanded, willing me therefore to abide and tarry for the said Christopher; I, for the avoiding of suspicion, showed myself content so to do, being nevertheless determined to proceed in my journey, if the said Christopher had not come the next day: and now your grace's pleasure known, my lord hath advised me to repair to Venice; which counsel cannot hinder your grace's purpose, for there being, if there be any possibility of access unto the pope, I have commodity to pass by the sea, till within one hundred miles of Rome.

He added that if a dispensation might be obtained *constante matrimonio*, of which he had doubt, he would soon obtain it; but 'if it cannot be impetrate *nisi soluto matrimonio*, less diligence may be suffered'.[1]

Wolsey thanked the king profusely for his letters and for the encouragement they had given him. He reported that he had despatched Knight to Italy, trusting that he would obtain access to the pope, and that he had given him 'the minute of the protestation, which I am informed, by my lord of Bath's letters, doth right well please and content your highness; as also the minute of the general commission; the same not to be set forth, impetrate, or sped by the said master secretary, afore he shall be advertised of your further pleasure in that behalf'.[2] Wolsey also furnished Knight with letters of recommendation to the pope, Clement VII, and to the cardinals.[3]

For Wolsey the despatch of Dr Knight to Rome had been disturbing enough. But the discovery that Knight was instructed to seek from the pope a dispensation to allow the king to marry a woman with whom he had contracted affinity caused him grave apprehension, since the woman referred to could be none other than Anne Boleyn. So disturbed was he that he was now extremely anxious to return to the side of the king and re-establish his influence; indeed, on the day that Knight reached Compiègne, Giovanni Salviati, the papal legate in France, was aware that the cardinal had abandoned his plans and sought to return to England as

---

[1] Knight to Henry VIII, 13 Sept. 1527 (*State Papers*, vii, 3; *L. & P.*, iv, 3422). By the last part of the letter he meant that a dispensation for affinity, to be used only if the marriage to Catherine were dissolved, would be easier to obtain than a dispensation to be used despite the existing marriage (a 'licence to commit bigamy').
[2] Wolsey to Henry VIII, 13 Sept. 1527 (*State Papers*, i, 277, 278; *L. & P.*, iv, 3423).
[3] *L. & P.*, iv, 3424-7.

quickly as he could.[1] Wolsey's anxieties were greatly increased when Christopher Mores arrived without the letters recalling Knight, for which he had hoped. Before setting out for England, Wolsey, with an Italian and three French cardinals, addressed a memorial to pope Clement VII, dated 16 September, in which, after assuring the pope that they were doing their utmost to secure his liberation, they protested that, should the emperor imprison the cardinals in Rome, the free cardinals would not recognize acts done under compulsion, or any cardinals created by the pope during his imprisonment.[2] This document, Wolsey hoped, would effectually support his legatine powers should the queen deny his jurisdiction in the marriage question and appeal to Rome. Wolsey was now determined to regain the full confidence of the king by using all his powers to procure for Henry what he wanted; but this was now a desperate course. It was dangerous to be half-hearted on the king's behalf and fatal to oppose the king's will; and Wolsey was now committed. He realized clearly that his only safety lay in vigorously promoting the king's great matter,[3] and with this object in view he began his journey back to England. He left Compiègne on 17 September,[4] and sailed from Calais on the 24th.[5] But when he visited the king, after his arrival in England, he found him closeted with Anne Boleyn. Any doubts that Wolsey may have had about the king's matrimonial intentions must then have vanished.[6]

[1] G. Salviati to Baldassare Castiglioni, nuncio in Spain, 10 Sept. 1527, from Compiègne (Ehses, 248); writing to Guicciardini on 14 Sept. he expressed the same opinion (Ehses, 249).

[2] *L. & P.*, iv, 3434; the text is in Le Grand, iii, 4-13. It is not certain that this document ever reached the pope.

[3] Later, Campeggio expressed the opinion that, although the cardinal appeared to be devoted to the king's cause, it was in fact distasteful to him; cf. Campeggio to J. Salviati, 9 Jan. 1529 (Ehses, 69): 'Al Rmo. Eboracense inf atto dispiace la cosa per quanto io comprendo, ma V. S. sia certa, che egli non ardirebbe di mostrarsi, nè ci può provedere, anzi è sforzato a dissimulare et mostrarsi fervente in procurare il desiderio del Re. Io con S. S. Rma. parlo liberamente per sapere già l'animo suo come io scrissi, et ella finalmente si stringe nè sa che dire, se non, che egli non ci è altro rimedio, che di satisfare aliquomodo al re, et valeat quantum valere potest, ch'il tempo poi porterà qualche rimedio.'

[4] Wolsey to Henry VIII, 21 Sept. 1527 (*State Papers*, i, 279; *L. & P.*, iv, 3441). It is amusing to note that this letter, written from Bologne, is subscribed by Wolsey, 'From Boleyn, the 21th day of September, by your Moste humble Chapleyn, T. Carlis. Ebor'.

[5] John Hacket to Wolsey, Nov. 1527 (*L. & P.*, iv, 3594).

[6] Hall stated that the cardinal 'returned wyth al his trayne and by jorneys the

2

The arrival of Knight at Compiègne made clear to Wolsey that he was no longer the sole directing influence in the king's great matter, and that, consequently, his personal position was one of great insecurity. He had proposed to make use of the services of Ghinucci, Gambara and Gregory Casale, to obtain from the pope a faculty which would enable him to exercise the plenitude of papal power and containing a clause forbidding any appeal from his decision to the pope. It was, of course, unlikely that such a faculty would be granted, but should the cardinal obtain what he asked, he would be in a position to pass an unassailable sentence in the king's matrimonial proceedings which would have been accepted both in France and in England. Accordingly, in a long letter to Henry written just before Knight's arrival at Compiègne, Wolsey told the king that he had had long conferences with Stafileo, the dean of the Rota, who was, he said, convinced that the bull of dispensation was invalid, and he assured Henry that 'there is perfect hope, if your grace will take a little patience, suffering such things to be experimented and done, which be and shall be devised for that purpose, by one way or other, your intent shall honourably and lawfully take the desired effect'.[1] Knight's arrival five days later, however, made it clear that Henry would not 'take a little patience', nor wait for Wolsey's schemes 'to be experimented and done'. Wolsey's advice had not been taken, and it was Knight who was to proceed to Rome on the king's business.

It may be thought that the most prudent course for Wolsey, after making his disagreeable discovery, was to abstain from any further action in the matter and leave the whole business to be transacted by those who were fully in the king's confidence. In Tudor times, however, it was not open to a minister whose advice was not accepted to resign.

[1] Wolsey to Henry VIII, 5 Sept. 1527 (*State Papers*, i, 273; *L. & P.*, iv, 3400).

last day of September, he came to Rychmond to the king of England' (Hall, *Chronicle*, ii, 105). The Spanish ambassador, Mendoza, reported that Wolsey went 'immediately' to the king at Richmond, and added that Anne Boleyn had demanded to be present at the first interview between the king and the cardinal, a request which Henry granted (Iñigo de Mendoza to the emperor, 26 Oct. 1527; *Span. Cal.*, iii, pt. 2, 224).

Ministers owed a continuing duty to serve their sovereign and might not escape responsibility by renouncing it. The rise of Anne Boleyn provided a great opportunity for those of the nobility who had long been excluded from what they regarded as their rightful places in the council, and who, in consequence, looked on Wolsey as their enemy. At the centre of the opposition to Wolsey was Anne Boleyn's father, ennobled in 1525 as lord Rochford, and her uncle, the duke of Norfolk, and they were vigorously assisted by the duke of Suffolk in total disregard of his personal obligations to Wolsey. If the king were to withdraw his support of Wolsey, the cardinal's fall was certain, and it seemed only too likely that his fall would be followed by his execution. For Wolsey, therefore, it was of the utmost importance to regain the king's confidence to the full.

Knight, it will be remembered, had left England with instructions to obtain from the pope a 'licence for bigamy' and a dispensation to allow Henry to marry Anne Boleyn. While he was still on his way the king had realized, evidently at the remonstrance of Wolsey, the imprudence of his demand for a licence to commit bigamy, and he sent a letter to Knight modifying his instructions. The bearer of this letter was John Barlow[1], a chaplain of lord Rochford, who caught up with Knight in Italy, probably at Foligno.[2] The letter told Knight that the proposal to obtain a licence to commit bigamy had become known to Wolsey, and he was instructed, if the cardinal asked about the matter, to say that the king had indeed sent a draft bull for the purpose but that the matter had been no part of Knight's original instructions. Knight was also ordered to do nothing further in the matter of the licence. Henry continued,

Nevertheless I do now send to you the copy of another [draft bull of dispensation] which no man doth know but they which I am sure will never disclose it to no man living for any craft the cardinal or any other can find; willing you both to keep it secret and to solicit that it may be in due form, keeping the effect and tenor thereof with all diligence, it once impetrate, to send it to us. Surely, to be plain with you, we are of the opinion that the cardinal is of touching the first bull [i.e. the draft of the licence for bigamy], for surely we thought it too much to be required and unreasonable to be granted, and therefore he and I jointly shall devise another, which hereafter we shall send to

[1] He was the brother of the notorious William Barlow who was afterwards successively bishop of various sees, the last of which was Chichester.
[2] On 4 Nov. 1527, Knight was in Foligno, waiting for Gambara who had gone to Rome to obtain a safe conduct; cf. *L. & P.*, iv, 3553.

you (and that or it be long), willing you to make all diligence to you possible
for impetrating of this first which presently I send you [i.e. the dispensation
for affinity], for that is it which I above all things do desire, and if you cannot
attain it, then solicit the other which my lord cardinal and I shall send you,
which, peradventure, shall not be much discrepant from this, but that shall be
made *pro forma tantum*—and so to cloak other matters if you possible [*sic*] may
attain this, desiring you heartily to use all ways to you possible to get access to
the pope's person, and then to solicit both the protestation and this bull with
all diligence; and in so doing I shall reckon it the highest service that you ever
did me. And if peradventure the pope do make any sticking at this bull,
because peradventure it is not yet to him known but that the marriage between
the queen and me is good and sufficient, you may show him that I doubt not
but if he ask the dean of his Roote,[1] which hath deeply seen the matter, he will
show him the truth thereof, and this bull is not desired except I be *legittime
absolutus ab hoc matrimonio Katherinae*.[2]

It is clear from this important letter that Wolsey's protests had induced
the king to abandon his proposal for a licence to commit bigamy.
Instead, another bull was to be obtained, which would dispense Henry
from the impediment of affinity with Anne Boleyn, so as to enable him
to marry her as soon as he was released from his marriage with Catherine;
and all knowledge of this bull was to be kept from Wolsey. Knight was
instructed to obtain the bull in the form of a draft supplied by Henry,
and if this proved to be possible he was to ignore the draft of another bull
that would be sent to him later. In giving Knight these instructions,
Henry's judgment appears to have been seriously at fault. Instead of
concentrating all his efforts upon his ultimate objective, the annulment
of his marriage to Catherine, Henry was seeking a dispensation that could
not be effective until the marriage had been annulled. Moreover, in
seeking such a dispensation he betrayed to the pope the real object of his
activities; he thus disclosed that his real purpose was to marry Anne

[1] Giovanni Stafileo was dean of the Sacred Rota. In a letter already cited (p. 25)
Wolsey informed Henry that Stafileo '(being by me ripely instructed of the
facte, with suche thinges as be dependaunt therupon) hath chaunged and
altered his opynyon, and nowe expresly affermeth that the Popes dispensacion is
clerely voyde and nought; aswel for that, that the impediment of affinite, *in
primo gradu*, is *de jure divino*; as also that the Pope can not, *nisi clave errante*,
dispense with the same; for the justificacion of whiche his opynyon, he hathe writen
a grete boke, right substancially and clerkely handeled, furnished plentuesly
with the decrees and auctorities of the lawe' (Wolsey to Henry VIII, 5 Sept.
1527; *State Papers*, i, 272; *L. & P.*, iv, 3400).
[2] Henry VIII to Dr William Knight, as printed in *E.H.R.*, xi, 685, 686. The
original letter is preserved in Corpus Christi College, Oxford (MS. 318, f. 3), and
was printed in *Academy*, xv, 239 (17 Mar. 1879).

Boleyn and not to ease his conscience, and thereby he rendered the papacy suspicious of his good faith in the matter. His want of judgment sprang, it seems, from impatience bred of his infatuation for Anne Boleyn.

Because of the urgency of the matter, Knight set out for Rome immediately he received the king's revised instructions, despite the disturbed state of the country. After an adventurous journey[1] he reached Rome, where he found many Spaniards, and took lodgings there. The pope, when he heard of his arrival, sent Gambara to him, but as Gambara did not dare to enter his lodgings, he went to Gambara and was told that it was impossible to gain admission to the pope. However, through cardinal Pisani, he contrived to send a packet to the pope containing the draft bull of dispensation and a letter in which he wrote what he would have said had he obtained an audience. That night he received word from the pope who advised him to withdraw from Rome but promised him that if he would remain in the neighbourhood of Narni his holiness, who had come to an arrangement with the Spaniards and hoped to be at liberty within a few days, 'would send unto me all your grace's requests in as ample form as they be desired'. Knight thereupon left Rome and by 4 December was back in Foligno.[2]

On 8 December the pope escaped to Orvieto,[3] and soon afterwards Knight had an interview with him. A little later Knight wrote to Henry and to Wolsey to report upon the business he had transacted with the pope, and from these letters we can obtain a fairly clear picture of what occurred.[4] Although the pope, while still a prisoner in the castle of St Angelo, had promised the king what he desired, once he was at liberty he showed some disinclination to fulfil his promise. He told Knight that

---

[1] He was set upon and nearly killed at Monterotundo, twelve miles from Rome.

[2] cf. Knight to Henry VIII, 4 Dec. 1527 (*State Papers*, vii, 16; *L. & P.*, iv, 3638). Cardinal Pisani is wrongly described in the calendar as 'cardinal [of] Pisa'; Knight wrote 'Cardinal Pisan'.

[3] On 8 Dec. 1527, Sir Gregory Casale and Sir Robert Jerningham wrote to Wolsey from Parma that the hostages given by the pope to the Spaniards had fled and that the pope himself had fled to Orvieto; on 9 Dec. Jerningham wrote to Henry VIII from Parma that news had come that the pope had escaped and the hostages had fled; and on 14 Dec. the pope himself wrote from Orvieto to Wolsey that he was sending Gambara to inform the king and Wolsey that he had regained his liberty (*L. & P.*, iv, 3650, 3652, 3658).

[4] Letters dated 1 Jan. 1528, printed in Burnet, i, Coll. of Rec., pp. 21-5, and in Pocock-Burnet, iv, 34, 37 (*L. & P.*, iv, 3749-51).

28

he had received the king's letters and asked him to depart, saying that he would send the dispensation. The pope begged that the king would have patience and not do anything in the matter of the marriage question for the time being, as he feared that the dispensation might encourage Wolsey, by his legatine authority, to hear and determine the cause; if the king were to have patience, Knight reported to Henry, 'it should not be long ere your highness should have, not only the dispensation, but anything else that may lie in his power'. Knight replied that, relying upon the pope's promise made in St Angelo, he had already sent off news of the dispensation, and he could not imagine how he could make the king believe that his holiness would perform a promise that he had already broken. After some argument, the pope expressed himself as content that Henry should have the dispensation, on condition that Gambara and Knight beseech the king not to proceed in the matrimonial cause until his holiness should be fully at liberty, a situation that could not be brought about while the Spaniards and Germans were still in Italy. Knight thought it best 'to be in possession of this dispensation'. Thereupon, the pope wished cardinal Pucci to revise the draft, and when that was done the pope showed it to Knight and asked him to leave, saying that Gambara would follow with the bull of dispensation. Knight did not proceed with the protestation and the commission for Wolsey since they were drafted on the assumption that the pope was a prisoner. In his letter to Henry, Knight enclosed a copy of the dispensation,[1] the text of

[1] The dispensation is dated at Orvieto, 23 Dec. 1527. For the text see Ehses, 14-16. Attention may be drawn to the following extracts: 'Exponi nobis super fecisti, quod alias tu et dilecta in Christo filia Catherina relicta quondam Arturi fratris tui germani, non ignorantes, vos primo affinitatis gradu invicem fore coniunctos, matrimonium per verba alias legitime de praesenti, nulla saltem canonica seu valida dispensatione desuper obtenta, quamvis de facto contraxistis illudque carnali copula consumastis ac prolem ex huiusmodi matrimonio suscepistis, excommunicationis sententiam incurrendo; . . . et in eventum declarationis nullitatis matrimonii huiusmodi tecum dispensari, ut cum quacunque alia muliere, etiamsi illa talis sit, quae alias cum alio matrimonium contraxerit, dummodo illud carnali copula non consumaverit, etiamsi tibi alias secundo vel remotiori consanguinitatis, aut primo affinitatis gradu ex quocunque licito seu illicito coitu coniuncta, dummodo relicta dicti fratris tui non fuerit, ac etiamsi cognatione spirituali vel legali tibi coniuncta extiterit et impedimentum publicae honestatis iustitiae subsistat, matrimonium licite contrahere et in eo libere remanere ac ex eo prolem legitimam suscipere possis . . . Ex praemissis et nonnullis aliis nobis notis causis huiusmodi supplicationibus inclinati tecum, ut si contingat, matrimonium cum praefata Catherina alias contractum nullum fuisse et esse declarari teque ab illius vinculo legitime

29

which had been revised not only by Pucci but by the pope himself in his own hand.[1]

Complying with the pope's request, Knight left Orvieto, but he was intercepted by a messenger from the king, named Thadeus, who delivered to him 'certain expeditions triplicate' for himself, Gambara and Gregory Casale. Included in the packet was the draft dispensation from the king and Wolsey which he had been instructed to ignore if he obtained the dispensation the draft of which had been brought by Barlow. There was also the draft of a commission to be obtained for Wolsey, but should objection be taken on the ground that he might be thought partial, it was to be obtained for Stafileo, the dean of the Rota who, Wolsey had assured the king, was favourably disposed towards Henry's opinions and had been visiting the French and English courts. It seems that the purpose of this commission was to authorize Wolsey to examine the grounds upon which the dispensation for Henry's marriage to Catherine had been obtained and, if they were found to be insufficient, to declare the marriage void.

---

[1] There is a copy of the dispensation in the Corsini library, which is in the handwriting of Pucci and shows corrections in the handwriting of Clement VII. This copy is docketed, 'Bulla scripta minuta manu propria Rev. cardinalis Laurentii SS. quatuor, de matrimonio Catherinae relictae quondam fratris regis Angliae . . . Correcta est minuta certis verbis in Margine per Clementem Papam manu sua secretissime' (cf. Ehses, 16, note).

absolvi, cum quacunque muliere ipsaque mulier tecum, dummodo a te propter hoc rapta non fuerit, etiamsi mulier ipsa talis fuerit, quae prius cum alio matrimonium contraxerit, dummodo illud carnali copula non fuerit consummatum, etiamsi illa tibi alias secundo aut remotiori consanguinitatis aut primo affinitatis gradu etiam ex quocunque licito vel illicito coitu proveniente invicem coniuncta, dummodo relicta dicti fratris tui non fuerit, ut praefertur, etiamsi cognationis spiritualis aut legalis et publicae honestatis iustitiae impedimentum subsistat et tibi coniuncta existat, matrimonium licite contrahere et postquam contractum fuerit, et in eo sic contracto, etiamsi illud inter te et ipsam mulierem iam de facto publice vel clandestine contractum et carnali copula consumatum fuerit, licite remanere valeatis, auctoritate apostolica et ex certa nostra scientia ac de apostolicae potestatis plenitudine tenore praesentium dispensamus, prolem inde forsan susceptam et suscipiendam legitimam fore decernentes. Non obstantibus prohibitionibus iuris divini ac constitutionibus et ordinationibus aliis quibuscunque in contrarium editis, quibus in quantum auctoritas apostolica se extendit, illis alias in suo robore remansuris, quoad hoc specialiter et expresse derogamus.' The last clause ('Non obstantibus') may be noted especially: in 1527 Henry was very ready to accept such a clause, since it operated to his advantage; when, however, such a clause operated to restrict his wishes, he denounced it as a blasphemous usurpation.

Thadeus also brought instructions from Wolsey to Gregory Casale.[1] Wolsey emphasized the secrecy with which the affair was to be conducted; he instructed Casale to change his dress and, after giving the appearance that he was in some other person's employ or had some commission from the duke of Ferrara, obtain a secret interview with the pope and discuss the matter with him. In order to obtain these ends he was to bribe those concerned with any sums that were necessary, and for that purpose a credit of 10,000 ducats had been arranged for him at Venice. Casale was told that the origin of the whole affair was the king's scruples which had arisen through his study of the scriptures. The king's doubts about the validity of his marriage had been reinforced by the opinions of the learned men he had consulted, who were of the opinion that the pope either had no power to dispense in such a case or could do so only for weighty reasons, and no such reasons appeared in the bull. Casale was instructed that, when he had gained access to the pope, and having ensured that no one else was present, he was to enlarge upon the grievous nature of the king's moral scruples and the evils likely to arise from the lack of a male heir. He was then to recall the great services which the king had rendered the church, services which gave him a claim on the pope's consideration; the point was, that when the pope knew of the insufficiency of the dispensation, he ought to offer, unsolicited, some relief for the king's conscience.[2] After these preliminaries had been disposed of, Casale was to request the pope to consider the great advantages likely to accrue to the holy see if, without disclosing the affair to anyone, he were to grant a commission in the form of a brief directing Wolsey to summon whom he pleased to inquire into the sufficiency of the dispensation, and Casale was told that the brief should be according to the tenor of the enclosed draft which was sent so as to avoid the need of the pope's consulting his advisers; rather than allow the matter to come to the ears of those who could offer any obstacle, Casale was to content himself with the pope's simple signature on the

[1] For these instructions, in Latin, see the long letter from Wolsey to Sir Gregory Casale, 5 Dec. 1527, printed in Burnet, i, Coll. of Rec., p. 12, Pocock-Burnet, iv, 19-23, and Pocock, ii, 19; *L. & P.*, iv, 3641. These were the first instructions about the divorce which Casale received. In this letter Wolsey set out the grounds on which the dispensation of Julius II was impugned, which are referred to later; see p. 35.
[2] 'Negotiumque hujusmodi est, ut cognita Dispensationis insufficientia, quamvis id non requisivisset Rex, ultro proponi offerique debuisset ab eadem Sanctitate tanquam a Patre Spirituali, in ejus salutis & conscientiae beneficium.'

31

draft, which could afterwards be confirmed by a subsequent instrument. After instructing Casale to make this outrageous request, Wolsey had the effrontery to add that, if objection were taken that he would not be impartial, being one of the king's subjects, Casale was to reply that Wolsey would do nothing inconsistent with his duty as a Christian, observing 'since I am a cardinal and legate *a latere* of the holy see, the honour of his holiness and the integrity of his conscience will be entirely preserved by me'.[1] Wolsey also told Casale that, because of the likelihood of difficulty or delay in gaining access to the pope, the king had also issued a commission to Knight; one or other of them was to try to gain admission, but in view of the urgency of the matter neither of them was to wait for the other.

When he received his new instructions, Knight returned to Orvieto and, accompanied by Sir Gregory Casale, visited the pope once more. After assuring his holiness of Henry's devotion to the church they pointed out how necessary it was to remove the danger of a disputed succession, which could only be done if the doubts which had been raised about the validity of the dispensation granted by Julius II were disposed of. Accordingly, they asked the pope to grant the commission to Wolsey in the terms of the draft sent from England. The pope was ready to admit the likelihood of the dangers they had mentioned, but he said that as he was not familiar with the granting of commissions, he would consult cardinal Pucci. Thereupon Knight and Casale visited Pucci and, after promising him 'a competent reward', put the draft commission before him. Cardinal Pucci studied it carefully and then expressed the opinion that such a document 'could not pass without perpetual dishonour unto the pope, the king and [Wolsey]'. He furnished Knight with a written statement of his objections, and, after reading it, Knight and Casale asked him to draw up the commission himself. Pucci set to work and made a number of drastic alterations, deleting some clauses and amending others, in order to remove objections to the document and to reserve to the pope the right to reconsider any decision given under its authority; and with the draft in this amended form Knight and Casale returned to the pope. The pope was extremely unwilling to grant what was asked; he said that, while in captivity, he had received representations on behalf of the emperor 'not to grant

[1] 'Et quin Cardinalis sim & Apostolicae sedis de latere Legatus, ejus Sanctitatis honor, integraque conscientia, a me omnino conservaretur.'

32

unto any act that might be preparative, or otherwise, to a divorce to be made between the king and the queen: and [the emperor] moreover desired an inhibition, that the said cause should not come in knowledge before any judge within the king's dominions'; and the pope protested that even yet he was not really free. He went on to say, however, that if the French forces under Lautrec were to approach, that fact would lend colour to an excuse to be given to the emperor that in granting the commission he acted under compulsion. He begged, with sighs and tears, not to be pressed in the matter and promised to send the commission when Lautrec should arrive. With this the English agents had to content themselves.[1] However, the commission in its amended form was of no material use to Wolsey or the king, since the provisions enabling Wolsey to give a sentence that could not be altered by the pope had been removed by Pucci.

The difference between the two letters, to the king and to Wolsey, written by Knight on 1 January 1528,[2] is significant. In his letter to the king, Knight was concerned principally with the dispensation that would enable Henry to marry Anne Boleyn once he were free from Catherine. In his letter to Wolsey, however, he did not enlighten the cardinal as to the nature of the dispensation[3] and dwelt chiefly on the commission, saying that he and Casale had 'desired his holiness to commit the knowledge of the dispensation that was obtained in the time of Julius, of famous memory, for matrimony to be had between the king and the widow, the relict late of prince Arthur; and that we might have it in form as that was that your grace [Wolsey] sent hither'.

[1] For the foregoing account, see Knight's letters, cited in note 4, p. 28, and the letter from Casale, Gardiner and Foxe to Wolsey dated 31 Mar. 1528, printed in Pocock, i, 95 (*L. & P.*, iv, 4120); cf. the pope's holograph letter to Henry VIII, dated 1 Jan. 1528 (*State Papers*, vii, 35; *L. & P.*, iv, 3756), in which he said that he had sent the dispensation and that he had also granted the demand in the king's subsequent letter, beyond the dispensation, though not without great hazard to himself, as a token of his affection for the king. It is of interest to note that cardinal Pucci declined the offered reward of 2,000 crowns, and so his secretary was given 30 crowns, the balance being retained by Gardiner to offer to Pucci again on a future occasion, should that be necessary; cf. *L. & P.*, iv, 3750.

[2] See p. 28, note 4.

[3] In a second letter to Henry, also written on 1 Jan. Knight told the king that he had written to Wolsey informing him that the commission and dispensation had been obtained, 'inasmoche as he sent hyther the mynute of a dispensacion to be spedd, but I specifye not aftyr what forme your dispensacion is graunted and passed' (*State Papers*, vii, 36; *L. & P.*, iv, 3750).

The dispensation which the envoys obtained[1] was a conditional one, and permitted the new marriage only in the event of the existing marriage with Catherine being declared void.[2] This may be compared with the draft bull sent to Knight by the king and Wolsey but which, in the event, was not used.[3] That draft was not drawn in a conditional form but, presupposing that Henry was otherwise free to marry, granted the necessary dispensation without reference to any sentence of nullity; but, of course, had the dispensation been granted in such a form, a sentence of nullity would still have been necessary for it to be effective.

The commission addressed to Wolsey which the envoys obtained from the pope seems to have disappeared. In all probability it authorized Wolsey to examine the objections which had been made to the bull of dispensation granted by Julius II; and it may, perhaps, have empowered the cardinal to determine the validity of Henry's marriage with Catherine. In that form it would have been of little use to Wolsey, for it is quite clear that it did not contain the clause which the cardinal regarded as essential, a provision that no appeal should lie to the pope from Wolsey's decision.[4] The failure of the envoys to obtain the commission in the form desired by Wolsey appears to be due, not only to the nature of the demand, but to the fact that the papal court were then aware of Henry's motives.

The point had not yet been reached when Henry would dispute the pope's power to dispense in cases of matrimonial impediments. So far from denying that the pope had such power, Henry had just obtained a dispensation and was anxious that the papal dispensing power should be of the greatest amplitude and used on his behalf. At this time it appears that Henry wished to raise two questions: first, whether the dispensation of Julius II was effective to remove the impediment to his marriage with Catherine and second, if the dispensation were not effec-

---

[1] See p. 29, note 1. It appears that the document was originally passed on 17 Dec. [16 calendas Januarii], 1527, but after further amendment was despatched by Gambara on 23 Dec. [10 calendas Januarii], 1527; cf. Ehses, 17 note.

[2] It is remarkable that such a document should ever have been issued. In the Public Record Office there is a copy of the bull of dispensation, containing marginal comments in which complaint is made (apparently by Wolsey) about the form of the preamble and desiring that it be expunged as reflecting unworthily on the king; cf. *L. & P.*, iv, 3686(2).

[3] Printed in *E.H.R.*, v, 544-50.

[4] cf. Casale, Gardiner and Foxe to Wolsey, 31 Mar. 1527 (Pocock, i, 95; *L. & P.*, iv, 4120).

tive, whether his marriage was thereby invalidated. The grounds upon which he sought to impeach the dispensation do not appear to have been very substantial and were almost entirely directed to the form of the document. In the first place, it was contended that the bull contained a false recital; whereas the bull recited that Henry desired the marriage, in fact he had never asked for it and was unaware that the dispensation was being obtained. Secondly, it was said that the reason recited in the bull for the contracting of the marriage, namely the preservation of peace and the promotion of an alliance, was insufficient, more especially as there had been no war and there was then no danger to peace. Thirdly, it was said that when the bull was obtained Henry was not of lawful age to marry, being then only twelve years old. Fourthly, it was contended that the bull must have been surreptitious because some of those named in it were dead before it was put into effect.[1] Lastly, it was contended that the written protest against the validity of his marriage contract which Henry had executed on the eve of his fifteenth birthday, had rendered void the dispensation which preceded it in date, so that a subsequent marriage would not be valid without a further dispensation.[2]

The last of these grounds is the most curious of all. In his examination by Wolman, the aged bishop of Winchester had expressed the opinion that the young Henry made his protest at the command of his father, Henry VII; he said that it was always Henry VII's intention that his son should marry Catherine but the solemnization of the marriage had been postponed only because of the disputes with the king of Spain touching the demand for the dowry.[3] Concerning this ground, the auditor of the Rota to whom the matter was referred,[4] objected that it was dishonourable for the king to say that he had renounced the dispensation

---

[1] All those named in the bull were alive when it was issued; Isabella of Castille and Henry VII died before the marriage took place.

[2] For these grounds, see Ehses, 21; cf. the draft bull which it was hoped to obtain from the pope (printed in Burnet, i, Coll. of Rec., p. 31), in which these grounds, in a different order, are recited; in the English documents the objection relating to the peace is always placed first. See also the record of the examination of Fox, bishop of Winchester, by Richard Wolman on 5 and 6 April 1527 (*L. & P.*, iv, 5791 (p. 2588)). Although none of these grounds is of much substance, they do not differ much in kind from many of the points that were then taken in ecclesiastical courts.

[3] *L. & P.*, iv, pp. 2588, 2589; cf. de Puebla to Almazan, 7 Sept. 1507 (*Span. Cal.*, i, 545).

[4] J. Simonetta, bishop of Pesaro.

but had afterwards contracted marriage. He went on to say that, even assuming that Henry had renounced the dispensation, Catherine had not and she had received no notice that Henry had done so; and in any case, the subsequent marriage must be deemed to have restored the dispensation to its full vigour if its efficacy had ever been doubtful.[1]

When Knight wrote his letters to the king and Wolsey, on 1 January, reporting the results of his mission, he despatched them immediately by the courier, Thadeus, and he himself left for home, passing through Florence, Genoa and Alessandria. At Alessandria he learned that John Barlow, who had again been sent to Rome, had left letters for him with Thadeus whose journey had been interrupted by floods in Lombardy and who was then at Asti. Knight reached Asti on 9 January, and there received a letter from Wolsey dated 27 December 1527.[2] When Wolsey wrote this letter he was not aware of the results of the interviews of Knight and Casale with the pope, but for some reason that is not entirely clear,[3] he decided upon a change of plan. The pope was now to be asked to send either cardinal Lorenzo Campeggio, cardinal Alessandro Farnese or the cardinal of Trani to England with a sufficient commission to determine the cause; in that way, all objections that might be urged by the queen against Wolsey as the king's subject, might be avoided. It was essential that this commission be granted to one of the three, Campeggio, Farnese or Trani, and the appointment of an imperialist cardinal was not to be agreed to. If the commission previously asked for had already been granted, it was to be sent to England with all speed, but the pope

---

[1] Ehses, 22. For authorities for the proposition, now generally accepted, that once a dispensation has been obtained it remains effective even though the person in whose favour it was granted renounces it, unless the authority granting the dispensation accepts the renunciation, see Sanchez, *De Matrimonio*, lib. viii, disp. 32, r. 5; cf. Bartholomaeus de Spina, *De Potestate Papae*, nn. 117, 118, which suggests that, in the early sixteenth century, there was some doubt on the point.

[2] See Knight's letters to Henry VIII and to Wolsey, both dated 9 Jan. 1528, printed in Pocock, i, 56, 57 (*L. & P.*, iv, 3784, 3785); Knight to Henry VIII, 10 Jan. 1528 (*State Papers*, vii, 46; *L. & P.*, iv, 3787); Knight to Wolsey, 10 Jan. 1528 (*L. & P.*, iv, 3788). For Wolsey's letter to Knight, of 27 Dec. 1527, of which a copy was sent to Gregory Casale and Gambara, see the letter to Casale printed in *State Papers*, vii, 29 (*L. & P.*, iv, 3693).

[3] When Wolsey wrote his previous instructions (5 Dec. 1527), the pope was still a prisoner. It seems likely, however, that the news of the pope's liberation on 8 Dec. caused him to think that there was little chance of obtaining the commission for himself in the form he wanted.

was to be urged to send a legate without revoking the prior commission.[1] If the pope were minded to send a legate merely to inquire into facts, reserving sentence to himself, he was to be told that the cause had been discussed and examined already and that the king could not assent to such a course without causing the greatest prejudice to the jurisdiction of the church.

Since Knight was informed that Gregory Casale, who was in touch with the pope, had received similar instructions, he saw no need to return to Orvieto but proposed to wait at Turin until he received further instructions. He expressed the opinion, however, that, since the pope had made so much difficulty about the commission for Wolsey which he had already granted, it would be extremely difficult to induce him to send a special legate.[2]

When Knight's reports reached England they were well received; Wolsey sent those addressed to himself to the king and remarked that 'there seemed to be good towardness in the affairs' in Italy.[3] This good impression does not seem to have survived the realization that Knight had, in fact, gained very little, and as late as 21 April Knight was still in France where the king wished him to remain. From there he wrote to the king in an attempt to mollify his displeasure, saying that it pierced his stomach that any charge committed to him should not be performed according to the king's pleasure, as chanced at his last journey.[4]

[1] Wolsey, of course, was not then to know that the amendments made to the commission by Pucci rendered it virtually useless for his purpose, that is, to enable him to declare the marriage invalid without the possibility of his sentence being reversed on appeal.

[2] cf. Knight's letters to Henry VIII and Wolsey, both dated 10 Jan. 1528 (*L. & P.*, iv, 3787, 3788).

[3] Wolsey to Henry VIII, 28 Jan. 1528 (*L. & P.*, iv, 3851).

[4] Knight to Henry VIII, 21 April 1528 (Pocock, i, 160; *L. & P.*, iv, 4185).

III

The Decretal Commission

I

The interval between Wolsey's return from France in September 1527 and his fall from power in 1529 was filled with the question of the divorce. During this period Henry again and again asked for what the pope could not grant and when, after each refusal, he renewed his demand the menace with which he made it became greater; it was the burden of the king's messages to the papacy that he asked only for what he had been promised, and had been promised only what he was entitled to expect. At the same time Wolsey exerted himself to the utmost to secure what the king wanted, for he well knew that failure would entail his utter ruin. The pope against whom the wiles and shifting policies of the two men were directed was, unhappily, a man of so weak and vacillating a character that he was the shuttlecock of European politics, pitched this way and that by the varying and various policies of the powers. Giulio de Medici, before his election to the papacy as Clement VII, was in no way remarkable, but he had the reputation of a hard worker with businesslike and temperate habits. His previous career had not imposed upon him any burdens that might have brought to light the latent defects of his character, but as pope his weaknesses were soon revealed.[1] Not only was he politically incompetent but his duplicity earned him almost universal distrust. His vacillations sprang from an inability to reach a firm decision, a weakness that the Venetian ambassador, Contarini, attributed, with some justification, to lack of courage. The results of these defects were further aggravated by an excessive love of secrecy and an inability to express himself with clarity. His weaknesses of charac-

[1] One is reminded of the severe judgment passed on the emperor Galba by Tacitus: 'et omnium consensu capax imperii nisi imperasset' (*Histories*, i, 49). Eustache Chapuys reported the opinion of the nuncio that Clement 'was influenced by timidity, which is constitutional with him'; see Chapuys to Charles V, 21 Feb. 1531 (*L. & P.*, v, 112). Earlier in the letter Chapuys had said that the pope's 'timidity [*doulceur*] and dissimulation would not only prejudice the queen's interests, but his own authority'.

ter rendered him incapable of remaining neutral in any dispute, and his habit of simultaneously engaging himself to each of the parties to a quarrel inevitably resulted in his incurring the enmity of both. It was with justice that Henry VIII remarked to Campeggio that Clement 'was a very worthy pontiff, but this way of his of dealing now with one side and now with another, and not being truly and sincerely neutral, was not pleasant'.[1] Such was the man from whom king and cardinal hoped to extract a commission which would enable them to stage the facade of a trial, with judges chosen by themselves who would deliver in the king's favour a judgment that had been determined before ever the proceedings began. But not even Clement VII could be induced to participate in such a villainous scheme.

When Wolsey's instructions of 27 December had been received, Knight, as previously noticed, left the matter to be dealt with by Gregory Casale. Casale had a long conference with the pope on 12 and 13 January at which they discussed the despatch of the legate whom Wolsey wanted. The pope expressed himself as being very anxious to satisfy the king, but said that he must consult Pucci and Simonetta as to the best method of proceeding. According to Casale, they recommended that Henry should commit his cause to Wolsey who would try it by virtue either of the commission which Knight had already obtained, or of his legatine authority; then, should the king find that his conscience had been unburdened by Wolsey's decision, he could marry again. In that case, if his marriage were questioned, a legate could be sent from Rome to decide the matter. This, it was said, was the most expeditious way of proceeding because, if the queen were cited, she would put in no answer but protest against the place of trial and the judges, and then the imperialists would demand a prohibition from the pope and so prevent the king's remarriage. On the other hand, if the king adopted the suggestion of Pucci and Simonetta and actually married again, the most the imperialists could put forward would be suspicions that Wolsey and the other cardinal were biased; in such a case, the pope would give sentence and so a judgment would be obtained to which neither Spaniard nor German could object. Casale added that the pope himself suggested

---

[1] As reported by Campeggio to Salviati, secretary of state, 26 Oct. 1528 (Ehses, 55): 'Soggiungendo, che essa era dignissimo Pontifice, ma che questo trattare hora con uno et hora con un altro et non esser neutrale vero et sincero non gli piaceva'.

39

this method of proceeding, but was anxious that the suggestion should not be thought of as coming from him.[1]

Whether the two cardinals, Pucci and Simonetta, proposed such a scheme in the form reported by Casale is, perhaps, open to doubt, but it seems clear that the pope was unwilling to send a legate, as demanded by Wolsey, since to do so would have angered the emperor whose prisoner he had so recently been. It may be supposed, however, that it would have suited the pope that Henry should accept the full responsibility and take matters into his own hands if he could not be induced to drop the matter altogether. The pope was anxious to satisfy Henry but he was afraid of the emperor; he did not refuse absolutely to send a legate but, as reported by Casale, put forward a number of difficulties: among the cardinals acceptable to Casale, de Cesis was a hostage at Naples, Caesarinus held a Spanish bishopric, Aracoeli had the gout, and even Campeggio, most suitable of all, could not leave Rome until Lautrec advanced further. In the event a legate was not sent.

The failure, so far, to obtain any commission that would enable Wolsey to dispose finally of the marriage question caused the cardinal and his master considerable concern. It was, therefore, determined to send a new embassy to the pope. The ambassadors selected were not, however, experienced diplomats but two young men, Stephen Gardiner, the king's secretary, and Edward Foxe. Each of them was a man of considerable ability and much ambition: Stephen Gardiner, subtle of mind, was an able advocate and the best canonist in England; Edward Foxe had considerable diplomatic gifts and in 1536 was to be employed on a mission to establish a rapprochement with the German protestants; both men subsequently became bishops. Foxe and Gardiner were instructed to obtain from the pope a commission that was entirely to Wolsey's liking, but the preceding activities of Knight and Casale were not the best of preparations at the papal court for such an embassy.

The king appears to have abandoned his scheme of dealing with the pope behind Wolsey's back, perhaps as a result of the failure of Knight's mission; at all events, the instructions of Foxe and Gardiner were drafted by Wolsey. They were instructed that on their arrival in Rome they were first to consult with Gambara, then bishop elect of Tortona, and Sir Gregory Casale. In particular, they were to ascertain from Gam-

---

[1] See Gregory Casale to Wolsey, 13 Jan. 1528 (*L. & P.*, iv, 3802); part of this letter is printed in Burnet, i, Coll. of Rec., p. 26, and Pocock-Burnet, iv, 41.

bara what were the pope's intentions in the matter, and what the pope desired of the king for the recovery of those places that had been taken from him. After these preliminaries they were to approach the pope himself. They were to thank him for the dispensation and commission already granted but they were to mention that these documents were not as effective as the pope, no doubt, intended them to be.[1] They were then to disabuse the mind of the pope of a misapprehension under which he seemed to be labouring. It appeared that the pope believed the king had set the matter on foot, not out of anxiety for the succession, but out of 'vain affection' for a lady who was not very highly esteemed.[2] They were to assure his holiness that Wolsey would not, for any consideration, swerve from the path of rectitude, and that the cardinal was convinced of the invalidity of the king's marriage to Catherine. As that marriage was contrary to God's law, the king's conscience was grievously troubled, but on the other hand,

the approved, excellent virtuous qualities of the said gentlewoman [Anne Boleyn], the purity of her life, her constant virginity, her maidenly and womanly pudicity, her soberness, chasteness, meekness, humility, descent of right noble and high through regal blood,[3] education in all good and laudable [qualities] and manners, apparent aptness to procreation of children, with her other infinite good qualities, more to be regarded and esteemed than the only progeny,

were the only grounds on which the king's desire was founded, and which Wolsey regarded as honest and necessary.[4]

[1] In his instructions to Gardiner and Foxe, Wolsey said that the dispensation and commission which had been granted 'in their present form, are as good as none at all'; an interesting echo of the disappointment felt at the failure of the efforts of Knight and Gregory Casale. And in a letter to Sir Gregory Casale of 12 Feb. 1528 (*State Papers*, vii, 50; *L. & P.*, iv, 3918), Wolsey said that the dispensation and commission already granted by the pope were of no effect.

[2] cf. Foxe to Gardiner, 11 May 1528 (*L. & P.*, iv, 4251 (p. 1872)): 'the pope declared to us he had been told, long before our coming, that the king wanted this only for private reasons, and that she was with child, and of no such qualities as should be worthy [of the king]'.

[3] Anne Boleyn's great-grandfather was mayor of London in 1457 and was knighted; his son, William Boleyn, married a daughter of the earl of Ormond and their son, Sir Thomas Boleyn, was Anne's father who had been created viscount Rochford as recently as 16 June 1525. Anne's mother was the daughter of a duke of Norfolk. The Boleyn wealth was commercial.

[4] *L. & P.*, iv, p. 1741. This description of Anne Boleyn serves to give some indication of the magnitude of Wolsey's anxiety to preserve his position by obtaining for the king what he wanted.

Gardiner and Foxe were then directed to express Wolsey's pleasure that the pope was aware of the dangers inherent in a disputed succession and was willing to provide a remedy. As he had already shown his good will by granting the dispensation and commission, he was to be asked to supply the defects in those documents and to ensure that they might be effectual. The ambassadors were therefore to beg the pope to grant the dispensation and commission, the so-called decretal commission, in the form devised in England, without alteration, and to send a legate. The commission was, preferably, to be directed to the legate to be chosen and to Wolsey and if such a commission were obtained, Foxe was to return with it immediately while Gardiner waited for the proposed legate. Rewards were to be offered and every effort made that, when the legate was appointed, cardinal Lorenzo Campeggio[1] be sent in preference to all others.

If they failed to obtain such a commission, the ambassadors were then to threaten the pope. They were to tell him that if the king could not obtain justice in the manner asked for, he would be compelled to seek it elsewhere and live out of the laws of holy church; and, however reluctant he might be, he would be driven to such a course in order to quieten his conscience. The ambassadors were to tell his holiness that the king intended to proceed, whether the pope acceded to his wishes or not, and they were to stress the danger to Wolsey that would necessarily ensue. If, however, the pope, despite the threats, would not agree to issue a commission to the legate and Wolsey jointly, they were to try and obtain a commission for one legate only, and, failing that, a commission addressed to the archbishop of Canterbury, William Warham, or some other bishop to be joined with him.[2]

So fearful was Wolsey that this embassy might not be successful and so bring disaster upon himself, that he addressed a personal letter to the pope in which he urged the importance of the king's cause, and pointed out that it concerned the safety of the king and the preservation of the kingdom, the public peace, the apostolic authority and Wolsey's very life. He implored the pope to grant the king's request, declaring that if it were not a just one he would undergo any punishment. He feared that unless the king were given what he wanted he would be driven by divine

[1] Campeggio had been appointed bishop of Salisbury in 1524; he was non-resident.
[2] Wolsey to Gardiner and Foxe, Feb. 1528 (*L. & P.*, iv, 3913).

42

and human law to seek his rights from the whole of christendom since, by the emperor's influence, justice was being denied him; and Wolsey warned the pope not to allow his authority to be thus injured.[1]

Gardiner and Foxe arrived at Dover on Tuesday, 10 February, and embarked the following day, but 'after getting half seas over', they were compelled to return and they did not get away until two in the morning of the following Saturday. After a tempestuous and 'very troublesome passage' they arrived at Calais at 8 p.m. on Sunday 15 February.[2] They did not reach Orvieto until Saturday 21 March, and they found the town in a sorry state. The pope was housed in the decayed palace of the bishop, but they could not tell how he could be described as being at liberty there, where hunger, scarcity, bad lodgings and ill air kept him as much confined as he had been in the castle of St Angelo.[3] Throughout the following month they had daily conferences with the pope, at which the discussions lasted for three or four hours without interruption, and on one occasion the conference was prolonged for five hours, until one o'clock in the morning. Their instructions required the ambassadors to use some audacity, and in their reports they were careful to convey the impression that audacity had been used. They appear to have made little attempt to spare the pope's feelings and, to use their own phrase, they 'spake roundly unto him'.[4]

[1] Wolsey to Clement VII, Feb. 1528, printed in Pocock-Burnet, iv, 45, and (from another draft, with variants) in Burnet, i, Coll. of Rec., p. 29, where the date 'Febr. 10. 1528' has been supplied from a note written in a modern hand (*L. & P.*, iv, 3912). Wolsey also sent letters to Giberto, bishop of Verona, urging him to take up again his public offices and assist the king, to the cardinal of Ancona, Pucci, Campeggio, and others (*L. & P.*, iv, 3903-6, 3908, 3920, 3921), and Henry himself wrote to the pope, Campeggio and other cardinals (*L. & P.*, iv, 3909-11, 3919). Wolsey had already, in Dec. 1527, told the pope that if he wished to keep the king and England devoted to him, and if he desired the restoration of the holy see, he must send a decretal commission in the amplest and strongest form, which Wolsey would keep secret; see the draft letter from Wolsey to Clement VII, printed in Pocock, i, 166 (*L. & P.*, iv, 3646).
[2] See the letters of Gardiner and Foxe to Wolsey, 13 and 17 Feb. 1528 (Pocock, i, 73, 75; *L. & P.*, iv, 3925, 3932). While waiting at Dover they had considered Wolsey's suggestion that Foxe, being the king's councillor and first named in the king's instructions, should have precedence, and that Gardiner should be spokesman; they had agreed that Gardiner should have pre-eminence both in place and speech (*L. & P.*, iv, 3925).
[3] Gardiner and Foxe to Tuke, 23 Mar. 1528 (*L. & P.*, iv, 4090).
[4] See Gardiner and Gregory Casale to Wolsey, 13 Apr. 1528 (Pocock, i, 120, at p. 127; *L. & P.*, iv, p. 1839).

It is unnecessary here to trace the day-to-day details of these conferences,[1] and it is sufficient to give a general account of their substance. It is, however, necessary to stress that the document chiefly desired by Wolsey and which their instructions required the ambassadors to obtain as the first of the possible alternatives open to them, was called a 'decretal commission', which they understood as 'a commission decretal *in eventum veritatis facti allegati*, defining the law'.[2] In other words, what was desired was a commission to enable Wolsey or other commissioner to ascertain facts, while the commission itself declared the law which determined the issue when the facts had been found. Thus the law applicable to the case was to be declared beforehand by the highest legislative authority in the church; a commission in this form virtually excluded the possibility of an appeal on a point of law, but the ambassadors were nevertheless instructed to take care that the commission should expressly exclude the possibility of an appeal from any judgment given under it.[3]

Accordingly, Gardiner and Foxe began to press the pope to grant a decretal commission, but the previous activities of Knight and Gregory Casale, while not producing the results looked for by the king and Wolsey, had put the pope and the cardinals on their guard. The demand made by Gardiner, who was the principal spokesman, was met by the offer of a general commission. Gardiner, however, continued to insist upon a decretal commission, answering one by one the objections made to it;

[1] The conferences may be followed in detail in the reports of the ambassadors, printed in Pocock, vol. 1, and calendared in *L. & P.*, vol. 4 (pt. 2), which should, however, be compared with the more sober accounts of Pucci printed in Ehses.

[2] Casale, Gardiner and Foxe to Wolsey, 31 Mar. 1528 (*L. & P.*, iv, p. 1820; Pocock, i, 95, at p. 101).

[3] By the sixteenth century such instruments were only rarely used. They derived their name, decretal commissions, from the fact that they were modelled upon the *literae decretales* which were the written decisions of popes in cases submitted to them. The nature of a decretal commission is adumbrated by the chapter *Veniens* of the title *De Sponsalibus* in the decretals of Gregory IX, the whole of which chapter Gardiner recited by heart as part of his endeavours to secure the grant of a decretal commission: 'As to the form of the commission, he [Pucci] rehearsed his old opinion. Whereunto we said, Answer was made there by the advice of sundry learned men, who thought that the form desired by the king's highness is conformable to such as be in the Decretals; and rehearsed by heart the chapter *Veniens*, in the title *De Sponsalibus*; which is in such like form as the king's highness desireth.' (Casale, Gardiner and Foxe to Wolsey, 31 Mar. 1528; Pocock, i, 95, at p. 103).

indeed, on one occasion he and Foxe discussed the matter with Simonetta, the dean of the Rota, from early in the morning until late at night.[1] They had a long discussion with the pope after dinner on Passion Sunday but his holiness, after consulting several cardinals, showed considerable reluctance to grant the commission. Gardiner said that there were only two questions: was the pope willing to grant the commission; and, if he were willing, had he the power to do so? Gardiner assured the pope that he did not doubt his good will, and so far as his powers to grant the commission were concerned, he considered that the offers already made were conclusive, since Pucci and Simonetta had said that once the sentence were pronounced the pope would confirm it. This implied that the cause was good, for if it were not good it ought not to be confirmed.[2]

The pope and his advisers continued to make objections, and Gardiner continued to press for a decretal commission, insisting that he sought nothing illegal. The point was reached when, after a long discussion, Gardiner desired the pope and the others present to note and ponder what he should say concerning the pope's authority, namely that, unless they took some other course than that they seemed inclined to take, it would create a 'marvellous opinion' of his holiness and the college of cardinals, for people would say that they either could not or would not make any certain reply; and if they refused to show the way to a wanderer, which was a task entrusted to them by God, especially when that wanderer was a prince to whom they were much indebted, the people would begin to exclaim against their cunning and dissimulation, and the king and lords of England would be driven to think that God had taken away from the holy see the key of knowledge and would begin to adopt the opinion of those who thought that pontifical laws which were not clear even to the pope himself might well be committed to the flames. To all this, the ambassadors complained, no answer was given except the old advice to come to a compromise. When, afterwards,

---

[1] See *L. & P.*, iv, p. 1820: 'From seven in the morning until night we discussed the commission with Simonett, until he descended to persuade us to be satisfied with a general commission, and not in the form we desired, being new and out of course. If so, it could be sped tomorrow, and within three months sentence be given in England, and remitted here to be confirmed.' Simonetta had, by then, succeeded Stafileo as dean of the Rota.

[2] *L. & P.*, iv, p. 1821. The flaw in this argument was, of course, that neither Pucci nor Simonetta could bind the pope, in advance, to confirm a sentence whether it were just or not.

Gardiner told the pope privately that he must see the justice of the king's cause, 'his holiness said that he was not learned, and to say the truth, albeit that it were a saying in the law that *Pontifex habet omnia jura in scrinio pectoris*, yet God never gave unto him the key to open *illud scrinium*'. The pope said he would consult the cardinals and auditors, and having done so, he announced that they had advised him not to grant a decretal commission in the form desired.

The next day the ambassadors told the pope flatly that 'the king's highness would do it without him'. The pope replied that he would it were done 'and to the other words [said] nothing but sighed and wiped his eyes, saying, that in a matter *in qua vertitur jus tertii* he could do nothing without the counsel' of the cardinals; he added that he wished it were in his power to do something for the king, if it were to his own hurt only.[1]

Thus far the account of these conferences has been taken from the reports of the English ambassadors which were written by Gardiner in a glowing style well calculated to display fully the force of his approach and his mastery of argument. It is, therefore, interesting and profitable to interrupt the narrative of the negotiations in order to compare Gardiner's account with the more sober memorandum of the foregoing conferences prepared by cardinal Pucci for the pope. In contrast to Gardiner's highly coloured accounts, Pucci's memorandum is a businesslike document which states clearly and concisely the points which were raised and the answers which were made to them.[2]

According to Pucci's memorandum the English ambassadors began by demanding a decretal commission, and the cardinal noted that they could not be persuaded that it was sufficient if the pope committed the cause to judges in the country concerned, to inquire not only whether the facts alleged were true but whether they were sufficient to render the dispensation invalid. The ambassadors objected that the king could obtain such a commission from his own ordinary, to which Pucci replied that it were better so. The ambassadors answered that they wished to obtain the commission from the pope on account of his greater authority,

---

[1] Gardiner and Gregory Casale to Wolsey, 13 April 1528 (Pocock, i, 120; *L. & P.*, iv, p. 1839). The quotations are at Pocock, i, 127.

[2] For Pucci's memorandum, see Ehses, 23-6. It appears from this memorandum, as it does not from Gardiner's reports, that the arguments of the Englishmen were fully and adequately answered. Gardiner gives the impression that the pope and his cardinals had no answer to the arguments put to them and sought merely to gain time by making captious objections.

for if it were done by the pope, all the people of England would approve of it and assent to it without difficulty, which would not be the case if a commission were obtained from the king's ordinary or from some other bishop of his kingdom. The English ambassadors further argued that there were ancient decretals which would provide a precedent.[1] To this Pucci replied that at the time when the decretals were made it was necessary to act in that way because no canons had then been published, but at the time when the discussion was proceeding, matters must be decided according to the canons then published. The memorandum referred to some of the arguments set out in a book drawn up by the king concerning his own case which Gardiner had presented to the pope,[2] and observed that the canons already published were sufficient to determine the question whether the facts of the case invalidated the dispensation. And Pucci remarked that should the pope, in the decretal commission demanded, declare to be law what should afterwards be found to be otherwise, it would be a scandal to the whole world.[3]

From this point onwards we are dependent upon Gardiner's reports, and allowance must be made for the characteristics already noted. Gardiner by now had reached the conclusion that it was useless to persist with the demand for a decretal commission, and the ambassadors turned their attention to the next alternative in their instructions, 'the second degree' Gardiner called it, and set about trying to obtain a general commission. To assist them in this task they called upon Sir Gregory Casale who opened the matter to the pope. However, hope of a decretal commission was not entirely abandoned; in a private conversation with his holiness Casale said, as of himself, that he would ascertain if his colleagues would be satisfied with a general commission,

---

[1] A reference, evidently, to Gardiner's recital of the chapter *Veniens* from the Decretals of Gregory IX; see p. 44, note 3.
[2] cf. *L. & P.*, iv, p. 1819.
[3] 'Et quia a Sanctitate Vestra in dicta commissione praecise petunt, illas declarari sufficientes ad inducendam nullitatem litterarum dispensationis, et solum mandari iudicibus, ut examinent, si sint verae vel non; et quoad hoc dicebatur eis: si Sanctitas Vestra hoc declarabat, et de iure aliter esset et per appellationem seu alias super veritate declarationis Sanctitatis Vestrae discuteretur et de iure contrarium esset, quod eadem Sanctitas Vestra declaravit, Sanctitas Vestra ab omnibus laceraretur et damnaretur, et per hoc scandalizaretur totus mundus, et revocaretur vigore commissionis, quam Sanctitas Vestra contra declarationem suam signare cogeretur in signatura iustitiae.' (Ehses, 24).

provided the pope would 'pass in secret manner the decretal commission; the same not to come *in publicum*' unless the pope did not confirm the sentence. The pope answered that it would be well to mention it to Casale's colleagues, and he himself would consider the matter.[1]

On Palm Sunday the ambassadors waited on the pope to receive his answer on this matter. The pope told them that he was in a dilemma: if it were just to issue the decretal commission it ought to be done publicly, but if it were unjust it would be a scandal and would trouble his conscience. Gardiner replied that it was just and should be done publicly, but since fear of the emperor prevented such a course, it could be done without fear in secret; and, no doubt, Wolsey's dexterity could induce the king to take it in good part. Nevertheless, the ambassadors had to leave empty-handed; Gardiner observed that the pope 'perceiveth better and sooner all that is spoken than any other, yet to give an answer yea or nay, *nunquam vidi tam tardum*'.[2]

The ambassadors then privately consulted Simonetta and, after expressing appreciation of his services which, they said, would be highly rewarded by the king, they asked him, as a friend and not in his judicial capacity, for his opinion of the king's matter; and they told him that he might safely give his opinion as they 'were not going to stick any further' in the matter of the decretal commission. They reported that Simonetta had replied that, assuming the facts were proved, he considered the cause great and just.[3]

Having now abandoned the attempt to obtain a decretal commission, Gardiner drafted a form of general commission, with the clauses contained in their instructions. Objections, however, were soon taken to this document. Gardiner complained that

hitherto we have done as they do; for they always praise the present flavour of the meat, though they are compelled to blame the cooking. Hitherto they have been quite in favour of a general commission, but when it comes to the point we find it is not agreeable. We had always been told it should be your own

---

[1] Gardiner and Gregory Casale to Wolsey, 13 April 1528 (Pocock, i, 120, at p. 127; *L. & P.*, iv, p. 1839.)

[2] Ibid. (Pocock, i, p. 1 *L. & P.*, 28; iv, p. 1839)

[3] *L. & P.*, iv, pp. 1839, 1840. This is Gardiner's version of the conversation. However, we know that a little earlier Simonetta had privately expressed to the pope an opinion in the exactly contrary sense (cf. Ehses, 22). Gardiner's version, therefore, may be an instance of his exaggeration, designed to please the eye of the king and Wolsey.

devising; but when we had made it they all took counsel to catch us in our speech, and prevent the meaning of the plainest words.[1]

At the pope's direction, they showed the draft to Simonetta who found only minor faults with it, but when they took it to cardinal Pucci he told them that it could not be granted, remarking that a sick man, on consulting his physician, did not prescribe the medicine himself. At length they left the draft with cardinal del Monte to be revised by him, and they were told by the cardinals that it would not be altered very much. On the Tuesday after Palm Sunday they were shown the revised draft, but when they saw the extent of the alterations that had been made in it, they accused the pope of breaking his promise to them.

There followed a series of long and heated discussions which reached their climax when Gardiner declared that when they reported what sort of men the pope had for his advisers, the only friend that his holiness had, the king of England, would be taken away and the holy see would fall to pieces with the consent and applause of everybody. 'At these words', Gardiner reported, 'the pope's holiness, casting his arms abroad, bade us put in the words we varied for, and therewith walked up and down the chamber, casting now and then his arms abroad, we standing in a great silence.'[2] In this fashion the commission was obtained. After

[1] *L. & P.*, iv, p. 1840. The quotation is from the calendar; the relevant portion of Gardiner and Casale's letter is as follows (Pocock, i, 129): 'Hitherto in our first letters and these we have in our writings done as they do, *qui dum comedunt, praesentem sibi saporem probant, quem in concoctione molestum improbare coguntur. Hactenus verba optima et dulcissima*, and specially for granting the general Commission, which in execution when it cometh to the point, we find *effectu amara*. Heretofore it was said unto us the Commission should be of your devising, now when we had made it, *Omnes inierunt consilium, ut caperent, in sermone, ut verbis optimis struant calumnias, et syncerissimo sensu scripta pervertant*, as I shall briefly note, and master Fox can more amply shew unto your grace.'

[2] *L. & P.*, iv, p. 1841. As to 'the words we varied for', see *L. & P.*, iv, p. 1840: 'Began a new discussion with Simonetta, the cardinals being absent. At last we differed but in two words, *omnem* to be added to *potestatem*, and *nolente* to the clause *nolente impedito*. This Simonetta would not do without the advice of the cardinals.' The commission as granted included the following clause (Ehses, 29, 30): 'Vobis coniunctim et altero vestrum nolente aut impedito divisim citra omnem personae aut iurisdictionis gradum omni recusatione et appellatione remotis vices et omnem auctoritatem nostram committimus et demandamus vosque etiam coniunctim et altero vestrum nolente aut impedito divisim ut praefertur, ad ea omnia, quae in hac commissione continentur, dumtaxat exequenda expedienda ac plenae finalique executioni demandanda vicegerentes nostros etiam ex certa nostra scientia creamus et deputamus'.

it had been written out and sealed, Gardiner and Foxe again resorted to the pope and cardinals, who expressed their great desire to satisfy the king; Gardiner and Foxe replied that the commission which had been granted would not satisfy him although they assured his holiness that they would do their best to make it acceptable. Gardiner, writing to Wolsey, expressed the view that it was as good as could be devised and was, in effect, all that could be wished save that there were no clauses providing for the pope's confirmation and against his revocation of the cause. Nevertheless, the pope told the English ambassadors to inform the king that he committed himself to his protection as the sending of the commission was, in effect, a declaration against the emperor.

The commission was dated 13 April 1528, at Orvieto, and was directed to Wolsey and Campeggio.[1] Campeggio was then in Rome and had not been consulted, and Gardiner left Orvieto to secure his consent. It was, perhaps, because of the uncertainties about Campeggio's position that an alternative commission, bearing the same date, was issued to Wolsey, with Warham as his coadjutor.[2] On the same day there was also issued a dispensation for the eventual marriage of the king to Anne Boleyn, in the form drafted by Wolsey; this was the document for which Knight had considered it unnecessary to apply after he had obtained a similar dispensation.[3]

Campeggio was not then able to act under the commission, as upon him fell the heavy responsibility for the civil government of Rome. The commission of 13 April was accordingly not despatched and still remains in the papal archives. In order to free Campeggio from these duties so that he might undertake the business of the divorce, the pope appointed cardinal Farnese to take his place as governor of Rome, by an instrument issued at Viterbo on 3 June.[4] Then, with Campeggio free

[1] For the text of the commission, see Ehses, 28-30.
[2] cf. Rymer, *Foedera*, xiv, 237. It is noteworthy that in his (and Casale's) long letter of 13 April 1528 (Pocock, i, 120; *L. & P.*, iv, 4167), Gardiner did not mention this commission; he evidently attached no importance to it (unless Gardiner sent another, private, letter to Wolsey which is now lost). The commission was directed solely to Wolsey but added 'adiuncto tibi venerabili fratre archiepiscopo Cantuariensi' (Ehses, 30).
[3] Henry's conscientious scruples about his marriage to Catherine are thus seen to be the preliminary to a series of manoeuvres designed to enable him to contract another marriage to which there was precisely the same objection. cf. Froude, *The Divorce of Catherine of Aragon* (London 1891), 55.
[4] For the text of the instrument appointing Farnese, see Ehses, 39.

and willing to act as commissioner, a new commission was issued, dated 8 June at Viterbo. This new commission was in all respects identical with the previous one of 13 April.[1] The effect of the commission was to appoint Wolsey and Campeggio to inquire into all the facts which had a bearing on the validity of the dispensation granted by Julius II, and, in the light of the facts so found, to pronounce sentence determining whether Henry's marriage were lawful or not. If the legates should pronounce the marriage to be null and void, they were empowered to declare legitimate the offspring of that marriage and of any subsequent marriage. And, not least important, there was a provision which enabled one legate to act alone if the other were unwilling or unable to act, and which clothed the legates with all the authority of the pope and forbade any appeal or refusal of jurisdiction.[2]

Meanwhile Foxe had returned to England to give an account of what had been done. He left Orvieto as soon as the commission of 13 April had been sealed and reached Paris on the 27th. He crossed from Calais and arrived at Sandwich on 2 May. He reached Greenwich late on the following afternoon. Wolsey had already left the court but Foxe was received by the king to whom he gave a full report. The king seemed 'marvellously well pleased' and, calling in Anne Boleyn, he made Foxe repeat all that he had said. The king then questioned him closely, and wanted to know what provision had been made against 'recusation' and appeal, and Foxe showed him the relevant clause. With this the king seemed to be satisfied, but said he would consult Wolsey. From Greenwich Foxe went at once to Durham Place to see the cardinal, and Wolsey, although it was late and he was in bed, received him immediately. When Foxe explained that they had not been able to obtain the decretal commission, Wolsey seemed much perplexed, thinking the commission that had been granted to be of no more value than that brought by Gambara. However, he told Foxe to leave the copy of the commission with him for

---

[1] The text of the commission of 8 June is identical with that of 13 April (printed in Ehses, 28-30), and was printed in Lord Herbert's *The Life and raigne of King Henry the Eighth*, p. 107, with some inaccuracies. It is also printed in Pocock, i, 167.

[2] For the text of this clause (which was the one that had caused Gardiner so much trouble), see p. 49, note 2. The provision forbidding appeal or refusal of jurisdiction merely prevented the competence of the tribunal being challenged; it did not prevent a person from objecting to the place of trial or to the judge or judges as being suspect of partiality.

E

the night, together with the letters from the pope and Gardiner. On the following afternoon Wolsey studied these documents with Foxe and Dr Bell, in the presence of lord Rochford, and expressed himself as satisfied.[1] The cardinal's disappointment must, however, have been intense, and since he had failed to obtain complete and absolute control of the marriage suit he was doubtless aware that his ruin was but a matter of time.

2

The depression which settled upon Wolsey as he studied the results obtained by Gardiner and Foxe served to spur him to further efforts. On Wednesday, 6 May, the day after he had looked at the documents with Dr Bell and lord Rochford, Wolsey summoned Foxe, together with Dr Wolman and Thomas Benet, his chaplain, for a conference, and in the afternoon the cardinal gave Foxe and Peter Vannes, one of his secretaries, further instructions to be sent to Gardiner; Foxe was ordered to convey these instructions.[2] Foxe was directed first to express to Gardiner the high appreciation of the king and Wolsey for his services, and then to tell him that Wolsey himself, for the discharge of his own conscience and considering the chances of mortality, was anxious that he should use all possible means to persuade the pope to grant the decretal commission, which was to be sent to the cardinal in the most secret fashion. Wolsey said that there were four reasons for renewing the demand for the decretal commission. First, it would provide his conscience with a rule to guide him in the proceedings, since it would determine the law on points that might be called in controversy, would enable a final sentence to be pronounced, and would prevent any subsequent attempts to set that sentence aside. Second, it would enable him easily to induce all those who 'be of the adversaries' part' to conform to the king's opinion.

[1] See Foxe to Gardiner, 11 May 1528 (Pocock, i, 141; *L. & P.*, iv, 4251).
[2] These instructions are contained in the same letter in which Foxe told Gardiner of his reception by the king and Wolsey (Pocock, i, 141; *L. & P.*, iv, 4251), cited in note 1, above. Although this letter was completed on Monday 11 May, the greater part (describing Foxe's arrival and setting out Wolsey's instructions for Gardiner) was drafted on Thursday, 7 May, and was read over to Wolsey, at his direction, on Friday, 8 May (see Pocock, i, 150; *L. & P.*, iv, p. 1873). Foxe, in his letter, complained that he was busy all Thursday penning the instructions which, for lack of experience, was a painful task for him.

Third, considering the uncertainty of life, Wolsey thought it better to enter that sea of judicial proceedings[1] by an open investigation of the cause, yet at that time everything hung upon the sole will of the pope, whether he would confirm the sentence or not, with which many things might interfere. Fourth, it would greatly conduce to the stability of the holy see if Wolsey's standing and authority with the king were such that Henry would readily agree to whatever Wolsey advised, and there were no better means to bring this about than by the grant of the decretal commission.[2]

When renewing his demand for the decretal commission, Gardiner was to assure the pope that Wolsey did not intend to 'make process by virtue thereof', and would not show the commission to any other person whereby the least slander might arise to the prejudice of the holy see; it would be shown to the king alone as a means of increasing the cardinal's influence with him. If, after three or four audiences, Gardiner saw no reason to expect that the pope would change his mind, he was to return home, leaving matters to be prosecuted by Sir Gregory Casale. Finally, as the lawyers in England were asserting that the queen had a right of appeal, Gardiner was to consult the most learned men at the papal court and discover whether she had such a right or not; and if so, what would be the effect of such an appeal, whether the legates might proceed notwithstanding an appeal, and whether, an appeal being made, the parties would be free to contract new marriages.

After the draft of these instructions had been read to Wolsey and he had approved them on Friday 8 May,[3] a further point occurred to him. On Saturday he summoned both Foxe and Dr Bell, and told Foxe to instruct Gardiner that he should consult Stafileo and others. The question on which he was to seek their opinion was whether the commission would be rendered invalid if the queen renounced, as Wolsey was informed she intended to do, all benefit under the dispensation of Julius II and relied solely on the allegation *quod non fuit cognita ab Arthuro*, in which case there would be no affinity at all. Wolsey himself thought that such a plea would fail, because the dispensation of Julius did not

---

[1] 'Pelagus illud judiciorum'.
[2] Foxe to Gardiner, 11 May 1528 (Pocock, i, 141, at pp. 147, 148; *L. & P.*, iv, 4251).
[3] Brian Tuke, one of Wolsey's secretaries, had also prepared letters from Wolsey to Gardiner which were read to Foxe (see *L. & P.*, iv, p. 1873) but these have not survived; presumably they contained further and more secret directions.

mention *publica honestas*,[1] and the mere fact that the dispensation was granted implied that the marriage itself was unlawful. Moreover, the wording of the commission required, first, that the validity or invalidity of the dispensation be determined, second that the lawfulness of the marriage should be determined, and third that sentence of divorce should be given if that appeared to be just. But the lawyers in England were doubtful whether three separate sentences were to be given or whether a decision that the marriage was a nullity would determine the other two questions. Wolsey asserted that he was determined to proceed conscientiously, and he thought that the king had one strong ground to go upon, namely, that at the time the dispensation was obtained he knew nothing of the matter, and the cardinal wished Gardiner, without appearing to doubt the justice of the cause, to obtain an opinion on the point from the bishop of Ancona or some other learned man.

These instructions, together with Wolsey's other despatches, were to have been sent off by Barlow on Sunday 10 May, but when Wolsey read them to the king, Dr Wolman raised a point which Gardiner was instructed to discuss with the papal lawyers. The point was concerned with the validity of the clause in the commission excluding appeal, and Gardiner was instructed to state his opinion boldly, as the king was determined to do nothing illegal and was persuaded that if the queen used her right of appeal she would do much to advance her cause, an opinion that Wolsey had by degrees instilled into his mind. Then followed a remarkable scene which was described by Foxe as follows:

Insomuch that yesterday to my great marvel, and no less joy and comfort, his grace [Wolsey], openly, in presence of Mr Tuke, Mr Wolman, Mr Bell, and me, made protestation to the king's highness, 'That although he was so much bound unto the same as any subject might be to his prince, and by reason thereof his grace was of so perfect devotion, faith, and loyalty towards his majesty that he could gladly spend goods, blood, and life in his just causes; yet sith his grace was more obliged to God, and that he was sure he should render an account *de operibus suis* before him; he would in this matter rather suffer his high indignation, yea, and his body jointly to be torn in pieces, than he would do anything in this cause otherwise than justice requireth; nor that his highness should look after other favour to be ministered unto him in this c use on his grace's part, than the justness of the cause would bear. But if the ll [of dispensation] were sufficient, he would so pronounce it, and rathei uffer *extrema quaeque* than to do the contrary, or else *contra conscientiam suam*.'[2]

[1] See p. 16, note 2.
[2] Foxe to Gardiner, 11 May 1528 (Pocock, i, 141, at pp. 153, 154; *L. & P.*, iv, 4251).

No doubt this extraordinary scene was merely a piece of play acting, performed so that it should be reported to Gardiner who would bring it to the notice of the pope. The object of the play acting was to increase the chances of obtaining the decretal commission, for if the pope retained the impression that Wolsey was no more than the king's creature ready to please him in all things, and that the king himself was not sincere, it was extremely unlikely that the pope would grant the decretal commission.[1]

As the result of an interview with the king on the morning of Monday 11 May, Foxe added a postscript to his long letter. The king wished Gardiner to know that he thought it important to obtain the decretal commission but that, if Gardiner despaired of obtaining it, he was to say to the pope that he was seriously afraid the refusal of the commission would so work upon the king as to alienate him from his holiness, seeing that he had never as yet done anything for the king's own sake, and such a result would be very prejudicial to the pope.

Wolsey was making a last determined effort to obtain the decretal commission that would enable him to pass the sentence desired by the king in a form that could not be questioned. Wolsey had, it is true, instructed Gardiner to promise that the commission, if granted, would be treated with the utmost secrecy and shown to no one save the king; but if those promises were kept the commission would not have been any more useful to Wolsey than the commission already obtained. It seems very unlikely that Wolsey intended to honour his promises in the event of the pope granting the decretal commission. The king's sole object was to obtain, somehow, a sentence having the authority of the holy see that would enable him to marry Anne Boleyn as soon as possible. It was vital for Wolsey, therefore, to obtain the means to pass such a sentence. However, it has been noticed that doubts concerning the good faith of Henry and Wolsey had already entered the minds of members of the papal curia, and these doubts were, in all probability, increased by a statement made to cardinal Pucci by Gardiner and Foxe in the course of

[1] cf. J. Gairdner in *E.H.R.*, xii, 4. In the course of the conferences between the pope and Foxe and Gardiner, the pope had questioned whether Wolsey would be objected to, as judge in the matrimonial cause, as being suspect, since by the opinions he had already expressed he might be considered to have given sentence beforehand and could not be considered impartial (cf. Casale, Gardiner and Foxe to Wolsey, 31 Mar. 1528; *L. & P.*, iv, p. 1819). It was important, therefore, to convince the pope of Wolsey's impartiality.

their negotiations. They had said that if the judges, to whom the sole investigation of the case was to be committed by his holiness, declared the dispensation invalid and the marriage with Catherine void, so that the king would then be free to marry some other woman, the people of England would care nothing for any declaration that might afterwards be made to the contrary, whether by other judges, a papal commission, a succeeding pope or Clement himself.[1]

John Barlow, bearing Foxe's long letter and Wolsey's private instructions for Gardiner, arrived at the papal court late in May. In view of the pope's earlier and long maintained resistance to the demand for a decretal commission, Gardiner's task was not an easy one. However, he managed to prevail upon the pope to write to Henry from Viterbo on 9 June saying that in order to show the gratitude of the holy see to the king, he would endeavour to discover some way to satisfy his majesty, however arduous the task might be; but he would need to proceed in the business with deliberation.[2] Two days later Gardiner wrote to the king to say that, after many altercations and many promises made to the pope, his holiness had at last consented to send the decretal commission by Campeggio. Gardiner said that he had urged the pope to express the matter in special terms but without success, the pope remarking that the king would understand his meaning by the words *inventuri sumus aliquam formam*, a reference to the pope's own letter of 9 June. Gardiner

[1] Ehses, 25, 26 (Pucci's memorandum already cited, p. 46): 'Nec his acquieverunt, replicantes, quod populi illi et status, tam ecclesiasticus quam nobilium et plebeorum viderit, quod Sanctitas Vestra approbaverit, dictas causas in litteris dispensationis expressas de iure reddere litteras surreptitias et nullas, et iudices quibus per Sanctitatem Vestram fuerit commissa sola inquisitio veritatis dictarum causarum, repererint illas esse veras, declarent litteras surreptitias et matrimonium nullum et concedant licentiam regi in Domino nubendi cum quacunque alia muliere, nullo subsistente canonico [impedimento], nuntiando prolem ex huiusmodi contrahendo matrimonio suscipiendam legitimam, fore dicunt, quod omnes status illius regni non curabunt, postea si contrarium vigore commissionis Sanctitatis Vestrae declararetur, nec etiam, si successores Sanctitatis Vestrae declararent, id quod Sanctitas Vestra iuris esse statuerit super dictis causis in litteris dispensationis expressis, videlicet quod de iure sint sufficientes ad reddendum litteras ipsas surreptitias et nullas, ex quo sequitur, quod matrimonium, illarum vigore contractum fuerit et est nullum. Et ex his Sanctitas Vestra intelliget, quare firmarunt pedes, velle omnino obtinere a Sanctitate Vestra, quod ipsa approbet causas in litteris dispensationis expressas iuridicas esse ad reddendum litteras dispensationis surreptitias et nullas.'
[2] Clement VII to Henry VIII, 9 June 1528 (*State Papers*, vii, 71; *L. & P.*, iv, 3448).

added that he might have been deceived but he thought that the pope meant well.[1]

It seems that the pope had been anxious to consult with Campeggio and would do nothing without his advice. It was, therefore, necessary to 'prepare' Campeggio, and for this purpose Sir Gregory Casale hastened to Rome. Arrived there, Casale urged Campeggio to support the king's request, not only because he would thereby merit the king's favour, but because his own honour was concerned in the confirmation of the sentence. Casale reported that Campeggio seemed anxious to accommodate himself to the king's will (an observation that Wolsey noted in the margin of Casale's letter), and that, in view of the urgency of the matter, he had persuaded Campeggio to change the route of his projected journey; instead of going to Bologna, which would have wasted time, he would obtain from Andrea Doria two galleys to take him from Corneto or Leghorn to Marseilles.[2] Casale then returned to Viterbo where he told the pope that Campeggio was not only pleased to take the decretal commission with him but approved of its being procured, and even wished to obtain it himself as he did not know a better way of making the sentence safe. To Campeggio, however, Casale had said that letters had been sent to England announcing that the pope would grant the commission if Campeggio would take it and thus the king knew that the matter depended upon him. (In the margin of Casale's letter, against his report of this piece of duplicity, Wolsey wrote in his own hand, *Prudenter factum*.) As a result of these manoeuvres a decretal commission was at last extracted from an unwilling pope, and so unwilling did the pope seem that Casale, in reporting the grant of the commission, remarked that he had feared the pope would not keep the promises he had made to him

[1] Gardiner to Henry VIII, 11 June 1528 (*State Papers*, vii, 77; *L. & P.*, iv, 4355). It must have been soon after the receipt of this letter that Anne Boleyn wrote to Wolsey (Burnet, i, 55; Pocock-Burnet, i, 103; *L. & P.*, iv, 4360) expressing her gratitude for the great pains he took for her and describing herself as 'alonely in loving you, next unto the King's grace, above all creatures living'; she also said that she longed to hear news of the legate. To this letter Henry added a note in which he said that the lack of news of the legate's arrival in France 'causeth us somewhat to muse', but he hoped that Wolsey would ease his mind on that score.

[2] Casale to Wolsey, 15 June 1528 (Pocock, i, 170; *L. & P.*, iv, 4379). Andrea Doria was a Genoese nobleman who became high admiral of the Levant. He resigned his command when Genoa was threatened by the French. In 1528 he expelled the French garrison and ruled Genoa on republican lines.

and Gardiner.[1] Wolsey's desperate appeal *ad misericordiam* had at length induced the pope to grant that which should never have been granted.

The grant of the decretal commission was, however, subject to a number of restrictions which, it was hoped, would ensure that it never became public and a source of embarrassment. Following on Wolsey's repeated assurances that he only wanted the document to increase his standing with the king and that it should be seen by no one other than himself and Henry, the pope gave the decretal commission into the sole keeping of cardinal Campeggio with strict instructions to show it to no one save the king and Wolsey, and never to let it out of his possession or to allow its contents to come to the knowledge of anyone else: no practical use was to be made of the document; it was granted solely because of Wolsey's insistence and to help him with the king.[2] Clement no doubt wished to save the cardinal from the disasters which, he had assured the pope, would undoubtedly overtake him if he were unable to satisfy his royal master.

Meanwhile the emperor, Charles V, had learned of the pope's intention to appoint Campeggio as commissioner to inquire into the validity of Henry's marriage, and he instructed his ambassador at the papal court, John Anthony Muxetula, to make a protest. Muxetula's protest was contained in a long document in Latin, dated 20 July 1528. The imperial protest requested the pope to forbid the marriage suit and to impose perpetual silence, since the only result of such a suit would be war between christian princes. On no account should the cause be heard elsewhere than in Rome, since the matter turned upon the interpretation of a papal dispensation. Least of all should the question be determined

---

[1] Sir Gregory Casale to Wolsey, 15 June 1528 (Pocock, i, 172; *L. & P.*, iv, 4380); cf. Casale's letter to Peter Vannes, one of Wolsey's secretaries (*L. & P.*, iv, 4168), announcing that the pope had passed the commission as desired; in this letter Casale said that before the pope would grant the commission, he had wept and said that it would be his utter ruin, since it would put him at the mercy of the imperialists and there was no hope from France; his sole hope had been from the emperor and that hope was now lost since the imperialists would say that the motive for what he had done for the king was hatred of the emperor. The pope asked Casale to write separately to Wolsey, making it plain that the pope had willingly incurred this danger, as he trusted in Wolsey's continual declarations of good will, without which he would never have dared to have done it.

[2] No doubt the commission was confided to Campeggio, and not to Wolsey, because it was felt in the papal curia that Wolsey's promises could not be relied on. See p. 67, for Campeggio's observations to Wolsey after the latter had been shown the decretal commission.

in England, where the queen feared the king and where she had no security for her defence; she was, however, ready to defend her rights in the pope's court. The protest went on to say that the legates were much suspected, especially Wolsey who was not only chancellor of England but councillor and vassal of the king and had often urged the pope to grant the king's request in the matter. The protest therefore petitioned the pope to revoke all commissions to try the cause away from Rome, and appealed to the pope's tribunal in the name of the queen and of the emperor.[1]

Despite this solemn warning from the emperor, the pope was induced by Sir Gregory Casale,[2] within a few days, to give a written promise that he would not revoke the commission, nor do anything to invalidate it, and would confirm the decision reached by the cardinals.[3] This document was written at Viterbo in the pope's own hand on a date that is, apparently, 23 July. It is to be noted that this promise (or 'pollicitation', as it is known) recited the issue of the decretal commission and, in its operative part, referred to 'the commission hitherto issued' in the marriage cause. A translation of the operative part of this important and remarkable document is as follows:

We vow and promise on the word of a Roman pontiff that at no one's prayers, request or petition, nor of our own mere motion, will we ever grant any letters, briefs, bulls and rescripts either by way of justice or by way of grace which shall contain any matter inhibitory of the commissions hitherto issued in the aforesaid cause or which shall delay or hinder or in any way oppose the full, perfect, final and due execution of the said commission, or revoke it; but we will preserve the commission given by us in its fullest force, authority, strength and efficacy.[4]

[1] *L. & P.*, iv, 4535. The protest is printed in full (from the notarial attestation among the Cottonian MSS) in *E.H.R.*, xii, 111-114.

[2] Gardiner had left Viterbo in the latter part of June for Venice (cf. the document with which the pope provided Gardiner for his journey, dated 17 June 1528; Ehses, 39), where he was going to urge, in the king's name, the restitution of Cervia and Ravenna to the pope (see Wolsey to G. Casale, 28 June 1528; *State Papers*, vii, 86; *L. & P.*, iv, 4430).

[3] The pope's promise is printed in Ehses, 30, 31. The original document (which no longer exists) was not signed but was written in the pope's own hand. The existing copies bear no date, but it is dated 23 July 1528 by Ehses. This 'pollicitation' is not the document, dated 23 July, printed by Lord Herbert of Cherbury and later by Burnet (Pocock-Burnet, vi, 26) which was never granted; see p. 90.

[4] Ehses, 31: 'Promittimus et in verba Romani Pontificis pollicemur, quod ad nullius preces requisitionem sive instantium merove motu ullas unquam litteras

These last words are particularly remarkable as they guarantee that the pope would preserve the full force and efficacy of a document that he was extremely anxious should not be used at all.[1]

The issue of the decretal commission and of the 'pollicitation' were serious political blunders. The folly of issuing a commission that was not to be acted upon, and whose existence it was hoped would remain secret, needs no emphasis. Moreover, it was inevitable that the existence of the secret decretal commission would become known and, being secret, it was equally inevitable that its nature would be misrepresented, as in fact occurred. The issue of the pollicitation extended the possible area of misrepresentation without in any way easing the pope's difficulties. Although, as a matter of strict language, the pollicitation was not an unqualified promise to ratify and uphold any decision that the cardinals might reach, even if there were good grounds of appeal, it would not have been difficult to give plausible reasons for supposing that to be its effect. Moreover, it was possible to assert that the opening words of the document (*Cum nos iustitiam eius causae perpendentes*) implied

[1] The preamble to the 'pollicitation' throws some light on the nature of the decretal commission, which, unfortunately, no longer exists: 'Whereas we, weighing carefully the justice of the cause, . . . have issued a decretal commission with clauses ratifying what our deputies shall have done in that behalf, whereby we may more certainly and clearly certify to the said king Henry our desire to administer speedy justice in that matter and render it more secure against a labyrinth of judicial proceedings . . .' (Cum nos iustitiam eius causae perpendentes, . . . commissionem decretalem emiserimus cum clausulis de rato habendo processu, quem nostri in ea parte fecerint deputati: quo animi nostri eidem Henrico regi in iustitia illa quam celerrime administranda propensionem certius et clarius attestemur securioremque reddamus de iudiciorum labyrintho . . .). The pope thus stated the object of the decretal commission to be the avoidance of 'a labyrinth of judicial proceedings', which was also Wolsey's object, save that he spoke of 'a sea of judicial proceedings' (see p. 53). The commission was one that set out the law relevant to the subject matter of the proceedings, and left it to the legates to determine the true facts of the case and give judgment in accordance with the law declared in the commission (cf. p. 44, note 3). It was not, what it was afterwards represented to have been, a secret bull that prejudged the whole case and declared the marriage invalid.

brevia bullas atque rescripta per modum vel iustitiae vel gratiae concedemus, quae materiam emissarum antehac in causa praefata commissionum inhibitoriam contineant quaeve dictae commissionis plenam perfectam ac finalem ac debitam executionem remorentur impediant aut in aliquo contrarientur eamve revocent; sed datam a nobis commissionem sua plenissima vi auctoritate robore et efficacia conservabimus.'

a papal acknowledgement of the justice of the king's cause.[1] It is, therefore, necessary to emphasize that, by the pollicitation, the pope only
promised not to interfere with the *due* execution of the commission, but
it did not exclude papal interference should the cardinals fail to proceed in accordance with the principles laid down in the commission or
where, for any reason, the proceedings were not in accordance with
canon law.

[1] This phrase, in reality, meant no more than that, in granting the decretal
commission, the pope had had regard to what was just and meet in the case put
before him, according to the requirements of canon law.

IV

The Spanish Brief

I

Campeggio embarked at Corneto for France on 25 July, and during his journey the prospects of the outcome were viewed very differently by those most concerned. Foxe's personal report and the enthusiastic despatches of Gardiner had induced the king and Anne Boleyn to believe that their case was progressing better than in fact it was. With the imminent arrival of a cardinal from Rome it seemed to them that a decision determing the invalidity of the king's marriage was not far off. Their only anxieties were occasioned by the sweating sickness which had dispersed the court in the summer and had attacked Anne Boleyn. However, Henry wrote to Anne that 'the legate, which we most desire, arrived at Paris on Sunday or Monday last past; so that I trust, by the next Monday, to hear of his arrival at Calais: And then I trust, within a while after, to enjoy that which I have so longed for, to God's pleasure and our both comforts'.[1]

Wolsey was not so sanguine; indeed, he gave every appearance of being a thoroughly worried man. He told du Bellay, the French ambassador, that he needed to use 'a terrible alchemy and dexterity' in his affairs, for there were men who watched him so narrowly that they would take the first opportunity of calumniating him as being too strong a partisan of France. The ambassador thought that Wolsey did not know where he stood, however much he might pretend; and he said that he had heard on good authority that the king had used most terrible language to the cardinal because he seemed lacking in enthusiasm and had tried to show him that the pope would not do what he wanted.[2] No doubt

---

[1] *Love letters of Henry VIII*, no. vi (and cf. no. xii); printed in *Harl. Misc.*, iii, 54 (see p. 57 for letter no. xii). Campeggio arrived in Paris on Monday 14 Sept. 1528 (Ehses, 41).

[2] du Bellay to Montmorenci, 20 Aug. 1528 (Le Grand, iii, 157, 158, 164, 165; *L. & P.*, iv, 4649): '... qu'il luy falloyt user d'un terrible alquemye & dexterité en ses affaires; car il y avoit des gens qui l'esclairoient si prés, que à la moindre occasion du monde qu'ils auroyent de calomnier sesdits actes, & de monstrer

Wolsey would have liked to have retired from the whole business had he been able to do so; as it was, he had to persist with his attempts to extract from a situation that he could not control a result that would please the king.

The pope, it seems, despite all the urgent demands that had been made on him on the king's behalf, still hoped that Henry might be persuaded to drop the matrimonial proceedings, and he seems to have believed that Wolsey would be ready to help in persuading the king to take such a course. With these ill-founded hopes in his mind, he instructed Campeggio to try to persuade the king to rid himself of his idea of proceeding with the suit and to persevere in his marriage; for these reasons Campeggio was to proceed as slowly as possible in the matter and defer as long as he could the pronouncement of a judgment.[1] Campeggio was suffering severely from gout, a circumstance that prolonged his leisurely journey to England, and he did not reach Paris until 14 September. His gout obliged him to remain there for a few days and then continue his journey by litter. He did not reach the outskirts of London until 7 October where, exhausted by his journey and the pain of the gout, he lodged at the house of the duke of Suffolk. He was unable to make his solemn entry into the city on the following day, but he eventually went by river to the lodgings assigned to him, Bath House, without pomp or ceremony.[2]

Despite his poor condition and the intensity of his pain, Wolsey visited him on the day after his arrival at Bath House and insisted upon discussing the business at hand, although Campeggio was very unwilling

---

[1] cf. Campeggio to J. Salviati, 21 June 1529 (Ehses, 107).
[2] Campeggio to J. Salviati; part of a letter written on 17 Oct. 1528 (Ehses, 47). This letter was written in four parts, dated respectively 17, 19, 26, and 28 Oct.; the whole was despatched on 28 Oct., presumably because a safe and reliable courier was not available before that date. Campeggio's despatches to Jacopo Salviati, the papal secretary of state, are our principal source of information for what passed at the discussions between Wolsey and Campeggio; the only reliable text of these despatches is that printed by Ehses (the calendared versions in *L. & P.*, which are taken from Theiner's *Vetera Monumenta*, are untrustworthy and even misleading).

---

qu'il fust trop formel pour nostre party'. 'Quant à Monsieur le Legat, je pense qu'il ne sçayt pas bien où il en est quelque dissimulation qu'il en faize'. 'Le Roy luy usa de terribles termes à cause qu'il sembloit l'en vouloir refroidir, & luy monstrer que le Pape ne se y vouloit condescendre.'

to transact any business at all. Campeggio discovered at once that the pope's belief that the king could be persuaded to drop the suit was quite unfounded, and he learned that Henry and Wolsey were both resolved to proceed to the dissolution of the marriage. He therfore presented the pope's letter of credence.[1] A long discussion took place in which Campeggio tried to move Wolsey from his resolution; but Wolsey would not move. Wolsey founded himself upon the invalidity of the marriage and the instability of the realm owing to the uncertain succession, and declared that if the king, who was fortified in his position by the opinions of many learned and God-fearing men, did not obtain what he desired, it would mean the ruin of the kingdom, of Wolsey and of ecclesiastical authority in England. To emphasize the urgency of the matter, Wolsey told Campeggio that the pope had advised the king to contract a second marriage, with promises that everything should afterwards be confirmed; that the king already had in his possession a dispensation for another marriage; and that they had the pope's written promise not to alter the legates' commission and to confirm whatever judgment they should give. These facts were unknown to Campeggio and must have astonished him when he learned of them; they also caused him some uneasiness.[2]

So insistent was Wolsey to proceed with the utmost speed to a judgment that Campeggio concluded that the only way to restrain him was to disclose the substance of a conversation that he had had with the pope just before his departure: when the pope had asked Campeggio for his opinion of the king's case he had answered that he had not made up his mind but that as soon as he did so he would inform his holiness before proceeding to judgment. This information greatly disturbed Wolsey, and he exclaimed '*Si sic est, nolo negotiare vobiscum sine potestate, neque sic agitur cum rege*' ('If it be so, I refuse to deal with you as you are without power, and the king should not be treated thus'). Campeggio assured him that he had not made this revelation because they had no powers but because it was necessary to carry out his promise to the pope. In a later conversation Wolsey repeatedly warned Campeggio to beware lest it might be said that, just as the greater part of Germany had become estranged from the apostolic see and from the faith because of the harsh-

---

[1] Ehses, 48: 'Ragionando et intendendo, quanto et S.S. Rma. et la Maestà del re erano resoluti in questa materia di venire alla dissolutione del matrimonio, le presentai la lettera di N. Signore'.

[2] Campeggio to J. Salviati; part of letter written on 17 Oct. 1528 (Ehses, 47, 48).

ness and severity of a certain cardinal, so another cardinal had given the same occasion to England with the same result. Wolsey often impressed upon him that if the divorce were not granted the authority of the holy see would be annihilated in England; whereat Campeggio observed that Wolsey was certainly very zealous for its preservation as all his grandeur depended upon it. These revelations of Wolsey's mind and intentions caused Campeggio a good deal of anxiety and he feared that he would be unable to carry out the pope's instructions; accordingly he told Salviati that if the pope considered delay to be imperative his holiness should send him a letter that he could show to the king, or should by some other means make his wishes known; and he recommended that the pope should write either to the king or to Wolsey to convince them that Campeggio had only done what he conceived to be necessary.[1]

Campeggio received another visit from Wolsey on 18 October. Wolsey gave him news from Spain and Italy which, he said, showed that, once England had made a firm alliance with France, a general league with the Italian states could be contrived against the emperor, and in the course of the negotiations for the league the Venetians could be persuaded to restore Ravenna and Cervia to the pope. Campeggio, however, did not regard these matters as germane to his mission, and was content to leave them to the papal curia.[2]

The king, with the queen, had now moved from Greenwich to the royal palace at Bridewell on the Thames, near Blackfriars.[3] This was not far from Bath House, where Campeggio was lodged, and, at the king's desire, although he could neither ride nor walk and could sit only with great discomfort, Campeggio went thither on 22 October for his first audience of the king. He was publicly received before a great gathering of notables, and warmly welcomed by Henry. Campeggio's secretary, Floriano Montino, made a speech on behalf of both legates, which received an attentive hearing and at one point moved the audience to tears. An elegant reply was made by Dr Foxe. After this public ceremony the king took Wolsey and Campeggio into another chamber; there Campeggio gave him the pope's letter and assured him of the pope's good will. At this first interview Campeggio did not descend to particular matters

---

[1] Campeggio to J. Salviati; part of letter written on 17 Oct. 1528 (Ehses, 49, 50).
[2] Campeggio to J. Salviati; part of letter written on 19 Oct. 1528 (Ehses, 50, 51).
[3] Iñigo de Mendoza to the emperor, 18 Nov. 1528 (*Span. Cal.*, iii, pt. 2, 586).

but spoke only of the general peace, and the king promised to do everything in his power to bring it about. There was a further conversation about the Venetians, of whom the king held a bad opinion, but he thought that they might be coerced into joining a league with England and France and be induced to give up Ravenna and Cervia; Henry added, however, that the French king agreed with him that his matrimonial question should first be settled.

On the following day, after dinner, Campeggio received a private visit from the king which lasted for four hours. In the course of this visit Campeggio urged the king to abandon the marriage suit and assured him that if he had any scruples about the validity of his marriage he could obtain a new dispensation. The king had clearly been forewarned of this approach, for Campeggio reported to Salviati that the king's reply had evidently been prepared beforehand, and he suspected the hand of Wolsey since Wolsey had used the same arguments.[1] The king and Campeggio then argued the question whether the prohibition against marriage with a deceased brother's wife was a prohibition of divine law or was a prohibition from which the pope could dispense. Campeggio reported that the king had diligently studied the matter and knew more than did many a theologian or jurist. The king told Campeggio plainly that he wanted nothing else than a declaration determining the question whether the marriage were valid or not; Campeggio observed that the king always presupposed its invalidity, and he thought that even an angel from heaven could not persuade him otherwise. Finding the king thus set in his mind, Campeggio put forward the proposal that the queen should be persuaded to enter some religious house. This suggestion seemed greatly to please the king who said that he would settle the succession on the queen's daughter, Mary, should he have no male heir by another marriage. It was therefore arranged that Campeggio and Wolsey should broach this proposal to the queen on the following day.

Accordingly, the next day, Saturday 24 October, Wolsey and Campeggio set out. But before speaking with the queen they had a further interview with Henry. Henry asked to see their commission and also the decretal commission. Campeggio read both these documents to him but was careful to keep them in his own hands, allowing no one but the

[1] 'Poi rispose come a cose premeditate. Et penso che *Eboracense lo havesse ben informato, perchè a Sua Signoria Rma. dissi le medesime ragioni*' (Ehses, 54; italicized words are in cipher in the original).

king and Wolsey to see them. Wolsey then said that 'this is all we need to inform our conscience', and Campeggio, as he had expected something of the kind, told Wolsey that the pope had sent the decretal commission, not because he thought it was right, but solely to satisfy Wolsey who had been so insistent about it; and he added that it would remain in his own hands until he received a new commission from the pope.[1] The king then said that he feared he might be abandoned in the affair; since his last interview with Campeggio some London merchants had told him that they would engage their credit that the pope would come to an agreement with the emperor. Campeggio replied that the pope would do nothing unworthy of a good pontiff, but he was bound to have regard to many things, not only for their own sake, but for the sake of the authority of the holy see; with which the king seemed satisfied.

Taking leave of the king, Campeggio and Wolsey repaired to queen Catherine, with whom they remained for about two hours. This difficult interview was conducted by Campeggio with much tact. After some preliminary greetings the queen read the pope's letter, and then asked Campeggio what it was that he had to say to her. Campeggio told her that as the pope could not refuse justice to anyone who demanded it, he had commissioned Wolsey and himself to inquire into the state of the question between herself and the king. He told her that as the matter was very important, the pope, relying upon her prudence, counselled her not to press the matter to trial but to take some other course which would give general satisfaction and greatly benefit herself. Campeggio did not explain his meaning further so that he might discover what she would demand; Wolsey spoke much to the same effect, but in English. The queen replied that her conscience did not trouble her, and that she wished to die in the faith and in obedience to the commands of God and of the church. She said that she would declare her conscience only to the pope, and that for the present she would give no other reply, as she intended to demand counsellors of the king and she would answer when

[1] 'Il qual volse *veder la bolla della commissione della causa, quale gli lessi; poi mi dimandò di vedere l'altra de la decretale, et così la mostrai et lessi, et sempre è stata et è in mano mia, nè altri l'ha veduta o letta, che S.M. et S.S. Rma.; et il Rmo. Eboracense letta che fu disse: questo ci basta al informare le nostre conscientie.* Il che havendo io già previsto, parlando con S.S. Rma. gli haveva detto, che *N. Signore l'haveva fatto expedire non perchè ita sentiret, ma per aiuto di S.S. Rma., vedendo la instantia che ne faceva. Detta bolla è in mia mano, nè più se vederà senza nuova commissione de Sua Beatudine'* (Ehses, 54, 55; the portions in italics are in cipher in the original).

she obtained them. The queen remarked that she had heard that the cardinals were to persuade her to enter some religious house. Campeggio did not deny it and urged on her the benefits that would follow from such a course. The cardinals then left.[1]

Despite the discouraging nature of this interview, Campeggio did not abandon hope of persuading the queen to enter a convent.[2] Knowing that she had a high regard for the bishop of Rochester, John Fisher, who was her confessor, Campeggio spoke with him the following day, and strongly recommended to him the advantages that would follow the queen's entry into a religious house; Campeggio subsequently informed Salviati that Fisher seemed well satisfied and well instructed. However, shortly after this interview, with the consent of the king, the queen came to Campeggio to make her confession. Although what Catherine said to Campeggio was told under the seal of the confessional, she gave him leave, and indeed besought him, to communicate to the pope the substance of what she said. She described to Campeggio the course of her life since her first arrival in England and she assured the cardinal that during the whole period of her reputed marriage with prince Arthur, less than five months, she had not slept with him more than seven nights, and that when she married Henry she was still a virgin.[3] Campeggio urged her to take a vow of chastity, but she repeatedly answered him that she intended to live and die in the state of matrimony, to which God had called her. Campeggio was impressed by her determination, as well as by her good sense and wisdom; but he thought it a pity that she should obstinately refuse to adopt a course that would have removed many difficulties without much loss to herself.[4]

---

[1] Mendoza, in giving his master an account of this interview, said that Catherine was convinced that Wolsey had 'blown this coal' between herself and the king (Mendoza to Charles V, 18 Nov. 1528; *Span. Cal.*, iii, pt. 2, 586 (p. 841). See p. 4.

[2] In his letter to Salviati, Campeggio said that as the queen was nearly fifty she would lose nothing by such a course and much good would ensue ('perchè sendo già presso alli cinquanta et non perdendo in cosa alcuna, secondo che è detto, et seguendone tanto bene'); Catherine was, in fact, forty-three, having been born in 1485.

[3] 'Et prima in conscientia sua affirma, che dalli XIV di novembre, ch'ella si sposò con il quondam Arturo, sino alli II d'aprile del seguente, che morì, non dormì seco salvo VII notti et che da lui restò intacta et incorrupta, come venne dal ventre di sua madre' (Ehses, 59).

[4] For the foregoing, see Campeggio to J. Salviati, 26 Oct. 1528 (Ehses, 53-9).

It is true that even had Catherine agreed to enter a convent, the king would not have been free to marry again, but such a course would have removed one of the principal difficulties that faced Wolsey and Campeggio and the marriage suit could then have proceeded in the absence of the queen and judgment by default could have been given against the marriage.[1]

On 27 October, at the king's request, Campeggio and Wolsey again visited Catherine. Once more Campeggio explained the reason for their legation and repeated much that he had already said to her. Once again he exhorted her to retire to a convent and dwelt at some length upon the advantages of so doing, mentioning that it would conduce to the tranquillity of the kingdom and enable her to obtain from the king all the material comforts that she desired, besides quieting her own conscience. Wolsey then addressed her in the same strain, but in English, and when he had done he knelt before her and begged her to accept the good advice of the legates and so secure the good will of the king and establish her own honour and advantage. The queen remained unmoved. She repeated that she would do nothing that would make for the damnation of her soul or was contrary to the law of God; she added that she would consult her counsellors and would then give the cardinals an answer. Campeggio then told his secretary to read the bull of the commission, and when that had been done the two cardinals withdrew.[2]

Campeggio's dilatory methods and his insistence upon proceeding in a way never contemplated by Wolsey, coupled with the queen's intransigence, served only to emphasize the difficulties that were crowding in upon Wolsey and to demonstrate more clearly the precarious nature of his position. On 1 November he sent a long letter of instructions to Sir Gregory Casale in Rome, which was, for the most part, a series of complaints to be passed on to the pope. Wolsey told Casale that the pope had granted to Campeggio a commission, the decretal commission, which was solely for his own instruction and that of the king's ministers, and was not to be used in the marriage suit; this, said Wolsey, had caused

---

[1] In any case, Henry was prepared, in the event of his marriage not being declared invalid, to press the pope for a dispensation to commit bigamy; cf. Henry's instructions to Sir Francis Bryan and Peter Vannes, in Nov. 1528 (*L. & P.*, iv, 4977 (p. 2158)); see, also, the instructions to Vannes later in the same month: 'That if the queen enter a monastery, the pope may enable him [Henry] to contract a second marriage' (*L. & P.*, iv, 4979); and Ehses, 63.
[2] Campeggio to J. Salviati, 28 Oct. 1528 (Ehses, 59, 60).

the king much dissatisfaction. Moreover, Campeggio had departed from his instructions and was attempting to dissuade the king and queen from proceeding with the marriage suit; worse still, he would not entrust Wolsey with the decretal commission, although Wolsey was his colleague in the matter. The result was, complained Wolsey, that the king, who had assured his privy council that the pope would not fail to do what he could in his cause, now found that he had been deceived, and those who had asserted that nothing but causes for delay would be invented had been proved right in their judgment. Casale was instructed to warn the pope of the gravity of the course he was pursuing which would probably drive the king to adopt those remedies which, injurious as they were to the pope, were constantly instilled into the king's ear. Wolsey asserted that it was useless for Campeggio even to think of reviving the marriage; let Campeggio, then, proceed to sentence in the marriage suit. Wolsey begged the pope to set aside all delays, for if the divorce were carried, then might be expected an alliance between the kings of England and France and the emperor who could take no offence at the king's honourable dealings.[1]

Wolsey's optimistic view of the international benefits that would flow from the divorce was reflected, no doubt, in the opinions that he had expressed to Campeggio, but it was in violent conflict with what he said to the French ambassador on 7 November, less than a week later. On that occasion he raised the question of the divorce with du Bellay and sought his interest by trying to show that the outcome would be a great rupture with the emperor and the perpetual confirmation of Anglo-French amity.[2]

When Wolsey's instructions reached Italy, Sir Gregory Casale was too ill to carry them out and, accordingly, his brother, John Casale, went to the pope and read to him Wolsey's letter. After presenting Wolsey's complaints to his holiness, Casale asked him whether he had intended to frustrate and delude the king with the commission. The pope became very angry and, laying his hand upon Casale's arm, forbade him to proceed. The pope declared that there was, indeed, ground for complaint, but that it was himself that had been deceived. He had

---

[1] Wolsey to Sir Gregory Casale, 1 Nov. 1528 (*State Papers*, vii, 102; *L. & P.*, iv, 4879).

[2] du Bellay to Montmorenci, 8 Nov. 1528 (Le Grand, iii, 197, at p. 200; *L. & P.*, iv, 4915 (p. 2133).

granted the decretal commission at Wolsey's most urgent entreaties in order to save him from ruin; he had granted it solely that it might be shown to the king and then burned immediately, but Wolsey now wished to divulge it to the king's councillors, a course to which the pope had never assented. His holiness went on to say with much feeling that he now saw what evil was likely to follow from the issue of the decretal commission, and that he would gladly recall what had been done, even to the loss of one of his fingers. When Casale suggested that the pope was shifting his ground, his holiness became more angry and more excited but refused to give way. Casale again visited the pope and pressed him to allow the decretal commission to be shown to the king's councillors but again the pope refused, and with that refusal Casale had to be content.[1]

2

The king's secret matter had not remained as secret as Henry wished. Although ignorant of the true state of affairs, the people were generally aware that the king was preparing to take some action against his wife, and, in the words of Edward Hall, 'in especial women and others that favoured the queen talked largely, and said that the king would for his own pleasure have another wife and had sent for this legate [Campeggio] to be divorced from his queen, with many foolish words, insomuch, that whosoever spake against the marriage was of the common people abhorred and reproved'.[2] This common talk and the rumours that were going round were brought to the knowledge of the king and caused him some anxiety. The queen was the object of a great deal of public sympathy while the king was incurring much odium due to his matrimonial proceedings. Matters came to a head when the queen, on her way through the gallery leading from the royal palace of Bridewell to Blackfriars priory, received an ovation from the crowd who wished her victory over her enemies. This striking display of affection for the queen greatly disconcerted Henry, and he gave orders that the place where it had occurred should be closed to the public.[3]

[1] John Casale to Wolsey, 17 Dec. 1528 (Burnet, i, Coll. of Rec., p. 41; Pocock-Burnet, iv, 64; *L. & P.*, iv, 5038).   [2] Hall, *Chronicle*, ii, 145.
[3] Iñigo de Mendoza to the emperor, 18 Nov. 1528 (*Span. Cal.*, iii, pt. 2, 586 (p. 845)).

In the face of these disquieting developments, the king deemed it expedient that some public statement should be made. Accordingly, on Sunday 8 November 1528, there assembled at the palace of Bridewell the judges, the lord mayor and corporation of London, the greater part of the nobility, and other personages of position and influence. To this gathering Henry made a speech that is notable for its sophistry. He told them of the great pains he had taken to preserve the peace of the realm and he informed them that he was anxious that that peace should not be disturbed at the time of his death by troubles arising from uncertainty as to the succession. He had been told, he said, by 'divers great clerks' that his marriage was unlawful so that he and the queen were then living together 'abominably and detestably in open adultery'. So much so, that when a marriage was proposed between the duke of Orleans and the princess Mary the councillors of the French king had said, 'It were well done to know whether she be the king of England's lawful daughter or not, for well known it is that he begat her on his brother's wife which is directly against God's law and his precept'.[1] This was a fiction which had, for some time, been in use by the king and his advisers, but this was the first time that it had been used publicly.

More serious matters than adverse public opinion now arose to claim Henry's attention. Hitherto attention had been focused on the bull of dispensation granted by Julius II, but, unknown to anyone in England or even to Clement VII, there existed in Spain a brief granting a dispensation for the marriage of Henry with Catherine. The brief had been issued prior to the bull and had been sent to Isabella of Spain on her death bed for her consolation; it had remained in Spain and had been forgotten.[2]

---

[1] Hall, *Chronicle*, ii, 145-7; cf. du Bellay to Montmorenci, 17 Nov. 1528 (Le Grand, iii, 209, at pp. 217, 218; *L. & P.*, iv, 4942). In reporting Henry's speech, the French ambassador, du Bellay, said, '& croy qu'il [Henri] usa de ces termes, Qu'il n'y auroit si belle teste qu'il n'en feist voller'. Edward Hall, an enthusiastic supporter of the Tudors, described the effect of this speech as follows: 'To see what countenaunce was made amongest the hearers of this Oracion, it was a straunge sight, for some syghed and sayd nothynge, other were sory to heare the kynge so troubled in his conscience. Other that favored the quene much sorowed that this matter was now opened, and so every man spake as his hert served him, but the kynge ever labored to know the trueth for discharge of his conscience' (Hall, *Chronicle*, ii, 147).
[2] The brief is printed in Burnet, i, Coll. of Rec., p. 39. It contains the following: 'Oblatae nobis nuper pro parte vestra petitionis series continebat, quod cum alias tu Filia Catharina, & tunc in humanis agens quondam Arthurus Carissimi in Christo Filii nostri Henrici Angliae Regis illustrissimus primogenitus, pro

But during the activity in Spain on the queen's behalf it had come to light and the Spanish ambassador, Iñigo de Mendoza, furnished Catherine with a copy which she showed to Campeggio.[1] Although the general purport and even the phraseology of the brief were very similar to those of the bull, the two documents were not identical.

At first sight the difference that is often cited as significant appears so trivial as to make it questionable whether it is capable of explaining the violent reaction of king and cardinal when they first learned of the existence of the brief.[2] The brief proceeded upon the assumption that Catherine's marriage to Arthur had been consummated (a fact which it took for granted) since it contained the passage *cum . . . matrimonium per verba legitime de praesenti contraxeritis, illudque carnali copula consummaveritis*; the bull, on the other hand, while granting the dispensation in the fullest terms, treated the consummation of the marriage to Arthur as a matter of doubt, stating *cum . . . matrimonium per verba legitime de praesenti contraxissetis, illudque carnali copula forsan consummaveritis*. Thus, it has been said that the only significant difference between the two documents is the presence in the bull of the word *forsan* which does not appear in the brief.

Dr Gairdner made the absence of the word *forsan* from the brief the basis of his explanation of the consternation caused by the production of the brief, and his explanation has achieved some popularity. For the purposes of this explanation it was necessary to postulate that, at the relevant time, the validity of the bull was challenged on the ground that it was only effective as a dispensation for Catherine to marry Henry if

---

[1] The brief had been found among the papers of Dr Puebla who had long been dead but who in 1503, as Spanish ambassador in England, had negotiated the marriage of Henry and Catherine (cf. *L. & P.*, iv, 2411). As early as 27 Jan. 1528, in the written answer made to Clarencieux king-at-arms, the emperor, Charles V, said, among other things, that he had in his hands the dispensations, which he was ready to show, and which were so ample that they allowed of no subterfuge without impugning the power of the pope (Le Grand, iii, 27, at p. 45; *L. & P.*, iv, 3844 (p. 1715)).

[2] cf. p. 72, note 2.

---

conservandis pacis & amicitiae nexibus & foederibus inter praefatum Angliae Regem, & Carissimum in Christo Filium nostrum Ferdinandum Regem, & Carissimam in Christo Filiam nostram Elizabeth Reginam Catholicos Hispaniarum & Siciliae, Matrimonium per verba legitime de praesenti contraxeritis, illudque carnali copula consummaveritis, quia tamen Dominus Arthurus prole ex hujusmodi Matrimonio non suscepta, decessit, . . .'

she were a virgin at the time of the marriage, a fact which Henry denied. The brief, however, by omitting the word *forsan* and thus proceeding on the footing that Catherine's marriage to Arthur had been consummated, destroyed this argument and cut away the ground upon which the king rested his case. It must be admitted that this explanation is not altogether satisfactory on its face, but its real weaknesses have been exposed by Fr Herbert Thurston, S.J., who has indicated much more plausible reasons for the sudden wish of the king and cardinal to postpone the opening of the legatine trial, for which they had hitherto been so eager.[1]

Dr Gairdner's explanation appears to require the assumption that Julius II had issued the bull in the belief that Catherine's marriage to Arthur had not been consummated, but it is not altogether easy to deduce this from the terms of the bull itself. It is perfectly true that had it been possible to prove that the bull had been issued in such circumstances and that the pope's belief was contrary to the fact, there would have been good reason to hope that the validity of the bull might successfully be challenged on the ground that it had been obtained by false representations or, to use the technical term of the canonists, was 'obreptitious'. There does not appear to be any evidence that, at this time, Henry was challenging the validity of the bull on any such ground, and the terms of the bull are such as to show, almost conclusively, that it was not obreptitious on this ground. The bull was asked for, and granted, in order to remove the impediment of affinity that stood in the way of the marriage of Catherine to Henry, and it was the universally accepted opinion that affinity only arose as the result of carnal knowledge; the impediment did not arise from a marriage that was *ratum sed non consummatum*, an unconsummated marriage.[2] It follows that, in granting the bull, the pope must have proceeded upon the footing that

---

[1] See, e.g. Gairdner, *History of the English Church in the Sixteenth Century*, 93; Gairdner, 'New light on the Divorce of Henry VIII', in *E.H.R.*, xii(1897), 237-53, at pp. 237, 238; cf. Constant, *Reformation in England*, i, 64. For Fr Thurston's observations, see Thurston, 'The Canon Law of the Divorce', in *E. H. R.*, xix (1904), 632-45.

[2] A definition of affinity that was common at this time was, 'Affinitas est personarum proximitas omni carens parentela, proveniens ex coitu maritali vel fornicaria'. See, e.g., Stephanus Costa, *De consanguinitate et affinitate* (printed in the Venetian collection of 1584, vol. ix, ff. 134 et seq.); cf. *Rosella Casuum* (Venice, 1495), s.v., *Impedimentum*, f. 275. See also the references cited in Sanchez, *De Matrimonio* lib. vii, disp. 64. The modern canon law is different; see *Corpus Juris Canonici*, Can. 97(i), quoted on p. 126, note 1.

the marriage to Arthur had been consummated since the impediment which the bull was designed to remove could not have arisen in the absence of consummation. It would, therefore, have been both difficult and ill-advised to argue that the bull was obreptitious on the ground that the pope had been falsely induced to believe that there had been no consummation. It should not be forgotten, however that the marriage to Arthur, even though not consummated, had been celebrated *in facie ecclesiae*, circumstance from which the impediment of *publica honestas*[1] could arise, and it was undoubtedly a weakness of the bull that it made no mention of this impediment.

It is not surprising, therefore, to find that the bull was not being attacked on the ground that the pope had been induced to believe, falsely, that the marriage to Arthur had not been consummated, and it should be noted that there is no mention of the question of consummation in the objections to the bull upon which reliance was placed at this time and for some time to come.[2] Dr Gairdner's explanation, therefore, must be rejected as unsatisfactory. The much more plausible explanation put forward by Fr Thurston is based in part on the existence of the secret decretal commission which had been wrung from an unwilling pope,[3] and in part on another difference between the bull and the brief.

A decretal commission, it will be recalled, set out the law by which the commissioners, after finding certain facts, were to be guided in their determination of the question referred to them; it was this characteristic that made a decretal commission so desirable to Wolsey because, by declaring the relevant law in advance, it virtually destroyed the possibility of appeal on a point of law. Unfortunately, we do not possess the text of the secret decretal commission, which was destroyed by Campeggio, but there is reason to think that it did not differ substantially from the form of the drafts submitted to the pope by the English ambassadors.[4] From these drafts it is clear that the decretal commission began with a

---

[1] See p. 16, note 2. It is curious that neither the brief nor the bull made any mention of the impediment of *publica honestas*, which may have been due to the close similarity of the impediment of *affinitas* to that of *publica honestas* which the canonists frequently termed *quasi-affinitas*. Wolsey was quick to notice this point in relation to the bull; see pp. 16, 54.

[2] See p. 35.

[3] See pp. 44, 57.

[4] cf. Thurston, op. cit., at p. 640. The differences between the three existing drafts are comparatively slight.

preliminary statement in which formal reference was made to the bull of Julius II, followed by the words *cuius quidem dispensationis tenor sequitur, et est talis*; the full text of the bull was then set out. The decretal commission then directed the legates to inquire into the validity of the recited bull, and throughout this part of the commission reference was made to 'the said bull of dispensation' which is the bull of Julius II set out earlier in the commission, but no reference is made to any other document.[1] The decretal commission thus declared the relevant law and restricted the investigation of the legates to certain defined issues of fact. The whole procedure was concerned only with the particular form of dispensation recited in the commission and had no application to any other dispensation. Accordingly, when Catherine produced the brief she disclosed the existence of another dispensation with which the decretal commission was not concerned. If the brief were authentic, its existence nullified the decretal commission because, even if the legates determined the bull to be invalid, the dispensation provided by the brief would remain unaffected by any judgment given by virtue of the decretal commission.[2] This consideration must have caused Wolsey great anxiety.

This, however, was not all; a further source of worry was provided by the terms of the brief itself. Despite the general similarity of the bull to

[1] The relevant text (quoted by Thurston, op. cit., 641, from the draft in B.M., MS Vitellius, B, xii, f. 133) is: 'Vobis [committimus vices nostras] coniunctim et ut prefertur divisim ad cognoscendum et procedendum summarie et de plano sine strepitu et figura iudicii in causa predicta, necnon de et super viribus sive validitate dicte bulle sive dispensacionis inquirendum, bullam sive dispensacionem, si vicia predicta aut eorum aliqua vera esse constiterit, et vel pacem que in bulla pretenditur sine matrimonio predicto continuari potuisse et permanere, vel dictum charissimum filium nostrum ut allegabatur non cupiisse contrahere matrimonium ad hoc ut pacis federa conservarentur, aut denique reges in bulla nominatos aut aliquem eorum ante mandatam executioni bullam fatis concessisse apparuerit, ipsam bullam nullam, minus validam, ex subreptione et obreptione inefficacem, irritam et inanem fuisse semper et esse pronunciandum et declarandum, matrimonium autem predictum, quod eiusdem virtute consistere videretur, nullum simul ac minus legitimum esse ac pro nullo minusque legitimo haberi debere decernendum, ipsos porro contrahentes ab omni contractu matrimoniali huiusmodi liberos et consortio coniugali quod hactenus observarunt separari deberi sentenciandos et auctoritate nostra separandos.'

[2] Fr Thurston aptly remarked (op. cit., 642) that even had the brief 'been a forgery one might feel a certain admiration for the smartness of the trick by which the king's carefully planned decretal commission was so simply rendered inoperative'.

the brief, there is a difference between the two documents which was, presumably, the principal reason for Wolsey's perturbation. This difference may best be seen by setting out the relevant portions of bull and brief side by side:

The Bull	The Brief
Cum autem . . . sicut eadem petitio subiungebat ad hoc ut huiusmodi vinculum pacis et amicitiae inter praefatos reges et reginam diutius permaneat, cupiatis matrimonium inter vos . . . contrahere . . . supplicari nobis fecistis. . . . Nos . . . huiusmodi supplicationibus inclinati . . . vobiscum . . . dispensamus.	Quia tamen . . . huiusmodi vinculum pacis et connexitatis inter praefatos reges et reginam ita firmiter verisimiliter non perduraret nisi etiam illud alio affinitatis vinculo . . . confirmaretur, ex his *et certis aliis causis* desideratis matrimonium . . . contrahere . . . supplicari nobis fecistis. . . . Nos . . . his *et ex aliis causis animum nostrum moventibus,* huiusmodi supplicationibus inclinati, vobiscum . . . dispensamus.

To appreciate the significance of this difference it is necessary to bear in mind the very great importance which the canonists attached to the *causa praetensa* or 'motive' set out in the grant of a dispensation; for it was a commonplace of canon law that if the motive assigned to the grant were fictitious or inadequate in the circumstances of the case the grant was null and void. It will be seen, from the passages set out above, that the *causa praetensa* expressed in the bull was the maintenance of peace between England and Spain; the bull granted the dispensation because the pope had been informed that the marriage was necessary to maintain peace between the two countries. The contention that this motive (the only one set out in the bull) was inadequate had all along been in the forefront of the English attack upon the bull.[1] Whatever one may think of the force of Henry's technical objections to the validity of the bull, it might well have been argued that, since Spain and England were at peace when the bull was issued and that peace was untroubled, the grant of the dispensation was unnecessary; it followed from this argument that the pope had been deceived in his grant and the bull was accordingly obreptitious.

The brief, on the other hand, set out the motive relating to peace in much less absolute terms; it did no more than state that the existing peaceful relations 'would probably not last so firmly' (*ita firmiter verisimiliter non perduraret*) if the proposed marriage were not celebrated,

[1] cf. p. 35.

77

a proposition that was not easy to dispute. Moreover, the brief granted the dispensation not only for the sake of maintaining peace but 'for certain other reasons' (*et certis aliis causis*). The inclusion of the words *et certis aliis causis* rendered nugatory the other objections alleged against the bull because, whatever the force of those objections might be, it was impossible to demonstrate the inadequacy or fictitious nature of the 'certain other reasons' since their nature was not stated, and it could still be said that the *causa praetensa* must be taken as affording valid grounds for the grant of the dispensation until the contrary were shown.[1]

Thus two matters emerge from a consideration of the brief: its effect on the decretal commission, and the change in the form of the *causa praetensa*. Either of these considerations was sufficient by itself to weaken very seriously the case put forward by the king; taken together they virtually destroyed all hope of success. Little wonder, then, that king and cardinal gave urgent thought to what they should do to meet this unexpected and devastating situation.

Catherine had always maintained that she had entered her marriage with Henry as a virgin and an immaculate woman. She was not disposed to accept the statement in the brief as true, and on 7 November she made a public protest that she did not admit that the brief showed that her marriage with Arthur had been consummated.[2] Such a protest did nothing to help Henry in his awkward predicament and he was anxious that a remedy be quickly found. He instructed the archbishop of Canterbury, William Warham, and the bishop of London, Cuthbert Tunstall, to visit the queen and to tell her that information had reached the king that certain ill-disposed persons were conspiring against him and Wolsey and it was thought that this conspiracy had been hatched on the queen's

[1] cf. the following passage in a summary of the divorce proceedings, apparently prepared for the pope in July 1530 by one of his consultors; after describing the action of the English ambassadors in Rome and Campeggio's eventual departure for England, the writer stated (Ehses, 157): 'Successive, cum in Anglia regina ostenderet copiam brevis obtentae dispensationis, cum dicta : *et ex aliis causis animum nostrum moventibus . . .* quae non est in autentico penes regem existenti, missi sunt a rege ad Sanctitatem Vestram oratores Dr Stephanus [Gardiner] et P[etrus] Vanni et D. Brianus, ut Sanctitas Vestra breve illud falsum pronuntiaret, quod negatum fuit, quia iustum non erat, quod illud, de quo non apparebat ni siper copiam, ac parte non citata nec audita falsum pronuntiaretur.' It seems clear that, for this writer, it was not the omission from the brief of the word *forsan* that was significant, but the presence of the words *et ex aliis causis animum nostrum moventibus*.

[2] For the text of Catherines protest, see Pocock, ii, 431.

account by those who favoured the emperor. Warham and Tunstall were then to warn the queen that if anything should be attempted against the king or Wolsey, the matter would be imputed to her, even if she were not guilty, and the result would be her utter undoing. Having delivered this shocking message Warham and Tunstall were then to urge the queen to enter a convent. In reporting the interview which took place the Spanish ambassador, Mendoza, somewhat exaggerated the matter so that it appeared even more outrageous than it was.[1]

As Catherine stoutly maintained her position, it was plain to Henry and Wolsey that their situation was a desperate one, for if the copy of the brief were accurate, the basis of Henry's case had been destroyed and the marriage suit seemed likely to fail. Wolsey was so painfully aware of the difficulties now facing him that, according to Mendoza, he was making strenuous efforts to rid himself of his responsibility by trying to persuade Henry that he could serve him better as advocate than as judge.[2] In the face of this awkward document the king and his advisers now found it inopportune to press for the speedy conclusion of the matrimonial suit, and the trial was postponed for a time. Efforts were now directed towards impugning the brief.

The nature of the first proposal that was made indicates the degree of panic into which the king and his advisers had been thrown by the production of the brief. Examination of the document had suggested to the lawyers concerned with the matter (who noted that it was a brief and not a bull) that there might be reasons for suspecting that the original had not been registered in Rome and that the copy produced by Catherine might not be a true copy. Accordingly they argued that if the brief had not been registered, as it should have been, and the original could by some means be extracted from the emperor, there would then be

---

[1] For Warham and Tunstall's instructions, see *L. & P.*, iv, 4981, where they are wrongly headed 'Intended address of the Legates to the queen'. According to Mendoza (Iñigo de Mendoza to the emperor, 18 Nov. 1528; *Span. Cal.*, iii, pt. 2, 586 (p. 845)), the queen was asked first, whether she had made an attempt on the king's life in order to enable her to arrange, at her own pleasure, her own and her daughter's marriage, and second, why she had not previously disclosed the existence of the brief and how it had come into her possession; she answered by saying that she could not believe that the first question came from the king, and that she had received a copy of the brief from Mendoza, six months previously.
[2] Iñigo de Mendoza to the emperor, 18 Nov. 1528; *Span. Cal.*, iii, pt. 2, 586 (p. 847).

79

no evidence available to Catherine that such a brief had ever been issued. The king therefore proposed to send a messenger (probably Fitzwilliam, the treasurer of the household) to Spain to discover whether the emperor did, in fact, possess the original document. The risks inherent in such a plan must have been soon realized, for it was discarded within a few days.[1]

The king next turned his attention to Rome. At the end of November 1528, two envoys, Sir Francis Bryan and Peter Vannes,[2] were sent there by way of Paris, with the ostensible object of making representations to the pope concerning the emperor's proposals for European peace; they were to warn the pope against these proposals. But the real object of their mission was very different. They were instructed to alienate the pope as much as possible from the emperor and to incline him towards Henry, so that he would be the more ready to grant any petition of the king such as in 'the great and weighty matter of the divorce'. This matter, however, the envoys were instructed not to mention at first, as if the purpose of their mission were solely concerned with the question of European peace. But, while remaining at Rome for the promotion of the peace, they were, by great and high policy, secrecy and circumspection, to endeavour to investigate the truth of 'the great and apparent craft and abusion' that seemed to have been used in disappointing the direct and due course of truth in the decision of the matter of the divorce by process and judgment. The envoys were instructed that it was obvious that 'some marvellous falsity and corruption' had been used because the queen had produced a copy of the brief. This brief, they were told, seemed totally to remove all the faults found in the dispensation of pope Julius II

remaining in the king's hands, the like of which have not been heard of to have been found or seen at any time either in king Henry VII's days, either in the court of Rome, in England, Spain or elsewhere, till now of late, that by such manner and circumstance as heretofore hath been declared unto the pope's

[1] Iñigo de Mendoza to the emperor, 23 Nov. 1528 (*Span. Cal.*, iii, pt. 2, 592); Iñigo de Mendoza to the emperor, Dec. 2 1528 (*Span. Cal.*, iii, pt. 2, 600).
[2] Sir Francis Bryan, Anne Boleyn's cousin, was a gentleman of the privy chamber and an intimate of the king; he was known as 'the king's vicar of Hell'. Peter Vannes was one of the king's secretaries. He was an Italian and, although a cleric, a polished man of the world; he was a man of no moral sense but was a skilled lawyer and a humanist, and he was, perhaps, the first professional diplomat. In Elizabeth's reign he was appointed a canon of one of the newly created cathedral chapters; cf. p. 78, note 1.

holiness the same happened to insurge and be brought in question, and consequently was a thing far unlike to have been thus in those special and material points only provided for by pope Julius by a brief apart from the principal bull, of the same date as the bull was, and that brief to be only in Spain, and none like in this country.

The envoys were told that the brief had never been previously mentioned or heard of in England which gave rise to great suspicion of forgery. They were to secure the services of some person from among the scribes and writers of the registers 'making sure of him either by ready money or continual entertainment' and do everything possible to provide evidence that the brief had been forged. Finally, the envoys were to inquire whether, in the event of the queen being induced to enter the religious life, the pope might *ex plenitudine potestatis* grant the king a dispensation for a second marriage; whether, if the queen refused to take religious vows without the king doing likewise, the pope would dispense him from the obligations of any such vow that he might find it necessary to take and grant a further dispensation to enable him to marry again; and whether, if the queen were still to be reputed his wife, the pope would grant a dispensation to enable the king to have two wives, making the children of the second marriage legitimate as well as those of the first 'whereof some great reasons and precedents, especially of the Old Testament, appear'. And since the pope knew how much the king took to heart the insufficiency of his marriage with the queen, and that such great consequences depended upon it, the envoys were to say to him that he could not do too much for so noble and loving a prince, and ought to show him a special and singular grace.[1]

At the same time Knight and Benet, accompanied by John Taylor, the master of the rolls, were instructed to follow Bryan and Vannes. On arrival at the French court they were to show the copy of the brief to Francis I, but merely as if their mission to the pope were for the purpose of obtaining the original as it was considered that such a document

---

[1] For the instructions to Bryan and Vannes, see *L. & P.*, iv, 4977; these instructions were very long, extending to 25 pages, and are signed at the beginning and the end by the king (B.M., Cotton MSS, Vitellius, B, x, 146). It seems that the envoys were to have been given a memorial for the pope, from the leading noblemen of the kingdom, stating that the king's divorce was greatly desired by all Henry's subjects; the king, however, failed to get many signatures; see Iñigo de Mendoza to the emperor, 2 Dec. 1528 (*Span. Cal.*, iii, pt 2, 600 (p. 861)).

should more fitly be in the hands of the king than in Spain. They were to take great care not to give Francis the smallest ground for supposing that Henry would be dissatisfied should the brief prove to be genuine, but they were to ask the French king to promote Henry's cause at Rome and obtain letters from him for that purpose without letting him know what use would be made of them. When they got to Rome they were to ascertain what had been done to prove the brief a forgery, and if that matter were clear, they were to deliver to the pope the letters of the king and of the two legates. They were then to rehearse to the pope the grounds upon which the brief might be declared spurious and obtain a decretal commission enabling the legates to pronounce the brief to be a forgery. At the same time they were to urge the pope to write peremptorily to the emperor requiring him to send the brief within three months. If the pope should not consent to this course, then Knight and Benet were to deliver two further letters from the legates asking for the 'avocation' of the marriage suit to Rome, at the same time obtaining from the pope a written promise that he would give judgment in Henry's favour on certain grounds, of which Knight and Benet were provided with a summary.[1] They were not, however, to consent to this course until hope of obtaining the commission had become desperate, but above all they were to make sure of the pope's promise. If all this proved impossible to accomplish, rather than return empty-handed they were to carry out the instructions given to Bryan and Vannes.[2] Bryan and Vannes arrived in Paris in the middle of December,[3] and Knight and Benet reached Calais soon afterwards.[4]

With the despatch of these envoys the king began to consider once more the possibility of gaining possession of the original brief. The

[1] For example, that the emperor would not send the brief; that the brief was false on its face; that the king was in great perplexity and his health in danger etc.
[2] Instructions for Knight, Benet, Bryan, Gregory Casale and Vannes, 28 Nov. 1528 (*State Papers*, vii, 117; *L. & P.*, iv, 4978).
[3] cf. Vannes to Wolsey, 17 Dec. 1528 (*L. & P.*, iv, 5041). Wolsey sent Vannes, Bryan and Casale further instructions, dated 19 Dec. 1528, chiefly concerned with the general European pacification; in this connection they were to offer to the pope 'a convenient presidy', that is, a bodyguard to defend the pope against the emperor and secure his independence, but which would also be used as a useful means of bringing pressure to bear upon his holiness; cf. Wolsey to Knight and Benet, Jan. 1529; *L. & P.*, iv, 5179 (p. 2278). The question of the 'king's cause of matrimony' was only briefly touched upon (*L. & P.*, iv, 5050).
[4] cf. Knight and Benet to Brian Tuke, 26 Dec. 1528 (*L. & P.*, iv, 5066).

scheme for sending a messenger to Spain had been abandoned because of the risk that suspicions might be raised in the minds of the Spaniards. Now a much more subtle plan was set in motion. The queen was coerced into writing a letter to the emperor in which she begged him, in her own interest and to enable her to obtain justice, to send her the original brief; she had been told, she wrote, that only the original document would be accepted as evidence in the matrimonial suit, so that, without it, she would lose her husband and her child would be prejudiced.[1] On 20 December the king sent for the French ambassador, du Bellay, and told him about the copy of the brief which the queen had put forward. The king went on to say that as the cardinals did not consider this document to be authentic, the queen intended to send to Spain for the original and he had consented to her sending a Spaniard in post; du Bellay was asked to provide a safe conduct through France for this messenger.[2] The messenger must have left England soon afterwards, but while he was making his way through Frence he fell and broke his shoulder blade. and consequently another messenger was despatched with a fresh copy of the letter on 9 January 1529.[3]

The new messenger was the queen's chaplain, Thomas Abell, and he was escorted by one of her household servants, Juan de Montoya. As soon as he was out of England Abell himself wrote a letter to the emperor in which he said that the queen earnestly requested the emperor not to give up the brief, notwithstanding what appeared in her own letter which she had been forced, against her wishes, to write.[4] In this manner Henry's second plan to obtain possession of the original brief was frustrated.

[1] cf. *L. & P.*, iv, 5154. There can be no doubt that not only cajolery but coercion was used to compel Catherine to write this letter; see 'The advice to be given to the Queen's grace by her counsellors' (*L. & P.*, iv, 5155), Abell's letter to Charles V (*L. & P.*, iv, 5154 (ii)), Mendoza to Charles V, 16 Jan. 1529 (*L. & P.*, iv, 5177), Mendoza to Muxetula, 25 Jan. 1529 (*L. & P.*, iv, 5211 (ii)).
[2] du Bellay to Montmorenci, 20 Dec. 1528 (Le Grand, iii, 245, at pp.251, 252; *L. & P.*, iv, 5033).
[3] cf. Campeggio to J. Salviati, 9 Jan. 1529 (Ehses, 68, at p. 70).
[4] For Catherine's letter and that of Thomas Abell, see *L. & P.*, iv, 5154. Catherine's letter was dated 9 Jan. 1529, and was written at Hampton Court. She had been compelled to leave Greenwich and go to Hampton Court early in December (she was still at Greenwich on 2 Dec.; cf. Iñigo de Mendoza to the emperor, 2 Dec. 1528; *Span. Cal.*, iii, pt. 2, 600 (p. 863)), in order to make way for Anne Boleyn for whom sumptuous apartments had been provided adjoining those of the king.

G

On the same day, 9 January, that Catherine wrote her letter to her nephew, the emperor, Campeggio sent a report to Jacopo Salviati, the papal secretary of state. He said that the king was more than ever desirous of making Anne Boleyn his wife and only refrained from doing so because he was awaiting a favourable reply from the pope which he was confident he would receive. Campeggio said that he had tried unavailingly to make plain to the king and Wolsey the difficulties of the case. The king resolutely closed his mind to all arguments that were opposed to his wishes and appeared to believe that the pope could not refuse the urgent appeals of a prince to whom he was so much indebted. Campeggio believed that Wolsey now found the whole business distasteful but was unable to extricate himself. Campeggio said that he had tried to discover what Wolsey really thought, but the cardinal of York had merely shrugged his shoulders and said that somehow the king must be satisfied and that time would bring a remedy. Campeggio had put the matter to Wolsey in political terms, and argued that the pope could not be expected to comply out of hand with the king's demands in a matter that touched so closely the honour of the emperor. To this Wolsey replied that the emperor would not really care what happened and that once the thing had become an accomplished fact there were a thousand ways of maintaining good relations with him. When Campeggio argued that the church had always regarded matrimony as indissoluble even in the case of persons of the least consequence, Wolsey answered that, at the least, the brief was doubtful and suspect and there were many authorities, great theologians both living and dead, who favoured the view that the dispensation was invalid; that being so, it would be no great thing to satisfy the king in this matter so as to avoid the greater scandal that would arise if the king married again on his own authority. Campeggio reported that he had several times told Wolsey of his belief that the pope would 'avoke' (*avocarà*) the cause to himself, and that there were good reasons for taking such a course.[1]

The avocation of the cause to Rome was precisely what the emperor and his ambassador in England, Iñigo de Mendoza, had been trying to bring about. On 16 January Mendoza wrote to the emperor saying that he had heard from Rome that if a request for the avocation of the suit had been made on behalf of Catherine herself, instead of, as had been done,

---

[1] Campeggio to J. Salviati, 9 Jan. 1529 (Ehses, 68).

the emperor, the case would already have been avoked to Rome. He added that it was essential that the queen should obtain the avocation of the cause, as neither she nor the judges were free.[1] Eventually, however, Mendoza managed to elude the watchfulness of those who guarded and spied upon the queen and he persuaded her to write in her own hand a letter to the pope setting out her real wishes, and disclosing the constraints imposed upon her.[2]

Meanwhile Henry and Wolsey, who were anxious that their schemes should not be forestalled by the emperor's agents, were becoming impatient at the slow progress made by the envoys in their journey to Rome.[3] Francesco Campano, the pope's chamberlain, and Vincent Casale, the half-brother of Sir Gregory Casale, arrived in England from Rome in the middle of January, and brought with them, among other things, letters from Bryan and Vannes.[4] The king learned from these letters that their journey had been slower than he had expected, and since difficulties had been encountered by Knight and Benet in their dealings with Francis I,[5] it was decided to send Stephen Gardiner immediately to Rome, riding post the whole way, to replace Knight and Benet who were to wait at Lyons.[6] Gardiner embarked for Calais on Friday 22 January.[7] Despite the secrecy with which Gardiner's journey

[1] Mendoza to Charles V, 16 Jan. 1529 (*L. & P.*, iv, 5177).
[2] Iñigo de Mendoza to Muxetula (*Span. Cal.*, iii, pt. 2, 618 (p. 882)). cf. Mendoza to Muxetula, 25 Jan. 1529 (*L. & P.*, iv, 5211 (ii)).
[3] There is in existence a 'Memorial of things to be said in answer to the Emperor by the English ambassadors, if the matter of the King's marriage be touched upon, and an appeal of the Emperor be spoken of'. The memorial instructed the ambassadors that they must take care to say nothing of themselves, but if anything be said by the emperor or his councillors calling for a reply, they were to adapt their answer from the long instructions (26 pages) which followed (*L. & P.*, iv, 5156).
[4] cf. *L. & P.*, iv, 5151, 5152.
[5] cf. *L. & P.*, iv, 5148, 5149, 5150.
[6] Wolsey to Bryan, Vannes and G. Casale, 17 Jan. 1529 (*L. & P.*, iv, 5178), and Wolsey to Knight and Benet, Jan. 1529 (*L. & P.*, iv, 5179). On 20 Jan. Henry wrote to Jacopo Salviati, the papal secretary of state, that he was sending Gardiner to the pope and had commissioned him to confer with Salviati on matters which concerned the king's health of soul and body, the security of his kingdom and the honour of the holy see (*L. & P.*, iv, 5188).
[7] Gardiner to Wolsey, 22 Jan. 1529 (*L. & P.*, iv, 5195). Sir Gregory Casale, Henry's resident agent in Rome, wrote an interesting letter to his half-brother, Vincent, which shows not only that he had a clear grasp of the realities of the situation but that he was well aware that there were limits beyond which a pope could not go. He wrote (as calendared): 'I do not know what to hope of Dr.

was carefully surrounded, news of it soon reached the French ambassador du Bellay, and he sent word of it to France on 25 January.[1] Before he had closed his packet, however, he had learned on what he described as good authority that Gardiner was instructed, among other things, to tell the pope that if he did not compel Campeggio to proceed with the divorce and conclude the matter, the king would throw off his allegiance.[2]

No sooner had Gardiner left England than news was received from Sir Gregory Casale of the pope's illness, and this was followed by a false report that his holiness had died.[3] This news caused consternation since Henry was afraid that all that had been done in connection with the commission to Campeggio and Wolsey would be frustrated and reversed by Clement's successor. Accordingly, a commission was issued to Gardiner, Bryan, Gregory Casale and Vannes empowering them to condole with the college of cardinals on the death of the pope and to treat with them concerning the election of a new pope,[4] and these commissioners also received instructions that they were to use every possible

[1] du Bellay to Montmorenci, 25 Jan. 1529 (Le Grand, iii, 281; *L. & P.*, iv, 5209).
[2] Du Bellay to Montmorenci (Le Grand, iii, 295; *L. & P.*, iv, 5210). In this letter du Bellay wrote: 'Et croyez, Monseigneur, que Monsieur le Legat [Wolsey] est en grand peine, car la chose en est si avant, que si elle ne vient en effet, le Roy son Maistre s'en prendra à luy, & là où elle s'achevera, encore void il qu'il aura à faire à forte partie'.
[3] See *L. & P.*, iv, 5147, 5161, 5162, 5187. The pope was 51 and his illness lasted for about six months; for a convenient summary of the progress of the illness, see Hughes, *Reformation in England*, i, 182, note 1.
[4] *L. & P.*, iv, 5269.

Stephen's [Gardiner's] mission, and how far the Pope ought to pronounce the brief produced by the queen a forgery. I think his holiness will do nothing; and you may tell Wolsey so, in the event of his desiring my opinion. I hear you have told him that if the Pope's fears were removed, he would do everything for the king, *licita et illicita*. But if you rightly remember, I told you that the Pope would do all that could be done; for there are many things which the Pope says he cannot do, *veluti esset bulla decretalis*; and so he will say of that brief, that he can pass no decision on a brief emanating from Pope Julius, in the event of its being brought from Spain. . . . When, therefore, you say that the pope will do *illicita*, that must be understood *quae aliquo modo possint colorari*. If you remember, one of the reasons for my sending you to England was to tell the king and Wolsey that they should make some other arrangement because, if the Pope's fear were altogether removed, he will never do what we should want of him. He will, however, use all his efforts for peace . . .; but I do not think he will consent to any of the terms brought by fellow ambassadors' (Gregory Casale to Vincent Casale, 16 Feb. 1529; *L. & P.*, iv, 5302).

means to secure Wolsey's election to the papacy, as upon that the making or marring of the king's cause depended.[1]

The pope's illness was a protracted one and the king's business was held up for some time.[2] However, in the middle of March the English ambassadors were received by the pope, but owing to his debility the audience was a short one. Although the pope wished to satisfy the king, the demands that were made by the ambassadors were such that his holiness could come to no determination in the matter without taking counsel with some of the cardinals and other learned men; and, because of the importance of the matter, such consultations would be lengthy and fatiguing and could not be undertaken in the then state of the pope's health.[3] The English ambassadors made a further visit to the pope on 1 April. This time they backed up their demands with threats, saying that if the king were disappointed there was a danger that England would join Luther and his sect.[4] Shortly afterwards the pope's secretary, Sanga, wrote to Campeggio to inform him that the pope had commissioned cardinals del Monte, Pucci and Simonetta to hear and report upon the petitions of the English ambassadors. Sanga went on to tell Campeggio of the annoyance caused to the pope by these ambassadors; his holiness could not imagine how it had happened that they should entertain hopes of the revocation of the brief and bulls of pope Julius II which stood in the way of the king's desires. The pope was highly displeased that such a hope should ever have been entertained. His holiness, said Sanga, was in great trouble because of Campeggio's inability to stem the torrent of the king's demands and the cardinal was instructed to do his best to remedy matters.[5]

The letters which Gardiner and his colleagues sent home while waiting to see the pope had been somewhat pessimistic in tone, and on 6 April Henry himself wrote to them, saying that he wondered at their

---

[1] Instructions to Gardiner, Bryan, Gregory Casale and Vannes (23 pages); *L. & P.*, iv, 5270.
[2] See, e.g., Paul Casale to John Casale, 28 Feb. 1529 (*L. & P.*, iv, 5329); Gardiner to Henry VIII, 3 Mar. 1529 (*State Papers*, vii, 152; *L. & P.*, iv, 5348).
[3] Sanga to Campeggio, 19 Mar. 1529 (*L. & P.*, iv, 5391). Giovanni Battista Sanga was the pope's secretary. cf. Vannes to Henry VIII, 23 Mar. 1529 (*State Papers*, vii, 154; *L. & P.*, iv, 5401).
[4] Mai to Charles V, 3 April 1529 (*L. & P.*, iv, 5417). Miguel Mai was the imperial ambassador at Rome.
[5] Sanga to Campeggio, 10 April 1529 (*L. & P.*, iv, 5447). For Campeggio's reply, dated 20 May 1529, see *L. & P.*, iv, 5572.

despair of any favour to be had from the pope when they had not yet spoken to him. Henry told them to use the utmost diligence in his cause, and urged them to retain some notable excellent divine, a friar or some other, who would firmly stick to the king's causes, relying on that *quod pontifex ex jure divino non posset dispensare &c.*[1] On the same day Wolsey sent the ambassadors a long despatch, urging them to use every possible means to press the matter forward with the pope, even if he were *in articulo mortis*. He enclosed a memorandum concerning the points which showed the brief to be a forgery, so that there could be no excuse if the pope refused to declare it spurious. Wolsey told the ambassadors that if the necessary decretals could not be obtained, they were to propose to the pope that the commission already granted to Campeggio and Wolsey should be amplified so as to enable them to do all that the pope himself might do in his ordinary and absolute power; there should be clauses enabling them to decide all questions relevant to the cause, and compelling princes and other persons, under certain penalties, to produce any necessary record or witnesses. Moreover, if the pollicitation were insufficient to oblige the pope to confirm all that the legates did by virtue of the commission, the ambassadors must take care to see that he was so obliged, either by the insertion of words in the commission or by obtaining a new pollicitation. Finally, Wolsey suggested that, if the pope were to die, the college of cardinals would have power to decide the king's matter *sede vacante*, and he asked Gardiner and his colleagues to consider certain relevant points of canon law.[2]

On 21 April the pope himself wrote to Henry to say that he had been unable to satisfy the king's wishes, as expressed by the ambassadors, although he had tried night and day to do so and had taken the best legal advice. Although he would have been glad to do what the king desired, the pope said that he could not declare the brief of Julius II to be false without hearing both sides.[3] Such a result was inevitable and even the ingenious and thrusting Gardiner scarcely hoped for anything better.

[1] Henry VIII to Gardiner and his colleagues, 6 April 1529 (Pocock-Burnet, iv, 115; *L. & P.*, iv, 5427).
[2] Wolsey to Gardiner, Bryan, Gregory Casale and Vannes, 6 April 1529 (*L. & P.*, iv, 5428). For the memorandum concerning the falsity of the brief, see *L. & P.*, iv, 5376; cf. Wolsey to Gardiner, Bryan, Gregory Casale and Vannes, 6 April 1529 (*L. & P.*, iv, 5429).
[3] Clement VII to Henry VIII, 21 April 1529 (*State Papers*, vii, 164; *L. & P.*, vi, 5474).

However, one crumb of comfort was forthcoming. Although the pope refused to dictate to the emperor and demand the production of the brief within a specified time,[1] he proposed to send his master of the household, Jerome Selade, bishop of Vaison, to Spain with instructions to use all diligence to procure production of the brief.[2]

Although the pollicitation had been issued in July 1528, it had never reached England and while Wolsey knew of its terms and had mentioned the pope's promise to Campeggio, he had never seen the actual document. It had been thought that Vincent Casale would bring it with him when he arrived in England, with Campano, in January 1529. The document, however, remained in Italy, and in his letter of 21 April Gardiner told Henry that Sir Gregory Casale was sending it.[3]

By the time the pollicitation reached England Wolsey had decided that Gardiner could be more usefully employed at home; and when the pollicitation came into his hands he realized that it was useless for the purposes for which he wished to use it. Early in May, therefore, he sent instructions to Gardiner, Bryan, Gregory Casale and Vannes. He told them that the king, in the face of the pope's ingratitude, was determined to dissemble with him and to proceed in England with the cause by virtue of the commission already granted to Campeggio and Wolsey. The king was therefore revoking the commission of all his ambassadors except that of Sir Gregory Casale, and Gardiner and Bryan were instructed to return immediately. Wolsey said that had it not been for the absence of Gardiner, whose services were so much needed, he would have begun the process before Whitsuntide. Before leaving Rome, however, they were to make every endeavour to obtain an amplification of the commission, stressing the disappointment of the king at finding the pope more anxious to please the emperor than Henry. Wolsey enclosed a copy of

---

[1] Salviati remarked that 'such a method of proceeding was never used with any prince, much less with the emperor' (J. Salviati to Campeggio, 21 April 1529; *L. & P.*, iv, 5480).

[2] Sanga to Campeggio, 21 April 1529 (*L. & P.*, iv, 5477); Sir Gregory Casale to Wolsey, 21 April 1529 (*L. & P.*, iv, 5478).

[3] Gardiner to Henry VIII, 21 April 1529 (*L. & P.*, iv, 5476). In this letter Gardiner said that the opening words of the pollicitation, *Cum nos iustitiam eius causae perpendentes* (see p. 60) made more for the king's cause than if the decretal commission in Campeggio's hands were shown; and the king was at liberty to show the pollicitation. On 3 Mar. Gardiner had written to Henry VIII that the pollicitation was safe at Bologna (*State Papers*, vii, 152; *L. & P.*, iv, 5348).

the pollicitation, with marginal notes showing where it was ineffectual,[1] and Gardiner was instructed to get it devised anew and regranted with additions. In order to achieve this, Gardiner was instructed to tell the pope that the original document had been much injured and defaced by damp in the course of transmission, and that it was still in the possession of the person to whom he had entrusted it. As he was likely to be blamed for its poor condition, it was necessary that the pope should grant a fresh document; Gardiner was to promise the pope that he would write it out afresh, according to the best of his recollection, but he was to take care to insert in it 'other pregnant, fat and available words as is possible'.[2]

Gardiner seems to have prepared a revised copy of the pollicitation, containing the insertions recommended by Wolsey. Gardiner's draft followed the original fairly closely so that, at a superficial inspection, it did not appear to differ substantially from the original document. Had Clement signed this draft, however, he would have committed himself to the assertion that Henry's marriage was a notorious transgression of both divine and human laws.[3] This was the 'pollicitation printed by Lord Herbert of Cherbury and by Burnet as a genuine document, but in fact it was never granted by the pope at all.[4]

In the middle of May the king and Wolsey received disturbing news from Gardiner and Bryan. Gardiner said that although they had done their best to obtain from the pope the accomplishment of the king's desires, they had not succeeded, and he added that now they saw it questioned whether the authority given to Campeggio and Wolsey should not be revoked. The ambassadors had, indeed, been asked why

[1] Wolsey here wrote: 'And amongst other things, whereas ye with these last Letters, sent the Pope's Pollicitation, for the non-inhibition or avoking of the Cause, the ratifying and confirming of the Sentence by us his Legates herein to be given, and other things mentioned in the same, ye shall understand, that the said Pollicitation is so couched and qualified, as the Pope's Holiness whensoever he will may resile; like as by certain Lines and Annotations, which in the Margin of a copy of the said Pollicitation I send you herewith, ye shall perceive more at large' (Burnet, i, Coll. of Rec., p. 64).

[2] Wolsey to Gardiner, Bryan, Gregory Casale and Vannes [May 1529] (Burnet, i, Coll. of Rec., pp. 60-7; *L. & P.*, iv, 5523).

[3] '. . . leges tam divinas quam humanas in ea parte notorie transgrediendo, prout revera sic transgrediebatur . . .'

[4] cf. Pocock-Burnet, vi, 26. For the genuine pollicitation, see p. 59.

the supplication presented by the imperial ambassador for the avocation of the cause should not proceed. Bryan said that neither fair means nor foul had served to obtain what the king desired.[1] The imperial ambassador at Rome reported to the emperor that the English ambassadors, using a threatening tone, had told the pope that if the queen did not consider England to be a safe place for the trial of the cause, just as little did they consider Rome a safe place, on account of the presence of the imperial army.[2]

The news that the possible revocation of the legates' commission was under discussion at Rome caused Wolsey the most lively apprehension, and to meet this new situation the king and the cardinal once more changed their plans. It now seemed to them imperative that the marriage suit should be begun under the authority of the legatine commission before that commission was revoked, and it was determined to press on with the proceedings in England. Accordingly, Dr William Benet, a man 'well learned in the laws', was sent to Rome to replace Gardiner and Bryan, since Gardiner's presence was now urgently required in England in connection with the marriage suit. Benet's principal task was to counter the activities of the imperial agents and to circumvent their attempts to obtain the avocation of the cause. If Gardiner and Bryan were still in Rome when Benet arrived they were to make a further attempt to obtain a more ample commission, while taking care that in doing so they did not alienate the pope or incline him towards avocation. So far as the brief was concerned, they were to dissuade the pope from sending to Spain for the original, and if a nuncio had been sent for that purpose they were to obtain from his holiness a command that no mention should be made of it.[3]

---

[1] See Gardiner to Henry VIII, 4 May 1529 (*L. & P.*, iv, 5518), and Bryan to Henry VIII, 5 May 1529 (*State Papers*, vii, 169; *L. & P.*, iv, 5519). Unfortunately, the joint letters of Gardiner and Bryan to Wolsey, to which each of them refers in the letters cited, have not survived. Some idea of the 'foul means' to which Bryan referred can be obtained from the fact that the rudeness of Gardiner and Bryan caused the pope to have a relapse in his illness (Mai to Charles V, 11 May 1529; *L. & P.*, iv, 5534). In his letter to the king, previously cited in this note, Bryan said that, during the interview with the pope, Gardiner 'so answered . . . that he made the pope ashamed of his own deeds', but Mai reported that they 'came away [from the interview] very angry and bullying' (Mai to Charles V, 9 May 1529; *L. & P.*, iv, 5529.)

[2] Mai to Charles V, 9 May 1529; (*L. & P.*, iv, 5529).

[3] For Benet's instructions, see *State Papers*, vii, 171; *L. & P.*, iv, 5575. See also Wolsey to Gardiner, Bryan, Gregory Casale and Vannes, 21 May 1529 (Burnet,

Meanwhile, Jerome de Ghinucci and Edward Lee had reported from Spain that they had examined the original brief and they expressed the opinion that it was probably not authentic.[1] The reasons which they adduced in support of their opinion were not, however, of a substantial nature, and this consideration, together with the fact that the emperor had put no difficulty in the way of the two English agents seeing the document, may well have caused Wolsey to believe that the brief was, in all probability, genuine and should therefore be kept out of sight so far as possible. But, more important, Henry now realized that the emperor and Francis I were considering the conclusion of a peace, and he was anxious that sentence in the marriage suit should be pronounced while they were still at war. Henry wished, therefore, to give his whole attention to the prosecution of the cause and was consequently ready to drop his attempts to secure the brief; this is probably the reason for the sudden change in the instructions to the ambassadors with regard to this document. When Campeggio told the king and Wolsey that the pope refused to issue a peremptory command to the emperor to produce the brief, they replied that they no longer cared whether the pope tried to obtain it or whether the emperor sent it to Rome or England; and Campeggio observed that the reason was, in all probability, their fear that the cause would be removed from England to Rome and the authority of the legates revoked.[2]

Campeggio was quite right in his belief that fear of the avocation of the cause was the principal motive now governing the actions of the king and Wolsey. And there was good cause for their anxiety. No doubt

[1] cf. Lee to Henry VIII, 20 April 1529 (*State Papers*, vii, 158; *L. & P.*, iv, 5470); Ghinucci and Lee to Wolsey, 20 April 1529 (*L. & P.*, iv, 5471); extracts from letters from Ghinucci to Nicolaus Rusticus, 21, 23 April 1529 (*L. & P.*, iv, 5486); Ghinucci and Lee to Wolsey, 23 April 1529 (*L. & P.*, iv, 5487). See also Campeggio to J. Salviati, 12 May 1529 (Ehses, 78, at p. 79); and Act for the Exhibition of the Dispensation Brief to the English Ambassadors, 3 April 1529 (*Span. Cal.*, iii, pt. 2, 662); cf. Mai's Report of Proceedings at Rome, April 1529 (*Span. Cal.*, iii, pt. 2, 664 (at p. 972)).
[2] Campeggio to J. Salviati, 18 May 1529 (Ehses, 82, at p. 85).

i, Coll. of Rec., pp. 71-4; *L. & P.*, iv, 5576). For Benet's letter of credence, see Henry VIII to Clement VII, 20 May 1529 (*L. & P.*, iv, 5574), and for the commission to the ambassadors, Benet, Gregory Casale and Peter Vannes, dated 21 May 1529, to treat, in conjunction with the French ambassadors, for peace with Charles V, etc., see *L. & P.*, iv, 5577.

it was not known in England that Catherine had already secretly despatched a letter to the pope setting out her position and describing the constraints to which she was subjected. Catherine had expressed her wish that the letter should be given to the pope very secretly, and in due course her letter was given to him together with one from Iñigo de Mendoza describing how the queen had been forced to write to Spain for the brief.[1] These letters do not appear to have had any immediate effect; after they had been handed to the pope, Salviati said to Mai, the imperial ambassador, two or three times, that it would be best for the queen to enter a convent where the dangers to her life would be reduced. The pope, too, told Mai that the English ambassadors had hinted at the use of poison and had said that, were not the king such a good man, he would long since have used other means to attain his end, adding that servants would not be wanting to do what was required. To this revelation Mai replied that the queen was ready to incur even that danger rather than be a bad wife and prejudice her daughter, and that if such a course were resorted to, the emperor would avenge it. Thereupon the pope told him to make his protestation and then the cause should be avoked. Soon afterwards Mai received a letter from Mendoza, reporting that everything was going wrong in England and that it was urgent that the avocation be obtained, and enclosing a letter from the queen which Mai described as "fit to break even a stone" (*yen verdad que era para quebrantar las piedras*)'.[2]

It was, however, known in England that the emperor was concerning himself with his aunt's affairs and that, since the queen had no proctor in Rome, imperial agents were taking action on her behalf. It has already been seen that, early in May, Gardiner and Bryan had been asked why the supplication for the avocation of the cause, presented by the imperial ambassador, should not be proceeded with,[3] and soon afterwards the imperial ambassador made, in the presence of the pope, a protest against the continuance of the cause in England which was notarially noted and subsequently published.[4] The news of these events was

[1] cf. Mai's letter of 9 Mar. 1529 (*L. & P.*, iv, 5356).
[2] cf. Mai's Report of Proceedings at Rome, April 1529 (*Span. Cal.*, iii, pt. 2, 664 (pp. 971, 974); *L. & P.*, iv, 5440).
[3] cf. Gardiner to Henry VIII, 4 May 1529 (*L. & P.*, iv, 5518), and Wolsey to Gardiner, Bryan, Gregory Casale and Vannes, 21 May 1529 (Burnet, i, Coll. of Rec., pp. 71-4; *L. & P.*, iv, 5576); see p. 91.
[4] Mai to Charles V, 9 May 1529 (*L. & P.*, iv, 5529).

immediately despatched to England by courier.[1] Campeggio, when he reached Richmond on 21 May, found Wolsey greatly exasperated at the citation of the English ambassadors, but Campeggio pacified him by explaining how judicial matters were conducted in the Roman curia.[2]

Wolsey's personal position was thus rapidly moving towards a crisis. To preserve his position with the king it was essential that he maintain control of the marriage suit, but if it were avoked to Rome this would become impossible. His position was also being weakened by the Boleyn faction who were openly saying that he had not done all that he might have done to further the king's great matter. The French ambassador was well aware of the straits into which Wolsey had been brought, and he noted that 'the cardinal of York is in the greatest trouble that ever he was. The dukes of Norfolk and Suffolk and others lead the king to think that he has not advanced the marriage as much as he could have done, had he so wished'.[3] Wolsey's enemies were crowding in upon him, and the Boleyns were bent upon his ruin. His only hope of extricating himself seemed to be the pronouncement of a favourable judgment as soon as possible. It was now imperative for both king and cardinal that the hearing of the marriage cause be begun immediately.

Speed, however, was not what the pope wanted. Before ever he left

---

[1] cf. Campeggio to J. Salviati, 18 May 1529 (Ehses, 82, at p. 87). Since the messenger arrived in England on 18 May (ibid) he must have made the journey from Rome to London in ten days. Campeggio said that he had heard that the messenger completed the journey in ten days (Campeggio to J. Salviati, 4 June 1529; Ehses, 98).

[2] Campeggio to J. Salviati, 22 May 1529 (Ehses, 95). On 4 June Campeggio wrote that his secretary had reported to him that the king was not much appeased with regard to the citation of the ambassadors (Campeggio to J. Salviati, 4 June 1529; Ehses, 98).

[3] du Bellay to ?, 22 May 1529 (Le Grand, iii, 313; *L. & P.*, iv, 5581): 'Je vous asseure, Monseigneur, que Monsieur le Cardinal d'Yorc est en la plus grant peine qu'il fut oncques. Les Ducs de Suffort & Norfoch & les autres mettent le Roy d'Angleterre en opinion, qu'il n'a tant avancé le mariage qu'il eust fait, s'il voulu, . . .' Even in February Mendoza had reported that 'This lady, who is the cause of all the disorder, finding her marriage delayed, that she thought herself so sure of, entertains great suspicion that this cardinal of England puts impediments in her way, from a belief that if she were queen his power would decline. In this suspicion she is joined by her father, and the two dukes of Suffolk and Norfolk, who have combined to overthrow the cardinal; but as yet they have made no impression on the king, except that he shows him in court not quite so good a countenance as he did, and that he has said some disagreeable words to him' (Mendoza to Charles V, 4 Feb. 1529; *L. & P.*, iv, 5255).

Italy, Campeggio had been instructed to proceed in the matter as slowly as possible, and since his arrival in England these instructions had been several times repeated in writing. Now, on 29 May, Salviati, writing in cipher, told Campeggio that the pope had always desired that the cause should be protracted in order that some means might be found by which the king could be satisfied without sentence being pronounced. Campeggio was assured that the avocation of the cause to Rome, which he had frequently insisted on, had been deferred, not because it was doubted that the matter could be treated with less scandal in Rome than in England, but because the pope had always shrunk from having to take a step that would offend the king. But since Campeggio had been unable to prevent the commencement of the proceedings, the pope wished to warn him that the process must be slow and that no sentence must be pronounced. The pope was confident that Campeggio would be able to prolong the proceedings until he was able to advise his holiness that the time was propitious for the avocation of the cause to Rome.[1] But before Campeggio received these instructions the trial had begun.

[1] Sanga to Campeggio, 29 May 1529 (*L. & P.*, iv, 5604); although the writer of this letter is stated in the calendar to be Sanga, the pope's secretary, it is clear that it was, in fact, written by J. Salviati. In his letter to Salviati of 21 June 1529 (Ehses, 107, at p. 108), Campeggio wrote: 'I wished to say this to your lordship because the bishop of Feltri writes to me that his holiness sent Campano to command me on no account to pronounce sentence before the business of the peace [between the pope and the emperor] had been settled, and that when the time for sentence came I was to tell the king openly that I could not do otherwise than pronounce against him, and that in this way I should sustain the matter. I cannot remember that Campano told me any such thing, . . .' (Questo ho voluto dire a Vostra Signoria, perchè Feltrense mi scrive, che N. Signore gli dice havermi mandato a dire per il Campano, che per niente io non dessi sententia prima che fusse resoluta la pratica de la pace, et che venendo il tempo de la sententia io dicessi apertamente al re, ch'io non la poteva dare, se non contra di lui, et in questo modo sostenessi la cosa. Io per me non mi ricordo che'l Campano mi habbia detto tal parole, . . .). The bishop of Feltri was Campeggio's brother. But, referring to Salviati's cipher letter of 29 May, Campeggio went on to say (Ehses, at p. 109): 'With reference to what your lordship writes in cipher, I say that I understand the wish of his holiness to be that we should not proceed to judgment and that I should continue to procrastinate as long as I can' (Concludendo a quanto Vostra Signoria scrive in cifra dico, che io intendo, la mente di N. Signore essere, che non si venga al iudicio et che io vada sostenendo quanto si può).

V

The Legatine Court

I

On 30 May 1529 a licence under the great seal was issued to cardinals
Wolsey and Campeggio authorizing them to proceed in the cause touch-
ing the validity of the king's marriage with queen Catherine according
to their commission from Clement VII dated, at Viterbo, 6 June 1528.[1]
On the following day the court assembled in the great hall, or 'Parlia-
ment Chamber', of the Dominican priory of Blackfriars, near Ludgate.
The setting for this momentous trial was graphically described by
Edward Hall as follows:

In the beginning of this year, in a great hall within the Black Friars of London,
was ordained a solemn place for the two legates to sit in, with two chairs
covered with cloth of gold, and cushions of the same, and a dormant table
railed before, like a solemn court, all covered with carpets and tapestry: on the
right hand of the court was hanged a cloth of estate, with a chair and cushions
of rich tissue, for the king, and on the left hand of the court was set a rich
chair for the queen.[2]

The proceedings at the first sitting of the court were purely formal.
After the legates had taken their seats, John Longland, bishop of
Lincoln, presented to the cardinal legates the commission from the pope
which was read by Floriano Montino, the Ferrarese notary who was
Campeggio's secretary. The commission was then accepted by the
legates in the presence of canon William Clayborough, a prothonotary,
Richard Watkins and William Clayton, notaries, John Islip, abbot of
Westminster, Cuthbert Marshall, archdeacon of Nottingham, William
Warham, archdeacon of Canterbury, Richard Doke, archdeacon of
Salisbury, William Franklin, chancellor of Durham, and Roger Edge-
worth, Henry Radclyff, John Sinclair and Thomas Arundel. The
cardinals then appointed the bishop of Lincoln and John Clerk, bishop

---

[1] Rymer, *Foedera*, xiv, 295; *L. & P.*, iv, 5611. On 29 May Wolsey and Campeggio had sent their commission to Henry and asked to learn his pleasure with
reference to its execution and their proceedings in the case (*State Papers*, vii,
177; *L. & P.*, iv, 5602).

[2] Hall, *Chronicle*, ii, 150. For Cavendish's description, see Cavendish, *Wolsey* 79.

of Bath and Wells, to summon the king and queen to appear on 18 June between the hours of nine and ten in the morning, and the bishops took an oath to perform their duty.[1]

Gardiner and Bryan left Rome early in June and soon after their departure instructions arrived addressed to Gardiner. These were opened by Gregory Casale who found that they commanded the ambassadors, if the pope should make any pronouncement against the king's cause, to appeal from his holiness to the true vicar of Christ.[2] On his arrival in England on 22 June,[3] one of Gardiner's first acts was to write to Vannes and his colleagues at Rome countermanding this order, saying that they were to forbear to make any protestation to the true vicar of Christ as such a protest was likely to irritate the pope.[4]

Although the legatine proceedings had commenced, the king was still uneasy that the imperial protests in Rome might result in the avocation of the suit.[5] But soon afterwards Henry and Wolsey learned, with a good deal of pleasure, that the imperial protests had not been signed.[6] This did not, however, allay Wolsey's anxieties and the matter continued to cause him considerable worry. On 22 June he wrote to Vannes and Gregory Casale to tell them that if the king's matter were avoked at the instance of the queen or the emperor, the greatest dishonour would accrue to the king and the judges. Vannes and Casale were to do all they could to prevent, and never consent to, the avocation of the cause, and they were instructed not to do anything that might suspend or hinder the action of the legates. Wolsey added that Casale and Vannes must now show the king that they were of some reputation in Rome and could do him some service.[7]

Meanwhile, on 15 June, the queen, who was anxious and perplexed about her affairs, visited Campeggio, who was in bed, suffering from gout and fever. The purpose of her visit was to tell him that her advocates

---

[1] *L. & P.*, iv, 5613; cf. Campeggio to J. Salviati, 4 June 1529 (Ehses, 98, at p. 99). Edward Hall (*Chronicle*, ii, 150) makes the curious error of stating that the king and queen were cited to appear on 28 May, which was three days before the court assembled.

[2] cf. Gregory Casale and Vannes to Henry VIII, 6 June 1529 (*State Papers*, vii, 184; *L. & P.*, iv, 5650).

[3] See Campeggio to J. Salviati, 24 June 1529 (Ehses, 111).

[4] Gardiner to Vannes, etc., 25 June 1529 (*State Papers*, vii, 190; *L. & P.*, vi, 5715).

[5] Campeggio to J. Salviati, 4 June 1529 (Ehses, 98). The calendared version of this letter is unsatisfactory (*L. & P.*, iv, 5636).

[6] Campeggio to J. Salviati, 21 June 1529 (Ehses, 105).

[7] Wolsey to Vannes and Gregory Casale, 22 June 1529 (*L. & P.*, iv, 5703).

who should have come from Flanders, had not arrived because, it seemed, the emperor had warned them not to set out on their journey as England was not safe.[1] As a result, the queen found herself without anyone to plead for her; she had no confidence in the counsel assigned to her by the king as she found it easy to believe that they would have greater regard to the king's pleasure than to her necessity. She went on to ask Campeggio what was the state of the case and inquired how it was possible for proceedings to begin in England while the trial of the cause was taking place before the pope in Rome. Campeggio explained that no proceedings had yet been started in Rome, and the pope would not avoke the cause without great forethought and consideration. He exhorted her to pray for enlightenment, that she might take some good course in her difficulties, and to commit her troubles to God; the queen, however, was far from accepting these hints that she should take religious vows, and she swore solemnly that from the embrace of her first husband she entered her marriage with Henry as a virgin and an immaculate woman. When the queen departed she left Campeggio in doubt as to the course she would pursue at the trial.[2]

On 18 June the legatine court reassembled. The proceedings began by the appearance before the legates of the bishops of Lincoln and of Bath and Wells who produced their commission to summon the king and queen. They declared that they had executed it by citing the king and queen in their privy chambers at Windsor on 1 June, and had endorsed their commission to that effect. For the king there appeared Richard Sampson, dean of the chapel, with letters of proxy for himself and Dr John Bell, the archdeacon of Gloucester. The great surprise however, was provided by Catherine herself. She appeared in person,[3] and read from a prepared script her protest against the jurisdiction of the legates which she desired to be registered and returned to her. The legates granted this request and appointed Montino, Clayborough and Watkins to act as notaries. They then appointed Dr John Hughes

---

[1] cf. Margaret of Savoy to Charles V, 27 May 1529 (*L. & P.*, iv, 5599 (p. 2476)).
[2] Campeggio to J. Salviati, 16 June 1529 (Ehses, 101). On 15 June Henry returned from Hampton Court to Greenwich, and the queen went to Baynard's Castle; it was while she was on her way that she crossed the river and visited Campeggio (ibid.).
[3] Up to the last moment it was not known what she would do and her personal appearance had not been foreseen. 'La personale comparitione di essa regina è stata improvista et incognita sino all' ultimo' (Campeggio to J. Salviati, in postcript dated 18 June, to letter dated 16 June 1529; Ehses, 101, at p. 104).

promotor or coadjutor, and cited the queen to appear again on Monday 21 June to hear their decision on her protest. Meanwhile Sampson was allowed copies of the proceedings.[1]

The court assembled again on 21 June. Both the king and the queen were present in person, and the proceedings began with a long speech by the king, spoken with much vehemence, in justification of the cause. He declared his devotion to the pope and the holy see, and protested that all he sought was the ascertainment of the truth and the relief of his conscience. He said that he had confidence in all that the legates should do and he urged all Englishmen to place a like confidence in them.[2] The legates then gave their decision on Catherine's protest against their jurisdiction; they rejected it, and pronounced themselves to be competent judges. Whereupon the queen appealed to the pope. Then, in a moment of high drama, she crossed the hall to Henry's chair and, kneeling before him, addressed him in a moving speech. She said that she was a poor woman and a stranger in the king's dominions where she had neither assured friends, unbiased advice nor indifferent judges. She had been the king's wife for a long time, had borne him several children and had always studied to please him. She protested that she had first come to the king a true maid, upon which she appealed to his own conscience. If there were anything she had done amiss, she was willing to be put away with shame, but she refused to submit to a court before which her lawyers, who were the king's subjects, were afraid to speak freely. Then, making the king a low reverence, she left the court.[3] The king remained silent until the queen had left the hall, and then he spoke a panegyric of her virtues, protesting that what he did was merely for the quieting of his conscience and the tranquillity of the kingdom, and saying that he would have been well content to have lived out the rest of his life with Catherine were it not for his conscientious scruples.[4]

---

[1] *L. & P.*, iv, 5694; Campeggio to J. Salviati, in postscript dated 18 June to letter dated 16 June, 1529 (Ehses, 101, at pp. 103, 104). For an account of the proceedings, signed by Montino, Clayborough and Watkins, see Pocock, i, 216. For the text of Catherine's protest, see Pocock, i, 219.

[2] cf. the postscript to Campeggio's letter to J. Salviati, dated 21 June, 1529 (Ehses, 105, at p. 106).

[3] See Campeggio to J. Salviati, 21 June 1529 (Ehses, 107, at pp. 108, 109); Cavendish, *Wolsey*, 80-2. In his letter Campeggio said that the queen had asked Henry for leave to write and send messengers to Rome and to the pope, and the king had granted her request.

[4] Cavendish, *Wolsey*, 82-4; du Bellay to Francis I, 22 June 1529 (*L. & P.*, iv, 5702).

The legates caused Catherine to be summoned three times, and when she did not appear they pronounced her contumacious and cited her to appear on the following Friday, 25 June.[1] Wolsey then asked the king to declare publicly whether it were true that he, the cardinal, had been the chief mover in the matter, 'for I am greatly suspected of all men herein'. The king replied that he could readily excuse the cardinal who, indeed, had always been against it. The matter had arisen, he said, in his own conscience which was first troubled by a remark made by one of the French ambassadors concerning the legitimacy of his daughter, Mary. He first mentioned the matter to the bishop of Lincoln, in confession, and subsequently asked the archbishop of Canterbury to consult the bishops about the matter; and he was able to show a writing, signed by all the bishops, which confirmed his scruples about his marriage. The archbishop acknowledged that it was so, but Fisher, the bishop of Rochester, immediately dissented, saying, 'You have not my consent thereto'. After some wrangling upon the point, the archbishop asserted that Fisher had agreed that the archbishop should sign his name and affix his seal which, said Warham, the bishop undertook to acknowledge; to that Fisher answered, 'Under your correction, my lord, and supportation of this noble audience, there is nothing more untrue'. The king, somewhat irritated by this turn of events, said that it made no matter; 'we will not stand with you in argument herein, for you are but one man'. And with that the court adjourned.[2]

After the close of this session, Campeggio wrote a long letter to Salviati which not only described the course of the trial but discussed the difficult position in which the legate found himself.[3] From this letter

---

[1] Henry VIII to Benet, Gregory Casale and Vannes, 13 June 1529 (Burnet, i, Coll. of Rec., p. 77; *L. & P.*, iv, 5707). Having protested against the jurisdiction of the legates and appealed to the pope, Catherine could not take part in the trial without, implicitly at least, acknowledging the competence of the judges.

[2] Cavendish, *Wolsey*, 82-5; *Life of Fisher*, 61-3. See also the draft of the method of procedure on 21 June (Pocock, i, 223).

[3] Campeggio to J. Salviati, 21 June 1529 (Ehses, 107-10); for a translation by Dr James Gairdner, see *E.H.R.*, xii, 249-52. In the course of this letter, Campeggio said: 'About this [the diligence to have the trial pushed on] I find myself in such trouble and anxiety that if your lordship saw me in bed with a cruel attack of gout in seven places, accompanied with fever, although only incidental, brought on by the pain, and surrounded by fifteen doctors with two piles of books to show me that all they conclude is according to law, and nothing else can or ought to be done, I am sure you would have compassion on me, especially as I am obliged to have myself carried to the place where the trial is held, God knows

certain conclusions may be drawn. Campeggio held the view, which appears to be correct, that the pope considered the case for the king to be so poor that, once it were submitted to judicial investigation, it was inevitable that judgment should be pronounced in favour of the marriage. It also appears that the pope, while desiring peace with the emperor, was anxious to maintain friendly relations with Henry, and for that reason he wanted no judgment at all to be given until peace with the emperor had been actually concluded. It is also clear that Campeggio was determined to do justice in the matter and to pronounce a sentence wholly consonant with the facts and the law, whatever might be the result. He had not prejudged the question and he appears to have thought that the pope might be wrong in his estimate of the strength of Henry's case. For Campeggio the question was solely one of canon law and the stresses imposed upon him by the directions he had received of a political nature added greatly to his difficulties. It also appears that the pope, like Campeggio, would have been glad if, by some means, the whole matter could have been shelved, and each of them would have welcomed a decision by the queen to retire into the religious life.[1]

The court sat again on Friday 25 June. Campeggio was suffering so severely from gout that he was carried in a litter to Blackfriars. It was necessary for the legates, that day, to obtain the king's oath with respect to the propositions and articles put forward on his behalf, and on their arrival they found him waiting for them in a chamber adjoining the great hall. The queen was again absent and she was again cited to appear.[2] The legates then began to receive evidence on behalf of the king and to hear argument from his counsel, a process that was to occupy them for another month. At the close of the proceedings Campeggio had a private discussion with the king, arising out of the latest despatches from Rome; from this discussion he concluded that Henry was exerting himself to prevent the conference then negotiating for peace at Cambrai reaching any conclusion for the time being, because he wished first to see the end of the marriage cause and then to send Wolsey to conclude,

---

[1] cf. Dr James Gairdner, *E.H.R.*, xii, 252.
[2] The citation was served upon her the following day 26 June, in her dining-room at Greenwich (Rymer, *Foedera*, xiv, 300; *L. & P.*, iv, 5716).

---

with what discomfort to me and danger in moving, in ascending and descending staircases, and in embarking and landing from the vessel. I pray God I may not have to remain forever in England!' (Gairdner's translation).

at one and the same time, fresh articles with the emperor and a league establishing universal peace.[1]

The court sat for the fifth time on 28 June. While the proceedings continued as usual in the queen's absence, her confessor, John Fisher, the bishop of Rochester, appeared and made a vigorous speech supporting the validity of Catherine's marriage. The bishop said that, pursuant to the king's commission, he had diligently studied the cause between the king and the queen and, as a result, he was positive that the marriage was holy and good and could be dissolved only by God. He asserted that he was prepared to die for his opinion, and that if he did die for such a cause he would not believe his death to be less unjust than the execution of St John the Baptist. Fisher then presented to the legates a book which he had composed upon the case, for them to study. He was followed by Henry Standish, the bishop of St Asaph, who expressed the same opinion, and by the dean of Arches, Dr Ligham. Wolsey replied to these speeches, and the proceedings then continued, and witnesses were heard at great length. Because of her non-appearance the queen was again pronounced contumacious and again cited to appear once and for all.[2]

In a letter to the secretary of the duke of Ferrara, describing the events of this session, Campeggio's secretary, Floriano Montino, said that the affair of the bishop of Rochester was unexpected and unforeseen, and consequently everybody had been kept in a wonder. Montino enclosed a copy of a letter from a friend in which the writer described Fisher as a man held in great esteem on account of his learning and pious life and said that the event had given rise to much discussion; because of Fisher's great reputation, however, he thought that the king could no longer persist in his desire to have the marriage declared void, adding that since Fisher was against it, the kingdom would not permit the queen to suffer wrong.[3] Fisher's dramatic intervention did, indeed, cause great

[1] Campeggio to J. Salviati, 25 June 1529 (Ehses, 112). In the last paragraph of this letter Campeggio wrote: 'Non so dire altro, salvo che io prego, V.S. consideri bene, in che travaglio mi trovo, et che non basta dire: dà la sententia contra il re; et per la contumacia della reina, et modo loro di procedere faranno il processo in modo, che secundum deducta facilmente non si potrà fare se non a lor modo per molti capi'. See also the articles of the process, 25 June 1529 (Pocock, i, 225). For the peace conference at Cambrai, see p. 111.
[2] Floriano Montino to secretary of duke of Ferrara, 29 June 1529 (Ehses, 116-18). The calendar (*L. & P.*, iv, 5732, 5733, 5734) is misleading here.
[3] Ibid.

anxiety to the king and Wolsey, and Gardiner, who had not been a week in England, was immediately ordered to prepare an answer to the bishop; and the bitterness with which Gardiner wrote indicates the effect of Fisher's statement.[1]

Fear that the cause might be avoked and uncertainty as to the result of the peace negotiations proceeding at Cambrai made the king and Wolsey anxious enough; but their anxiety was greatly enhanced by the unexpected declaration of the bishop of Rochester. Accordingly, with the field left open to them by Catherine's refusal to take part in the trial they redoubled their efforts to bring the proceedings to an end and secure the sentence they wanted. Campeggio, whose objective was procrastination, was becoming seriously alarmed. He wrote to Salviati that the lawyers were proceeding with inconceivable urgency in the king's cause and expected to come to the end within twenty days. He complained that since the queen had not appeared after presenting her appeal, the king's advocates had a wide field for action, with the result that they did what they liked and conducted the trial with all those arts which could influence the result in their favour. And after discussing some matters connected with the conference at Cambrai he added a postscript: 'I hear the king has had much discussion with his grace [Wolsey], proposing, as his grace is unable to go in time, to send to Cambrai the bishop of London [Cuthbert Tunstall], a man of worth and merit, and More, a layman, and a man of like learning and merit.'[2] Campeggio's information was reliable; on 30 June Tunstall, More and Hacket were appointed to treat for peace with the French and imperial ambassadors.[3] Tunstall and More left London on 1 July.[4]

[1] Gardiner's reply is in the Public Record Office (S.P., Hen. VIII, 54) and is calendared at *L. & P.*, iv, 5729. For Gardiner's authorship of this document, see *Obedience in Church and State: Three political tracts by Stephen Gardiner* (ed. P. Janelle; Cambridge 1930), pp. xvii-xx.

[2] Campeggio to J. Salviati, 29 June 1529 (Ehses, 114); the postscript is as follows (Ehses, 115): 'Ho inteso, questa Maestà essere in molta consulta col Rmo., pensando, che S.S. Rma. più non possa andare a tempo, di mandare a Cambrai il vescovo di Londra, persona degna et di valore, et il Moro laico, persona di dottrina et valore similmente'.

[3] Their commission is printed in full in Rogers, 406-8; cf. *L. & P.*, iv, 5744. The three were also commissioned to treat about the debts due from the emperor to the king; to treat for peace with the ambassadors of Clement VII, Charles V, Francis I, Venice and other states; and to treat about commercial disputes. John Hacket was the English ambassador to Margaret of Savoy in the Netherlands.

[4] Campeggio to J. Salviati, 13 July 1529 (Ehses, 119, at p. 120).

The court continued to sit at intervals and in the course of its proceedings a very large body of evidence was put before the legates.[1] The sense of urgency increased. On 13 July Campeggio wrote to Salviati that the case was proceeding with greater celerity and more urgency than ever, and that it made such strides, always faster than a trot, that some people expected the sentence within ten days; and he complained that the legates had many things to do—writings, allegations and processes to see and examine—yet the urgency and diligence was so great that nothing sufficed to bring them a moment's breathing time. He warned Salviati that it would be impossible for him not to declare his opinion, but he assured him that he would not fail to do his duty and office, and that when he gave sentence he would have before his eyes only God and the honour of the holy see.[2]

On 19 July the proceedings were largely concerned with the brief of Julius II, and a number of certified extracts from the records, together with several depositions, were put in evidence. Among the documents so put in was the record of the examination of the bishop of Winchester by Richard Wolman in April 1527.[3] Since the bishop had declined to sign the deposition on account of his great age and failing sight, Wolman said that he was instructed to sign it, if necessary, in the bishop's name; whereupon, out of deference to the king's command, he signed it. On the following Wednesday, 21 July, there was put in the protest against the marriage which Henry, as prince of Wales, had executed on the eve of his fifteenth birthday.[4]

On 23 July the court sat again, and it was confidently expected that on this occasion the legates would give judgment.[5] Accordingly, the king was present to hear sentence pronounced in his favour, and when the court sat, counsel for the king formally asked for judgment. Campeggio, however, declined to give judgment until he had made a report to the pope, saying that having regard to the great mass of evidence, the high

---

[1] Not all of this evidence survives; but see, e.g., *L. & P.*, iv, 5751, 5768, 5773, 5774, 5778, 5783. See, also, Wolsey's notes of the proceedings (Pocock, i, 229, 230, 231).

[2] Campeggio to J. Salviati, 13 July 1529 (Ehses, 119). In this letter he wrote: 'Rofense et Asavense [the bishops of Rochester and St Asaph] parlano in favore del matrimonio et hanno dato alcun libri, etiam alcuni dottori, ma con timore et come da se, nè a nome de la reina parla più alcuno. Si aspettava un' avocatione o suspensione'.

[3] See p. 12.   [4] See p. 7.

[5] cf. du Bellay to Brion, 22 July 1529 (*L. & P.*, iv, 5789); Cavendish, *Wolsey*, 89.

dignity of the parties and the nicety of the arguments, it was improper to give judgment hastily. He therefore adjourned the court until 1 October. The adjournment was in accordance with the practice of the Roman curia, which did not sit from the end of July until October, but the point of Campeggio's action was not lost upon the king. The announcement of the adjournment caused stupefaction among those present, and in the silence the duke of Suffolk stepped forward and said, 'It was never merry in England whilst we had cardinals amongst us', words which must have sounded ominously in Wolsey's ears.[1] It was now clear to everyone that the days of Wolsey's power were nearly over.

2

Meanwhile Benet, who had been sent to Rome to replace Gardiner and Bryan,[2] arrived there on 16 June. He found that the imperial ambassadors were strongly urging the avocation of the suit and he feared that the departure of Gardiner might cause the pope to suspect that the king would proceed without waiting for the production of the original brief. He and Gregory Casale therefore decided that it would be best to assure the pope that the cause was not in progress, despite the fact that it had already begun; but it could scarcely be expected that this puerile lie would have any effect. Benet and his colleagues were received in audience by the pope on 21 June, but they contented themselves with the discussion of generalities. Before another audience could be arranged a recurrence of the pope's illness prevented any further discussion with him. However, Benet and Casale told Salviati that proceedings had not yet been started. Salviati was considerably surprised by this statement as he knew, from Campeggio's letters and from Campano who had arrived in Rome on 22 June, that the proceedings had commenced on 31 May. Whereupon Benet told Salviati that he had left

[1] Cavendish, *Wolsey*, 89-91; Hall, *Chronicle*, ii, 153; Burnet, i, 77. For the dates, see *L. & P.*, iv, 5791 (p. 2589); Hall's dates are wrong. According to Cavendish's account, Wolsey made a reply to Suffolk, but Cavendish is the sole authority for the reply, and it may be doubted whether any answer was actually given (cf. Pollard, *Wolsey*, 234, note 4). Pollard (ibid. 234) observed that the duke's outburst 'was the only remark of Suffolk's that anyone ever remembered. For once in his life he had given public expression to public opinion in a way to make it decisive. Wolsey's power was gone.'

[2] See p. 91.

England at the same time as Campano and pledged his word that nothing had been done. Upon this dubious foundation Benet and Casale urged Salviati to persuade the pope not to order the avocation of the cause.[1]

About 28 June news reached Rome that the French army had been defeated by imperial troops; however, it was some days before those in Rome learned the full extent of the disaster at Landriano on 21 June when Francis I lost his entire army under St Pol. Charles V was now master of Europe and Francis I had no choice but to conclude peace upon the emperor's terms. A little while before this momentous event, the pope had sent a nuncio to Barcelona to negotiate an alliance between himself and the emperor. The negotiations came to a successful conclusion on 29 June when the treaty of Barcelona, between Clement VII and Charles V, was signed. The treaty provided, among other things, for the marriage of the pope's nephew to the emperor's natural daughter, for the re-establishment of Medici rule in Florence and for the restoration to the pope of Cervia and Ravenna and other papal towns in the hands of the emperor, and for the absolution from ecclesiastical censures of all those who had taken part in the sack of Rome.[2]

The English ambassadors continued their efforts to prevent the avocation of the cause.[3] On 6 July the pope, who had now recovered something of his health, sent for them. He told them of the imperial demands for avocation and that he had received from the queen herself an appeal demanding that the cause should be avoked; and he added that the imperial ambassadors were complaining that he had allowed the marriage suit to proceed in England despite his promises to the contrary. The Englishmen replied that they knew nothing of the process, adding,

[1] Benet, Gregory Casale and Vannes to Wolsey, 28 June 1529 (*L. & P.*, iv, 5275). Concern that the pope was about to avoke the cause was felt early in June, before Gardiner had left Rome; Gardiner and Gregory Casale then told Salviati that unless the pope were prevented from signing the avocation, which would inflict a serious injury on the king's cause, the king and Wolsey would have reason to neglect the pope's authority and proceed in some other way (which many learned men, both in England and France, had advised him to do) and the holy see would thus be ruined (Gregory Casale to Wolsey, 5 June 1529; *L. & P.*, iv, 5461).
[2] It is idle to suggest, as is sometimes done, that the treaty of Barcelona was the result of the battle of Landriano. For one thing, the negotiations had begun before the battle was fought, and, moreover, the distances involved are too great and the time interval too short, for the one event to have determined the other.
[3] One of the means employed to this end was interference with correspondence destined for Salviati and the pope; cf. *L. & P.*, iv, 5725, 5763, 5764, 5769, etc.

somewhat lamely, that if it had indeed begun the legates had probably commenced the proceedings on hearing of the pope's illness in order to preserve their jurisdiction in the event of his death. They reminded the pope of the purpose for which he had granted the legatine commission and mentioned the evils that would follow the avocation of the cause. The pope replied, with lamentations, that he was placed between the hammer and the anvil; he foresaw the general ruin of christendom but had no power to apply a remedy. Hitherto, he said, when pressed by the imperial ambassadors for the avocation of the cause, he had restrained them by saying that he had no mandate from the queen, but now they were able to point to an appeal by the queen herself. After much further discussion, the pope said that he would postpone for a few days the consideration of the avocation, and would study the queen's appeal which had not yet been read; then he might devise means for deferring the avocation. With this the ambassadors had to be content. In their despatch to Wolsey describing the audience they said that, since they could now serve the king only by postponing the avocation, they had deliberated what should be done to gain time. As a result, they thought it best to advise the pope to send a courier to England to discover the true state of affairs, because such a course would enable his holiness to tell the imperial ambassadors that nothing could be done in the matter of the avocation until the courier's return. In a personal letter to Wolsey, Benet wrote, 'seeing that we could obtain nothing of the pope for stopping the avocation, we consulted and devised for the deferring of it, till such time as your grace might make an end in the cause there [i.e. in England]'.[1]

The ambassadors' letters, which reached Wolsey on 22 July, convinced

---

[1] Benet, Gregory Casale and Vannes to Wolsey, 9 July 1529 (*L. & P.*, iv, 5762); Benet to Wolsey, 9 July 1529 (Burnet, i, Coll. of Rec., p. 80; *L. & P.*, iv, 5761). In their joint letter, the ambassadors wrote that Salviati had told Sir Gregory Casale that there was no need to deceive him about the process, as Campeggio had written all the actions and mind of the king. See also Vannes to Henry VIII, 9 July 1529 (*State Papers*, vii, 191; *L. & P.*, iv, 5763), in which he wrote: 'You can tell him [Campeggio], although it is not true, that we have no fear of an avocation, lest he should defer judgment in expectation of it' (Poterit etiam dicere, licet non verum est, quod nos nihil timemus de avocatione; ne ipse, ea spe detentus, sententiam differat). And he went on to warn the king that, if he were afraid of the avocation, the cause must be hurried on; cf. Vannes to Wolsey, 9 July 1529 (*L. & P.*, iv, 5764), and Gregory Casale to Wolsey, 9 July 1529 (*L. & P.*, iv, 5767).

him of the impossibility of preventing the avocation, and he realized that it was merely a matter of time. He wrote to the ambassadors to say that it was difficult to carry out their advice to bring the suit to a conclusion as speedily as possible because 'such discrepance and contrariety of opinions hath here ensued in the said cause', that it would be long delayed. He went on to say that other counsels were therefore necessary and it was important to act as if the avocation had been granted. If the avocation, he said, were merely intended to tie his hands without preventing the king from taking any other remedy, it might be allowed to pass, but a citation of the king to Rome, or a threat of excommunication, was no more tolerable than the whole loss of the king's dignity. If, therefore, the pope had granted any such avocation, it must be revoked; and the ambassadors were told not to consume time but to apply themselves to the matter.[1]

But it was too late. Even before Wolsey had written his letter the matter had been decided. For some weeks the imperial ambassador in Rome, Miguel Mai, had been pressing the pope to avoke the cause, only to be told that nothing could be done in the absence of an appeal from Catherine herself. When Catherine's appeal reached Rome matters took a different turn.[2] At the instance of Mai the appeal was referred to the *Signatura*[3] which decided that the cause should be avoked. The pope, however, wished the decision to be confirmed in a consistory of cardinals, but on the day appointed for the consistory the pope was too unwell to attend, and the decree for the avocation of the cause and its reference to the Rota was passed, on 16 July, seven days before the legatine court was adjourned, in a congregation appointed by the pope for the

[1] Wolsey to Benet, Gregory Casale and Vannes, 27 July 1529 (*State Papers*, vii, 193; *L. & P.*, iv, 5797).
[2] For the text of Catherine's appeal, see Ehses, 122-5; see pp. 85, 93.
[3] In the early Middle Ages, as the number of petitions to Rome increased, certain officials were appointed to examine and report upon them; these officials became known as *referendarii apostolici*. The brief in reply to a petition was known as a *signatura*, and this term became applied to the body of *referendarii*. Petitions fell into two classes, those asking for favours and those asking for justice, and Alexander VI (1492-1503) accordingly divided the *referendarii* into two bodies, the *Signatura* of Grace (for petitions asking for favours) and the *Signatura* of Justice (for petitions asking for justice); the former gradually disappeared, but the latter was reorganized by Gregory XVI in 1834, while St Pius X, by the apostolic constitution *Sapienti consilio* (29 June 1908), made the *Signatura* one of the three tribunals of the Roman curia, the others being the *Penitentiaria* and the *Rota*.

purpose.[1] Six copies of the decree were made, one of which was posted in Rome on 23 July, two were sent to Flanders to be posted in Bruges and Dunkirk, and the remainder were sent to Catherine.[2]

On 18 July the pope communicated the decision to Wolsey. He said that hitherto he had exceeded the limits of condescension in acceding to the demands of the English ambassadors, but now, in order to avoid giving scandal to the whole of christendom, he wished to provide for an impartial judgment, adding that, so far as possible, due regard would be had to the king's desires.[3] On 19 July he wrote to the king to tell him that, by the unanimous advice of the auditors and *referendarii* of the *Signatura*, the queen's appeal had been allowed.[4] On the same day he wrote again to Wolsey to express his sorrow at having been compelled to avoke the cause; he hoped that Wolsey would feel no regret, considering how much the pope had done to delay matters, and he urged Wolsey to keep the king well disposed to the holy see.[5]

Henry now realized, with shock, that despite all the fair promises made to him in the course of the past two years, the pope was not disposed to allow a decision to be given against the queen without permitting her to be heard in her own defence. A supreme egoist, Henry's capacity for believing in his own righteousness was almost unlimited, and that the pope should feel bound to consider the queen's claims to justice appeared to him as the blackest ingratitude; in the shock of realization, he placed much of the blame upon Wolsey. From the day when Campeggio adjourned the court, Henry had no further personal communication with Wolsey save for a long conversation on the occasion of Campeggio's leave-taking. One man, however, had contrived to turn matters to his own advantage; Stephen Gardiner left Wolsey's service to enter that of the king, and on 28 July he went to court for the first time to enter upon his duties as secretary.[6]

On 29 August the pope issued a brief suspending the further hearing of the king's cause until Christmas, which was presented to Henry by

---

[1] cf. Ehses, 122-5.
[2] See Mai to Charles V, 4 Aug. 1529 (*L. & P.*, iv, 5827).
[3] Clement VII to Wolsey, 18 July 1529 (Ehses, 118). The pope also wrote to the king on the same day; cf. Ehses, 119.
[4] Clement VII to Henry VIII, 19 July 1529 (Ehses, 120).
[5] Clement VII to Wolsey, 19 July 1529 (Burnet, i, Coll. of Rec., p. 81; *L. & P.*, iv, 5785).
[6] Gardiner to Vannes, 28 July 1529 (*L. & P.*, iv, 5798).

Campeggio, and he wrote once more to Henry to tell him of the avocation of the cause.[1] On 1 September the pope wrote to Wolsey and Campeggio to inform them of what had been done.[2] There was now nothing to detain Campeggio longer in England and his departure was taken by Henry as occasion to write to the pope, complaining of the conduct of his holiness. He could have wished, he said, that all things had been so expedited as to have corresponded with his expectations which were founded on the pope's promises. As it was, he was compelled to regard with grief and wonder the incredible confusion that had occurred. If the pope could relax divine laws at his pleasure, he surely had as much power over human laws, and Henry went on to complain that he had been deceived by the pope, on whose promises no reliance could be placed; moreover, his dignity had not been considered in the treatment he had received. But if the pope would now perform what he had promised and keep the cause, now avoked to Rome, in his own hands until it could be decided by impartial judges and in an indifferent place and in a manner satisfactory to the king's scruples, Henry would forget what was past and repay kindness with kindness.[3]

The pope thereupon wrote once more to Henry, assuring him that he had but suspended the cause. He went on to point out that the dispensation was a matter of positive, not divine, law, and if the queen, as she affirmed, had not been known by prince Arthur, there could be no doubt that the dispensation was perfectly sound *in foro conscientiae*. Finally he begged Henry to consider the danger in which christendom stood from the Turks, and how greatly that danger was increased by the marriage dispute.[4]

3

Tunstall and More had left London on 1 July to take part, with John Hacket, in the peace negotiations proceeding at Cambrai.[5] The close

---

[1] *L. & P.*, iv, 5878 (cf. Ehses, 125) Campeggio to J. Salviati, 7 Oct. 1529 (Ehses, 132-5). It is of interest to note that there exists a draft, in Gregory Casale's hand, of a promise by Clement VII that in three months after the avocation of the cause he would pronounce a sentence of divorce and give the king licence to contract a second marriage (*L. & P.*, iv, 5878(2)).
[2] Ehses, 126.   [3] Henry VIII to Clement VII, 30 Sept. 1529 (Ehses, 130).
[4] Clement VII to Henry VIII, 7 Oct. 1529 (Ehses, 132). This letter was written shortly before the pope's departure from Rome for his long conference with Charles V at Bologna; see p. 133.   [5] See p. 103.

alliance existing between England and France had led to a joint declaration of war against the emperor in January 1528. The English ambassadors in Spain had, against Henry's wishes, allowed the French ambassador to draw them into this declaration,[1] and Wolsey had been hard put to it to pacify the king. The news of the declaration of war was received in England with violent opposition, especially among the clothworkers whose prosperous industry was likely to be ruined by a war in Flanders.[2] No hostilities, however, actually occurred and discussions for peace were soon taking place; an agreement was reached that trade should continue as usual with Flanders,[3] and in June a truce was arranged.[4] The real contest was between the emperor, Catherine's nephew, and Francis I of France who was the only supporter of Henry's marriage scheme to be found outside England.

Wolsey's policy had been to support French power in Italy as a counterpoise to that of the emperor in the belief that so long as this delicate balance was maintained, England (and Wolsey) would have a large, and perhaps decisive, voice in the affairs of Europe. Should the emperor and Francis I come to terms, Wolsey's policy would collapse like a house of cards. And now the disquieting news came that 'the ladies', Louisa of Angoulême, mother of Francis I, and Margaret of Savoy, aunt of the emperor and regent of the Netherlands, were meeting at Cambrai to bring about an arrangement between Francis I and Charles V. These rumours greatly disturbed Wolsey and he told the French ambassador, du Bellay, that he would 'stake his head' to Henry that the rumours of a separate peace were without foundation and an invention of the enemy.[5] Nevertheless it soon became plain that negotiations were actually taking place, and in the summer it was clear that they had resulted in a project of peace which would not only leave England out of account, but free the emperor to espouse fully the cause of his aunt before sentence had

---

[1] See the emperor to Iñigo de Mendoza, 5 July 1528 (*Span. Cal.*, iii, pt. 2, 483); Ghinucci and Lee to Wolsey, 28 July 1528 (*L. & P.*, iv, 4564).
[2] cf. *L. & P.*, iv, 4012, 4040, 4043, 4044, 4239, 4310.
[3] Hacket to Wolsey, 6 April 1528 (*L. & P.*, iv, 4147).
[4] Treaty signed at Hampton Court, 15 June 1528 (*L. & P.*, iv, 4376). For the proclamation announcing the truce, see *T.R.P.*, i, 175 (dated 17 June 1528, and proclaimed in London on 19 June 1528). See also the proclamation continuing the truce, dated 18 Mar. 1529 (*T.R.P.*, i, 187).
[5] Du Bellay to Montmorenci, 28 Jan. 1529 (Le Grand, iii, 289, at p. 293; *L. & P.* iv, 5231).

been pronounced in the marriage suit. Accordingly, since Wolsey was occupied with the divorce, Tunstall and More were hastily despatched to join Hacket.

More and Tunstall left England in circumstances that did not augur well for the success of their mission. Nine days before their commission was issued to them, the French army had been destroyed at Landriano, and Charles had become master of Europe. It was a less spectacular defeat than that at Pavia, four years before, but its effects were final, and Francis I accepted the decision brought about by the imperial forces. The task of More and his fellow ambassadors was a thankless one, and they achieved little. A treaty (the *Paix des Dames*, as it is known) was signed at Cambrai on 5 August 1529, which settled for some years the peace of Europe. Francis I renounced all his claims in Italy, as well as his rights of suzerainty in Flanders and Artois, and in return Charles V did not press his claims to Burgundy. Francis I was required to pay a ransom of two million crowns for the return of his sons, and a marriage was arranged between Francis and Eleanor of Austria. In addition to a number of treaties with minor princes, a treaty was concluded between Henry VIII and the emperor, with provision for mutual aid and defence, but Henry was required to release the sums due to him from the emperor and look to Francis I for satisfaction, as a condition for the liberation of the sons of the French king.[1] Wolsey's policy had collapsed. Whatever of Wolsey's ruin had not been effected by the sudden adjournment of the legatine court, had been completed by the Peace of Cambrai.

More and Tunstall returned to England towards the end of August, and reported to the king.[2] Their report could not have contained much to Henry's liking; their one considerable gain was a commercial agreement that re-established trade with Flanders and Spain.

[1] The Treaty of Windsor (19 June 1522) provided for the invasion of France by Charles V and Henry VIII, and Charles V undertook to pay to Henry 133,305 gold crowns as indemnity for the money owed to him by Francis I, the payment of which would be prevented by the declaration of war (cf. *L. & P.*, iii, 2333). Francis, by the Treaty of Cambrai, undertook to discharge these obligations of the emperor to Henry, and to pay the sum at the rate of 50,000 crowns p.a. in consideration of the deliverance of his children (cf. *L. & P.*, iv, 5832). For the proclamation announcing peace with the emperor (dated 27 Aug. 1529, and proclaimed in Calais on 30 Aug., 1529) see *T.R.P.*, i, 189.

[2] More reached Woodstock by 3 Sept.; on that day he wrote a letter from Woodstock to his wife (see Rogers, 422). For the despatches of Tunstall, Hacket and More to Henry VIII during their absence abroad, see Rogers, 408, 415, 418, 421.

VI

Parliament

Henry reacted swiftly to the momentous events that have just been described. On 9 August 1529, four days after the signature of the treaty of Cambrai, writs were issued for the election of members of a parliament that was summoned to meet on 3 November.[1] The significance of the step was unmistakable; Henry was appealing from the pope to his people. This is not the place to trace the details of the fall of Wolsey. He himself knew that he had lost the confidence of the king, and it was clear that no one but the king was now master; in a letter addressed to Montmorenci, du Bellay observed that the king now took the management of everything, and he added, in a postscript, that he saw clearly that on account of the parliament Wolsey would lose his influence entirely.[2]

Henry did not wait for parliament to bring Wolsey to account. Proceedings in *praemunire* were begun against him on 9 October, and on 22 October the cardinal, in a written instrument, acknowledged his guilt.[3] A few days previously he had been deprived of his office of lord chancellor; on 17 October the dukes of Suffolk and Norfolk visited him and took possession of the great seal, which was delivered to the master of the rolls, Dr John Taylor, on 20 October at Windsor. On 25 October, at Greenwich, the king delivered the seal into the hands of Sir Thomas More, and on the following day More took the oath as lord chancellor in the great hall at Westminster.[4] The choice of a layman was significant. Three days before More received the seal du Bellay had written, with prophetic insight, that 'it is not yet known who will have the seal, but

---

[1] Rymer, *Foedera*, xiv, 302; *L. & P.*, iv, 5837.
[2] du Bellay to Montmorenci, 4 Oct. 1529 (Le Grand, iii, 359, at pp. 361, 363; *L. & P.*, iv, 5983).
[3] *L. & P.*, iv, 6017. For the indictment, see *L. & P.*, iv, 6035.
[4] Rymer, *Foedera*, xiv, 349; *L. & P.*, iv, 6025.

I believe the priests will never have it again and that in this parliament they will have terrible alarms'.[1]

At first sight it might appear that in summoning parliament Henry was courting disaster. The treaty of Cambrai had put an end to the enmity between France and the emperor upon which England had largely depended for her safety, and had freed Charles to stir up trouble in Ireland and Scotland; Charles and his advisers believed that they could drive Henry out of England without much difficulty.[2] At home, the king's attempt to put an end to his marriage was extremely unpopular, and Catherine was enthusiastically received wherever she went, while Anne Boleyn was met with insults. In the matter of the divorce popular feeling seems to have been compounded of a firm belief that Catherine was a wronged and injured woman, and a fear that if Henry persisted in his efforts to obtain a divorce he would alienate the emperor who would then destroy the wool trade with the Low Countries. To the casual observer, Henry's position seemed to be one of great insecurity.

In reality, parliament was the means that enabled Henry to ride the whirlwind. The latent anti-clericalism of the laity, which had been fed by taxation and Wolsey's magnificence, could be easily stirred to active expression, as the affair of Richard Hunne had shown. And now the most prominent anti-clericals were the close relations of Anne Boleyn, whom Wolsey had kept in check only with difficulty. A summons to the king requiring him to appear before the papal court to whom the pope had remitted the marriage suit, would be well calculated to exacerbate popular feeling. Even to so well disposed a person as George Cavendish, the summoning of the king and queen to appear before the legatine court at Blackfriars had seemed an outrage;[3] how much more outrageous

---

[1] du Bellay to Montmorenci, 22 Oct. 1529 (Le Grand, iii, 377; *L. & P.*, iv, 6019): 'On ne sçait encores qui aura le Sceau, je croy bien que les Prestres n'y toucheront plus, & que à ce Parlement ils auront de terribles alarmes'.

[2] cf. Sylvester Darius to Wolsey, 5 Nov. 1528 (*L. & P.*, iv, 4909); Sylvester Darius to Brian Tuke, 5 Nov. 1528 (*L. & P.*, iv, 4911); Mendoza to Charles V, 28 April 1529 (*L. & P.*, iv, 5501). Sylvester Darius was an auditor of the Rota.

[3] Cavendish, *Wolsey*, 78: '. . . thes ij legattes sat In Iugeme^t as notable Iuges, byfore whome the kyng & the Quene were dewly Cited and Sommoned to appere, W^{che} was the strayngest & newest sight & devyse that euer was rede or hard in any history or Cronycle in any Region, That a kyng and a quene, to be convented and constrayned by processe compellatory to appere in any Court (as comen persons) w^t in ther owen Realme or domynyon to abyde the Iugeme^t & decrees of ther owen subiectes . . .' (commas have been substituted for the virgula employed by Cavendish).

would it seem, that the king of England should be summoned to appear before a foreign court held in a distant land that was dominated by the armies of the emperor.

Should he summon Henry to appear in Rome the pope would provide the king with a most powerful weapon. Only a short while before the news of the avocation of the suit reached England, Wolsey, with truth, had written to the ambassadors in Rome that

if either it [the avocation] be already passed, or shall now or at any time hereafter pass, with citation of the king in person or by procurator to the court of Rome, or with any clauses of interdiction, excommunication, incurring into contempt, *vel cum invocatione brachii secularis aut penis pecuniariis*, whereby the king should be secluded from the taking his advantage otherwise, the dignity and prerogative royal of the king's crown, whereunto all the nobles and subjects of this realm will adhere and stick unto the death, may not tolerate nor suffer that the same be obeyed. . . . Nor shall it ever be seen that the king's cause shall be ventilated or decided in any place out of this his own realm, but that if his grace at any time should come to the court of Rome, he would do the same with such a main and army royal, as should be formidable to the pope and all Italy.[1]

And there would have been few Englishmen who would not have been angered by the petition presented to the pope on behalf of Charles V and Ferdinand, praying that the English parliament should be forbidden to discuss the divorce.[2] The divorce was no longer the simple question whether the king's marriage were valid or not; it had now become inextricably interwoven with the more fundamental question of papal jurisdiction in England, which had for so long been the begetter of difficulty and dispute. And there could be no doubt that, on the question of papal jurisdiction, Henry was enthusiastically supported by most of the laity. On parliament, therefore, Henry could confidently rely for support in any struggle with the papacy, and, now that Wolsey had gone, parliament would provide a rallying ground and a forum for those anti-clerical forces that the cardinal had hitherto kept at bay. The divorce was unpopular, it is true, but the main tide of popular feeling was now flowing strongly in Henry's favour. Henry could, with confidence, turn to his people for support against the pope.

[1] Wolsey to Benet, Gregory Casale and Vannes, 27 July 1529 (*State Papers*, vii, 193, at p. 194; *L. & P.*, iv, 5797). Almost the whole of the letter is in cipher.
[2] Petition of the Imperial Ambassadors respecting the Divorce Case, 15 [?], April 1529 (*Span. Cal.*, iii, pt. 2, 667).

The composition of this parliament, which has come to be known as the 'Reformation Parliament', has been the subject of much controversy, and the extent to which it was 'packed' by the king's supporters is still a question of partisan contention. It would appear that the extreme view that the parliament consisted almost entirely of royal nominees is greatly exaggerated and there is evidence that the election of the country members was marked by genuine popular liberty.[1] Since Henry and the country at large were of an anti-clerical cast of mind, their identity of interest produced an harmony of opinion that can easily be mistaken for servility, and Henry was sufficiently skilful to make use of this harmony to manipulate both houses of parliament.

The parliament met on Wednesday 3 November 1529, in the hall of Blackfriars, and the king himself was present.[2] Sir Thomas More, the new chancellor, made 'an eloquent oration' in which he said that, just as a shepherd seeks to preserve and defend his flock against all perils, so the king,

vigilantly foreseeing things to come considered how divers laws before this time were made now by long continuance of time and mutation of things, very insufficient, and unperfect, and also by the frail condition of man, divers new enormities were sprung amongst the people, for the which no law was yet made to reform the same, which was the very cause why at that time the king had summoned his high court of parliament.

More went on to make a severe attack upon Wolsey, 'the great wether which is of late fallen [who], as you all know, so craftily, so scabbedly, yea and so untruly juggled with the king.' More then directed the com-

---

[1] For this topic, see Pollard, *Henry VIII*, 252 et seq.; Neale, *The Elizabethan House of Commons*, 282 et seq.; Mackie, *The Earlier Tudors, 1485-1558*, 349 et seq.; cf. Hall, *Chronicle*, ii, 169 ('but the moste parte of the commons were the kynges servauntes'). The theory that the house of commons consisted of royal nominees is based largely on the letter of Ralph Sadler to Thomas Cromwell, 1 Nov. 1529 (*L. & P.*, iv, App., 238). This letter is much too inconclusive to serve as the foundation for such a theory; cf. Pollard, op. cit. 254. The progress of the elections caused Catherine anxiety as to the intentions of the king in summoning parliament, but Chapuys, now imperial ambassador, thought her fears to be exaggerated (Chapuys to Charles V, 21 Sept. 1529; *Span. Cal.*, iv, pt. 1, 160 (p. 235)); towards the end of the year, however, he changed his mind, and believed that the majority of members had been bribed in favour of the king (Chapuys to Charles V, 8 Dec. 1529; *Span. Cal.*, iv, pt. 1, 228 (p. 361)).
[2] *L. & P.*, iv, 6043.

mons that it was the king's pleasure that they should resort 'to the nether house' and there elect a speaker.[1]

The references to reform in More's speech were in general terms, but there could have been little doubt that those to be reformed were the ecclesiastics. Henry's purpose was to subject the church to his own temporal power. The church was subject to the spiritual authority of the pope and at the same time to the temporal authority of the king, and the relationship of church to state had for long been a source of dispute. But the idea of the universal church was being submerged by that of the national state, and the spirit of nationality had no patience with what seemed a divided allegiance. An *imperium in imperio* could not be countenanced; henceforth Henry must be head of a single body comprising both church and state.

After the first sitting parliament adjourned to Westminster, on account of the plague, and met there the next day, 4 November. The commons presented Thomas Audley to the king as their speaker, and two days later, on 6 November, the king signified his approval. Edward Hall recorded that the commons, after the king had approved their choice of speaker, 'began to common of their griefs wherewith the spiritualty had before time grievously oppressed them, both contrary to the law of the realm, and contrary to all right';[2] it appears that these 'griefs' were embodied in a petition, but the petition was never presented. After these general grumbles there was introduced into the commons house a bill to regulate the practice of mortuaries which were the cause of the crisis that had arisen in the case of Richard Hunne.[3] Two days

---

[1] Hall, *Chronicle*, ii, 164, 165. Hall sat in this parliament as one of the members for Wenlock (*L. & P.*, iv, 6043(2) (ii)), and presumably heard More's speech; his account of it is confirmed by the summary sent by Chapuys to Charles V, 8 Nov. 1529; (*Span. Cal.*, iv, pt. 1, 211 (pp. 323, 324)). The rolls of parliament state that More 'declared the cause of its [the parliament's] being summoned, viz. to reform such things as have been used or permitted in England by inadvertence, or by the changes of time have become inexpedient, and to make new statutes and laws where it is thought fit' (*L. & P.*, iv, 6043).
[2] Hall, *Chronicle*, ii, 166.
[3] A 'mortuary' was a kind of ecclesiastical heriot; it was a customary gift claimed by and due to the rector in many parishes on the death of a parishioner. In origen they were, like heriots, voluntary gifts intended as a kind of quittance to the clergy for personal tithes and other dues not paid during the lifetime of the dead man. What was claimed by the clergy was the most valuable article belonging to the dead person; the identification of the article was a source of much argument and ill feeling, but the clerical claim led to the contention that

after this bill had reached the lords, the commons sent up another bill to regulate the fees exacted by the ecclesiastical courts for probates. The second bill caused considerable dissatisfaction among the spiritual lords, and the bishop of Rochester, John Fisher, protested, saying, 'My lords, you see daily what bills come hither from the common house and all is to the destruction of the church; for God's sake see what a realm the kingdome of Boheme was, and when the church went down, then fell the glory of the kingdom; now with the commons is nothing but down with the church, and all this meseemeth is for lack of faith only'. The commons protested to the king at this statement and the bishop was constrained to explain it away. The spiritual lords, however, succeeded in securing the rejection of both bills. The king thereupon proposed a conference between eight members of each house, and as a result the bills were passed.[1]

[1] cf. Hall, *Chronicle*, ii, 167-70. Since all the commons' representatives and half of the lords' representatives were laymen, the result was a foregone conclusion. (At about this time the imperial ambassador observed that 'nearly all the people here hate the priests'; Chapuys to Charles V, 13 Dec. 1529; *Span. Cal.*, iv, pt. 1, 232 (p. 367)). The bill relating to mortuaries became the act 21 Hen. VIII, c. 6 (Mortuaries Act 1529). It imposed limits upon the amount of mortuaries that might be demanded; no mortuary might be demanded where the deceased died worth less than 10 marks; 3s. 4d. where he died worth from 10 marks to £30; 6s. 8d. where he died worth from £30 to £40; and 10s. where the deceased was worth more than £40. Mortuaries for married women and children were forbidden, and mortuaries for travellers were to be paid 'where they had their most habitation'. Section 1 of the act was repealed in part by the Statute Law Revision Act 1948, and s. 6 was repealed by the combined effect of 13 Ann., c. 6, s. 1, and 28 Geo. II, c. 6, s. 1; the remainder was repealed by the Ecclesiastical Jurisdiction Measure 1963, which came into force on 1 Mar. 1965. The bill relating to probate fees became the act 21 Hen. VIII, c. 5, and established a scale of fees for probate of wills: no fees were to be charged where the estate was worth £5 or less ('except only to the scribe to have for writing of the probate', 6d.); a fee of 3s. 6d. where the estate exceeded £5 but not £40; and

mortuaries were illegal when a person died without property. It was common to bring the mortuary to the church when the corpse was brought for burial, and for this reason it was sometimes called a 'corpse present'; cf. Blackstone's Commentaries 425; Stephens, *Practical Treatise of the Laws relating to the Clergy*, (London 1848), 808. For the case of Richard Hunne, see Jeffries Davies, 'The Authorities for the case of Richard Hunne (1514-15)', *E.H.R.*, xxx, 477-88; *V. C. H., London*, i, 236-50; Pollard, *Wolsey*, 31-42; Ogle, *Tragedy of the Lollards' Tower* (Oxford 1949), Part I; Deanesly, *The Lollard Bible* (Cambridge 1920), 369, 370; Milsom, 'Richard Hunne's "Praemunire" ', in *E.H.R.*, lxxvi, 80-2.

A further bill, introduced into the commons and considered by the conference of both houses, provided for the abolition of clerical pluralities and non-residence. This bill was the boldest of all the anti-clerical measures introduced in 1529, and it excited much clerical opposition; nevertheless, its passage was secured by the device already mentioned, and it became an act.[1] In the course of this session the lords drew up the articles in which they set out the charges against cardinal Wolsey. These articles, forty-four in number, were substantially a list of grievances against the cardinal; they were not couched in the form of a bill of attainder or an act of parliament, nor did they accuse Wolsey of either treason or felony, but merely requested that 'he be so provided for that he never have any power, jurisdiction, or authority herafter to trouble, vex, and impoverish the commonwealth'. They were presented to the king and then sent to the commons house where they were read. No further proceedings appear to have been taken on them and it seems to have been merely a question of communicating information to the commons.[2] Parliament was prorogued on 17 December 1529.[3]

[1] Hall, *Chronicle*, ii, 170. The bill became the act 21 Hen. VIII, c. 13. The act restrained pluralities and dealt with non-residence, and prohibited farming and trading by the clergy. It also dealt with the special case of absenteeism by parish priests who served chantries, and provided that spiritual persons with a benefice having cure of souls should not 'take any particular stipend' to 'sing for any soul'. It imposed a fine of £10 per month upon holders of benefices who were non-resident, and provided that it should be an offence to obtain from the pope a dispensation to hold more than one benefice in plurality or to retain a benefice without residing therein. Provision was made for dispensations in certain circumstances, but it was evidently envisaged that such dispensations should be obtained from the king (two licences from the crown, in 1535, are quoted in Amos, *Observations on the Statutes of the Reformation Parliament* (London 1859), 239).
[2] Hall, *Chronicle*, ii, 170, 171. For the articles against Wolsey see *L. & P.*, iv, 6075. For a discussion of this matter, see Pollard, *Wolsey*, 258-63.
[3] cf. Hall, *Chronicle*, ii, 171.

5s. where the estate exceeded £40; cf. Pollard, *Henry VIII*, 272: 'Englishmen . . . began their Reformation not with the enunciation of some new truth, but with an attack on clerical fees'. The act relating to probate fees was repealed by 15 & 16 Geo. V, c. 23, s. 56, Sch. 2, pt. 1. See Hall, *Chronicle*, ii, 167, 168. The version of Fisher's words is from Hall's Chronicle, but see *Life of Fisher*, 69.

VII

The Consultation
of the Universities

I

Meanwhile, an idea matured that was to have important consequences. In the spring of 1529 there was an outbreak of the sweating sickness in Cambridge where the two sons of a certain Master Cressey were receiving instruction from their tutor, Thomas Cranmer, a fellow of Jesus College, who was related to Cressey's wife. Because of the danger to their health the boys returned to their father's house at Waltham and Cranmer went with them. By the middle of July the pestilence had abated sufficiently to allow the university to reassemble and Cranmer returned to Cambridge. Within a short while, however, he was back at Waltham, and he was there at the beginning of August when Henry arrived at Waltham Abbey to hunt. Henry was accompanied by the court who were accommodated in neighbouring houses, and Edward Foxe, the king's almoner, and Stephen Gardiner, the king's secretary, were lodged by the harbingers in Master Cressey's house.[1]

Foxe and Gardiner were old acquaintances of Cranmer from their Cambridge days, and at supper on the first night, 2 August 1529,[2] they fell into talk concerning the state of the university. Since discussion of the divorce then took a prominent place in Cambridge life, as it did

[1] Morice, *Anecdotes and Character of Archbishop Cranmer*, printed in Nichols, *Narratives*, 238-72, at pp. 240, 241; Cooper, *Annals of Cambridge*, i, 330; Foxe, *Acts and Monuments*, viii, 6, 7; and see generally, Ridley, *Thomas Cranmer*, 25 et seq., with regard to Cranmer's meeting with Foxe and Gardiner at Waltham, and his subsequent meeting with the king.
[2] According to Ralph Morice, who subsequently became Cranmer's secretary and confidant, the meeting took place 'the firste night at supper' (see Nichols, *Narratives*, 241); the court arrived at Waltham on 2 Aug. 1529 (see Note on the King's Progress, *L. & P.*, iv, 5965), which is, presumably, the date to which Morice refers.

everywhere else, the talk naturally turned to this subject and 'they debated amongst themselves that great and weighty cause of the king's divorcement'.[1] In the course of this discussion Cranmer told Foxe and Gardiner that, although he had not studied the matter, it seemed to him 'that you go not the next way to work, as to bring the matter unto a perfect conclusion and end'. He believed that, because of the 'frustratory delays' that characterized proceedings in the ecclesiastical courts, the suit would 'linger long enough, and peradventure in the end . . . come unto small effect'. He went on to say that it was most certain that there was 'but one truth in it, which no man ought or better can discuss than the divines'. A theologian himself he was distrustful of the canonists, and he expressed the view that the whole matter could be brought to a speedy conclusion if the king were to refer the question to theologians for their decision; once they had pronounced their opinion Henry could, in conscience, act upon their advice, and it would be unnecessary to obtain a judgment from an ecclesiastical court.[2]

The suggestion that the king, without any pronouncement by a court of competent jurisdiction, could treat as null and void a marriage of long duration that had been publicly celebrated and subsequently consummated, was startlingly novel and very unorthodox, but it seems to have aroused the interest of Foxe and Gardiner. It seems probable that, as a result of the conversation over Master Cressey's dinner table, they persuaded Cranmer to study the whole question of the divorce; however that may be, Cranmer was subsequently engaged in arguing the king's case with his fellow members of Cambridge University. Not long after he had begun these propagandist activities, a disputation took place between six theologians from Oxford and six from Cambridge, who unanimously reached the conclusion that the king's marriage to Catherine was lawful and valid. Cranmer had been chosen as one of the Cambridge theologians but, before the disputation took place, he was called away from Cambridge, and his place had been taken by one of his colleagues. On his return, however, he engaged the six Cambridge men in argument, and he put the king's case with such vigour and dexterity that all but

[1] Morice, op cit., in Nichols, *Narratives*, 241.
[2] Morice, op. cit., in Nichols, *Narratives*, 241, 242. Mr Ridley (*Thomas Cranmer*, 25) rightly rejects Foxe's story that Cranmer proposed that Henry should appeal from the legatine court to the English and foreign universities; cf. Foxe, *Acts and Monuments*, viii, 6, 7. Foxe derived his information from Morice, but the story which he tells differs from Morice's account.

one of them recanted their former opinion and agreed with Cranmer that the marriage was unlawful.

Cranmer's triumph at Cambridge was reported to the king who recognized his qualities as a propagandist and determined to make use of his services.[1] He was summoned to court and met Henry at Greenwich, probably towards the end of October 1529. According to Foxe, the martyrologist, the king told Cranmer that he was much troubled in conscience because of his marriage with the queen and he commanded Cranmer to take pains to further his cause. He protested, however, that he sought

not to be divorced from the queen, if by any means I might justly be persuaded that this our matrimony were inviolable, and not against the laws of God; for otherwise there was never cause to move me to seek any such extremity: neither was there ever prince had a more gentle, a more obedient and loving companion and wife than the queen is, nor did I ever fancy woman in all respects better, if this doubt had not risen; assuring you that for the singular virtues wherewith she is endued, besides the consideration of her noble stock, I could be right well contented still to remain with her, if so it would stand with the will and pleasure of Almighty God.

He therefore instructed Cranmer to study the whole matter with 'an indifferent eye' and to put his conclusion into writing.[2] Mr Ridley aptly observed that 'Henry may well have said this to Cranmer, for he frequently expressed these hypocritical sentiments when he spoke about the divorce; but he would not have asked Cranmer to write a book about his marriage unless he had known the conclusions which Cranmer would reach'.[3]

The king arranged that Cranmer should pursue his studies in London, within easy reach of the court, and the place chosen for this purpose was Durham House, the London home of Sir Thomas Boleyn. Cranmer remained there for two months while he composed the book which Henry had ordered him to write, and he wrote it primarily to influence

---

[1] Mr Ridley is surely right in suggesting that the king's interest was aroused by Cranmer's demonstration of his ability as a propagandist for the king, rather than by the suggestion made to Foxe and Gardiner. He also rightly rejects John Foxe's story that Foxe and Gardiner, on the day after the dinner table discussion, told the king what Cranmer had said, whereupon the king exclaimed, 'I perceive that that man hath the sow by the right ear: and if I had known this device but two years ago, it had been in my way a great piece of money, and had also rid me out of much disquietness' (Foxe, *Acts and Monuments*, viii, 7). See, generally, Ridley, *Thomas Cranmer*, 26-9.
[2] Foxe, *Acts and Monuments*, viii, 8.
[3] Ridley, *Thomas Cranmer*, 28.

the theologians of Cambridge University. But, as matters turned out, Cranmer's services were not used in Cambridge; instead he joined the embassy of Sir Thomas Boleyn, newly created earl of Wiltshire, who was sent to Bologna on a diplomatic mission to the emperor, and he left London on 21 January 1530.[1]

Cranmer's literary activity was directly related to a proposal put forward some two years earlier. It had then been suggested that the king should obtain the opinions of all the universities in christendom,[2] and, following the adjournment of the legatine court, the proposal had been given a more immediately practical appeal by Cranmer's suggestion to Foxe and Gardiner that the king might act on such opinions without the necessity of obtaining a judgment from an ecclesiastical court. The proposal was now taken up in earnest and arrangements were made to consult the universities.[3] Before the year was out Henry's agents were

---

[1] See p. 133.

[2] cf. R. Wakefield to Henry VIII, 5 July 1527 (printed in Blunt, *Reformation of the Church of England*, i, 130; Pocock-Burnet, iv, 21): 'I ... can defend your cause or question in all the universities in Christendom against all men, ...'; at the time the letter was written, Wakefield was a monk of Syon, and he was subsequently appointed Regius Professor of Hebrew at Oxford. See also Wolsey to Sir G. Casale, 5 Dec. 1527 (Burnet, i, Coll. of Rec., 12, at p. 13): 'Super qua re maturum sanumque judicium consuluit clarissimorum celeberrimorumque Doctorum aliorumque complurium in omni eruditionis genere excellentiorum virorum ac Praelatorum, partim Theologorum, partim Jurisperitorum, tum in suo Regno, tum alibi existentium, ut aperte vereque cognosceret, an Dispensatio antea concessa pro se & Regina, ex eo quod Regina Fratris sui uterini Uxor antea extiterit, valida & sufficiens foret, necne demumque a variis multisque ex his Doctoribus asseritur, quod Papa non potest dispensare in primo gradu affinitatis, tanquam ex jure Divino, moraliter, naturaliterque prohibito, ac si potest, omnes affirmant & consentiunt quod hoc non potest, nisi ex urgentissimis & arduis causis, quales non subfuerunt'.

[3] cf. du Bellay to Montmorenci, 23 Aug. 1529 (Le Grand, iii, 337, at p. 339; *L. & P.*, iv, 5862): '. . . car mondict sieur le Legat & pareillement le Roy son Maistre, monstroyent de desirer fort que je feisse ung tour jusques de là, pour secretement fair veoir par les plus scavans du Royaume, la matiere de ce divorce où ils sont autant fondez que jamais, & la debattre avec eulx, leur communiquant les raisons de partie adverse pour en tirer d'eulx quelque bon advis & raison'. See also du Bellay to Montmorenci, 18 Sept. 1529 (Le Grand, iii, 354, at p. 355; *L. & P.*, iv, 5945): 'La cause, Monseigneur, pourquoy principalement m'avoyt envoyé querir ledict sieur Legat, estoit pour encores me communiquer bien au long de la matiere de ce divorce, me faisant toute l'instance du monde tant de la part du Roy son Maistre que de la sienne, de vouloir leur ayder à faire consulter cette matiere avec nos Theologiens, me pryant vouloir trouver moyen de faire ung voyage de là la mer soubs couleur d'autre chose, afin d'en communiquer par

travelling throughout Europe to obtain from the universities opinions that would support Henry's contention that his marriage to Catherine was invalid. All these agents were liberally supplied with money and were lavish in their promises of rewards; it was said that Ghinucci, the bishop of Worcester, had sufficient funds to bribe all the Italians.[1] They pursued their scandalous and sometimes comical activities for some nine months, but the results of their labours must have seemed satisfactory to Henry. After proceedings that can only be described as extraordinary, the theologians of Cambridge University expressed themselves as satisfied that a marriage with the widow of a deceased brother was forbidden by divine law in such manner that not even a papal dispensation could render it lawful. A month later Oxford University gave a similar opinion, but only after three demands had been made by the king who described those who opposed him as rebellious youths.[2] Opinions favourable to the king were obtained in France from the universities of Paris, Angers, Bourges, Toulouse and Orleans, although only Toulouse and Orleans, and the theologians of Paris, went to the full length of asserting that marriage could in no wise be validly contracted with a brother's widow, even if the first marriage had not been consummated; Angers, on the other hand, was of opinion that the pope had power to dispense in such a case.[3] In Italy, the universities of Padua, Pavia, Ferrara and Bologna were favourable to the king,[4] but, curiously enough, he failed to obtain a single favourable opinion in the whole of

---

[1] cf. the draft (never sent) of a reply from Clement VII to the letter of Henry VIII dated 6 Dec. 1530 (Ehses, 170, at p. 172), in which it was said that 'there are not wanting those who assert that a great sum of money was sent by you into Italy to entice and even to bribe writers, but we can by no means persuade ourselves to credit this' (Non desunt, qui asserant, magnam pecuniae quantitatem in Italiam a te transmissam ad alliciendos, quin potius corrumpendos scribentes, quod tamen nobis nullo modo persuadere possumus). For the methods used to obtain the opinions of the universities, see the documents printed in Pocock, i, 272-333, 400-592.

[2] The date of the Cambridge opinion is 9 Mar. 1530; that of Oxford is 8 April 1530. For texts of the opinions, see Tierney-Dodd, i, 369-70.

[3] The dates of these opinions are: Paris 23 May and 2 July; Angers 7 May; Bourges 10 June; Toulouse 17 Sept.; Orleans 5 April. For the texts of these opinions, see Tierney-Dodd, i, 376-8.

[4] For texts of the opinions of Pavia and Bologna, see Tierney-Dodd, i, 376, 377.

---

le congié du Roy & de Madame secretement à ceulx qui les y peuvent ayder, me usant là dessus des termes mesmes qu'il usa à mon frere estant icy, dont ne vous feray aultre redite.'

The Consultation of the Universities

Germany.[1] Those opinions that were favourable were collected together
and subsequently published.[2]

At the time when these opinions were being solicited, the great Dominican theologian, Francisco de Vitoria, was lecturing at Salamanca
university, and it was his custom, in the course of his lectures, to discuss
questions of the day that involved moral issues. When, therefore, the
question of Henry's marriage came before the senate of the university
for its opinion, Vitoria's friends asked him to consider it in his lectures.
Vitoria's treatment of the question occupies the last part of his *Relectio
de Matrimonio* and is a lengthy discussion of the question, *An gradus
prohibiti in Levitico sint contra ius divinum, et omnes de iure canonico
illegitimi?*—whether the forbidden degrees in Leviticus are against divine
law, and whether all are illegal in canon law? Ultimately he came to
three conclusions, which are today the universal view of the question:
first, that the marriage of a man with the widow of his dead brother
was not contrary to natural law; second, that marriage with the childless
widow of his dead brother was at no time forbidden by the divine law
of the Old Testament; third, that in the absence of human law, marriage
with the widow of a deceased brother, whether she be childless or not,
was lawful without the necessity of a papal dispensation.[3]

Hitherto Henry's attack upon the validity of his marriage had been
virtually confined to the canonical validity of the dispensation of Julius
II. But latent in Henry's argument were the seeds of another that rested
upon a matter of fundamental importance; this was the argument now
raised publicly by the universities, that the pope had no power to dispense, which ultimately led to the breach with Rome since it involved a
point of faith.[4] Henry's approach to the problem of the validity of his

[1] Le Grand, i, 187: 'De sorte qu'il ne put trouver personne dans toute l'Alle-
magne qui voulust écrire pour luy. Les Lutheriens furent même plus fermes en
cette occasion que les Catholiques.' It is also interesting to note that William
Tyndale pronounced against the divorce.
[2] *The Determinations of the most famous and most excellent Universities* was the
work of Foxe, Stokesley and Nicholas de Burgo; it was altered and augmented
by Cranmer and published in London in 1531.
[3] For the text, see de Vitoria, *Relecciones Téologales* (ed. Getino; Madrid 1934),
ii, 440-504. For Francisco de Vitoria, see Scott, *The Spanish Origin of International Law*, vol. 1, *Francisco de Vitoria and his Law of Nations* (Oxford 1934).
[4] This had been hinted at much earlier. For example, in the course of his letter
to Sir Gregory Casale, dated 5 Dec. 1527, Wolsey wrote: 'a variis multisque ex
his doctoribus asseritur, quod Papa non potest dispensare in primo gradu
affinitatis, tanquam ex jure Divino, moraliter naturaliterque prohibito, ac si

own marriage was characterized by extraordinary shifts. First he asserted that study of the text in Leviticus had shown him that the validity of his marriage was doubtful and furnished an explanation of his lack of a male heir. From this he turned to a consideration of the dispensation which he then asserted was of no effect on account of its legal defects. This position was in turn abandoned and he took his stand upon the fundamental proposition that the pope had no power to grant the dispensation; whether it contained defects or not, it was of no force and was ineffectual to render his marriage lawful.

The dispensation of 1503, granted by Julius II, was however, something of a novelty. The law which prohibited marriage between persons within certain degrees of affinity[1] took its origin from the Levitical code,[2] which comprehended nine persons and, in particular, prohibited marriage between a man and his deceased brother's wife.[3] The church

---

[1] 'Affinity' is the relationship that exists between a husband and his wife's blood relations and between a wife and her husband's blood relations. cf. *Corpus Juris Canonici*, can. 97: '(1) Affinitas oritur ex matrimonio valido sive rato tantum sive rato et consummato. (2) Viget inter virum dumtaxat et consanguineos mulieris, itemque mulierem inter et viri consanguineos. (3) Ita computatur ut qui sunt consanguinei viri, iidem in eadem linea et gradu sint affines mulieris, et vice versa.' This is the modern law, which is not entirely the same as that recognized in the sixteenth century; cf. p. 74, note 2.

[2] The Levitical list of prohibited marriages is: (1) step-mother: Lev. xviii, 8; xxii, 11; Deut. xxii, 30; xxvii, 20; (2) wife's mother: Lev. xviii, 17; xx, 14; Deut. xxvii, 23; (3) son's wife: Lev. xviii, 15; xx, 12; (4) wife's daughter: Lev. xviii, 17; (5) wife's son's daughter: Lev. xviii, 17; (6) wife's daughter's daughter: Lev. xviii, 17; (7) father's brother's wife: Lev. xviii, 14; (8) brother's wife: Lev. xviii, 16; xx, 21; (9) step-sister [i.e. daughter of step-mother and of her former husband]: Lev. xviii, 11 (LXX).

[3] This was the prohibition on which Henry had founded, and the text (in the Clementine Vulgate) upon which he had meditated was as follows (Lev. xx, 21): 'Qui duxerit uxorem fratris sui rem facit illicitam, turpitudinem fratris sui revelavit: absque liberis erunt' (The man who takes his brother's wife in marriage does a forbidden thing, bringing shame on his own brother; children they shall have never—Knox translation).

---

potest, omnes affirmant et consentiunt quod hoc non potest, nisi ex urgentissimis et arduis causis, quales non subfuerunt' (Burnet, i, Coll. of Rec., 12, at p. 13). On 6 April 1529 Henry VIII wrote to Gardiner and his colleagues, then in Rome: 'And by your next letters, we will that ye advertise us what advocates ye have on our part, with their names and qualities; finding the means also, if it be possible, to retain some notable and excellent divine, a frere, or other that may, can, or will firmly stick to our causes, in leaning to that *quod pontifex ex jure divino non potest dispensare*' (Pocock-Burnet, iv, 115, at p. 117; *L. & P.*, iv, 5427). See pp. 88, 123.

accepted these precepts but imposed them with greater strictness.[1] In the course of the seventh century, however, the opinion began to prevail that the impediment of affinity arose as a result of physical union; in other words, that when a man and wife became 'one flesh' (*una caro*), the relatives of one became the relatives of the other.[2] So it came about that affinity and consanguinity were put upon an equality. It followed from this theory that an impediment arose if the affinity were produced, not only by lawful marriage, but by an illicit union (*copula illicita*).[3] The canonists went on to deduce further conclusions from the principle of *una caro*, and they produced a second and third kind of affinity;[4] but these did not endure for long, for one of the decrees in the Lateran Council issued by pope Innocent III in 1215 confined the impediments of affinity and consanguinity to the first four degrees of canonical computation and abolished altogether the second and third kinds of affinity. The law remained unchanged, however, in so far as it equated affinity arising *ex copula illicita* with affinity arising from lawful marriage.[5]

Until the fifteenth century marriages within the first and second degrees of affinity were regarded, it seems, as prohibited by divine law. The teaching of Duns Scotus, however, gradually made headway, and

[1] The Levitical code did not forbid a man to marry his deceased wife's sister, but from a very early date the church prohibited such marriages; and although Leviticus only prohibited marriage with the widow of a paternal uncle, the church prohibited marriage with the widow of a mother's brother.

[2] The earliest document in which *una caro* is regarded as the real ground for the prohibition of marriages between *affines* appears to be St Gregory I's letter to St Augustine of Canterbury (see Haddan and Stubbs, *Councils and Ecclesiastical Documents, etc.*, iii, 20).

[3] The impediment of affinity arising *ex copula illicita* was definitely recognized by the law of the church under Alexander III (1159-81).

[4] The second kind of affinity arose because the kindred of a man's wife are equivalently his own kindred and therefore, if his wife should die, he may not marry any person so connected with him. This was a diriment impediment to the fourth degree. The third kind of affinity arose where a person who was connected with a man by the second kind of affinity was left a widower and his new partner became an *affinis* of the third kind. This was an impediment to the second degree but was not, apparently, diriment. Affinity of the second and third kind arose from affinity of the first kind.

[5] This could cause great difficulty in domestic life; if a man committed adultery with a woman related to his wife an affinity thereby arose between himself and his wife, so that if he resumed conjugal relations with his wife without obtaining a dispensation he committed the sin of incest. The council of Trent, however, decreed that the impediment of *affinitas ex copula illicita* should extend only to the second collateral degree, instead of the fourth.

in 1418 Martin V was advised by most of the theologians assembled at the council of Constance that it was within his power to grant a dispensation that would enable the count de Foix to marry his deceased wife's sister, Blanche of Navarre.[1] No dispensation of such a kind, however, seems to have been actually granted before the beginning of the sixteenth century. In 1500 pope Alexander VI granted a dispensation to king Manoel of Portugal to marry Maria, the youngest daughter of Ferdinand and Isabella of Spain, who was the sister of his first wife, Isabella. The second instance of such a dispensation was the very dispensation, granted to Henry by Julius II, from which arose the controversy.[2] There were many later instances and the fact that the development of the law took the course it did is good evidence that the theologians were convinced that the impediment was *de iure ecclesiastico* and not *de iure divino*; had this not been the case, subsequent popes would have treated the dispensation granted by Alexander VI in 1500 as an abuse of power and have refused to follow such a precedent.[3]

It will be seen that when Henry raised the fundamental question of the power of the pope to grant a dispensation from the impediment of affinity in the first or second degree, he was, at first, doing no more than reopening an old controversy which the pope had settled by granting the dispensation. But the path on which Henry thus set foot led him, ultimately, to refuse to acknowledge the supreme spiritual authority of the pope.

The precise question raised by the consultation of the universities, whether the pope had power to dispense, had been exhaustively discussed some twelve years previously by one of the greatest of theologians, Tommaso de Vio, Master General of the Dominicans and better known as Cajetan, in the course of his commentary on the *Summa* of St Thomas Aquinas. Cajetan was considering the validity of certain objections

[1] It is very doubtful whether a dispensation was actually granted in this case; in any event, the marriage never took place.

[2] Thus Henry was quite right when he said to the speaker, Thomas Audley, on 'the last daie of Aprill' 1532: 'Savyng in Spayne or Portyngall it hath not bene sene, that one man hath maried twoo sisters, the one beyng carnally knowen before: but the brother to mary the brothers wife was so abhorred amongest all nacions, that I never hearde it, that any Christen man did it, but my selfe' (Hall, *Chronicle*, ii, 209, 210).

[3] For a detailed treatment of the question of the prohibited degrees of affinity, upon which the foregoing account is substantially based, see Joyce, *Christian Marriage: an historical and doctrinal study* (London 1948), 534-45.

that had been made against the doctrine of Aquinas, that the quality of the sinfulness of incest was the same whether the parties were related by blood or by marriage. These criticisms of Aquinas ultimately raised the question of marriages within the forbidden degrees of kindred since such marriages, if they were not valid, were indistinguishable from incest. Consequently, in his defence of the thesis of Aquinas, Cajetan was led to discuss the question whether, apart from the case of parent and child, there was any relationship of such a nature that sexual intercourse between those so related was contrary to the natural law, and could not be rendered lawful by the dispensation of any human authority.[1] This was, of course, the very point raised by Henry VIII.

In discussing this problem Cajetan proposed a principle to form a rational basis of distinction separating unions between parent and child from all other unions. He argued that the prohibition of marriages within certain degrees of kindred arose from the unseemliness of the unions concerned; in the case of parent and child that unseemliness was inherent in the very nature of the relationship, but in other cases the unseemliness arose from law or custom. This distinction led him to the formulation of his principle, that unions which are rendered unseemly only by custom or law are not, of themselves, contrary to the natural law. Cajetan then turned to an objection that might be considered as invalidating his principle; whether, for example, the prescriptions of the eighteenth chapter of Leviticus were of such a nature that no human authority had power to grant a dispensation from them, for if they were moral precepts, as the language used seemed to imply, then it could be objected that the moral precepts of the divine law, as set out in Leviticus, formed part of the natural law. To dispose of this objection, Cajetan cited the current practice of the church, and argued that the prescriptions of Leviticus could form no part of the natural law since dispensations from their requirements had, in fact, been granted. In other words, the interpretation of Holy Scripture was a matter for the pope, and the pope had decided the interpretation of the text in Leviticus by granting the dispensations.

For Cajetan, developing his academic argument, the novelty of the dispensations was irrelevant; what was decisive for him was the fact

---

[1] Every human authority is subject to the natural law, and no dispensation from a law can be granted by an authority itself subject to that law, unless the law itself explicitly so provides.

that they had been granted. It is interesting to note that this was the substance of the argument of St John Fisher when he had answered Wolsey's inquiry as to his opinion of the validity of Henry's marriage.[1] Cajetan cited three examples of such dispensations, and his second example was that granted by Julius II for the marriage of Catherine to Henry VIII.[2] For him it was axiomatic that the decision of the pope to grant dispensations in the cases cited conclusively proved that the pope had power to dispense in such cases; he alone could determine his own jurisdiction. In this way Cajetan eventually reached his conclusion that the prescriptions of the eighteenth chapter of Leviticus were not precepts in an absolute sense but only in a restricted sense, and from this it followed that they were only binding in so far as they were made so by the legislation of the church.[3] Thus, the position was that all theologians of eminence were agreed that it was part of the papal office to decide the true meaning of ambiguities in Scripture, and the pope had decided the meaning of the ambiguity vexing Henry by granting the relevant dispensations.

It is of interest to compare Cajetan's argument with the argument that Henry himself had advanced in 1521 in his famous book, *Assertio Septem Sacramentarum*, written in answer to Luther's even more famous book, *The Babylonian Captivity of the Church*. In the course of his book Henry wrote that the pope is 'Christ's vicar in that church over which Christ is head', and that 'the whole church, not only is subject to Christ, but, for Christ's sake, to Christ's only vicar the pope of Rome'. He went

---

[1] See p. 13.

[2] 'In oppositum est quod Papa potest in his dispensare. Constat autem quod non potest in naturali iuri dispensare: quoniam Papa est subditus naturali iuri; et non est supra ipsum, ut possit illud tollere, aut mutare, sicut potest tollere aut mutare ius positivum. Et quod Papa possit, ex gestis Romanorum Pontificum patet. Nam modernus Rex Portugalliae duas sorores, quarum altera superest, successive uxores habuit, ita quod etiam cum prima consummaverat matrimonium. Moderna quoque regina Angliae consummaverat prius matrimonium cum olim fratre istius regis Angliae sui mariti. Ferdinandus quoque Iunior, Rex Siciliae citra Pharum, sororem fratris sui Ioannam, quae adhuc superest, in uxorem duxit, dispensante Alexandro VI. Haec autem constat esse in divina lege prohibita, in dicto capitulo.'

[3] For Cajetan's argument, see his *Commentaria in Summam Theologicam D. Thomae*, printed in the Roman edition of the *Opera Omnia* of Aquinas, vol. 10 (1899), pp. 238-42. The relevant portion of Cajetan's commentary was published in Venice on 20 Aug. 1518. See, also, Hughes, *Reformation in England*, i, 168-72, where Cajetan's argument is discussed at some length.

on to say that the church 'has from God not only the power of discerning God's word from that of men . . . but also the discerning betwixt divine and human senses of Scripture . . . betwixt divine institutions and the traditions of men . . . Christ's care being that his church may not err in any manner whatsoever'.[1]

Thus, the consultation of the universities had brought into public controversy the question of the papal dispensing power which, as we have seen, depended upon the fundamental point of faith that the primacy of the pope was of divine institution. The question had been hinted at by the king and those advising him, as we have noted, but one and all had hitherto shirked raising the fundamental issue latent in the question, for 'a sure instinct told them that once raised, a head-on collision with the papacy was unavoidable.'[2]

2

So long as the marriage suit was proceeding before the legatine court at Blackfriars, Henry might hope, with the aid of Wolsey, to confront the pope with a *fait accompli* that would give the king what he wanted, while

---

[1] The quotations are from Webster's translation (1687) in *Miscellaneous Writings of Henry the Eighth* (ed. F. Macnamara; London 1924) 128, 129. The *Assertio* was in Latin.

[2] Hughes, *Reformation in England*, i, 177. Henry himself had raised the point with Campeggio on 23 Oct. 1528 (see p. 66). But once Catherine had produced the copy of the brief which, if genuine, destroyed Henry's argument that the dispensation was invalid, the king had no case unless he could show that the pope had no power to grant the brief. Campeggio warned Wolsey that no discussion of the pope's powers would be tolerated, and the danger was appreciated by Wolsey who preferred to continue the case on the basis that the dispensation was invalid because of its form, rather than raise the dangerous question of the pope's power to dispense. du Bellay reported: 'Quant, Monseigneur, au mariage de deczà, on actend ce conseil de Flandres dont vous ay escript, qui est en partie d'Espaignols. J'en ay esté en propos avec le Cardinal Campege longtemps, . . . A la fin nous en demourasmes, qu'il deist des deux opinions la mienne estre invincible, l'autre neanmoins est fort soustenable; mais d'en venir là, de dire que le Pape n'ayt peu dispenser, seroit subvertir sa puissance qui est infinie, comme monstrant craindre qu'on veüille prendre la chose par là, parquoy Monsieur le Legat [Wolsey] voyant ces termes, vouldroyt qu'on luy poussast cela royde, afin de le faire tomber à declarer la dispense mal fondée plustost que de tomber en l'autre inconvenient' (du Bellay to Montmorenci, 17 Nov. 1528; Le Grand, iii, 209, at pp. 216, 217).

K

the queen's case went by default. Hence, once the court had begun its work, every effort had been made to bring matters to a speedy conclusion. The avocation of the suit to Rome, however, produced a very different state of affairs. There was now no Wolsey, anxious at all costs to please the king, sitting as judge, and the queen's case would now be heard. When the cause was removed to Rome on 16 July 1529, Henry's hopes of a favourable result were destroyed, and there was now scarcely a possibility that Henry could obtain, from an ecclesiastical court (the only court competent to give a binding judgment in such a cause), the decision that he wanted. If Henry wished to obtain a decision enabling him to marry Anne Boleyn he must look elsewhere. On the other hand it now seemed that, if the marriage cause proceeded to judgment in Rome, judgment would be given in favour of the validity of Henry's marriage. Henry was in an agony of indecision as to his future course of action, and at the turn of the year, in a conversation with the French ambassador lasting more than four hours, he said that he was in such a state of perplexity that he could continue no longer.[1] Until he could find a way out of his perplexities he must postpone as long as possible the day when judgment should be given. The need now was not urgent haste but prolonged delay.

The canonists advising Henry had no difficulty in providing him with the means to delay the prosecution of the marriage suit before the Roman court. Before the proceedings could begin in Rome it was necessary to serve on Henry, as a party to the suit, the order avoking the case and the citation requiring him to appear before the Roman judge either in person or by proctor. It was not difficult to ensure that service of the documents was not effected, for so long as the king remained in England, and no appropriate representative was abroad, no practical method of service could be found. So matters remained for some six months until Henry himself incautiously provided the opportunity for service of the documents.

Fortunately for Henry, the pope was equally reluctant to see progress made in the marriage suit. Hitherto his holiness had been subjected to unceasing pressure from both Henry and the emperor, and his defects of character prevented him taking any action that was

[1] du Bellay to Montmorenci, 27 Jan. 1530 (Le Grand, iii, 425, at p. 426; *L. & P.*, iv, 6169): 'En substance, il advoуё & dit clairement qu'il se trouve en telle perplexité, qu'il ne luy est possible de plus vivre en cette sorte'.

entirely independent of either. He was anxious to avoid being forced by one into a course of action that would precipitate a crisis with the other, and it would clearly have suited him very well if the troublesome question of the divorce could have been solved by some means that did not involve the papacy. Heavy pressure from Charles V had induced him to accord some measure of justice to Catherine and to avoke the cause to Rome, but he shrank from the decisive moment when judgment would have to be given. After the conclusion of the proceedings in London, he appears to have entertained a hope that, despite the avocation, Wolsey would have proceeded, by virtue of his jurisdiction as legate *a latere*, to pronounce judgment in Henry's favour, thus enabling the king to contract another marriage without seeking papal consent.[1] Buoyed up by some such hope as this, the pope delayed the hearing of the suit before the Rota.

The reconciliation between the pope and the emperor effected at Barcelona was followed by a long meeting at Bologna where, for four months, Clement VII and Charles V lived under the same roof.[2] To Henry this meeting appeared to offer a favourable opportunity to attempt to remove imperial opposition to the divorce. He appointed ambassadors, led by Anne Boleyn's father who had recently been created earl of Wiltshire, to negotiate with the emperor.[3] Wiltshire was instructed to tell the emperor that Henry now wished to open to him the depths of his conscience in the weighty matter of the divorce, assuring him that no earthly consideration had affected his judgment in such a matter, and the arguments on which Henry relied were to be set out in full. He was also instructed not to lose an opportunity to show the emperor how he could bind himself to the king and the whole realm of England if the matter were decided with his consent, while, on the other hand, his opposition to the king's purpose would diminish their friendship and give Henry just cause to complain of ingratitude. Finally, Wiltshire was to declare that Henry, on mature deliberation, had fixed his cause upon the express words of God, that the marriage

---

[1] cf. the bishop of Tarbes to Francis I, 27 Mar. 1530 (Le Grand, iii, 394, at p. 400; *L. & P.*, iv, 6290): '. . . & à ce qu'il m'en a declaré des fois plus de trois en secret, il seroit content que ledit mariage fust ja faict ou par dispense du Legat d'Angleterre ou autrement, mais que ce ne fust par son auctorité, ny aussi diminuant sa puissance'.

[2] cf. Contarini to the Signory, 5 Nov. 1529 (*Ven. Cal.*, iv, 524).

[3] Sir Thomas Boleyn had been created earl of Wiltshire on 8 Dec. 1529.

was against the divine commandments and that he did not see what judgment was needed to delay the case longer, considering that Scripture said *Ubi Spiritus Domini, ubi libertas*[1] and that the pope's laws approved the acts of one who suffered the extremity of ecclesiastical censures and conformed to the decision of his own conscience. The king was, therefore, resolved to conform himself to the words of our Saviour, *Nolite timere eos qui occidunt corpus, animam autem occidere non possunt. Sed eum potius timete qui potest corpus et animam perdere in Gehennam;*[2] and so the emperor was to be informed.[3]

It is not easy to see how Henry could have had much hope of the success of such a mission, with its inept choice of ambassador, but he was reported to have said that if Wiltshire were unsuccessful he would settle the matter within his own kingdom by the advice of his council and parliament.[4] The prospects of success were further reduced when, on 7 March, a few days before Wiltshire's arrival at Bologna, the pope issued a bull which recited that on the appeal of queen Catherine from the judgment of the legates, who had declared her contumacious for refusing their jurisdiction on the ground of their lack of impartiality, the pope had committed the cause, at her request, to Dr Paulo di Capisucchi,

---

[1] 2 Cor. iii, 17: in the Clementine Vulgate, 'Dominus autem spiritus est; ubi autem Spiritus Domini, ibi libertas'.

[2] Matt. x, 28; cf. Luke xii, 4.

[3] For the instructions to Wiltshire, see *L. & P.*, iv, 6111. Wiltshire was accompanied by John Stokesley, the bishop elect of London, Edward Lee, the king's almoner, and Benet, and a number of divines including Thomas Cranmer and Edward Carne.

[4] de Vaux to Francis I, 4 April 1530 (*L. & P.*, iv, 6307): 'He [i.e. Henry VIII] also says if his ambassadors with the pope do not report a good conclusion he intends to settle the matter within his realm by the advice of his Council and Parliament, so as not to have recourse to the Pope, whom he regards as simoniacal and ignorant, and consequently no good father. And he thinks that if he thus refuse to recognize the court of Rome, other kingdoms will do the same.' For the full text of the original see Le Grand, iii, 412, at p. 418: 'Apresso S. M. mi disse se li suoi ambassiatori, si come la dubita, tocante la sua causa d'al PP. non riporterano qual che buona resposta & conclusion', ch'in tal caso la pensa nel suo regno pigliar tal ordine qual al suo consiglio & parlamento parera conveniente, per non haver da ricorrer' dal PP. havendolo & per simoniaco & per ignorante & in consequentia per non buon pastore & Padre universale &c. ne in materia beneficiale alcunamente riconoscer lui ne la Romana corte, da tempo in qua governata come si scia & stima ley che da quetsa sua fatta apertura, o, daro Principio cio e del haver' in questo suo regno con la conveniente auctorita un Provinciale o sia Patriarca che l'altri regni & Provincie questo imitando debino far' el medesimo.'

with power to cite the king and others; that the auditor, ascertaining that the access was not safe, caused the citation, with an inhibition under censures, to be posted on the doors of the churches in Rome, at Bruges, Tournai and Dunkirk, and the towns of the diocese of Terouenne; but the queen having complained that the king, notwithstanding the inhibition, had boasted that he would proceed to a second marriage, the pope therefore issued a further inhibition, to be fixed on the doors of the churches as before, under the penalty of the greater excommunication and interdict to be laid upon the kingdom.[1]

Wiltshire was graciously received, both by the emperor and by the pope, but when he began to discuss the divorce with Charles V, the emperor told him sharply not to speak but to leave that matter to others, as he was an interested party. Wiltshire replied that he did not stand there as a father but as a subject and servant of his sovereign, doing his master's bidding. He went on to say that if the emperor would consent to the divorce, the king would rejoice, but if the emperor did not agree the king would not be dissuaded from attempting to obtain justice; and he offered the emperor 300,000 crowns, the return of Catherine's marriage portion, and security for the suitable maintenance of Catherine during the remainder of her life. The emperor replied that he was not a merchant to sell his aunt's honour, adding that if the pope gave a decision against her, he would remain silent, but if the decision were in her favour he would support her with all the means at his disposal.[2] Wiltshire's embassy had achieved nothing, but his presence at the papal court enabled the papal officials to serve him, as the properly accredited representative of the king, with the citation to appear before the Rota. The pope, however, offered to suspend the hearing of the cause until September if Henry undertook to do nothing in the matter until then. Henry accepted this offer.[3] Nevertheless, on 21 March the pope issued a second bull that prohibited all ecclesiastical judges, doctors, notaries, advocates, and others, from speaking or writing about the validity of the marriage under pain of excommunication.[4]

---

[1] *L. & P.*, iv, 6256; Le Grand, iii, 446.
[2] cf. bishop of Tarbes to Francis I, 27 Mar. 1530 (*L. & P.*, iv, 6290; Le Grand, iii, 394); bishop of Tarbes to Montmorenci, 28 Mar. 1530 (*L. & P.*, iv, 6293; Le Grand, iii, 454). Both letters were written from Bologna.
[3] Clement VII to Henry VIII, 26 Mar. 1530 (Ehses, 140-2); Henry VIII to Clement VII, 10 April 1530 (*L. & P.*, iv, 6324).
[4] *L. & P.*, iv, 6279.

3

The favourable opinions which Henry had received from a number of European universities induced him to make one further attempt to move the pope to accede to his wishes. On 12 June Henry summoned a number of notables to draw up a joint address to the pope urging him to decide the cause in Henry's favour. The king secured the first signatures to this address by means of personal interviews and it was then sent into the country for further signatures to be appended.[1] When the signatures had been collected the letter was dated 13 July 1530. Sir Thomas More did not sign this document and it seems that he was in some danger of losing his office of lord chancellor because of his refusal to sign.[2] The memorial began by declaring that the signatories were moved to address the pope because of their close connection with the king. They asserted that the king's cause had now been found just, not only by many learned men, but in the opinions of universities in England, France, and Italy, and their judgment ought to be confirmed by the pope's own authority, without anyone moving him to do so and despite all protests to the contrary; the pope was especially bound to do this as the matter touched a king and a kingdom to whom he was under great obligations. But since neither the justice of the king's cause nor the king's most earnest desires had prevailed with the pope, the signatories were compelled to complain of the usage accorded to their king. The king had defended the apostolic see and the Catholic faith both

---

[1] cf. Chapuys to Charles V, 29 June 1530 (*Span. Cal.*, iv, pt. 1, 366 (p. 616)). The signatures were not very numerous: there were the signatures of the two archbishops, Warham and Wolsey, of the dukes of Norfolk and Suffolk, of two marquesses, thirteen earls, four bishops, twenty-seven barons, twenty-two abbots, and eleven members of the house of commons; cf. *L. & P.*, iv, 6513. For a description of Wolsey signing the document, see Cavendish, *Wolsey*, 139, 140; cf. Pollard, *Wolsey*, 287. Eustache Chapuys succeeded Iñigo de Mendoza as imperial ambassador in September 1529, soon after the adjournment of the legatine court. Being a Savoyard, a layman and a commoner he was regarded by Charles V as being more capable of taking a detached view of Catherine's affairs than a Spanish aristocrat or cleric.

[2] cf. Chapuys to the emperor, 15 June 1530 (*Span. Cal.*, iv, pt. 1, 354 (p. 599)); 20 Sept. 1530 (*Span. Cal.*, iv, pt. 1, 433 (p. 727)); 15 Oct. 1530 (*Span. Cal.*, iv, pt. 1, 460 (p. 762)).

with his authority and with his pen, yet he was denied justice. The signatories feared great calamities and civil wars, and these could be prevented only if the king were to marry another wife by whom he might have issue; but this could not be done until his present marriage was annulled. If the pope continued in his refusal to annul the marriage they must conclude that he had abandoned them, and so they would be forced to seek a remedy elsewhere. They earnestly prayed the pope to prevent such a thing, as they did not wish to go to extremities until nothing more was to be hoped for at his hands.[1]

To this discourteous communication Henry added a personal letter of his own. He wrote, ostensibly, in reply to the pope's letter of 7 October 1529.[2] He said that inasmuch as the pope had appeared anxious 'to vanquish those doubts and to take away inquietations which daily do prick our conscience', he heartily thanked him, but since nothing had in fact been done in the matter he must require the pope 'to provide us other remedies'. The fault lay with the temerity and ignorance of the councillors of his holiness, but it was a great fault in Christ's vicar that he should 'have dealt so variably, yea rather so inconstantly and deceivably'. The king then gave an account of the course of the proceedings in the marriage suit which, he said, demonstrated the great inconsistency of the pope's conduct; he referred to the commission granted to Wolsey and Campeggio and the pope's promise not to revoke it, and to the decretal commission which was burned, and he added, 'if your holiness did grant us all these things justly, ye did unjustly revoke them; and if by good and truth the same was granted, they were not made frustrate nor annihilate without fraud; so that if there were no deceit nor fraud in the revocation, then how wrongfully and subtilly have been done those things that have been done!' The king went on to say that the deplorable conduct of the pope had compelled him to take the advice of 'every learned man', but their opinions differed greatly 'from that that those few men of yours do show unto you', and they held that 'by no means it is lawful to dispense with that, that God and nature hath forbidden'. In this respect, the universities of Cambridge, Oxford, Paris, Orleans, Bourges, Angers, and Bologna were at one. Henry declared that he wrote thus with a heavy heart, but 'if we should obey the letters of

[1] For the text of this letter, see Rymer, *Foedera*, xiv, 405; Tierney-Dodd, i, 378. cf. Ehses, 153.
[2] See p. 110.

your holiness, in that they do affirm that we know to be otherwise, we should offend God and our conscience, and we should be a great slander to them that do the contrary, which be a great number'. Henry therefore urged the pope to take in good part what he had written, declaring that should he dissent from the pronouncements of the pope, he would account it unlawful if there were no 'cause to defend the fact, as we now do, being compelled by necessity, lest we should seem to contemn the authority of the see apostolic'.[1]

These letters were conveyed to Rome by Guron Bertano.[2] Meanwhile the pope had been seeking a way out of the impasse, and had secretly suggested to Henry's agents in Rome that a possible solution was for the king to be allowed two wives.[3] Despite his earlier demand for a dispensation to commit bigamy, Henry did not respond to this suggestion, probably for the reason indicated by Benet, that acceptance of such a dispensation would tacitly admit the power of the pope to grant a dispensation in his own case, and such an admission would destroy the sole ground upon which Henry now relied for the invalidity of his marriage.[4]

The pope delayed his answer to the letter of the English notables until 27 September. His reply to their discourtesies and menaces was a lengthy document that was remarkable not only for its temperateness but for

---

[1] Burnet, i, Coll. of Rec., 107 (the date is wrong); *L. & P.*, iv, App. 260; cf. Ehses, 154, 155. The date of the letter is 13 July 1530.

[2] *Trevelyan Papers* (ed. Collier; Camden Soc.), i, 169.

[3] Gregory Casale to Henry VIII, 18 Sept. 1530 (*L. & P.*, iv, 6627): 'A few days since the pope secretly proposed to me the following condition;—that your Majesty might be allowed to have two wives. I told him I could not undertake to make any such proposition, because I did not know whether it would satisfy your Majesty's conscience'. Benet to Henry VIII, 27 Oct. 1530 (*L. & P.*, iv, 6705, at p. 3023): 'Shortly at Benet's coming there, the pope spoke to him of a dispensation for two wives, but so doubtfully, that Benet suspects he spoke it for two purposes; one was that he should break it to the king, and see if it would be accepted, "thereby he should have gotten a mean to bring your Highness to grant that if he might dispense in this case, which is of no less force than your case is, consequently he might dispense in your Highness' case". The other was to entertain the King, and defer the cause.' Ghinucci to Henry VIII, Sept. 1530 (*L. & P.*, iv, App. 261); in the course of this letter Ghinucci said that he had remonstrated with the pope against his refusal to grant a decretal commission or remit the cause to England, and reported upon a further interview in which the pope had 'said that he could with less scandal give the King a dispensation for two wives, than grant what the writer asked.'

[4] cf. Benet's letter of 27 Oct. 1530, quoted above.

its firmness. The pope began by acknowledging the merits of the king, as set out by the notables, but he rejected their assertion that he had denied the king justice; indeed, the matter was far otherwise, for so anxious had been the pope to grant Henry what he desired that he had been accused of partiality. When the case had first been laid before him, three years previously, he had submitted the determination of it to Wolsey and Campeggio, judges chosen by Henry. The queen, however, had suspected them of partiality and had appealed to him. Nevertheless, out of regard for Henry, he had done all he could to delay matters and had refused to act upon the appeal until he had been charged by the college of cardinals with injustice; and it was not until all the cardinals in consistory had unanimously decided that the appeal should be heard that the pope gave way. In such a cause the pope could not act otherwise than with deliberation. His holiness went on to remark that the king had sent no proctors to appear on his behalf in Rome, so that blame for any delay in the determination of the king's cause could not be attributed to the pope. Moreover the king's ambassadors at Bologna had themselves demanded the delay, and the king's complaints of delay appeared therefore to be without substance. The notables, continued the pope, apprehended great calamities if the king were not permitted to marry again and beget a male heir, but if the pope were to neglect his duty and depart from the requirements of justice, the resulting calamities would be much greater. Turning to the threat of the notables that if their requests were not granted they would be left to take care of themselves and seek a remedy elsewhere, the pope retorted that such a resolution was unworthy of them and he could not believe that it was sanctioned by the king. In conclusion, the pope said that he was anxious to comply with the king's requests in so far as they were compatible with justice, but he should not be asked to do anything that would violate the immutable commands of God.[1]

But before the pope's letter had been despatched, Henry had learned

---

[1] For the text of the letter, see Ehses, 163; Pocock, i, 434. cf. Tierney-Dodd, i, 381-4; it is calendared in *L. & P.*, iv, 6638. The letter is addressed: 'Venerabilibus fratribus, archiepiscopis et episcopis, ac dilectis filiis, abbatibus, nobilibusque viris, ducibus, marchionibus, comitibus, baronibus, militibus, ac doctoribus parlamenti regni Angliae'. Clement's answer to Henry's personal letter, if there ever was an answer, has not survived; but cf. the draft reply to Henry, prepared by cardinal Pietro Accolti but not sent, printed in Ehses, 170-4 (cited p. 124, note 1).

of the bulls of 7 and 21 March,[1] and he issued a proclamation, dated 12 September, forbidding the purchase from the court of Rome, or the publication, of anything containing matter prejudicial to the realm or to the king's intended purposes.[2] The king now had thoughts of having his case decided in England.[3] In the early part of September he summoned the nuncio, baron Antonio Borgho, and after complaining of the avocation of the cause and its committal to the Rota, he said that unless the case were committed to the archbishop of Canterbury or the church courts in England, he was determined to deal with the matter himself, since he knew that the pope had already promised to give judgment in favour of the queen. The nuncio proposed that the matter should be determined by four judges, two to be chosen by Henry and two by the queen. The discussion of this proposal went on far into the night, and then Henry asked the nuncio to speak with the duke of Norfolk about it. When the nuncio did so, the duke professed himself devoted to the holy see, but he said that when the king had distinctly declared his will he must support him, and the king would never agree to the cause being judged outside his kingdom. The duke's personal opinion was that the king would do nothing if nothing were done at Rome.[4]

But this suggestion was merely one of many that passed through the king's mind; in reality he was gravely perplexed as to what his next move should be. He had instructed his ambassadors in Rome that if the pope refused to grant a decretal commission for the cause to be decided in England, they should protest that justice was denied them and appeal

---

[1] See pp. 134, 135.
[2] *L. & P.*, iv, 6615. Edward Hall noted that 'Thys proclamacion was muche mused at and every worde of the same well noted. Some sayd that it was made because that the quene had purchased a newe Bull for the ratifycacyon of her mariage, other sayde that it was made because the Cardinall [Wolsey] had purchased a Bull to curse the kyng, yf he would not restore hym to hys old dignities, and that the king should suffer him to correct the spiritualtie, and he was not to meddle wyth the same' (Hall, *Chronicle*, ii, 180). At the time Chapuys could discover no reason for the proclamation, and conjectured that it might be to spite the pope, but he learned later from the nuncio that the sole object of the proclamation was to forestall measures against the king on the queen's behalf: cf. Chapuys to the emperor, 1 Oct. 1530; *Span. Cal.*, iv, pt. 1, 445 (p. 735). For the text of the proclamation, see *T.R.P.*, i, 197.
[3] cf. J. Salviati to Campeggio, 21 Oct. 1530 (Ehses, 165).
[4] Letter from Borgho, 16 Sept. 1530 (*L. & P.*, iv, 6618). For other references to this suggestion, see Mai to Charles V, 15 Oct. 1530 (*L. & P.*, iv, 6685); Benet to Henry VIII, 27 Oct. 1530 (*L. & P.*, iv, 6705).

to a future general council; the ambassadors, however, informed the king that they had not carried out these instructions as appeals to general councils had been forbidden, under pain of excommunication, by bulls of Pius II and Julius II.[1] They also told Henry that they had not thought it prudent to allege, as instructed, the custom of England whereby no one could be compelled to go to law out of the kingdom, since the doctors in Rome had cast doubt on the privilege.[2] The ambassadors' letter was received in London on 30 September, and Henry wrote to them, on 7 October, to complain about the fruitlessness of their activities. They were once more instructed to raise the question of the English custom and to put the matter strongly before the pope. They were also told that if the pope remained unmoved by their arguments and the opinions of the universities, they were to request the pope not to proceed in the matter before the end of January, so that, both sides abstaining from proceeding either at Rome or in England, an interval would be obtained during which the privileges of the king and of the pope might be examined. The king also complained that the ambassadors had not taken counsel with learned men to discover what should be done in the last resort, in declining the pope's judgment, or what should be done to stave it off; and they were told peremptorily to obtain such advice.[3]

But before the end of October it was clear that the pope could not be induced to change his determination. On receiving the king's instructions, Benet, Ghinucci and Casale had immediately conferred with cardinal Gabriel de Grammont, bishop of Tarbes and French ambassador. As a result de Grammont told the pope that the French king had resolved to join Henry in his great cause and it was the duty of the pope to satisfy both kings in order to keep them in obedience to the holy see.

[1] See the bull *Execrabilis* of Pius II, 18 Jan. 1460 (*Bullarum Diplomatum et Privilegiorum Sanctorum Romanorum Pontificum*, Taurinensis editio, v, 149b; Denzinger, no. 717), and the bull *Pastor Aeternus* of Julius II, 19 Dec. 1516, in the 11th session of the fifth Lateran Council (Mansi, xxxii, 967; Denzinger, no. 740).
[2] The ambassadors at Rome to Henry VIII, Sept. 1530 (*L. & P.*, iv, App. 262).
[3] Henry VIII to Ghinucci, Benet and Casale, 7 Oct. 1530 (*State Papers*, vii, 261; *L. & P.*, iv, 6667). According to the imperial ambassador at Rome, Miguel Mai, Henry's ambassadors, at this time, were suggesting that the pope should dissolve the king's marriage without any legal process or, at least, should promise not to proceed against Henry if the king were to marry again; cf. the letters of Mai to Charles V, 2 and 10 Oct. 1530 (*L. & P.*, iv, 6661, 6675). On 3 Oct. 1530, Catherine wrote from Windsor to the cardinal Sanctae Crucis to ask him to use his influence with the pope so as to ensure that the cause should remain in the Rota and not be removed, on any pretence, to England (*L. & P.*, iv, App. 263).

In a further interview with the pope de Grammont proposed that the marriage suit should be referred to a commission consisting of the archbishop of Canterbury and two other English bishops for hearing in England, but the pope replied that he could give no other answer than what he had already given to this suggestion, that as the queen had alleged that the place was suspect he could not again commit it thither without her consent. de Grammont then suggested a commission of learned clergy from the province of Canterbury, but the pope returned the same answer. Benet thereupon intervened to say that the pope could not, with reason or justice, hear the cause at Rome or commit it to any other place than England, because of the privileges and customs of the realm which did not allow any man of the realm to be 'convented out of it', and undoubtedly the king would not suffer any violation of those prerogatives that he had sworn to maintain. The pope answered that if these matters were alleged in the cause the king should be heard and should have as much as the law allowed.

de Grammont then turned to the third proposal, that if the king should provide a remedy for his great cause and should follow such means as were approved by learned men and universities in all christendom, the pope should forbear from molesting him by censures and other means. To this the pope answered that he would consult his advisers. de Grammont then told the pope that it was necessary that his holiness should satisfy Henry in some of these matters or else he would see a greater ruin in christendom than he had seen hitherto. With some heat the pope replied that he would be sorry for that and he would do all he could to prevent it, but if such ruin were to follow he would rather it were the result of his doing his duty than of his omitting to do it; in any event, he was unalterably determined to proceed in the matter according to law and justice. Further argument failed to move the pope, and de Grammont left for France. Two days later the Englishmen went once more to the pope to urge the custom of England and to tell his holiness that he would not do well if he sought to question it after it had been established for so long a time, but the pope refused to give them further audience except in the presence of his advisers. It was now plain that the pope would not proceed except according to law, and the ambassadors, in reporting to Henry, told him so.[1]

[1] Benet to Henry VIII, 27 Oct. 1530 (*L. & P.*, iv, 6705; Pocock, i, 448; Tierney-Dodd, i, 384-95).

The ambassadors' report made it clear that the pope would do nothing to interfere with the due hearing of the cause before the Rota; and Henry realized that it would be fatal to his case, such as it was, should the hearing be concluded in Rome. Henry's perplexity and uncertainty increased. His agents told him that the imperialists were urgent in their solicitations at the Vatican and that the pope would soon be compelled to issue an inhibition, prohibiting all bishops and ecclesiastical courts from coming to a decision in the matrimonial cause. Henry could neither remove the opposition of the emperor nor bend the pope to his will and, after years of endeavour, he found the difficulties in his way were greater than ever. He began to waver, telling his confidants that he had been greatly deceived; he told them he would never have sought a divorce had he not been assured that papal approval might easily be obtained, but the assurance had proved false; and he even considered abandoning the attempt.[1] At this critical moment there appeared the man who was to provide Henry with a solution to his problem.

[1] cf. Lingard, *History of England* (ed. 1826 Paris), vi, 193. Lingard is here summarizing Pole, *Apologia ad Carolum Quintum*, c. xxvi, where Pole declared that he had his account from one of those to whom the king had discharged his mind. It was about this time that Pole made his great appeal to Henry to abandon the divorce suit.

VIII

Delays in Rome

Thomas Cromwell, like his master, Wolsey, was a man of mean birth. He was born in 1485 and his father was a blacksmith. In 1503 he had served in the French army and fought against the Spaniards in Italy. After his military service he was employed as an accountant by a Venetian merchant, and on his return to England in 1512 he settled in London, earning his living as a lawyer and moneylender and engaging in the cloth trade; and he married a wealthy woman. Later he entered Wolsey's service, serving him faithfully as his principal man of business, and was chiefly responsible for the detailed work connected with the dissolution of the religious houses whose estates and revenues went to the endowment of the colleges that Wolsey was then founding at Oxford and Ipswich. He was a man of large administrative skill, great ability and no moral scruples.

In October 1529 the fall of Wolsey seemed likely to bring disaster to Cromwell. On the morning of All Saints' Day, 1 November, Cavendish came into the great chamber of the house at Esher where Wolsey and his household were then lodged, and found Cromwell leaning in the embrasure of a window, reading the Little Office of Our Lady, with tears streaming down his face. Cavendish was touched at the sight and said; 'Why, master Cromwell, what meaneth all this your sorrow; is my lord [Wolsey] in any danger for whom ye lament thus, or is it for any loss that ye have sustained by any misadventure'. Cromwell replied; 'Nay, nay, it is my unhappy adventure, which am like to lose all that I have travailed for all the days of my life for doing of my master true and diligent service.' He went on to tell Cavendish 'that I do intend (God willing) this afternoon when my lord hath dined to ride to London and so to the court, where I will either make or mar ere I come again'.[1]

That afternoon Cromwell left Esher for London, and there he contrived to insinuate himself into the service of the duke of Norfolk, one of the principal figures of the Boleyn faction and the chief enemy of

---

[1] Cavendish, *Wolsey*, 104, 105.

Wolsey. With Norfolk's influence he obtained a seat in the parliament that was then assembling.[1] His next step was to persuade the stricken cardinal to attempt to buy off his enemies with what could be salvaged from the surrender of his property and patronage. 'For his efficiency in winding up Wolsey's complicated political bankruptcy, in knowing just where this sum or that had slid to and how to recover it, and just what profitable disposition could be made of the leases, rights and pensions which had accumulated in the Cardinal's hands, Cromwell won golden opinions',[2] and, it might be added, gained much profit for the Boleyn faction and the notice of the king for himself. During the following months his activities in the disposal of Wolsey's property afforded him 'a great occasion of access to the king . . . by means whereof and by his witty demeanour, he grew continually into the king's favour'.[3]

Cromwell's inspiration was the conception of a strong, centralized state functioning through a well ordered administration, and the favour shown to him by the king seemed to indicate that this conception could now be made a practical reality. Cromwell's conception of government was the fruit of his study of a small treatise, *Il Principe*, by Niccolò Machiavelli, whose thesis was very congenial to the mind of a man like Cromwell. *Il Principe* was not printed and published until five years after Machiavelli's death in 1527, but copies of it had long circulated in manuscript and one copy was Cromwell's constant companion and political textbook.[4] The aim of Machiavelli was to teach the reality of statecraft, deduced from practical experience and unencumbered by moral precepts for which the Florentine could find no practical authority. The real originality of the book lay in the analytical method by which the author developed his ideas, pursuing them with a rigid and penetrating logic. Machiavelli attempted to base his theories and arguments solely upon ascertainable fact, and when he had ascertained the facts he

[1] He sat as one of the members for Taunton, one of Norfolk's boroughs (*L. & P.*, iv, 6043(2) (ii)).
[2] Mattingly, *Catherine of Aragon*, 227.
[3] Cavendish, *Wolsey*, 126.
[4] cf. the long conversation between Reginald Pole and Thomas Cromwell, set out in Pole, *Apologia R. Poli ad Carolum Quintum Caesarem supra quattuor libris a se scriptis de Unitate Ecclesiae*, Louvain 1569; reprinted in Quirini, *Epistolae Reginaldi Poli* (1744-57), i, 166. cf. van Dyke, *Renascence Portraits* (New York 1905), appendix (which first appeared in *Amer. Hist. Rev.* (1904), ix, 696-724), in which the suggestion is made that the book in question was *Il Cortègiano* and not *Il Principe*.

analysed the manner in which they had happened and demonstrated the lessons which they taught. This practical and realist approach to statecraft subordinated everything to the test of expediency and eliminated, as irrelevant, all moral considerations. For Machiavelli, the proper question was always, 'Is the proposed course of action conducive to the end in view?'; it was unnecessary to ask, 'Is it right?' The prince who wished to govern was, therefore, counselled to dissimulate his true motives, to learn that fraud and deceit can be useful tools, and that to be feared was better than to be loved; in so far as they conduced to the achievement of the end in view, all things were grist to the mill of the prince, and only failure was to be eschewed. Such was the teaching that first fired the imagination of Thomas Cromwell.

Cromwell was also well acquainted with another work which had a profound influence on English constitutional ideas, the *Defensor Pacis* of Marsiglio of Padua. This book was completed in 1324, but it had never sunk into oblivion. In this work Marsiglio constructed an ideal scheme for the perfect form of government. He held that the community was composed of several classes of men that were defined by their functions in the community, and the priesthood formed one of those classes. The most important part of the community, however, was the *principans* which exercised the executive power. Nevertheless, the source of power, and that which controlled it, was the legislator which was no less than the whole body of the citizens in their general assembly; the laws of the community were established by the legislator, whence they derived their binding power, and the function of the *principans* was to carry them out. The crucial tenet of Marsiglio was that the *principans* was a unity, whether a single man or a body of men, which was supreme over all classes of persons in the community, including the priesthood.

Marsiglio was even more radical in his conception of the church. He developed an argument that purported to prove that canon law and the papal power were no more than a perversion of the true principles of Christianity; and that this perversion, gradually brought about, had resulted in the subordination of the true rights of the legislator. For Marsiglio the church comprised the whole body of believers, and the priesthood consisted only of priests and deacons, for bishops were no more than priests with supervisory duties; and he held that the functions of the priesthood were confined to the celebration of Mass, the administration of the sacraments, and the teaching of revealed divine law.

Priests had no power of coercion, such as excommunication and interdict, and were incapable of owning property. In all things the priesthood was entirely subject to the legislator, for the priesthood was no different from any other class of citizens. Thus the church was wholly dependant upon the state and the prince was supreme over the church. So greatly did Cromwell admire this book that in 1534, after he had achieved supreme power, he arranged for its translation and publication in England.[1] It is an interesting speculation how far Cromwell derived from the *Defensor Pacis* the idea which he placed before Henry in the late autumn of 1530.

Like many things of a fundamental nature, the idea was a simple one. It was now clear that Henry's way to a second marriage was blocked by the papacy, and, to Cromwell's mind, this was due to the fact that there operated in England a power over which there was no control within the realm. Since, by virtue of his crown, Henry was the ruler of all his subjects including the clergy, legislation should declare that the king was supreme not only over the laity but over the clergy as well; in other words, Henry should be declared head of the church within his own dominions. Once that was established the question of his marriage could be decided by the church whose head he was declared to be.

These ideas, here stated in all their stark simplicity, were much to Henry's liking and put an end to the months of vacillation and indecision. When he again addressed himself to the pope, the change is immediately apparent. On 6 December Henry wrote to Clement a letter in which he began by saying that although he found that his demands were put aside, the requests of the French king of no avail, and the intercession of his nobles despised and derided, the result seemed to be so opposed to common sense that he could scarcely believe that the pope could have done what he knew he had done. Who could have believed that his holiness would have denied his petition for judges? The king certainly expected otherwise, as did the French king who supported his request, the counsellors who advised him, and the whole nobility and leading men of England. The queen's bare assertion that England was an unsafe place in which to judge the cause was accepted in the face of the clearest evidence to the contrary. Henry thought it best, in so grave a matter, that he and the pope should communicate their views to each other by means of formal demands and replies. Henry therefore demanded once

[1] cf. William Marshal to Cromwell, April 1534 (*L. & P.*, vii, 423).

L

more than the pope should allow the cause to be decided in England by the judges named by his ambassadors. It would be difficult to maintain the queen's objection, and the infamy it ascribed to the king was intolerable. Henry said that he did not wish to judge the pope rashly and went on to set out a number of 'very serious charges' against him. If the pope desired his own rights to be respected, let him not interfere with those of Henry. Let him not receive appeals to Rome in the king's cause, but remit them for hearing in England; and if he had issued inhibitions he must revoke them. The pope should not suppose that either the king or his nobles would allow the fixed laws of England to be set aside. Henry sought only to preserve what was his own, and he sought it in accordance with the laws of the church, the authority of councils, and the opinions of St Cyprian and St Bernard; he sought it because the laws of England would not suffer the contrary and he himself abhorred contention; but he would brook no denial.[1]

On the same day Henry also wrote to Benet and Carne in Rome. Carne, who had been sent to Rome to ensure delay in the marriage suit,[2] had written to the king's secretary to say that the learned men they had consulted on the king's behalf were of opinion that Rome was not a safe place for the hearing of the marriage suit, and this, he thought, would be a good ground on which to obtain a stay of proceedings. Henry informed Benet and Carne that his council were of the same opinion, but he himself declined to use any means that would acknowledge the pope's jurisdiction and he preferred that they should use other objections, according to the form which he enclosed; they were at liberty, however, to modify such objections at their discretion, as Henry did not doubt that they would prefer 'to be taken and reputed entire Englishmen than Englishmen papisticate'.[3] The new temper of affairs in England was noted by a Florentine, Francesco Bardi, who, after a long conversation with Henry, remarked that 'nothing else is thought of in that island every day, except of arranging affairs in such a way that they do no longer be in want of the pope, neither for filling vacancies in the church, nor for any other purpose'.[4]

[1] Henry VIII to Clement VII, 6 Dec. 1530 (*L. & P.*, iv, 6759; cf. Ehses, 167).
[2] See p. 150.
[3] Henry VIII to Benet and Carne, 6 Dec. 1530 (*State Papers*, vii, 269, at p. 271; *L. & P.*, iv, 6760).
[4] See the letter of Luigi Alamani to the Republic of Venice, 25 Dec. 1530 (*L. & P.*, iv, 6774).

Henry's letter to the pope was considered at a secret consistory, over which Clement presided, on Friday 23 December, but nothing was concluded and no vote was taken, the pope declaring that the business ought to be ripely discussed and treated with the greatest consideration in future consistories. At the same consistory the pope ordered the cardinals to consider the report of Dr Paulo di Capisucchi, auditor of the Rota, concerning the marriage suit. From this report it appeared that the queen's proctors had asked that the pope should forbid the archbishop of Canterbury to take cognizance of the suit, and had likewise asked that the pope should repeat and confirm all the inhibitions which the auditors of the Rota, to whom the cause was entrusted, had directed to all the prelates of England. The queen's proctors had further petitioned that the pope should forbid the king, while the suit was pending, either to cohabit with any other woman, and especially 'a certain lady Anne',[1] or to contract marriage, and, in case such a marriage should be contracted, to declare it null and void. Lastly, the proctors had prayed that the pope should forbid the lady Anne, and all women in general, to contract, *pendente lite*, a marriage with the king of England. After a lengthy discussion the cardinals concluded that these petitions were justifiable in law and that briefs should be granted.[2]

In accordance with this decision the pope issued a brief on 5 January, 1531, forbidding Henry to remarry until the cause should be decided, and declaring that should he do so any issue of the marriage would be illegitimate. The brief also prohibited anyone in England of ecclesiastical dignity, universities, parliaments, courts of law, and the like from pronouncing any decision in a matter of which judgment was reserved to the holy see; and it was declared that the foregoing was binding under pain of excommunication.[3] Two days later the pope sent a mild and conciliatory reply to Henry's angry letter of 6 December.[4]

The pope had promised to delay the hearing of the marriage suit by the Rota until September 1530,[5] but the hearing did not begin even then for Henry's strenuous efforts to secure the hearing of the case in England, although unsuccessful, served to prolong the delay already granted by

---

[1] 'Ne cum alia muliere et praecipue cum quadam Dna. Anna cohabitaret'.
[2] Ehses, 206 (Acta consistorialia); *L. & P.*, iv, 6772.
[3] Le Grand, iii, 531-9; Pocock, ii, 104; cf. Ehses, 175; *L. & P.*, v, 27.
[4] Clement VII to Henry VIII, 7 Jan. 1531 (Pocock, ii, 111; *L. & P.*, v, 31).
[5] See p. 135.

the pope. But these delays could only be temporary, and it was vital for Henry's purposes that the Rota should not hear the case at all. Accordingly, to ensure a prolonged and indefinite delay, Henry adopted an ingenious device. According to the citation issued by the Rota, Henry was required to appear either in person or by proctor; this he did not do, but instead sent to Rome Dr Edward Carne, a layman and doctor of civil law, who was instructed to appear before the Rota in a private capacity and there complain of the unseemliness of the action of the Rota in citing the king to appear before it.[1] During the next two years the activities of Carne were chiefly responsible for the long delay in the hearing; the period was largely devoted to discussion of the question whether Carne had a right to be heard, and until that question was settled little could be done to prosecute the divorce case. Carne's task was by no means an easy one; he was required to use all means to hinder the hearing before the Rota, but it was necessary that he should avoid any action that might acknowledge the jurisdiction of the Rota in the marriage cause, for once the king acknowledged the jurisdiction he was lost.

On 10 February 1531 Paulo di Capisucchi told Benet of the Rota's opinion that Carne might act as *excusator* without a proxy from the king, but, reported Benet, 'We, perceiving the resolution of the Rota alonely to be upon this point, *quod excusator non est audiendus sine mandato*, doubting how they would resolve themselves upon the other things contained in the matter, and perceiving also that they desired very greatly to have a proxy, my lord of Worcester, Mr Carne and I thought it very expedient not to disclose, in any manner of wise, that we had any'. On the previous day, when the pope had made it clear that there would be no delay in the hearing and that the excusator could not be heard without authorization from the king, Benet had asked for a period in which to consult Henry, and the pope replied that he would raise the matter in consistory. When Benet urged the pope to suspend

[1] cf. *L. & P.*, v, 75(1): Henry, cited to appear at Rome personally or by proxy, sent Edward Carne as *excusator*. The memoir presented by him declared that Henry would not plead by proxy in a cause on which the ease of his conscience depended, as it would be necessary for him to communicate personally with his judges. Neither could he appear in person, as it was unseemly for a king to abandon his kingdom to the disorders produced by absence. Such a citation was contrary to the customs of the church and to the privileges of christian sovereigns.

the cause, his holiness answered, 'Nay, my son, for if the king, your master, had once answered by his proctor in the cause here, the cause should depend then here *suo consensu, et sic a fortiori* he might not attempt anything at home *de facto*.'[1] At a consistory on 12 February Capisucchi reported that there had appeared 'a certain Englishman, merely as one of the people', in order to make excusatory allegations on behalf of the king of England, for whom, however, he did not appear in the matrimonial cause.[2] After discussion, and the matter having been put to the vote, the pope decreed that the excusator could not be admitted *sine mandato*;[3] and this decision was conveyed to Henry on the following day.[4] These events were also reported to the emperor by his ambassador who urged that everything should be done to press on with the cause.[5] But nothing was done until after Ash Wednesday, 22 February, and there was so little prospect of an early hearing[6] that in the middle of March the imperial ambassador complained that everyone in Rome seemed ready to give their blood to prolong the case, but his work was to bring it to a conclusion.[7] The delays, however, continued for two years.

[1] Benet to Henry VIII, 10 Feb. 1531 (*State Papers*, vii, 281; *L. & P.*, v, 93); cf. Muxetula to Charles V, 10 Feb. 1531 (*L. & P.*, v, 92): 'An Englishman has appeared before the pope and the Rota to excuse the king, and many practices are set on foot by him and the ambassadors'.
[2] '. . . fuit consistorium, in quo R. D. Capisuccius retulit, quendam Anglicum comparuisse, tamquam unum de populo, ad excusandum regem Angliae, eo quod non comparebat in causa matrimonii; . . .'
[3] Ehses, 207 (Acta consistorialia).
[4] Ghinucci and Benet to Henry VIII, 13 Feb. 1531 (*L. & P.*, v, 98).
[5] Mai to Charles V, 13 Feb. 1531 (*L. & P.*, v, 102).
[6] Benet to Henry VIII, 6 Mar. 1531 (*State Papers*, vii, 287; *L. & P.*, v, 122), a letter in which Benet described the difficulties of Carne in executing his office.
[7] Mai to Francisco de los Cobos, 13 Mar. 1531 (*L. & P.*, v, 137).

IX

The Clergy Attacked

Meanwhile in England the new influence in state affairs was strongly felt. The first step towards the solution of Henry's matrimonial difficulty was to bring the clergy into a compliant mood. On 12 January the duke of Norfolk sent for the imperial ambassador in England, Eustache Chapuys, and told him of 'a constitution made by the states of the realm' against bringing bulls or provisions from Rome. The duke was evidently referring to the statute of Praemunire,[1] and he told Chapuys that he had recently learned that, at the solicitation of the queen, the pope had issued some very injurious mandates; he warned Chapuys of the dangers attached to the execution of these documents in England, saying that even if the pope himself came to execute them, nothing could save him from the fury of the people. In former times, said Norfolk, the pope had tried to usurp authority in England, but the people would not suffer it; still less would they suffer it now. On the following day Norfolk drew the attention of the nuncio to the penalties attaching to the execution of the papal decrees against the king, and expressed his surprise that the pope had ordered the cause to proceed.[2]

The threats of proceedings in praemunire were not idle threats. Such

---

[1] The statute of Praemunire (1393) is 16 Ric. II, c. 5, which was incorporated by reference in many later statutes (e.g. 25 Hen. VIII, c. 20, s. 6; 13 Car. II, c. 1, etc.). The offence of praemunire is so called from the words of the writ preparatory to the prosecution of the offence: *praemunire facias A. B.* (cause A. B. to be forewarned) that he appear before us to answer the contempt wherewith he stands charged; particulars of the contempt were recited in the preamble to the writ. Blackstone defined the essence of the offence as 'introducing a foreign power into the land and creating *imperium in imperio*, by paying that obedience to alien process which constitutionally belonged to the king alone' (4 Bl. Comm. 103). The statutes of praemunire are 25 Edw. III, stat. ii, c. 22, known as the statute of Provisors (1351), and 16 Ric. II, c. 5, the statute of Praemunire. The punishment for the offence of praemunire was that the offender was put out of the crown's protection and his lands and goods were forfeited to the crown. Until the passing of 5 Eliz. I, c. 1, now repealed, the killing of a person convicted of praemunire may, perhaps, have been lawful; cf. Co. Litt. 391a. Chapuys had succeeded Mendoza in Sept. 1529; see p. 136, note 1.

[2] Chapuys to Charles V, 13 Jan. 1531 (*L. & P.*, v, 45).

proceedings had been taken against Wolsey on the ground that by the exercise of his legatine authority he had brought himself within the terms of the statute; and to that charge he had pleaded guilty.[1] The penalties of praemunire were severe, and involved forfeiture of lands and goods to the king, imprisonment, and outlawry.[2] When Wolsey pleaded guilty the crown profited substantially by the forfeiture of his possessions; and it was in securing the fruits of the judgment against Wolsey that Cromwell attracted the attention of the king. If so much could be wrung from one cleric, albeit the greatest, what could not be obtained from the whole body of the clergy; for had they not involved themselves in Wolsey's acknowledged crime, as aiders and abetters, by submitting to his legatine authority and obeying the mandates which he issued by virtue of that authority.

The plan first considered, which appears to have been under discussion in the autumn of 1530, was on a limited scale. There exists a memorandum concerning the taking of proceedings in praemunire against the bishops of Coventry and Lichfield, Norwich, St Asaph, Ely, Bangor, Rochester, Bath and Wells, and of Chichester, and against the abbots of Bury, Waltham and Westminster, the archdeacon of Wiltshire, the dean of Hereford, and the sub-dean of Sarum.[3] On 21 October, however, Cromwell told the fallen Wolsey that he should be 'out of all doubts for all the king's officers in the mean season', and he added that the 'prelates should not appear in the praemunire. There is another way devised in place thereof, as your Grace shall further know.'[4] The new device was designed to involve the prelates not only in a praemunire but in much else besides. In December 1530, a few days after Wolsey's death, the

---

[1] Wolsey had, of course, exercised his legatine authority with Henry's express leave and licence.

[2] cf. 16 Ric. II, c. 5 (Statute of Praemunire, 1393): 'If any purchase or pursue, or cause to be purchased or pursued in the court of Rome, or elsewhere, . . . processes, and sentences of excommunications, bulls, instruments, or any other things whatsoever, which touch the king against him, his crown, and his regalty, or his realm, . . . and they which bring within the realm, or them receive or make thereof notification or any other execution whatsoever within the same realm or without, . . . shall be put out of the king's protection, and their lands and tenements, goods and chattels, forfeit to our lord the king; and that they be attached by their bodies, if they may be found, and brought before the king and his council, there to answer to the cases aforesaid, or that process be made against them by praemunire facias, in manner as is ordained in other statutes of provisors. . . .'

[3] cf. *L. & P.*, iv, 6488.

[4] Cromwell to Wolsey, 21 Oct. 1530 (*L. & P.*, iv, 6699).

preliminary steps for proceedings in praemunire were taken against the clergy.[1] This move differed from the preceding scheme, however, because it was intended that when the clergy should plead guilty and seek to compound with the king for the penalties, their pleas of guilty should contain a declaration of the king's position as head of the church. Thus the king would obtain the two things he wanted: money, and the clergy's recognition of his supremacy. The ingenious mind from which this scheme sprang could, surely, be none other than that of Thomas Cromwell.

Parliament re-assembled on 16 January 1531[2] and, as was customary, the convocation of Canterbury assembled at the same time, meeting in the chapter house of Westminster Abbey on 21 January. A few days later there began a long discussion of the means to meet the threat against the clergy embodied in the proceedings in praemunire. No doubt it was realized in convocation that, in the event of judgment against them, it would be a practical impossibility to deprive every cleric of his possessions and imprison him; but no doubt it was also realized that certain individuals would be chosen to suffer the penalties and that, as the fate of Wolsey had so clearly shown, the highest would be chosen to suffer first. It was clear that a concerted attack was being made upon the church but those who were the leaders of the clergy, the bishops, were not, save for the bishop of Rochester, of the stuff of which martyrs are made. It was not, therefore, to be expected that the proctors of the clergy, in the convocation of Canterbury, would vigorously oppose the king, nor make a determined stand on a question of principle. The clergy would follow their bishops, and their bishops were for the most part royal servants of long experience in secular affairs.

Although the charge against the clergy was based on their acknow-ledgement of and participation in Wolsey's legatine authority, it does not seem to have occurred to those in convocation that they might defend themselves on the ground that Wolsey had acted throughout with the licence of the king;[3] had not Wolsey himself pleaded guilty? A charge involving praemunire was a terrifying one. Chapuys, when he had con-

---

[1] cf. Burnet, i, 106; Hall, *Chronicle*, ii, 183. But see Scarisbrick, 'The Pardon of the Clergy, 1531' in *Camb. Hist. Jo.* (1956), xii, 22-39, which should, however, be read with circumspection. [2] cf. *L. & P.*, v, 48.
[3] Stephen Gardiner, writing much later, from the Fleet, where he had been imprisoned after his protests against the injunctions of Edward VI, evidently thought that the licence of the king was no defence to a charge of praemunire:

sulted lawyers, observed that the law of praemunire was one that 'no person in England can understand, and its interpretation lies solely in the king's head, who amplifies it and declares it at his pleasure, making it apply to any cases he pleases';[1] the uncertainties served only to increase the terror of the charge, but there was no uncertainty about the penalty. For convocation it was, at first, merely a question of the amount of money that would be necessary to satisfy the king, and after much discussion they decided to offer him £40,000.[2] The imperial ambassador was much disturbed by what was happening, and he persuaded the nuncio to go to convocation and urge them to stand up for the immunity of the church, promising them that he would intercede for them with the king about the 'gift' with which Henry wished to charge them. When, however, the nuncio appeared the clergy were astonished and scandalized; without allowing him to open his mouth they begged him to leave them in peace, since they had not the king's leave to speak with him. The nuncio was, perforce, obliged to return without achieving his purpose, and had to content himself with explaining his intention privately to the bishop of London.[3]

Before convocation had time to make their offer of £40,000 they received a strong hint that nothing less than £100,000 would be accepted. Accordingly, on 24 January they voted that sum, and in the text of the grant they described it as being offered to the king in acknowledgement of his defence of the catholic faith against heresy; they did not make any reference to the proceedings in praemunire then pending, nor did they acknowledge their guilt. A fortnight passed, and on 7 February they

[1] Chapuys to Charles V, 14 Feb. 1531 (*Span. Cal.*, iv, pt. 2, 635; *L. & P.*, v, 105).
[2] For the proceedings in convocation, see Wilkins, *Concilia*, iii, 724, 725; *Life of Fisher*, 76-81; Hall, *Chronicle*, ii, 183. Unfortunately there does not exist any full record of the debates in convocation, either official or unofficial.
[3] Chapuys to Charles V, 23 Jan. 1531 (*L. & P.*, v, 62).

'Fyrst, my Lord Cardynal that obteyned his legacie by our late souverain lordes request at Rome, yet bicause it was against the lawes of the realme, the judges concluded thoffense of premenire; which matier I bare awaye, and toke it for a lawe of the realme, bicause the lawers said soo, but my reason digested it not' (Gardiner to Somerset, 14 Oct. [1547]; printed in J. A. Muller, ed. *Letters of Stephen Gardiner*, 379, at p. 390). The reference to the conclusion of the judges is a curious one; Wolsey pleaded guilty and therefore the judges would have had no occasion on which to make a decision on the point. A. F. Pollard (*Wolsey*, 253, note 1) considered, with some justification, that after eighteen years Gardiner's recollection had become confused.

were informed that the king had refused their grant in the terms in which it was made. They were informed that if the 'gift' were to be accepted, they must acknowledge, in the grant, that it was offered in consideration of the king's pardon for their breach of penal law, and they were to describe the king, not only by his usual style, but with the addition of the words, 'protector and supreme head of the church and clergy of England'.[1]

The implications of the title now demanded by the king were evident to all, and three days were spent in fruitless discussion. Conferences were held with Cromwell and with other royal councillors, and expedients were proposed in convocation only to be rejected. It was proposed that there should be added to the clause demanded by the king the words *quantum per leges canonicas liceat* (so far as canon law allows); the meaning of this addition was, however, too precise for the king's liking and he rejected it.[2] A message was brought by the viscount Rochford that the king would tolerate no other alteration than the addition of the words 'under God', but the bishops were of opinion that such an addition did little to modify the original phrase. After further discussion, and when threatening messages had failed to bend convocation to the royal will, a group of bishops and others were summoned by the king who gave them his personal assurance, 'on the word of a king', that by insisting upon the addition to his style and title he had no thought of making any innovation. On their return to the chapter house of Westminster Abbey they repeated the king's assurances to the assembly, and thereupon the members of convocation were disposed to meet the royal demand and agreed to vote the grant in the form required by the king. But Fisher, in order to preserve at least the appearance of decency, proposed the addition, *in quantum per Christi legem licet* (in so far as the law of Christ allows).[3] Ultimately Warham, as archbishop, put the clause with Fisher's

---

[1] The king also demanded that the clergy should recognize that it was by him that they were able 'inservire curae animarum majestati ejus commissae'. The clergy avoided this by amending the phrase to read 'inservire curae populi majestati ejus commissi'. cf. Wilkins, *Concilia*, iii, 725, 743.

[2] Scarpinelli to Francesco Sforza, duke of Milan, 19 Feb. 1531 (*Ven. Cal.*, iv, 656).

[3] The *Life of Fisher*, 80, reports Fisher as saying that, although the king had by his own mouth and by his councillors, solemnly sworn as a king that he did not require more than the law of God allowed and had no intention to meddle in spiritual matters, 'yet for a more trewe and plaine exposition of your meaninge towardes the kinge and all his posterritie, let these condicionall wordes be expressed in your graunt, *quantum per legem dei licet*, which is no otherwise (as the kinge and his counsellors say) then themselves meane.'

addition to convocation as follows: ' . . . of which church and clergy of England we acknowledge his majesty to be the chief protector, only and supreme lord and also, in so far as the law of Christ allows, supreme head'. Warham's motion was followed by a long silence. At length, using a maxim of the common law, the archbishop said, *Qui tacet consentire videtur*, and an unknown prelate answered: 'Then are we all silent.' In this ambiguous manner the grant was made on 11 February.[1]

Three months later, on 7 May, the convocation of York adopted the same language and voted for the same purpose the sum of £18,800.[2] However, the clause containing the addition to the king's style did not pass without a protest from Cuthbert Tunstall, now bishop of Durham. If the clause meant no more than that the king was the head of the church in temporals, why, asked the bishop, did the clause not say so? But if it meant that he was head in spirituals, it was contrary to the doctrine of the Catholic Church; and accordingly he dissented from it lest he be thought to dissent from the Catholic Church 'outside which there is no salvation for any christian'. He called upon all present to witness his dissent, and he required his protest to be entered in the acts of convocation.[3] Tunstall's protest drew from the king a lengthy letter of reply.[4]

---

[1] See Wilkins, *Concilia*, iii, 724 (*L. & P.*, v, 928). For the text of the grant, printed from the Close Rolls, see Rymer, *Foedera*, xiv, 413; Wilkins, *Concilia*, iii, 742-4. The crucial clause was introduced, in parentheses, into that part of the grant where convocation acknowledged the great services which Henry had rendered to the church and clergy: 'sic impraesens quamplurimos hostes, maxime Lutheranos, in perniciem ecclesiae et cleri Anglicani (cujus singularem protectorem unicum et supremum dominum, et quantum per Christi legem licet, etiam supremum caput ipsius majestatem recognoscimus) conspirantes . . .' (see Wilkins, *Concilia*, iii, 742).
[2] See Wilkins, *Concilia*, iii, 744 et seq. The precise sum was the curious one of £18,840 os. 10d.; see p. 159, note 2.
[3] Wilkins, *Concilia*, iii, 745. In the course of his protest Tunstall said, 'If these words [*quantum per Christi legem licet*] are understood of spiritual matters, the king is not supreme head of the church, since this is not lawful according to Christ's law' (Si vero de spiritualibus intelligantur ea verba, rex non sit supremum caput ecclesiae, cum hoc per Christi legem non liceat).
[4] For the text, see Wilkins, *Concilia*, iii, 762 (*L. & P.*, v, App. 9). The terms of Tunstall's protest, and of Henry's reply, strongly suggest that, at any rate up to this point, the question exercising the minds of the clergy was not one that explicitly bore upon the authority of the holy see. Tunstall was not so much protesting at an encroachment upon papal authority as at the ambiguity of a phrase that would enable heretics to reject episcopal jurisdiction and appeal from ecclesiastical censures to the royal courts.

The ambiguity of the saving clause, 'in so far as the law of Christ allows', is plain for all to see. It enabled those who, like Tunstall and Fisher, held to the traditional opinion and rejected the king's supremacy, to maintain that it destroyed any implication of royal supremacy that there might be in the terms of the grant of convocation; but for others who were imbued with the ideas of Machiavelli and of Marsiglio of Padua, the clause, which did not define what was the law of Christ nor what it forbade, had little meaning, and the grant was no more than the first step on the road leading to the supremacy of the king. The astute Chapuys regarded the saving clause as valueless; 'it is all the same,' he wrote, 'as far as the king is concerned, as if they [the clergy] had made no reservation; for no one now will be so bold as to contest with his lord the importance of this reservation'.[1] When the nuncio broached the subject of 'this new papacy made here', the king said that it was nothing and was not intended to infringe the authority of the pope, provided that his holiness paid due regard to him; otherwise the king would know what to do.[2]

When the convocation of Canterbury agreed to compound with the king for their liability in praemunire, and made a grant in terms acceptable to him, it was determined that the royal pardon should be granted to them by means of an act of parliament, and a bill for this purpose was introduced into the house of lords. The bill there passed without difficulty, as might be expected in an assembly composed largely of bishops and abbots,[3] but matters were different when the bill reached the commons. The terror inspired by the proceedings in praemunire affected the commons who feared that they might be in like case with the clergy, and when they perceived that they were not included in the bill they refused to pass it. In the commons 'divers froward persons would in no wise assent to it, except all men were pardoned, saying that all men which had anything to do with the cardinal were in the same case'.[4] The king at first refused to listen to the protests of the commons, saying

---

[1] Chapuys to Charles V, 14 Feb. 1531 (*Span. Cal.*, iv, pt. 2, 635; *L. & P.*, v, 105).
[2] Chapuys to Charles V, 21 Feb. 1531 (*L. & P.*, v, 112).
[3] But cf. Chapuys to Charles V, 8 Mar. 1531 (*L. & P.*, v, 124), when the ambassador wrote that the clergy were more conscious every day of the great error they committed in acknowledging the king as sovereign of the church, and were urgent in parliament to retract it.
[4] Hall, *Chronicle*, ii, 184.

that an act of parliament was unnecessary as he could effectively pardon the clergy by an instrument under the great seal; but the king's haughty attitude led to

great murmuring among them in the chamber of the commons, where it was publicly said in the presence of some of the privy council that the king had burdened and oppressed his kingdom with more imposts and exactions than any three or four of his predecessors, and he ought to consider that the strength of the king lay in the affections of his people. And many instances were alleged of the inconveniences which had happened to princes through the ill treatment of their subjects.[1]

The sound political sense of this plain speaking was not lost upon Henry who recognized that his chief support was derived from the commons, and he yielded immediately. A further bill for the pardon of the laity was at once introduced and the two bills passed without further difficulty.[2]

The proceedings in convocation had caused the chancellor, Sir Thomas More, a great deal of distress. The imperial ambassador reported that he was so mortified by the actions of the clergy that he was anxious above all things to resign his office, and Fisher was ill with disappointment. More and Fisher were closely linked to the championship of the queen, the emperor's aunt, and despite his discretion and loyalty it was impossible for More to conceal his opposition to the divorce. The news of the distress of these two men moved the emperor to write to More, sending the letter to Chapuys for delivery.[3] But when Chapuys

[1] Chapuys to Charles V, 2 April 1531 (*L. & P.*, v, 171).
[2] cf. Hall, *Chronicle*, ii, 184, 185. Hall, who greatly admired Henry, recorded that when the king gave his assent to the bill for the pardon of the laity, 'the commons lovingly thanked the king, and much praised his witte, that he had denied it to them when they had unworthely demaunded it and had bountifully graunted when he perceyved that they sorowed and lamented'. The two acts were 22 Hen. VIII, c. 15 (pardon of the clergy of the province of Canterbury; *Statutes of the Realm*, iii, 334), and 22 Hen. VIII, c. 16 (pardon of the laity; *Statutes of the Realm*, iii, 338). In 1532 a further act was passed pardoning the clergy of the province of York (23 Hen. VIII, c. 19; *Statutes of the Realm*, iii, 383); the sum to be paid by the province of York, described in the act as 'a subsidy', was £18,840 0s. 10d. These three statutes were repealed by the Statute Law Revision Act, 1863. Difficulties were experienced in collecting the money; for example, on 30 Aug., after the bishop of London had attempted to assess the clergy of his diocese for the purpose of this 'subsidy', there was a riot at St Paul's and the bishop was seriously assaulted: see Bill filed in the Star Chamber (*L. & P.*, v, 387), and Hall, *Chronicle*, 200, 201.
[3] Chapuys acknowledged the receipt of this letter on 22 Mar.; see Chapuys to Charles V, 22 Mar. 1513 (*Span. Cal.*, iv, pt. 2, 664 (p. 98); *L. & P.*, v, 148).

sent to tell More that he had letters for him from the emperor, More begged him 'for the honour of God' to forbear, saying that although he had given such proof of his loyalty that he ought to incur no suspicion whoever came to visit him, yet a visit from the imperial ambassador might deprive him of the liberty he had always used in speaking of matters concerning the queen and the emperor. More begged Chapuys to keep the letter until a more suitable time, for if he received it he must communicate it to the king.[1]

More's mortification at the action of convocation was shortly afterwards increased by the action of the king. The last business of the session was to acquaint each house of parliament, in a formal manner, with the opinions of the universities that were favourable to Henry. Despite the king's promise that he would not ask More to act in any way contrary to his conscience, More, as lord chancellor, was required to speak as the king's mouthpiece on this occasion. His unwilling participation in this task was not only distasteful to him but resulted in an incident that caused him great embarrassment. On Thursday, 30 March, More rose in the house of lords to inform the house, by command, of the things that the king wished them to know. He began by saying that there were some who put it about that the king pursued the divorce out of love for some lady; but this was not true, for the king's only concern was to discharge his conscience which, as he had learned from what he had read and discovered from doctors and universities, was in an evil condition because he had lived with the queen who was a woman with whom it was sinful to marry, even with the dispensation of the pope, as the house would learn from the opinions of the universities that were to be read to them. Sir Brian Tuke, the clerk of the parliament, then proceeded to read the opinions in a loud voice. When the reading was done the bishop of Lincoln spoke in favour of the king and was followed by the bishop of London. Immediately the bishops of Bath and Wells and of St Asaph protested that it was not the place to discuss such a question and that time was too short to demonstrate the justice of the queen's cause. The duke of Norfolk hastily interrupted to say that the documents had been read, not as a basis for discussion, but for the purpose set out by the lord chancellor. More was then asked for his opinion. To this embarrassing question he replied that he had many times already declared his opinion to the king, and said no more; an answer that made his disapproval clear,

[1] Chapuys to Charles V, 2 April 1531 (*L. & P.*, v, 171).

for had he approved the divorce he could scarcely have refrained from saying so. Then More, accompanied by several members of the house of lords, both spiritual and lay, and Sir Brian Tuke, descended to the commons and repeated what he had said in the lords. When Tuke had finished reading the documents, More added that the king wished them to be acquainted with the matter so that when they returned to their homes they might inform their neighbours of the truth. More and those accompanying him then departed, without a word from the commons. On the following day parliament was prorogued to October, and in his speech on behalf of the king, More told the members that the king was very well satisfied with them.[1]

[1] See Chapuys to Charles V, 2 April 1531 (*L. & P.*, v, 171); Hall, *Chronicle*, ii, 185-95.

X

More Delays in Rome

I

That parliament had met and been prorogued without discussing the divorce was a matter of great satisfaction to the queen.[1] Ever since the avocation of the marriage cause she had been anxious for judgment to be given in Rome and fearful of what might be done in England. In April 1530 she had written, in her breathless Spanish, to Dr Pedro Ortiz, the emperor's proctor in Rome:

I do not know what to think of his holiness; but on this side, the heretics who are in the christian world, seeing that this cause, as it is, in suspense, gives room that there should be more suspense; and he being the head and protector of the church, he wished the church to have a great fall. I cannot do more, as I have written to his holiness, than to inform him of the truth, and have represented to him the evils I see if they follow the course of not bringing to an end this cause, and procure that there shall be an end to it through the means which appear to me the proper ones. . . . I have seen a copy of the brief which his holiness has issued, and I have shown it to learned persons, and they have told me that the medicine which is to cure this wound must be stronger, and that remedy is the sentence, and anything else will bring anger and little profit for a few days only.[2]

[1] cf. Chapuys to Charles V, 2 April 1531 (L. & P., v, 171): 'The Queen lately left Richmond, where she left the Princess [Mary], and she is now at Greenwich, in great spirits at having escaped the determination of Parliament on the divorce, of which she was always afraid'.

[2] Catherine of Aragon to Ortiz, 14 April 1530. The Spanish original of this letter, with a translation, is printed in Manchester (duke of), *Court and Society from Elizabeth to Anne* (1864), i, 165-7 (the quotation above is taken from the English translation); the letter is calendared at L. & P., iv, 6337. The relevant portions of the Spanish original are: 'No se que me diga de Su Santidad syno que allende los hereges que ay en la Christianidad teniendo esta causa como la tiene suspensa quiere dar lugar a que aya mas y seyendo caveça y protector de la yglesia la quiere hazer dar una gran cayda y no puedo hazer mas como a Su Santidad escrybo syno ynformale de mi verdad y representarle los daños que veo se siguen por nodar fin a esta causa y procurar que se acabe por las vias que me parescera . . . yo he visto la copia del breve que Su Santidad otorgo y helo mostrado a personas doctas y anme respondido que la medicina que esta llaga a de curar a de ser mas fuerte y quel remedio es la sentencia y lo demas trahera enojo y aprovechera poco . . .'

She instructed Ortiz to communicate to the pope what she had written. But despite the frequent appeals to the pope which she sent through Chapuys and Ortiz nearly eighteen months had passed and her case had not even been opened at Rome. To all her appeals and to the frequent remonstrances made on behalf of the emperor, the same reply was made: that she be patient and refrain from vexing the king.

At the beginning of January 1531, just before convocation began their proceedings, she wrote once more to the pope. She declared that her complaint was not against the king but against the instigators and abettors of the marriage suit.

From these people spring the threats against your holiness. Therefore, put a bit in their mouths! Proceed to sentence! Then their tongues will be silenced and their hopes of mischief vanish; then they will set my lord at liberty and he will become once more the dutiful son of your holiness, as he always was.[1]

As soon as parliament had been prorogued she appealed to the emperor for help. She told him that she believed that the opinions of the universities had been read in parliament for two reasons: first, on account of the shameless life the king was leading with the woman he kept with him; and secondly, because the king believed that their publication would be enough to make the kingdom consent. She expressed her anxiety about the delays in Rome and besought the emperor to procure a sentence from the Rota before parliament re-assembled in October.[2] Catherine was demanding that the pope should come to a decision, but no request more difficult to satisfy could have been made to Clement VII.

Henry's agents in Rome, however, were exerting themselves to delay the opening of the marriage suit before the Rota, and now that the English clergy had been tamed, the king was seeking other means to secure a declaration of the invalidity of his marriage; his immediate plan was the institution of proceedings in the archiepiscopal court of Canterbury. Since the collapse of the clergy in convocation, in face of the threat of the penalties of praemunire, Chapuys had feared that some such move would be made. At the queen's request he did what he could to prevent it, and he urged the nuncio to intervene with the archbishop to persuade him not to entertain any such cause and, if necessary, to serve upon the archbishop the papal inhibitory briefs should that prove

---

[1] Catherine of Aragon to Clement VII, 6 [?] Jan., 1531 (quoted, from the Vienna archives, in Mattingly, *Catherine of Aragon*, 236).
[2] Catherine of Aragon to Charles V, 5 April 1531 (*L. & P.*, v, 176).

practicable. On 13 January, accordingly, the nuncio called upon Warham to exhort him to have regard to God, his conscience, the authority of the pope, and to the justice, welfare and tranquillity of the kingdom. They were interrupted, however, by the arrival of the bishop of Lincoln, John Longland, who was the king's confessor. But the archbishop told the nuncio that the king had come in person to induce him to comply with his wishes; Warham nevertheless assured the nuncio that he would on no account disobey the pope's prohibition.[1]

Efforts were made in Rome, with French support, to obtain an order committing the hearing of the cause to a place near England. In April Henry instructed Benet to delay the commencement of the marriage suit until Michaelmas, at the earliest, and the pope should therefore be told that the summoning of the king to Rome would do much to destroy papal authority. Benet was also to tell the pope that, in order to allay public anxiety, he should arrange a hearing at a neutral place and by impartial judges, and inform the French king of his having done so, in order that Francis might mediate. Benet was told that, by thus allowing his holiness to hope that Henry would condescend to appear in the suit if it were heard under such conditions, the process might be delayed.[2] Early in May Gabriel de Grammont, the bishop of Tarbes, arrived in Rome with a demand that the cause be heard in some place near England, such as Cambrai, so that the king might know what was going on;[3] and once again the English ambassadors in Rome were instructed to insist upon the removal of the cause to England.[4]

However, the king learned from his ambassadors that the pope appeared unwilling to grant an indefinite delay in the cause, and no progress had been made with the proposal for a hearing at Cambrai. Accordingly Henry, after consulting his council, determined to bring pressure upon the queen to induce her to agree to the hearing of the cause at a place other than Rome. On the Tuesday after Whitsunday, 30 May, the queen was secretly apprised of what was afoot, and on the following day she caused her chaplain to offer a votive Mass of the Holy Ghost, begging for guidance. That night, at about eight or nine o'clock, as the

---

[1] Chapuys to Charles V, 13 Jan. 1531 (*Span. Cal.*, iv, pt. 2, 598 (pp. 27, 28); *L. & P.*, v, 45).

[2] Henry VIII to Benet, 23 April 1531 (*State Papers*, vii, 297; *L. & P.*, v, 206).

[3] Ortiz to Charles V, 25 May 1531 (*L. & P.*, v, 255).

[4] Instructions to the English ambassadors with the pope (*L. & P.*, v, 274).

queen was retiring to rest, she was visited by the dukes of Norfolk and Suffolk, and some thirty privy councillors, together with the bishops of Lincoln and London, and Dr Sampson, Dr Lee and Stephen Gardiner. Norfolk made a long and somewhat rambling speech in which he urged the queen to consider that it was neither right nor seemly that the king should be forced to abandon his kingdom and appear in the marriage suit at Rome. He had the effrontery to say that it would be much better if the matter were not carried on with so much precipitation at Rome, and he urged the queen to agree that a place and judges that were above suspicion should be chosen by common accord. The queen was asked to remember that the king could not be dragged to Rome by judicial process without his own consent, for he was entirely sovereign in his own kingdom, as well in regard to the temporalty as to the spiritualty, as had lately been recognized and approved by parliament and the clergy of England.

When Norfolk had finished his harangue, Catherine made a dignified speech to the assembly. No one, she said, had greater cause than she had to regret any pain or shame that the affair might have caused the king, but she could not suppose that her proctors would solicit any unjust process, and still less that those to whom cognizance of the cause was committed would grant such process. In summoning Henry to appear either in person or by proctor no injustice had been done to anyone. She went on to recite the different favours granted by the pope to the king and the lack of favour that she herself had received. Turning to Norfolk's assertion that the king was supreme head in both temporal and spiritual matters, Catherine declared that she considered the king to be her sovereign, and would therefore serve and obey him. He was sovereign in his realm so far as temporal jurisdiction went, but where spiritual matters were concerned it was not pleasing to God either that the king should intend to exercise a sovereignty or that she should consent thereto; for the pope was the only true sovereign and vicar of Christ who had power to judge spiritual matters, of which marriage was one.

Dr Lee broke in to say that the marriage between herself and the king was detestable and abominable before God and the world. Then Dr Sampson told her that she would do best if she agreed to the selection of judges as Norfolk had proposed, and he was followed by Longland, the bishop of Lincoln. To each of them the queen replied, but she was unshakable in her determination that the case should proceed in Rome.

Her replies were made with simplicity and directness, so that Chapuys, in reporting the interview to the emperor, observed that the deputation, if they had had the liberty of speaking their thoughts, would, for the most part, have inclined to the queen's side; but as they could do no more they indicated their satisfaction at the queen's answers by nudging one another when any point struck home. The queen was more than a match for her interlocutors, and, as they left her presence, Sir Henry Guildford observed that it would be the best deed in the world if all those who had suggested and supported the affair were tied in a cart and sent to Rome, there to maintain their opinions or meet with the confusion they deserved. When the king, who had been waiting anxiously to learn the result of the interview, was told what had occurred, he said that he had feared it would be so, considering the courage and fantasy of the queen, but it would now be necessary to provide other remedies.[1]

This interview provoked a crisis in Catherine's relations with Henry. For months she had been living in hope that the suit would be decided in Rome before parliament assembled again, but the continuing delay depressed her spirits and she feared that the pope had no intention of ensuring that justice be done to her. She saw, too, that Anne Boleyn spoke with ever greater assurance, and she believed that the king made difficulties only in order to get the suit tried in England.[2] Henry, for his part, was increasingly anxious for a speedy determination of the cause in his favour, a thing he could not hope for in Rome. The queen's refusal to assist him in securing the transfer of the case to Cambrai or some other place put an unendurable strain upon their relations which had for long been little more than formal. In the middle of June Henry went to Windsor, accompanied by Anne Boleyn. In the middle of July he left on a hunting expedition, taking Anne Boleyn with him, but he rode off without taking leave of the queen. It was, in fact, their final parting. The queen waited until the twenty-fifth of the month, when she sent to the king to inquire of his health and to tell him of the concern she had felt at not having been able to speak to him before his departure. On receiving the message the king, after consulting Norfolk and Stephen Gardiner, recalled the messenger and in great anger commanded him

---

[1] Chapuys to Charles V, 6 June 1531 (*Span. Cal.*, iv, pt. 2, 739; *L. & P.*, v, 287); cf. Hall, *Chronicle*, ii, 196.
[2] cf. Chapuys to Charles V, 17 July 1531 (*L. & P.*, v, 340).

to tell the queen that he had no need to bid her adieu nor to give her any other consolation. She had wished to bring shame on him by having him personally cited to Rome and had refused, like the obstinate woman she was, to accede to the reasonable request of his councillors. Henceforth she must desist from sending him messengers or visitors. Catherine wrote again, saying she was sorry for the anger and illwill he had against her without cause, for all she had done had been by his leave and for his honour. But, she said, her hope depended, not on the king, but only on God who was the real protector of justice and truth.

The king delayed three days before replying to Catherine's second letter, and then, after taking advice, sent her a harsh answer that made it plain that he did not wish to see her again.[1] In August, because the king was accustomed to hunt near Windsor, the queen was ordered to move to The More, Wolsey's old house in Hertfordshire, and to send her daughter, Mary, to Richmond.[2] On 13 October, while she was still at Windsor, Catherine was visited by Dr Lee, now archbishop-elect of York, the earl of Sussex, Sir William Fitzwilliam the treasurer, and Dr Sampson, at the order of the king. They made her a long discourse setting out the inconvenience that would arise if the differences between herself and the king proceeded according to the full rigour of the law. It would be much better, they said, if the matter could be settled in an amicable way, and that could be done if it were left to the bishops and others of the kingdom, since there was no reason why the cause should be decided at Rome where justice could not be obtained. These were much the arguments addressed to her by Norfolk in May, and once more they failed to move her from her decision. At the close of the interview she was told that the king would allow her the choice to remain where she was or to retire to a small house of his or to an abbey of nuns. She replied that it was not for her to choose, and wherever the king

---

[1] Chapuys to Charles V, 24 June 1531 (*L. & P.*, v, 308); Chapuys to Charles V, 17 July 1531 (*L. & P.*, v, 340); Chapuys to Charles V, 31 July 1531 (*L. & P.*, v, 361). In his letter of 31 July Chapuys noted that Henry's last letter had no address, which he took to be an indication that Henry had decided to change Catherine's title but had not then determined what title to give her.

[2] Chapuys to Charles V, 19 Aug. 1531 (*L. & P.*, v, 375); Chapuys to Charles V, 10 Sept. 1531 (*L. & P.*, v, 416); Hall, *Chronicle*, ii, 197. Hall, after recording the parting of the king and queen, sententiously observed: 'Wherfore the Commen people dailye murmured and spake their folysh fantasies. But the affayres of Princes be not ordered by the commen people, not it were not convenient that all thynges were opened to theim.'

commanded, thither would she go. Catherine moved to The More at the end of October.[1]

The remainder of the queen's life was one of solitude, deprived of her daughter and publicly insulted. But Anne Boleyn was triumphant. In July she was boasting that she would be married within three or four months. She had engaged an armourer and other household officers and was thus setting about her preparations for her royal station.[2]

2

In Rome the refusal of Henry to appear in the marriage suit caused much irritation to the imperialists who wished to bring the suit to a conclusion as quickly as possible. The continued delays exasperated them, and by the spring of 1531 means were being sought to force the Rota to give judgment by default.[3] The imperial ambassador was consequently distressed to learn of the opinion of the cardinal of Trent who had expressed the view that, unless some agreement could be reached, it would be well for a delay of two years to occur in the king of England's marriage suit.[4] Carne's activities, however, ensured that the delay should continue. Henry was appreciative of his activities and wished him to continue the defence of the king that he had undertaken in his own name.[5] The exceedingly equivocal position of Carne caused the cardinals much trouble,

[1] Chapuys to Charles V, 16 Oct. 1531 (*L. & P.*, v, 478); Chapuys to Charles V, 4 Nov. 1531 (*L. & P.*, v, 512). In November the serjeants-at-law gave a feast at Ely House, which extended over five days, from Friday the 10th until the following Tuesday; on Monday 13th the king and queen Catherine dined there, but in separate chambers (see *L. & P.*, v, 531).

[2] Chapuys to Charles V, 17 July 1531 (*L. & P.*, v, 340).

[3] Ortiz to Charles V, 16 Mar. 1531 (*L. & P.*, v, 144): 'If [Henry] perserveres in his refusal, the intention of the queen of England must be proved, and the sentence called "por contradictas" given as against a person who fails to appear. Then his Holiness should be required to hear the examination of the merits of the cause, and the Consistory would determine by an "extravagante" that this grade of affinity between brother and sister-in-law does not impede marriage, except by human law, with which the pope can dispense. By this means the justice of the cause will be well determined and founded for ever.' Unfortunately Ortiz, a lawyer who had been sent to Rome to assist in the marriage suit, was not on good terms with the ambassador, Miguel Mai; cf. Ortiz to the archbishop of Santiago, 11 April 1531 (*L. & P.*, v, 188).

[4] Mai to de los Cobos, 28 Mar. 1531 (*L. & P.*, v, 158).

[5] Henry VIII to Carne, 23 April 1531 (*L. & P.*, v, 208).

but his vigorous attempts to secure the revocation of the papal decree avoking the cause to Rome and summoning the king, so that the cause might be heard in England,[1] were fruitless. On 10 May a secret consistory decided that, notwithstanding the arguments of the excusator, the decree concerning the matrimonial cause should remain in full force and effect.[2] Nevertheless Carne's mere presence was enough to ensure prolonged delay. At the beginning of June Ortiz heard a rumour that Carne had received full authority from the king to appear on his behalf, but in reporting the rumour he added, gloomily, that 'he must be heard first, and replying to him will occupy the time until the vacation'.[3] The rumour, of course, proved false.

In July Henry instructed his ambassadors to protest to the pope against the injuries done to him by the citation to appear in Rome, and he enclosed the opinions of French lawyers who held that the pope had no power to cite the king to Rome.[4] On the same day he wrote to Benet, in rather different terms. Benet was instructed to speak to the pope and then to ask *ex abrupto* why the cause should not be remitted to the archbishop of Canterbury. Benet was to do his utmost to secure the pope's consent to the remission of the cause to the archbishop, but should he fail he was to suggest that the matter be committed to certain abbots; if the pope objected to this proposal also, Benet was to suggest a hearing by the bishop of London and other bishops. The pope, said Henry, was to be earnestly pressed in these matters, and he was to be told that if he would have his laws observed he must respect the king's privileges.[5]

The activities of Henry and his agents to secure the hearing of the cause in England, or at Cambrai or some other neutral place,[6] caused a reaction on the part of the emperor, and of Catherine who had been led

[1] cf. Instructions to the English ambassadors with the Pope (*L. & P.*, v, 274): 'On these grounds you shall also insist on the reasons alleged by our excusator for remitting our cause to England'.

[2] Ehses, 207 (Acta consistorialia); cf. *L. & P.*, v, 234. Ortiz reported that the consistory decided once more that the *excusator* should not be heard unless he showed full powers to appear on the king's behalf; Ortiz to Charles V, 15 May 1531 (*L. & P.*, v, 239). cf. Benet to Henry VIII, May 1531 (*State Papers*, vii, 299; *L. & P.*, v, 245).

[3] Ortiz to Charles V, 4 June 1531 (*L. & P.*, v, 284); cf. Mai to Charles V, 9 June 1531 (*L. & P.*, v, 289).

[4] Henry VIII to Ghinucci, Benet and Casale, 10 July 1531 (Pocock, ii, 283; *L. & P.*, v, 326).

[5] Henry VIII to Benet, 10 July 1531 (*State Papers*, vii, 305; *L. & P.*, v, 327).

[6] See p. 163.

to suppose that her nephew was actually negotiating with the pope for the trial of the cause at Cambrai.[1] The emperor, in a formal communication, told the English ambassador that he wished to remain on terms of friendship with Henry and he assured the ambassador that he had acted throughout with moderation. But he pointed out that it would be most unfair to the queen if the trial should take place in England or even at Cambrai, and that the king had no grounds for suspecting the partiality of Roman justice. The ultimate decision would be that of the pope himself and there was no other tribunal to which the king could so safely commit his conscience. To the pope the emperor protested that it was hard to see how the cause could be decided elsewhere than in Rome.[2] The vacation, however, intervened and prevented any further progress with the cause.[3] The king was well satisfied with the dilatory course of the suit, and when he heard that it was the pope's intention to proceed with the cause after the vacation he instructed his ambassadors that if that were done they were to leave Rome before judgment was given, because, he said, 'we do not think that our ambassadors should attend the court of one who shows such hostility to us.'[4]

Meanwhile the king had been concerned to make a reality of the title of supreme head of the church and clergy of England which both convocations had acknowledged to be his. The jurisdiction to try questions of heresy belonged exclusively to the ecclesiastical courts, although persons convicted of heresy were handed over to the secular power for the execution of the sentence imposed. However, in the spring of 1531 matters took a different turn when one of the leading preachers was detained in prison, pending his trial on a charge of heresy in having

---

[1] See Catherine of Aragon to Charles V, 28 July 1531 (*L. & P.*, v, 355). cf. Benet to Henry VIII, 12 Aug. 1531 (*State Papers*, vii, 316; *L. & P.*, v, 369), in which Benet reported that the pope had received a letter from his ambassador stating that Catherine complained of the pope's delay and that she could not obtain justice from him.

[2] cf. *L. & P.*, v, 352, 353, 354. Meanwhile the emperor was busy securing documents relevant to the marriage suit; see *L. & P.*, v, 362.

[3] Ortiz to Charles V, 22 Aug. 1531 (*L. & P.*, v, 378).

[4] Henry VIII to Ghinucci, Benet and Casale, 2 Oct. 1531 (*State Papers*, vii, 323; *L. & P.*, v, 464). The quotation is from the calendar; the original letter is in Latin: 'Neque enim convenire putamus, illius Nos aulam oratoribus ornare nostris, atque maximis nostris sumptibus honorare, qui Nobis inimicissima queque molitur'. The news of these instructions caused great uneasiness in the Vatican; see p. 174.

set forth Lutheran opinions. When this man was brought before the archbishop of Canterbury he refused to answer any interrogatories and demanded, in the first place, that secular members of the council should be present at his trial. Accordingly, the duke of Norfolk and some others were deputed to attend, and they heard several of the accused man's errors in the course of the preliminary hearings. Two days later he appealed to the king as the archbishop's sovereign, perhaps because he feared the outcome of a trial in the ecclesiastical court. The king immediately ordered that he be brought before him, and in the royal presence several bishops disputed against him. When the king read the articles of heresy charged against him and noticed that the preacher was alleged to have said that the pope was not head of the christian church, he observed that such a charge ought not to have been entered among the articles as the statement was undoubtedly true. After hearing the preacher in his own defence Henry set him at liberty and dismissed him to his own house, on condition that he preached a further sermon retracting certain points which the king did not consider to be correct. Chapuys gave it as his opinion that the preacher owed his liberty to the intervention of Anne Boleyn and her father who were, he said, 'more Lutheran than Luther himself'.[1]

Henry now busied himself in such matters and took pride in the zeal with which he repressed heresy by means of exhortation and proclamation, by argument and punishment. For example, Wolsey's former physician, the Italian Augustine de Augustinis, told the emperor in May 1531 that the king had spent the whole of one day, from nine in the morning till seven at night, examining a heretic, news which caused the emperor some wonderment.[2] The king's zeal for religious orthodoxy,

---

[1] Chapuys to Charles V, 22 Mar. 1531 (*L. & P.*, v, 148). A year later Chapuys reported that the king wished bishops not to have power to lay hands on persons accused of heresy, saying that it was not their duty to meddle with bodies, for they were merely doctors of the soul; Chapuys added that the chancellor, More, and the bishops opposed the king who was very angry, especially with the chancellor and the bishop of Winchester (see Chapuys to Charles V, 13 May 1532; *L. & P.*, v, 1014); see p. 191. In the following June Ghinucci and Benet reported to the king that the pope had complained that a priest in England had been thrown into prison for maintaining the papal authority, and that a clerk detained in the Lollards' Tower for Lutheranism had appealed to the king as head of the church (see Ghinucci and Benet to Henry VIII, 15 June 1532; *L. & P.*, v, 1096).

[2] Augustine de Augustinis to duke of Norfolk, 3 June 1531 (*L. & P.*, v, 283).

however, was tempered in favour of any heretic who expressed opinions favourable to the king in his great matter. Thus Robert Barnes, an Austin friar from Cambridge who became, under the influence of Thomas Bilney, one of the most active of the English Lutherans, had escaped in 1528 to the continent and lodged for a time with Luther, writing tracts on such subjects as justification by faith, the marriage of priests and the like. As he had expressed opinions favourable to the divorce, he was persuaded to return to England to assist in the dispute with the pope, and there, wearing secular dress, he remained unmolested for some years.[1]

When in the spring of 1532 a preacher ventured to speak against the divorce he was arrested on the king's orders and examined by the council to whom he declared that he had been moved to do what he did by the truth, the service of God and the honour of the king;[2] but when, a few weeks later, the nuncio complained that the king and council had allowed a preacher to call the pope a heretic, the duke of Norfolk told him that he need not be surprised, since the man owed his immunity to Anne Boleyn and her father.[3]

During the earlier part of this period of royal ecclesiastical activity three important sees were vacant: York, Winchester, and Lichfield and Coventry.[4] Henry requested the pope to fill two of these sees with his nominees, and in October 1531 his holiness appointed Edward Lee to York and Stephen Gardiner to Winchester, the two men on whom Henry had chiefly relied in the matter of the divorce; and in making the appointments the pope was careful to comply with the king's request that the heavy fees customarily paid on such occasions should be substantially reduced.[5] It was usual for a see to remain vacant for at least a year, and the exceptional speed with which the sees of York and Win-

---

[1] For Barnes, see Foxe, *Acts and Monuments*, v, 414-38; *D.N.B.*, art. Barnes, Robert. cf. Chapuys to Charles V, 21 Dec. 1531 (*L. & P.*, v, 593). Friar Barnes was ultimately condemned for heresy in 1540, when the divorce was a thing of the past.

[2] Chapuys to Charles V, 20 Mar. 1532 (*L. & P.*, v, 879).

[3] Chapuys to Charles V, 13 May 1532 (*L. & P.*, v, 1013).

[4] Cardinal Wolsey, who died in 1530, held the see of York and, after the death of Richard Foxe in 1528, the see of Winchester as well. Geoffrey Blythe, of Lichfield and Coventry, died in 1530.

[5] cf. Henry VIII to Clement VII, 12 Sept. 1531 (Pocock, ii, 137; *L. & P.*, v, 418); Clement VII to Henry VIII, 23 Oct. 1531 (Ehses, 183); Clement VII to Gardiner, 23 Oct. 1531 (Ehses, 184). See also Ehses, 207 (Acta consistorialia; 20 Oct. 1531), and *L. & P.*, v, 483 (bull appointing Lee to York), and *L. & P.*, v, 627(3), (8) (restitution of temporalities of York and Winchester).

chester had been filled caused Catherine to fear that it had been done to secure the presence in parliament of two more prelates who were well disposed towards the king's divorce. Her fears were increased by the suspicion that there was some new understanding between the pope and the king because, despite the fact that the king had declared himself to be supreme head of the church of England, he had sent to Rome for these appointments.[1]

3

It was tolerably clear to the lawyers of the Roman curia that, if the marriage case proceeded to judgment, sentence was likely to be pronounced in favour of Catherine. It was believed in Rome that Henry had the same expectation of the outcome, and it was feared that should he reach the point where he despaired of obtaining his desires by means of the law, he would provide his own way to his goal, and such a move was likely to involve the abolition of papal jurisdiction in England. Jacopo Salviati, the secretary of state, was acutely apprehensive that Henry would take matters into his own hands,[2] and the nuncio in England was convinced that the abolition of papal jurisdiction was threatened.[3] These opinions were no new growth. As early as the autumn of 1528 Campeggio himself had reported that Wolsey had often told him that if the divorce were not granted the authority in England of the holy see would be finished.[4] In the following spring the legate in Paris, Giovanni Salviati, reported that the French king had told him that Henry was determined upon a new marriage and that if the matter could not be arranged in Rome he would settle it in England.[5] In 1530 the nuncio

[1] Chapuys to Charles V, 26 Sept. 1531 (*L. & P.*, v, 432).
[2] J. Salviati to Campeggio, 9 June 1531 (Ehses, 176, at p. 177): 'È pericolo grande, che disperato quel re, di poter ottener per via iudiciaria quel que desidera, si risolva a far di fatto . . .'
[3] Baron Borgho to Salviati, 1 July 1531 (Ehses, 178): ' . . . che siamo minacciati di esserne levata la iurisdittione, . . .'
[4] Campeggio to J. Salviati, 17 Oct. 1528 (Ehses, 47, at p. 50): ' . . . et [Wolsey] spesso mi replica, si hoc non fiat, actum esse de auctoritate Sedis Apostolicae in hoc regno . . .'; cf. p. 65.
[5] Giovanni Salviati to Jacopo Salviati, 20 May 1529 (Ehses, 264): 'Il Cristianissimo ha opinione, che il re d'Inghilterra farà il nuovo matrimonio in ogni modo, tanto più, quanto adesso si pratica la pace, volendo haver lasciata la regina innanzi ch'ella si concluda, et pensa, che non potendo per via di Roma la farà risolvere in Inghilterra.'

in England, in the first despatch that he wrote after his arrival, reported that the king was determined that, should he not obtain a favourable decision from the pope, he would himself provide for his own case; Jacopo Salviati passed this opinion on to Campeggio.[1]

The news of Henry's last instructions to his ambassadors, at the beginning of October 1531,[2] caused great uneasiness in the Vatican, and in November Campeggio, in Brussels, was inquiring whether the emperor would be willing to execute a sentence of excommunication against Henry if such a course should prove necessary; for, said Campeggio to the emperor, the pope had learned of the instructions given to the English ambassadors requiring them to leave Rome if sentence were given against the king, and that, he said, 'might be the beginning of the abolition of obedience to his holiness and the holy see'.[3] But against these fears, which urged delay, there was the pressure of the imperialists demanding a speedy judgment, and the vociferous appeals of Catherine herself. Nevertheless, despite this pressure, the pope clung to the opinion that delay would serve best.[4] The continued delay, however, exasperated the emperor and he complained to Jerome Aleander, the nuncio, that 'it was a very strange and abominable thing, that the lust of a foolish man

[1] J. Salviati to Campeggio, 21 Oct. 1530 (Ehses, 164, at p. 165): 'Con le ultime di Vostra Signoria Rma. si sono haute lettere del Signor barone [Borgho], che son le prime dopo l'arrivar suo in Inghilterra; . . . Mostrava quella Maestà esser determinata, quando non potesse ottener questo da N. Signore, di proveder per se stessa a casi suoi . . .'

[2] See p. 170.

[3] Campeggio to Jacopo Salviati, 25 Nov. 1531 (Ehses, 189): 'Quando dissi ad S. M. la commissione, che li Signori ambasciatori Anglici tengono, di domandar licentia et partirsi in evento, che la sententia si desse etc., se ne maravigliò et disse, che potria bene esser, ma che quando non procedesse più oltre, non era di molta importantia; sopra le quali parole io come da me discorrendo dissi, che potria esser un principio di levar l'obedientia ad Sua Santità et Sede Apostolica, il che quando seguisse, saria cosa di mala natura, et che Sua Santità saria sforzata procedere contro di quel re et regno per defensione dell' auctorità et libertà ecclesiastica, il che però saria con poco effecto, quando non le fusse apparecchiata l'executione, et che questo toccheria ad S. M. come primogenito della chiesa'. Campeggio was now legate to Charles V.

[4] Jacopo Salviati to Campeggio, 24 Oct. 1531 (Ehses, 185): 'Si procede tuttavia nella causa d'Inghilterra, et poichè cosi piace a Sua Maestà Cesarea et alla Serma. regina, Sua Santità lascia andar la iustitia per il corso suo; vero è, che lei è della medesima opinione, che la vera cura di questo male fusse il guadagnar tempo et maximamente si vero fusse quello che di qualche luogo, non so però quanto degno di fede, s'intende che quella Signora Anna comincia a declinar quel tanto favor, nel qual era appresso il Sermo. re'.

and a foolish woman should hold up a lawsuit and inflict an outrageous burden upon such a good and blameless queen'.[1]

To the pope, anxious to avoid proceeding with the marriage cause, the unofficial presence in Rome of Carne, the excusator, was not altogether unwelcome, for the wrangles before the Rota about his status and his capacity to be heard effectively served to block the progress of the suit. The discussions concerning Carne, with their attendant delays, occupied the greater part of October; as Benet reported to the king, 'as yet we be here in disputation upon your highness's letters, whether by them Mr Carne should be admitted to lay in the matter excusatory or not, and so all this while the party adverse is stopped from their process'.[2] At the same time the emperor was maintaining his pressure to secure, if possible, a speedy decision in the marriage cause;[3] but the activities of the Spanish ambassador, Miguel Mai, and the lawyer, Dr Ortiz, to procure the exclusion of Carne served only to prolong the delay.[4] Benet was pleased with the way things were going and reported to the king that Carne had 'aquitted himself like a clerk'.[5] At the beginning of November, however, the king wrote to the pope recalling Benet,[6] and the latter left Rome in the middle of the month bearing a letter of commendation from his holiness.[7]

The Rota continued to hear representations throughout November, and Carne's position was the principal matter discussed. But however much the pope might wish to postpone the conclusion of the case, some

---

[1] Aleander to Sanga and J. Salviati, 19 Nov. 1531 (Ehses, 188): The emperor's words, as reported by Aleander, are: 'Alhora S. M. mi disse, ch'era una cosa molto strana et abominevole, al appetito di un folo et di una fola tenersi suspesa la iustitia et farsi tanto oltraggio et stracio ad una sì buona et sancta regina.'
[2] Benet to Henry VIII, 21 Oct. 1531 (*State Papers*, vii, 327; *L. & P.*, v, 484).
[3] cf. Charles V to Mai, 22 Oct. 1531 (*L. & P.*, **v**, 485).
[4] cf. Ortiz to Charles V, 24 Oct. 1531 (*L. & P.*, v, 489); Mai to de los Cobos, 24 Oct. 1531 (*L. & P.*, v, 491); Ortiz to Chapuys, 24 Oct. 1531 (*L. & P.*, v, 492); Mai to de los Cobos, 6 Nov. 1531 (*L. & P.*, v, 516: 'In the English cause they make me mad. They pass us on from one audience to another. I have been continually busy about the legal allegations (*de dreccho*), and in soliciting them, but I do not make much progress.'); Ortiz to Charles V, 6 Nov. 1531 (*L. & P.*, v, 517); Ortiz to the Empress, 7 Nov. 1531 (*L. & P.*, v, 518); Mai to Charles V, 30 Nov. 1531 (*L. & P.*, v, 556); Catherine was still protesting to the emperor in November; cf. Catherine of Aragon to Charles V, 6 Nov. 1531 (*L. & P.*, v, 513).
[5] Benet to Henry VIII, 7 Nov. 1531 (*State Papers*, vii, 328; *L. & P.*, v, 520). Carne was a layman.
[6] Henry VIII to Clement VII, 4 Nov. 1531 (Pocock, ii, 141; *L. & P.*, v, 511).
[7] Clement VII to Henry VIII, 19 Nov. 1531 (Pocock, ii, 142; *L. & P.*, v, 539).

decision could not be endlessly avoided. The majority of the Rota was, by now, of the opinion that Carne should not be heard further.[1] The decision, however, must be that of the cardinals in consistory, and in order to stave off a decision the English representatives requested that the point should be argued by lawyers. When the Spanish ambassador agreed to this proposal, rather than waste further time by disputing it, the Englishmen demanded an adjournment of four to six months in order that they might bring lawyers to Rome for the purpose. On 11 December an English orator appeared before the consistory seeking the adjournment, but it was decreed that an adjournment should be granted only until the Epiphany (6 January); the lawyers were directed to be ready for public argument on the first day after that feast, and they were told that they could expect no further adjournment.[2]

Towards the end of December William Benet left England to return to his post in Rome. Henry wrote to the pope to tell him that he had read the letter which Benet had brought and that Benet was returning to his embassy. But the greater part of Henry's letter was devoted to his insistence that he should not plead his case in Rome either personally or by proctor, a point on which the king asserted that books and doctors were unanimous. The king instructed Benet to repair to Rome as quickly as possible and there 'besides the special matter contained in these instructions, by all other ways and means that can be excogitated or devised, practice the delay and putting over of the process there, until such time as the emperor be passed into Spain'. Henry was of opinion that if Benet carried out his instructions satisfactorily a delay of six months

---

[1] cf. Ortiz to the Empress, 23 Nov. 1531 (*L. & P.*, v, 545); Ortiz to Charles V, 28 Nov. 1531 (*L. & P.*, v, 553); Cardinal of Osma to Charles V, 4 Dec. 1531 (*L. & P.*, v, 565); Mai to Charles V, 12 Dec. 1531 (*L. & P.*, v, 580). Ortiz was anxious that the emperor should be in no doubt as to his zeal; on 28 Nov. he wrote, not altogether truthfully, that his 'zeal in the matrimonial cause of the queen of England has had the result that great progress has been made' since the end of the vacation (*L. & P.*, v, 553), and on 10 Dec. he wrote to the empress saying that his 'services in the matrimonial cause of the queen of England have been attended with complete success', and he went on to claim the whole credit for a number of things (*L. & P.*, v, 575). The emperor commended him for his valuable services but warned him not to do anything which he had not first concerted with the ambassador, for otherwise he would commit a grave error (Charles V to Ortiz, 28 Jan. 1532 (*L. & P.*, v, 761).

[2] Ehses, 207, 208 (Acta consistorialia; Dec. 11, 1531); cf. Mai to Charles V, 12 Dec. 1531 (*L. & P.*, v, 580).

might be gained.[1] Benet reached Rome on 3 February and Muxetula, reporting his arrival, remarked that he 'seemingly brings nothing but the usual delays'.[2]

When the consistory met on 8 January 1532 the imperial ambassador and queen Catherine's advocate appeared and demanded that the cause should proceed. Called upon by the pope to reply, the English ambassadors put forward Carne to speak on their behalf. He said that his efforts to bring skilled lawyers to Rome had been hampered by the adverse party and he asked the pope for a remedy. In the result both parties were ordered to put their contentions in writing. A further consistory on 12 January was adjourned, but at a consistory on 15 January it was ordered that there should be a final adjournment until the end of the month, a delay that was accepted by the Spanish ambassador with a bad grace.[3] But before Henry could learn of these proceedings he had despatched Edmund Bonner to Rome, with full instructions concerning every point of his affairs there; Carne and Benet were instructed to keep Bonner fully informed, and Bonner himself was instructed to consult with Gardiner, then at the French court, on his way to Rome.[4]

Meanwhile the pope had learned from his nuncio in England that the king had finally separated from Catherine. When the nuncio remonstrated with Henry concerning his treatment of the queen, Henry had replied that she was his wife and was bound to obey him in all things, yet she had refused to meet his wishes with regard to the marriage cause and he had therefore been forced to live apart from her. When the nuncio remarked that the pope could not defer judgment but must give a decision, and urged Henry to send a mandate to Rome

[1] Henry VIII to Clement VII, 28 Dec. 1531 (Pocock, ii, 148; *L. & P.*, v, 610; cf. Ehses, 191); Henry VIII to Benet, Dec. 1531 (Pocock, ii, 144; *L. & P.*, v, 611).
[2] Bishop of Auxerre to the cardinal Tournon, 7 Feb. 1532 (*L. & P.*, v, 781); Muxetula to Charles V, 8 Feb. 1532 (*L. & P.*, v, 790). cf. Muxetula to Charles V, 24 Jan. 1532 (*L. & P.*, v, 744); Mai to Charles V, 25 Jan. 1532 (*L. & P.*, v, 747); Benet and Casale to Henry VIII, n. d. (*L. & P.*, v, 777).
[3] Ehses, 208, 209 (Acta consistorialia); Carne to Henry VIII, 20 Jan. 1532 (*L. & P.*, v, 731); Mai to Charles V, 25 Jan. 1532 (*L. & P.*, v, 747); Ortiz to Charles V, 25 Jan. 1532 (*L. & P.*, v, 748); and cf. the enclosure in Ortiz's letter of 25 Jan. to de los Cobos (ibid. 738).
[4] Henry VIII to Benet and Carne, 21 Jan. 1532 (*L. & P.*, v, 732); Henry VIII to Ghinucci and Casale, 21 Jan. 1532 (*State Papers*, vii, 337; *L. & P.*, v, 733); Henry VIII to Gardiner, Jan. 1532 (*L. & P.*, v, 742).

enabling his representatives there to appear on his behalf, the king remarked that the pope was not learned enough to judge the cause and his advisers were venial.[1] The nuncio's report was distressing enough, but more serious was the rumour that Henry was cohabiting with Anne Boleyn.[2] The cardinal of Ancona,[3] the principal lawyer in the consistory, who had throughout been a zealous supporter of Catherine, had come to the opinion, which he communicated to the pope, that matters had reached such a pass that the king should be ordered, under pain of excommunication, to restore the queen to her position and to dismiss Anne Boleyn.[4] Pressed by Dr Ortiz, the pope despatched a brief addressed to Henry urging him to recall Catherine and to 'restore to her the honour as a queen, and the affection as a wife, which she ought to have from you, and to send away Anne, till our sentence between you has been given'; and the pope went on to say that he would be grieved should it become necessary to have recourse to law to compel the king's compliance.[5] This brief was not sent direct to the king but was despatched to the emperor who, in his turn, forwarded it to Catherine herself; the queen, however, retained it in her possession until the following May.[6]

The consistory met again on Wednesday 7 February, 1532, and there appeared Antonio Muxetula on behalf of the emperor and Juan Aloisio on behalf of queen Catherine who asked that the cause might proceed

---

[1] Chapuys to Charles V, 4 Jan. 1532 (*L. & P.*, v, 696); paper by Ortiz, dated 22 Jan. 1532, and enclosed in a letter to de los Cobos dated 25 Jan. 1532 (*L. & P.*, v, 738). In the marriage cause, Henry was asserting that his marriage to Catherine was invalid.

[2] cf. Ortiz to Charles V, 30 Dec. 1531 (*L. & P.*, v, 615); Ortiz reported the rumour that Anne Boleyn, to whom he referred as *la manceba*, had miscarried; *L. & P.*, v, 628 (the case of Roger Dycker who had spread the rumour that the king was about to take another wife). The bishop of Bayonne, who returned to Rome from England towards the end of 1531, led the pope to suppose that the king might have gone so far as to marry Anne Boleyn; see the cardinal of Osma to Charles V, 4 Dec. 1531 (*L. & P.*, v, 565).

[3] Pietro de Accolti, bishop of Sabino and cardinal of Ancona; he was called 'the old man', to distinguish him from his nephew Benedict de Accolti, Cardinal of Ravenna, who was called 'the young man'.

[4] cf. Ortiz to Charles V, 30 Dec. 1531 (*L. & P.*, v, 615).

[5] Clement VII to Henry VIII, 25 Jan. 1532 (Le Grand, iii, 560-5; Pocock, ii, 166; *L. & P.*, v, 750); cf. Mai to Charles V, 25 Jan. 1532 (*L. & P.*, v, 747), and Ortiz to Charles V, 25 Jan. 1532 (*L. & P.*, v, 748).

[6] Ortiz to Charles V, 16 Feb. 1532 (*L. & P.*, v, 809); see p. 193.

without delay. Carne appeared as excusator and complained that he had been prevented by the emperor from bringing lawyers on behalf of the king from Padua and Bologna, which were within the imperial dominions. Carne, however, expressed himself ready to discuss the 'matters excusatory' in a public audience if means were provided to enable him to obtain the services of the Italian lawyers. It was accordingly determined that a public disputation should be held before the pope at the end of the following week.[1]

The consistory met again on 16 February, the Friday after Ash Wednesday, for the purpose of holding the disputation, and there were present, as well as the pope and the cardinals, the auditor of the Rota and certain prelates and learned men. On the one side there appeared the advocates for the emperor and queen Catherine, and on the other the excusator, Carne. Carne put forward twenty-five propositions and he proposed that each of them be argued for a day.[2] Such a programme involved a very lengthy delay and was strenuously opposed by the queen's advocates who argued that the only point for discussion should be whether the excusator was entitled to be heard. In the outcome it was ordered that all the propositions should be discussed but that three

[1] Ehses, 209, 210 (Acta consistorialia); bishop of Auxerre to Montmorenci, 7 Feb. 1532 (*L. & P.*, v, 782); Muxetula to Charles V, 8 Feb. 1532 (*L. & P.*, v, 790); Carne to Henry VIII, 11 Feb. 1532 (*State Papers*, vii, 346; *L. & P.*, v, 797). In a letter from Rodrigo Niño, the imperial ambassador at Venice, to Mai, dated 3 Feb. 1532, Niño reported that the English agents had 'been very urgent with the Signory to send some professors of Padua to Rome to support the king's cause'. Niño told the Signory that they had nothing to do but stand to their determination not to allow any of the professors to meddle with the matter, adding that he had, however, no commission to speak with them on the subject (see *L. & P.*, v, 770). Since the validity of Carne's mandate was being attacked, and it was contended that he could not be heard without a valid mandate, Carne asked for 'a more exact mandate' to be sent; meanwhile the English agents decided that they would not only not use the existing mandate but would refuse to acknowledge that they possessed it; cf. Ghinucci and Benet to Henry VIII, 8 Feb. 1532 (Pocock, ii, 174; *L. & P.*, v, 785); Carne to Henry VIII, 11 Feb. 1532 (*State Papers*, vii, 346; *L. & P.*, v, 797); English ambassadors at Rome to Henry VIII, 13 Feb. 1532 (*L. & P.*, v, 800). This led Henry to complain to the pope that Carne was not admitted as excusator (Henry VIII to Clement VII, 28 Feb. 1532; Pocock, ii, 207; *L. & P.*, v, 829), and he informed Ghinucci, Benet and Casale that he had supplied the defect in the mandate, but he told the ambassadors to urge the pope not to rest the king's cause upon such a trifle (Henry VIII to Ghinucci, Benet and Casale, 29 Feb. 1532; *State Papers*, vii, 350; *L. & P.*, v, 833).
[2] For Carne's propositions, see Pocock, ii, 663, 664.

N

were to be considered at each consistory[1]. Accordingly three of Carne's propositions were discussed on 28 February[2], and a further three on 6 March.[3] Further consistories were held during March, April, May and June, but in that held on 8 July the pope decreed that the process should be adjourned until the following October to enable the king to produce his mandate for a proctor in the principal cause, and ordered that otherwise the case should proceed.[4]

[1] Ehses, 210; bishop of Auxerre to du Prat, 22 Feb. 1532 (*L. & P.*, v, 815); cardinal of Osma to the Commendador Mayor, 29 Feb. 1532 (*L. & P.*, v, 835).
[2] Ehses, 210; the propositions were those numbered 4, 5 and 2 in Pocock, loc. cit.
[3] Ehses, 211; the propositions were those numbered 1, 3 and 15 in Pocock, loc. cit.
[4] Ehses, 211; Benet, Carne and Bonner to Henry VIII, 23 Mar. 1532 (Burnet, i, Coll. of Rec., 111 (wrongly dated); *L. & P.*, v, 892); Carne and Bonner to Henry VIII, 23 April 1532 (Burnet, i, Coll. of Rec., 116; *L. & P.*, v, 972); Ortiz to Charles V, 9 July 1532 (*L. & P.*, v, 1160); bishop of Auxerre to Montmorenci, 13 July 1532 (*L. & P.*, v, 1170); Ghinucci, Benet and Sir Gregory Casale to Henry VIII, 13 July 1532 (Burnet, i, Coll. of Rec., 118; *L. & P.*, v, 1171); Carne and Bonner to Henry VIII, 15 July 1532 (Pocock, ii, 292; *L. & P.*, v, 1172); Benet and Casale to Henry VIII, 15 July 1532 (Pocock, ii, 288; *L. & P.*, v, 1173); Sir Gregory Casale to Henry VIII, n. d. (*L. & P.*, v, 1174). The papal decree of 8 July is printed in Pocock, ii, 280. In June the cardinal of Siguenza, who was well disposed towards Catherine, had complained: 'In the cause of England I am not an agent, but a judge. God knows the grief it has caused me since I have been here [Rome]. The chief obstacles are the continued threats of the king to renounce obedience to the Holy See, the coming of the Turk, and the Pope's cowardice' (cardinal of Siguenza to the Commendador Mayor, 22 June 1532; *L. & P.*, v, 1112).

XI

The Submission
of the Clergy

Meanwhile, parliament had re-assembled. In the spring it had been prorogued to 14 October without discussing the question of the divorce;[1] it was further prorogued to 6 November and, on account of the insalubrity of the air in London and Westminster, was again prorogued to 15 January, 1532.[2] Accordingly, parliament met at Westminster on Monday 15 January, and the session proved to be a notable one. Members were already in an ill humour at being summoned once again from their homes, and they had no liking for much of the legislation that was put before them. Their grumbling discontent continued throughout the session and the king had, perforce, to accept much plain speaking on many subjects, even his marriage. But a new influence in English politics was now making itself felt.

In the late autumn of 1531 Thomas Cromwell became one of the inner circle of councillors who were the real advisers of the king, exercising the predominating influence in government;[3] Norfolk and Gardiner were no longer the king's principal advisers. Hitherto the king's policy, if such a word can be applied to the shifts and turns of the preceding years, had been to force the pope to act as the king wished. He sought to carry

---

[1] See p. 161.

[2] See *L. & P.*, v, 559(5) (writ to Sir Thomas More, chancellor, duke of Norfolk, treasurer, and the earl of Sussex and the bishop of London, for the further prorogation of parliament); cf. Chapuys to Charles V, 24 Oct. 1531 (*L. & P.*, v, 488). For the text of the proclamation (dated 4 Oct. 1531) proroguing parliament to 6 Nov., see *T.R.P.*, i, 204; the subsequent prorogation was on 21 Oct.

[3] cf. Elton, *Tudor Revolution in Government* (Cambridge 1953), 90, 91. Cromwell was not yet, however, the dominating influence, for in Jan. 1532, in a letter to Gardiner, who was not only ambassador to the French king but still principal secretary, he found it prudent to minimize his own importance; see Merriman, *Life and Letters of Thomas Cromwell* (Oxford 1902), i, 344.

out this policy, which had throughout been futile and doomed to failure, by diplomatic pressure at Rome and by clumsy attempts at bribery designed to secure sufficient royal adherents among the cardinals to ensure that a decision was not reached in consistory.[1] Under Cromwell's direction the old policy was not completely abandoned, it is true, but new means were adopted to accompany and supplement the old. Parliament was now to be turned against the pope, and under Cromwell's guidance Henry learned what could be done by statute and how great a source of power he could find in parliament. Parliament had already dealt roughly with the English clergy, it is true, but it had not yet touched the papacy; in 1532 it began the process that culminated in the complete destruction of papal jurisdiction in England and the withdrawal of Englishmen from obedience to the pope.

The first few weeks of the new session were devoted to the discussion of a bill whose purpose was to strengthen the feudal rights of the king. The king's right of *primer seisin* enabled him to exact a year's profits from a tenant in chief upon descent of lands to an heir of full age. If, however the lands were held to uses and so did not pass by descent, the king's right was rendered nugatory, and so it became a widespread custom for tenants in chief to make feoffments of land to uses in order to avoid the heavy feudal payments due upon a succession.[2] The purpose of the bill was to put a stop to such conveyancing practices, and it is perhaps not surprising that it met with determined opposition from a body of men whose pockets it would hit severely if it passed into law; after much discontented discussion it was rejected.[3] And when the commons were asked for an aid for the defence of the Scottish border they refused to vote more than a fifteenth, although a tenth had been asked for. In the course of the later discussion of the aid, one member, Temse, stated that the fortification of the Scottish border was needless because the Scots could do no harm without foreign aid. He asserted that the best defence was to maintain justice in the kingdom and friendship with the emperor, and for that purpose parliament should petition the king to take back his wife and treat her well; otherwise the kingdom

---

[1] cf. Pocock, ii, 144 ff., 213 ff., 252 ff., 339.
[2] cf. Hall, *Chronicle*, ii, 203, 204.
[3] Chapuys to Charles V, 30 Jan. 1532 (*L. & P.*, v, 762); Chapuys to Charles V, 14 Feb. 1532 (*Span. Cal.*, iv, pt. 2, 899; *L. & P.*, v, 805); cf. Hall, *Chronicle*, ii, 203, 204 (as might be expected, Hall deplored the refusal to pass the bill relating to *primer seisin*).

would be ruined and the emperor, who would not abandon the rights of his aunt, would do them more harm than any other.[1]

By the middle of February the commons had discussed little more than the bill relating to *primer seisin* and the fifteenth; and they were in an ill humour.[2] The council, however, were ready to take advantage of the bad temper into which the commons had been thrown. Towards the end of February there were introduced into the house of commons a bill relating to the payments of annates, which was anti-papal, and a petition, to be presented to the king, which was markedly anti-clerical. In their exasperation at the feudal and fiscal demands of the king the commons readily gave sympathetic attention to anti-clerical grievances.

The petition, which came to be known as the 'Commons' Supplication against the Ordinaries', was, in the main, the work of Thomas Cromwell.[3] He took as his foundation an existing parliamentary paper which was, in all probability, the petition listing the grievances of the commons against the ecclesiastics drawn up during the session of 1529 but never presented.[4] As revised by Cromwell, in successive drafts that are still extant, the document became a violent attack upon clerical jurisdiction and emphasized the one point that touched the crown directly and was well calculated to appeal to Henry, namely, that the laws by which the church was governed, affecting clergy and laity alike, did not depend upon the assent of either king or commons. It seems fairly clear that the

---

[1] Chapuys to Charles V, 2 May 1532 (*L. & P.*, v, 989); cf. Le Grand, i, 223, 224, and Hall, *Chronicle*, ii, 205, 210.

[2] Chapuys to Charles V, 14 Feb. 1532 (*L. & P.*, v, 805; *Span. Cal.*, iv, pt. 2, 899 (p. 383)): 'Nothing else [besides the bill relating to *primer seisin*] has been done in the said parliament except the prohibition of importing new wines before Candlemas. . . . They have also tried for some days to prohibit the importation of silk cloth . . .' (*Span. Cal.*) In the same letter Chapuys reported that the duke of Norfolk had convened a meeting of a number of persons, whose identity was unknown, at which he sounded them upon the question of jurisdiction in the marriage suit, asserting that the jurisdiction in matrimonial causes was a temporal one and not spiritual, and so belonged to the king who was emperor in his kingdom, and not to the pope.

[3] For the genesis and development of the Supplication, see G. R. Elton, 'The Commons' Supplication of 1532: Parliamentary Manoeuvres in the Reign of Henry VIII', in *E.H.R.* (1951), lxvi, 507-34, which should be read in conjunction with J. P. Cooper, 'The Supplication against the Ordinaries Reconsidered', in *E.H.R.* (1957), lxxvii, 616-41.

[4] See p. 117.

greater part of Cromwell's redrafting was done during 1529.[1] Cromwell's drafts remained in his possession and it seems that at the very beginning of 1532 he brought them forward and they were considered by the council. The council subjected Cromwell's work to further revision, and, to judge by the existing draft upon which they worked, most of this revision was done by Thomas Audley who, although speaker of the house of commons, was also chancellor of the duchy of Lancaster and a king's serjeant. In all probability the final draft was in existence before the session of 1532 began.[2] Thus the Supplication, which originated with a petition by the commons in 1529, was given its final form by the council in 1532.

After the unpalatable financial measures which the council had tried, in vain, to get through the house, the Supplication proved to be a welcome relief, and the commons turned to it with relish. Hall, a member of the house, recorded that they 'sore complained of the cruelty of the ordinaries' and that 'when this matter and other exactions done by the clergy in their courts were long debated in the common house, at last it was concluded and agreed, that all the griefs which the temporal men were grieved with, should be put in writing and delivered to the king, which by great advice was done'.[3] Accordingly, on 18 March, a deputa-

[1] cf. Elton, op. cit. *E.H.R.*, lxvi, 515-20. The drafts in question are (using Dr Elton's sigla): A (the original commons' petition of 1529), containing about half the points of the Supplication; it is in P.R.O., State Papers, Henry VIII, vol. 50, fos. 203, 204, and is calendared at *L. & P.*, v, 1016(3). A was supplemented by B which contains the remainder of the Supplication; B is in P.R.O., State Papers, Henry VIII, vol. 56, fos. 40-3, and is calendared at *L. & P.*, v, 6043(7) (misplaced in the calendar). At this stage the document was thus in two parts. Further drafts were made of each part (C_1 and C_2) which, though written separately, belong together (C); C is in P.R.O., Theol. Tracts, vol. 7, arts. 21, 22, and is calendared at *L. & P.*, v, 1016(4); C is the draft printed by Merriman, *Life and Letters of Thomas Cromwell* (Oxford 1902), i, 104 et seq. and it is also the basis of the version of the Supplication printed in *G. & H.*, 145-153. All these drafts (A-C) belong to 1529.

[2] cf. Elton, op. cit. *E.H.R.*, lxvi, 511 et seq. The drafts C1 and C_2 (see preceding note) were further corrected and the next draft (D) combined the two separate parts into one document; D is in P.R.O., State Papers, Henry VIII, vol. 50, fos. 193-202, and is calendared at *L. & P.*, v, 1016(2). From D a fair copy (E) was made. E is in P.R.O., Theol. Tracts, vol. 1, art 22, and is calendared at *L. & P.*, v, 1016(1); it is printed, with modernized spelling, in Ogle, *The Tragedy of the Lollards' Tower* (Oxford 1949), 324-30.

[3] Hall, *Chronicle*, ii, 202. Meanwhile the policy of putting pressure upon the pope was not abandoned. Writing to Benet, ambassador in Rome, on 28 Feb. 1532, Norfolk said, 'For, notwithstondyng the infenyte clamours of the tem-

tion from the commons, led by the speaker, presented the Supplication to the king.[1]

Immediately afterwards, parliament passed the anti-papal statute in restraint of annates.[2] Annates, or first fruits, were the first year's profits of a spiritual preferment and were payable to the pope, forming part of the papal revenue.[3] The payment of annates was not popular,[4] but the preamble to the act, as was the way with Henrician preambles, undoubtedly exaggerated the grievance when it asserted that

there hath passed out of this realm unto the court of Rome since the second year of the reign of the most noble prince of famous memory King Henry VII unto this present time, under the name of annates or first fruits paid for the expedition of bulls of archbishoprics and bishoprics, the sum of eight hundred thousand ducats, amounting in sterling money at the least to eight score thousand pounds, besides other great and intolerable sums which have yearly been conveyed to the said court of Rome by many other ways and means, to the great impoverishment of this realm.

The act then recited that

albeit that our said sovereign lord the king and all his natural subjects as well spiritual as temporal be as obedient, devout, Catholic, and humble children of God and Holy Church as any people be within any realm christened, yet the said exactions of annates or first fruits be so intolerable and importable to this realm that it is considered and declared by the whole body of this realm now represented . . . in this present parliament that the king's highness before

[1] Hall, *Chronicle*, ii, 202, 203.
[2] 23 Hen. VIII, c. 20 (*Statutes of the Realm*, iii, 385). The act is printed in *G. & H.*, 178-86, and (in part) in Tanner, *Tudor Constitutional Documents*, 25-9. In the house of lords the bill was opposed by all the bishops and abbots present, but by only one lay lord; cf. Chapuys to Charles V, 20 Mar. 1532 (*L. & P.*, v, 879).
[3] See *Termes de la Ley*, s.v.; the amount of the annates was calculated according to a valuation made in 1292. Annates were introduced into England by Pandulph, the papal legate during the reigns of John and Henry III (cf. 1 Bl. Com., 274; *Bishop of Rochester* v. *Le Fanu*, [1906] 2 Ch. 513). Although annates were, theoretically, payable in respect of any spiritual preferment, they were of practical importance only in the case of bishoprics.
[4] Annates had formed the subject of grievances in the past; a statute of 1404 (6 Hen. IV, c. 1) referred to them as a 'horrible mischief and damnable custom'.

poraltye here, in Parlment, agaynst the mysusyng of the sprytuell jurysdiccion; yet in His Highnes doth remayne to stop all such effectes, and woll do so, onles ill and unkynde handlyng enforce him to consent to the same. I asseure you this realme dyd never grudge the 10th part agaynst the abusys of the Churche at no Parlment in my days, as they do now' (*State Papers*, vii, 349).

Almighty God is bound as by the duty of a good christian prince, for the conservation and preservation of the good estate and commonwealth of this his realm, to do all that in him is to obviate, repress, and redress the said abusions and exactions of annates or first fruits.

It was then provided that the payment of annates should cease and that no one thereafter appointed to a bishopric or archbishopric within the realm should pay annates, upon pain of forfeiture of all his property. The act then went on to provide that if the court of Rome should delay or deny, in consequence of the non-payment of annates, 'bulls apostolic and other things requisite' for the consecration of a prelate presented to a see, that prelate should be consecrated without such bulls; it was, however, provided, for the recompense of the court of Rome, that fees should be paid for the preparation of the necessary bulls and documents, calculated at the rate of five per centum of the annual revenue of the see in question.

Then followed a singular innovation in English statute law. It was recited that parliament, being unwilling to use extremity without urgent cause, had committed the matter to the king, who was authorized to try to reach a composition with the pope over the payment of annates; and if such a composition were concluded it should have all the force and effect of law; in this connection it was further provided that the king should, at any time before the feast of Easter 1533, or before the beginning of the next parliament, declare by letters patent whether the act should have effect or not. The act concluded by providing that should an amicable arrangement between the pope and the king not be reached and the pope attempt to vex the country by interdict, excommunication or other censures, 'all and all manner sacraments, sacramentals, ceremonies or other divine service of Holy Church' should continue to be ministered, and the interdicts and censures should not be published or executed.[1]

The act was designed as a bargaining counter by means of which it was hoped to extort concessions from the pope in the marriage cause.

---

[1] The clauses of the act whereby its operation was postponed and the king empowered to bring it into force by letters patent, were the work of Cromwell; see Elton, 'Note on the first Act of Annates', in *B.I.H.R.*, xxiii (1950), 203, 204, where there is printed the original draft of the clauses in Cromwell's hand, and corrected by him. When it became plain that the hoped for concession from Rome would not be forthcoming, the act was brought into force by letters patent dated 9 July 1533 (see *L. & P.*, vi, 793, and p. 251).

Writing to his ambassadors in Rome immediately after the act had been passed, Henry sent them a copy so that they might explain 'to the cardinals who are moved by their interests how this statute will be to their advantage or disadvantage'; and the ambassadors would easily see, said Henry, that the act was so contrived that the cardinals favourable to him would rejoice at it. The pope and the cardinals were to be assured that Henry had taken care that the question of annates should be referred to his decision and the 'mouth of parliament stopped'; the pope and cardinals need not fear his decision, but if they wished to derive advantage from the statute they would have to show themselves deserving of it.[1]

While the act in conditional restraint of annates was anti-papal in character, the Commons' Supplication was the means by which the clergy were reduced to complete subjection. After reciting that the 'uncharitable behaviour and dealing of divers ordinaries, their commissaries and substitutes' had caused much vexation to the king's subjects in the spiritual courts, from which much discord had arisen, the Supplication proceeded to set out twelve 'special particular griefs'.

The most important of these 'particular griefs', and the one that determined the principal character of the whole Supplication, was the first:

First, the prelates and other of the clergy of this your realm, being your subjects, in their convocations by them holden within this your realm, have made and daily make divers fashions of laws and ordinances concerning temporal things: and some of them be repugnant to the laws and statutes of your realm, not having nor requiring your most royal assent to the same laws by them so made, nor any assent or knowledge of your lay subjects is had to the same, nor to them published and known in the English tongue: Albeit divers and sundry of the said laws extend in certain cases to your excellent person, your liberty and prerogative royal, and to the interdiction of your lands and possessions: and some likewise to the goods and possessions of your lay subjects, declaring the infringers of the same laws so by them made not only to incur into the terrible censures of excommunication, but also into the detestable crime and sin of heresy: by the which divers of your most humble and obedient lay subjects be brought into this ambiguity, whether they may do and execute your laws according to your jurisdiction royal of this your realm for dread of the same pains and censures comprised in the said laws so by them made in their convocations, to the great trouble and inquietation

[1] Henry VIII to Ghinucci, Benet and Casale, 21 Mar. 1532 (*State Papers*, vii, 360; *L. & P.*, v, 886). The letter is in Latin.

of your said humble, loving and obedient lay subjects: and as they suppose, under the supportation of your majesty, the same laws so made are against your jurisdiction and prerogative royal.[1]

The Supplication went on to complain of such grievances as the trivial and vexatious nature of many of the causes promoted by ordinaries against laymen, especially the poor; the citation of laymen before ecclesiastical courts out of their dioceses; the excessive fees taken in ecclesiastical courts; the delays and fees in connection with the probate of wills; the exaction of mortuaries and tithes; the methods by which ecclesiastical persons obtained prescriptive titles against the laity; the fees, first fruits and private arrangements exacted and made at institutions to benefices; the provision of infants to benefices by ordinaries; the excessive number of holy days that must be observed; and the intrusion of ecclesiastical persons into lay offices. The Supplication accordingly prayed the king, as 'the only sovereign lord, protector and defender' of both the clergy and the laity, to remedy the matters complained of and to 'bring into perpetual unity your said subjects spiritual and temporal'.[2]

When the Supplication was presented to the king on 18 March[3] he received it with moderate graciousness, although he remarked that the commons could scarcely expect much consideration of their grievances so long as they refused to pass the bill concerned with *primer seisin*; and he made some observations on the inconsistency displayed by their petition for the early dissolution of parliament and their expressed desire to bring about peace between clergy and laity. According to Hall, when the king received the Supplication he paused a while before addressing the speaker, and then, in the course of his remarks, he said.

I will hear the party that is accused speak before I give any sentence: your book [i.e. the Supplication] containeth divers articles of great and weighty matters,

[1] Where quotations are made from the Supplication they are taken from Ogle, *Tragedy of the Lollards' Tower*, where it is printed, with modernized spelling, from the final fair copy, E (see p. 184, note 2); the version in *G. & H.*, 145, is based on an earlier draft, C (see p. 184, note 1). A comparison of the two texts is interesting and instructive. The above passage is at Ogle, op. cit., 325.
[2] In relation to the complaint about citation before ecclesiastical courts, parliament passed the statute 23 Hen. VIII, c. 9, which provided that no person should be cited out of the diocese in which he dwelt, except in certain cases. The act was repealed by the Ecclesiastical Jurisdiction Measure 1963, which came into force on 1 Mar. 1965.
[3] See pp. 184, 185.

and as I perceive, it is against the spiritual persons and prelates of our realm, of which thing you desire a redress and a reformation, which desire and request is more contrariant to your last petition: for you require to have the parliament dissolved and to depart into your countries [i.e. counties], and yet you would have a reformation of your griefs with all diligence: . . . For I have sent to you a bill concerning wards and *primer seisin*, in which things I am greatly wronged: wherefore I have offered you reason as I think, yea, and so thinketh all the lords, for they have set their hands to the book [i.e. the bill]: therefore I assure you, if you will not take some reasonable end now when it is offered, I will search out the extremity of the law, and then will I not offer you so much again: with this answer, the Speaker and his company departed.[1]

Soon afterwards, as Easter was approaching, parliament was prorogued to 10 April.[2]

The king passed the Supplication to Warham who brought it before convocation on 12 April; the answer was ready on 19 April.[3] Warham's part in drafting the Answer is unknown to us, but it is clear that the principal part was taken by Stephen Gardiner, still only thirty-four years of age and recently appointed bishop of Winchester as a reward for his services as the king's secretary. Fisher, the one tower of moral strength among them, took no part, for he was not present at this convocation, having been barred from parliament in 1532 by the king's orders; in May he was ill at his house in Lambeth. The Answer of the Ordinaries is a very lengthy document in which the bishops, describing themselves as the king's 'orators and daily bounden bedesmen', began by assuring Henry that there was 'no such discord, debate, variance, or breach of peace on our part' against the laity as the commons had asserted. Each of the commons' 'griefs' was then dealt with in general terms, for such general allegations as appeared in the Supplication could only be refuted by general denials. They expounded matters of principle soundly and well, but the underlying assumption of the whole Answer is that all was well and could not be bettered. The general line of defence was that the bishops were blameless; if the matters complained of had actually occurred the bishops did not know of it, but in any case the fault must be imputed to the individual concerned and could not be laid to the blame of the whole clergy. On reading the Answer one is left

---

[1] Hall, *Chronicle*, ii, 203.
[2] Hall, *Chronicle*, ii, 204.
[3] Wilkins, *Concilia*, iii, 748. The Answer of the Ordinaries is printed, correctly, in *G. & H.*, 154-76.

with the impression that the bishops were uneasily aware that there was substance in the Commons' Supplication but were determined, somehow, to deflect the attack.

On 30 April the king sent for the speaker and some others of the house of commons and delivered to them the Answer of the Ordinaries. According to Hall, Henry said to them: 'We think their answer will smally please you, for it seemeth to us very slender.' Hall's own opinion of the Answer was that it 'was very sophistical, and nothing avoiding the griefs of the lay people'. And Henry, alluding to Temse's outburst, took occasion to express his astonishment that open comment should have been made in parliament on the absence of the queen from the king's side, remarking that it was not a matter for discussion in parliament since 'it touched his soul'.[1] Henry told the speaker's deputation that, being 'a great sort of wise men', he did not doubt that they would look circumspectly into the matter and that he himself would remain indifferent between clergy and laity. The commons took the hint and expressed their dissatisfaction with the Answer.

The discussion was thereupon resumed in convocation and several drafts, in varying degrees of defiance of the commons, were produced.[2] However, on 8 May it was decided to imitate the example of the commons by presenting a petition to the king complaining of the things done to the prejudice of the clergy, and asking for the favour of the king. A deputation was sent to present this petition to Henry, but it was an utter failure. Henry had other ideas for the clergy. On 10 May Edward Foxe, one of the ecclesiastical deputation,[3] returned with three demands from the king. Convocation was now required to promise that they would not, in future, assemble without the king's writ; that they would not enact, publish or enforce any constitutions without the royal authority and consent; and that they would submit all those constitutions then in force to the scrutiny of a commission of thirty-two members, half clerics and half laymen, appointed by the king, and would accept the determination of the commission as to which constitutions should be abolished and which should be retained.[4]

---

[1] Hall, *Chronicle*, ii, 209, 210.
[2] See, e.g. the drafts printed in Atterbury, *Rights, Powers and Privileges of Convocation* (1700), App. III, pp. 464-71, and calendared at *L. & P.*, v, 1018.
[3] And also an enthusiastic supporter of the king.
[4] Wilkins, *Concilia*, iii, 748, 749.

Chapuys reported that parliament was discussing a proposal to prohibit the holding of ecclesiastical synods without the express licence of the king. This he regarded as a 'strange thing', saying that churchmen would be of less account than shoemakers who, at least, had the power of assembling and making their own regulations. He also reported that the king wished to deprive the bishops of their power to try persons for heresy on the ground that it was not their duty to meddle with bodies, for they were only doctors of the soul. Chapuys said that the king was opposed by More and the bishops, and that he was very angry, especially with More and Gardiner.[1]

With the adroitness that had characterized the actions of the king and his council throughout this session, Henry reinforced Foxe's approach. On the following day, 11 May, he summoned the speaker and twelve of the commons, and addressed them in words that left little doubt that the real issue was one of sovereignty:

Well beloved subjects, we thought that the clergy of our realm had been our subjects wholly, but now we have well perceived that they be but half our subjects, yea, and scarce our subjects: for all the prelates at their consecration make an oath to the pope, clean contrary to the oath that they make to us, so that they seem to be his subjects and not ours; the copy of both the oaths I deliver here to you, requiring you to invent some order, that we be not thus deluded of our spiritual subjects.[2]

The threat was effective and all resistance collapsed. On 15 May, within a very few days of Henry's speech, convocation voted the Submission of the Clergy, accepting Henry's demands and setting forth the complete surrender of their legislative independence. By this short document the clergy promised, with all confidence in the king, first, that new canons should not be made without the king's licence and ratification, and, secondly, that canons already enacted should be submitted

---

[1] Chapuys to Charles V, 13 May 1532 (*L. & P.*, v, 1013); cf. p. 171, note 1. The king was indeed angry with Gardiner from whom he had expected support, but who had taken a principal part in drafting the Answer. Gardiner wrote to the king in an attempt to excuse himself (Gardiner to Henry VIII, May 1532; Wilkins, *Concilia*, iii, 752; *L. & P.*, v, 1019) but it was of no avail and at the end of the session he was sent to his see in disgrace. It was during this period that he held the only ordination of his long episcopate extending over nearly a quarter of a century.

[2] Hall, *Chronicle*, ii, 210. According to Foxe, the martyrologist, it was Cromwell who suggested this manoeuvre to the king; see his *Life of Lord Thomas Cromwell* in *Acts and Monuments* (ed. Pratt 1870), v, 367.

to a committee of revision,[1] on condition that only those approved by the committee be put in force.[2] On the following day the Submission was presented to the king at Westminster in the presence of Lord Abergavenny, Lord Hussey, Lord Mordaunt, Sir William Fitzwilliam and Thomas Cromwell.[3]

With the presentation to the king of their Submission, the bishops ceased to be masters in their own house. All ecclesiastical legislation was to become dependent upon the king, with the necessary corollary that the government of the church in England would be subordinated to the crown. The ancient, and at times troublesome, distinction between church and state had been so greatly blurred as to have been virtually removed. The capitulation of the bishops was ignominious and complete. It is instructive to compare the Answer of the Ordinaries with the manner of their Submission. When they were considering their Answer the bishops were concerned only with the commons, and although the Supplication, which they were called upon to answer, was grounded on real grievances, the bishops replied with assurance. The tone of their Answer was that of a schoolmaster addressing his charges; the bishops were unconcerned that such grievances should be laid to their charge for they felt safe in the knowledge that their house was in excellent order, and when they did not deny the charges they were content to brush them aside. But when the king himself intervened the ordinaries suffered a sudden change of heart. The king, without any reference to the lay grievances that were the subject of dispute, demanded that the bishops should renounce their independent legislative power, and they capitulated almost at once; there was an interval of but five days between the king's demand and the bishops' submission. The language of the Answer was confident and even stubborn; the Submission was couched in the servile terms to be expected from men who had lost their nerve.

[1] 'It be committed to the examination and judgment of your grace and of thirty-two persons, whereof sixteen to be of the upper and nether house of the temporalty, and other sixteen of the clergy, all to be chosen and appointed by your most noble grace.'
[2] The Submission of the Clergy, 1532 (Pocock, ii, 257; Wilkins, *Concilia*, iii, 754; *G. & H.*, 176-8; *L. & P.*, v, 1023).
[3] See *L. & P.*, v, 1023(1). The list of persons present is an interesting one. Cromwell had only recently become an office holder, and of the remainder, Abergavenny and Hussey, soldiers and old servants of Henry VII, were household officers, Mordaunt, a friend of Cromwell, was associated with the household, while Fitzwilliam, the treasurer of the household, had yet to achieve prominence. None of the leaders of the council was present.

XII

The Archbishop of Canterbury

I

On the day after the bishops made their submission to the king Sir Thomas More resigned his office. In reporting his resignation Chapuys remarked to the emperor that if he had remained lord chancellor he would have been obliged to act against his conscience or incur the king's displeasure, as he had already begun to do by refusing to take any part against the clergy; and the ambassador added that everyone was concerned at the resignation for there had never been a better man in the office.[1] More surrendered the great seal in the afternoon of Thursday 16 May 1532,[2] two days after parliament had been prorogued to the following February.[3] On 20 May Thomas Audley was appointed lord keeper and knighted, and on 5 June, in the court of Chancery at Westminster, he took his oath of office.[4]

The pope's brief of 25 January had not been presented to the king while parliament was still sitting.[5] The emperor had forwarded it to Chapuys towards the end of April, but the queen did not think it advisable to present it to the king while the session continued lest it might drive Henry to seek a remedy from parliament.[6] The prorogation of parliament ended the queen's fears on this score, and Chapuys arranged that the brief should be presented to the king by the nuncio. The nuncio went to court for this purpose on 13 May, but he experienced some

[1] Chapuys to Charles V, 22 May 1532 (*L. & P.*, v, 1046).
[2] Rymer, *Foedera*, xiv, 439; *L. & P.*, v, 1075. Foxe, in a letter written to Benet on the day of More's resignation, informed him of the fact (Foxe to Benet, 16 May 1532; *State Papers*, vii, 370; *L. & P.*, v, 1025).
[3] Hall, *Chronicle*, ii, 212; cf. Chapuys to Charles V, 22 May 1532 (*L. & P.*, v, 1046); Chapuys erroneously stated that parliament was prorogued to November (so did Foxe: see Foxe to Benet, 16 May 1532; *State Papers*, vii, 370, at p. 371; *L. & P.*, v, 1025).
[4] Rymer, *Foedera*, xiv, 433; *L. & P.*, v, 1075.   [5] See p. 178.
[6] cf. Chapuys to Charles V, 29 April 1532 (*L. & P.*, v, 973).

difficulty in obtaining an audience. When he asked the duke of Norfolk for audience he was told that the king could not see him and that the duke was commissioned to report what he had to say. The nuncio replied that he had no authority to speak with anyone but the king, and at length Norfolk, after a fruitless attempt to discover the reason for the nuncio's visit, went into the king's chamber, where he stayed about an hour. When Norfolk left, the nuncio was summoned to the king. After discussing the current news the nuncio repeated the tenor of the pope's letter to the king and then gave it to him. The nuncio afterwards told Chapuys that the king seemed 'astonished and troubled'. Henry said that he was surprised that the pope should persist in his fancy of wishing him to recall the queen, for if the queen were his wife, as his holiness had said, then it was none of the pope's business to meddle with the way in which he punished her for the rude behaviour that she daily used to him. When the nuncio retorted that the pope could not refuse justice, especially as the case concerned the emperor and the king of the Romans, Henry repeated several times that the way he treated his wife was his own affair and did not concern anyone else. Ultimately Henry said that he would read the brief and send an answer. In sending a report of this interview to the emperor, Chapuys observed that he did not know what the answer would be, but he was sure that the king would not obey the pope's letter; he added that it would not be surprising if the king were to ignore the letter as the pope could not have made it weaker than it was.[1] Henry's only reply was to move Catherine further from the court; she was moved from The More to Buckden, a much inferior house belonging to the bishop of Lincoln whom the queen believed to be one of the principal promoters of the divorce.

The archbishop of Canterbury, William Warham, was now an old man, but in the last moments of his life he gave evidence of a spirit that was characteristic rather of the independence of his predecessor, St Thomas Becket, than of the servility of the majority of the Henrician bishops. On 24 February he had signed a formal protest against all the enactments made in the parliament which commenced on 3 November 1529, in derogation of the pope's authority or of the ecclesiastical prerogatives of the province of Canterbury.[2] And later in the year, when he

[1] Chapuys to Charles V, 22 May 1532 (*L. & P.*, v, 1046).
[2] For the text see Wilkins, *Concilia*, iii, 746; Pocock-Burnet, vi, 54; calendared at *L. & P.*, v, 818.

was threatened with proceedings in praemunire because he had, in 1518, consecrated Henry Standish as bishop of St Asaph before the bishop had exhibited his bulls to the king, he prepared the draft of what may have been a speech that he intended to deliver in the house of lords. The draft contains a vigorous restatement of the traditional Catholic position with regard to the relationship between church and state in its classic form.

After declaring that he meant to say nothing to the king's prejudice, Warham protested that archbishops had never been bound to discover, by examining bishops requiring consecration, whether they had exhibited their bulls or not, and he asserted that if metropolitans had been so bound the fact that they had made the necessary inquiries would have appeared on record. He then turned to the general proposition that if the spiritual powers of archbishops depended upon the temporal power of the prince they would be of little effect: if the archbishops cannot give the spiritualities

to him so promoted a bishop till the king's grace had granted and delivered to him his temporalities then the spiritual power of the archbishops should hang and depend of the temporal power of the prince, and so should be of little or none effect which is against all law. . . . And so it were in a manner as good to have no spiritualities as to have such spiritualities as he might not give but at the prince's pleasure.

Warham went on to declare that an archbishop had no right to keep the spiritualities in his hands after an elect had been pronounced bishop, for a man was not made a bishop by consecration but by the pronouncement in Rome in consistory; consecration did not give him jurisdiction but only the rights of his order. If the archbishop were to withhold the spiritualities until the king had granted the temporalities an elect might be deprived of both, for there had been kings, such as Henry II, who had retained the temporalities for many years.

Warham argued that the king was not injured by the consecration of a bishop before he had exhibited his bulls to the king and done homage, for the king could still keep the temporalities in his hands; and there had been many archbishops and bishops whose temporalities had been detained for a long time. If the king were right, then, by parity of reasoning, the pope should not be consecrated or crowned until he had sued of the emperor for those temporalities which Constantine had given to the see of Rome; and if that were so there would be no pope save at the emperor's pleasure. Apart from law, a spiritual man ought first to seek what was necessary for his spiritual functions and not go after temporal things; he should be consecrated first and afterwards sue for his temporalities. In consecrating the bishop of St Asaph, Warham had been but the pope's commissary and the act was that of the pope; he did only what he was bound by oath to do.

And then memories of Warham's great predecessor, Thomas Becket, crowded in upon him as he went on to show that the point for which the king contended was one of the articles which Henry II sought to extort at Clarendon and which Becket opposed to the extent of dying as a martyr; and even Henry II afterwards relinquished the point. He quoted from the Life of the archbishop by Henry of Bosham and from Becket's own letters. He quoted, too, from Magna Carta which guaranteed the liberties of the church, and protested; 'But *ecclesia anglicana non habet libertates suas illaesas*[1] when the church hath not its liberty to consecrate bishops but at princes' pleasures, for in case it should not please princes to have any bishops consecrated so the church should cease'. And he recalled the several kings who had violated the liberties of the church and come to an evil end: Henry II, Edward III, Richard II and Henry IV.[2] Warham then referred to a brief of Pope Martin to Henry IV concerning a praemunire against the liberties of the church, and he warned the lords, in answer to their threat that they would defend the matter with their swords, of what befell those knights who drew their swords against St Thomas of Canterbury. He had already said that St Thomas 'was rewarded of God with the great honour of martyrdom, which is the best death that can be. Which thing is the example and comfort of others to

[1] The first article of Magna Carta is as follows: 'In primis concessisse Deo et hac praesenti carta nostra confirmasse, pro nobis et haeredibus nostris in perpetuum, quod Anglicana ecclesia libera sit, et habeat jura sua integra, et libertates suas illaesas; et ita volumus observari; quod apparet ex eo quod libertatem electionum, quae maxima et magis necessaria reputatur ecclesiae Anglicanae, mera et spontanea voluntate, ante discordiam inter nos et barones nostros motam, concessimus et carta nostra confirmavimus, et eam optinuimus a domino papa Innocentio tertio confirmari; quam et nos observabimus et ab haeredibus nostris in perpetuum bona fide volumus observari. Concessimus etiam omnibus liberis hominibus regni nostri, pro nobis et haeredibus nostris in perpetuum, omnes libertates subscriptas, habendas et tenendas, eis et haeredibus suis, de nobis et haeredibus nostris'.

[2] Henry II was the author of the Constitutions of Clarendon; Edward III was responsible for the Statute of Provisors (1351), and Richard II for the Statute of Praemunire (1392).

196

speak and do for the defence of the liberties of God's church'; and now, he added, 'I think it were better for me to suffer the same than against my conscience to confess this article to be a praemunire for which Saint Thomas died.'

Warham concluded by saying that he would not refuse the lay counsel offered him. He added, however, that he expected little from them, for two reasons: first, because laymen advanced their own laws rather than those of the church.

And in this behalf I understand that such temporal learned men as have been assigned of counsel with spiritual men lately in cases of praemunire (as it was surmised) for the advancing of their temporal laws, and for the derogation of the laws of the church have counselled them and induced them to confess and grant a praemunire. Whereto peradventure, they would advise me in likewise. Which if I were so minded to confess, I needed not to have their counsel.

Secondly, he understood that temporal men defending their clients, when they spoke anything against the minds of the king's council, had been called fools and put to silence, and Warham would be sorry that they should be so rebuked for defending him. As the matter was spiritual, he desired spiritual counsel.[1]

Warham died on 23 August 1532, without delivering his speech in defence of the liberties of the church. Had Warham lived and continued in the firmness of mind he had recovered during the last months of his life, Henry's path might have been more difficult. But now that convocation had surrendered its legislative independence to the king and so taken the first step towards the destruction of papal authority in England, the death of Warham, so soon afterwards, presented Henry with the opportunity to appoint, at such a critical time, an archbishop who would be wholly subservient to him.

2

The king's treatment of Catherine and his open flaunting of his association with Anne Boleyn were the occasion of some outbursts of popular feeling. It was difficult for Anne to appear in public without being greeted

---

[1] Warham's draft speech is calendared at *L. & P.*, v, 1248, and is printed in full in *Dublin Review*, cxiv (1894), 401-14 (appendix to Moyes, 'Warham, an English Primate on the Eve of the Reformation').

with abuse, and sometimes popular disapproval took a more menacing form. For instance, towards the end of 1531, when she was dining at a place on the river, a hostile and threatening mob of women assembled in boats and she only escaped by hastily crossing over when warned of their approach.[1] And when the abbot of Whitby, on his return from convocation in the early spring of 1532, was asked what news he brought, he replied, repeating the common gossip of the day: 'Evil news; for the king's grace was ruled by one common stued huer, Anne Bullan, who made all the spiritualty to be beggared, and the temporalty also.'[2] It was, no doubt, but natural that the king's favourite, who accompanied him from place to place after he had parted from his wife, should be spoken of as a common prostitute, especially when many sermons were preached against the king's great matter. It was at about the same time that the king ordered the arrest of a preacher who had spoken against the divorce; on being examined by the council the preacher said he was moved to speak as he did by the truth, the service of God and the honour of the king.[3] The popular expression of opinion adverse to the king was such that compulsion was necessary to induce preachers to speak in favour of the divorce.[4] But when, in May, a preacher at Paul's Cross obeyed the king's instructions, a woman stood up and told him that he lied and that the king's example would be the destruction of the law of matrimony. The woman was arrested, and so were several of the clergy who had preached in favour of Catherine a few days previously.[5]

Henry's instructions to the clergy did not prevent some of them from voicing their disapproval even in the presence of the king. It is well known that, on Easter Sunday 1532, William Peto, the provincial of the Friars Minor, angered the king by the sermon which he preached in the royal presence at the Franciscan convent at Greenwich. Peto preached on

[1] Advices from France, received by the French ambassador in Venice, dated 24 Nov. 1531 (*Ven. Cal.*, iv, 701).
[2] *L. & P.*, v, 907.
[3] See p. 172.
[4] Chapuys to Charles V, 20 Mar. 1532 (*L. & P.*, v, 879). cf. Hall, *Chronicle*, ii, 209: 'In the begynnynge of this xxiiii yere [of the king's reign] the Ladye Anne Bulleyne was so moche in the Kynges favoure, that the commen people whiche knewe not the Kynges trew entent, sayd and thought that the absence of the Quene was onely for her sake, which was not trew: for the kyng was openly rebuked of Preachers for kepyng company with hys brothers wyfe, which was thoccasyon that he eschued her company, tyll the truth were tryed.'
[5] Carlo Capello to the Signory, 16 May 1532 (*Ven. Cal.*, iv, 768).

the twenty first and twenty second chapters of the third book of Kings and, after recounting the history of Ahab, he applied to the king the threat of the prophet, Elijah: 'Here, where the dogs licked the blood of Naboth, they shall lick thine'.[1] He went on to say that, like Ahab, the king was deprived of the truth by his false counsellors, and he urged the king to separate from Anne. He concluded: 'I am that Micheas whom thou hate because I must tell thee truly that this marriage is unlawful, and I know that I shall eat the bread of affliction and drink the water of sorrow, yet because our Lord hath put it into my mouth I must speak it'. After strongly inveighing against the king's second marriage, he said,

There are many other preachers, yea too many, which preach and persuade thee otherwise, feeding thy folly and frail affections upon hope of their own worldly promotion, and by that means they betray thy soul, thy honour and posterity, to obtain fat benefices, to become rich abbots, and get episcopal jurisdiction and other ecclesiastical dignities. These, I say, are the four hundred prophets who, in the spirit of lying, seek to deceive thee; but take good heed lest you being seduced, you find Ahab's punishment, which was to have his blood licked upon the dogs, [for] it was one of the greatest miseries in princes to be daily abused by flatterers.

While still in the chapel the king suppressed his anger, but afterwards he sent for Peto and sharply rebuked him for what he had said. Peto was not to be browbeaten, and he answered that the king was endangering his crown, for both great and small were murmuring at the marriage. Then, to be rid of him for a while, the king gave him leave to go to Toulouse to attend a chapter of his order. During Peto's absence, the king arranged for one of his own chaplains, Dr Richard Curwen, to preach before him at Greenwich. Curwen's sermon was a bitter attack on Peto and a paean of praise of the king. Finally he said: 'I speak to thee, Peto, which makest thyself Micheas, that thou mayest speak evil of kings, but now thou art not to be found, being fled for fear and shame, as being unable to answer my arguments'. This was too much for the warden of Greenwich, Henry Elstowe, who shouted to him that it was not so. Elstowe waxed so hot in defence of his provincial that the king himself had to bid him be quiet.

When Peto returned from Toulouse he was told by the bishops, at

---

[1] 3 Kings xxi, 19 (Knox translation); the reference in A.V. is 1 Kings xxi, 19.

the king's command, that he must degrade Elstowe. When he refused to do so he and Elstowe were summoned before the council and imprisoned. During Elstowe's imprisonment William Curson was appointed vicar of the convent at Greenwich, and he was staunch in the support he gave to his superior; he encouraged a friar of Richmond, Father Robinson, to preach in favour of the queen at Paul's Cross.[1] But, although the greater part of the friars of Greenwich strongly supported their warden and provincial, there were some, such as friar John Lawrence, who, anxious to curry favour at court, were ready to betray their brethren in letters to Cromwell and the king.[2]

The popular feeling against Anne Boleyn was given strongest expression, as might be expected, by women. For instance, in July the king went northward on a hunting tour but, although great preparations had been made, he suddenly turned back. Several explanations of this strange behaviour were put forward, but the most probable cause of his unexpected change of plan seems to have been the displays of popular feeling with which he was confronted and for which he was unprepared. In two or three places through which he passed the inhabitants urged him to take back the queen and the women openly insulted Anne Boleyn who rode with him.[3] While the king was still away on this tour a writ was issued from Ampthill on 24 July directing a commission of oyer and terminer to the chief justice of the King's Bench, the chief baron of the Exchequer and others, to hold an inquiry at Yarmouth, immediately after the assizes at Norwich, concerning a great riot and unlawful assembly of women at that town, 'which it is thought could not have been held without the connivance of their husbands'.[4] The general public indignation must have been considerable for such exceptional measures to have been taken.

[1] See Chapuys to Charles V, 16 April 1532 (*L. & P.*, v, 941); Stow, *Chronicle of England* (ed. 1631), 562 (Stow's dates are unreliable). See also Chapuys to Charles V, May 1532 (*L. & P.*, v, 989); William Curson to Sir John Dyve, 22 May 1532 (*L. & P.*, v, 1043); Friar John Lawrence to Cromwell, June 1532 (*L. & P.*, v, 1142). cf. Gasquet, *Henry VIII and the English Monasteries*, cap. v.

[2] cf. Friar John Lawrence to Cromwell, June 1532 (*L. & P.*, v, 1142); Friar Lawrence to Cromwell, June 1532 (*L. & P.*, v, 1143); Friar Lawrence to Cromwell, Aug. 1532 (*L. & P.*, v, 1208); Friar Lawrence to Cromwell, Aug. 1532 (*L. & P.*, v, 1260), in which he complains that he has been forbidden by his superior to write to the king.

[3] Chapuys to Charles V, 29 July 1532 (*L. & P.*, v, 1202).

[4] See *L. & P.*, v, 1207(45).

Indications of the popular feeling were to be found even in the king's household. It seems that one of the court fools had been so handled by several of the king's servants that he fell from his horse; and when he mounted again he observed that the king, too, would have a fall shortly. The incident was bruited abroad and came to the notice of John Driver, the prior of the Crutched Friars in London, who used it as a text with which to urge his brethren to 'keep good religion'. The prior told them of a rumour that the king, because of the opposition to him, was planning to pull down certain religious houses; if he did so, said the prior, he deserved to be called not *defensor fidei* but *destructor fidei*. For his part in this incident the prior was examined before Thomas Cromwell and John Alleyn and confessed on oath that it was true.[1] The current opinion of Anne Boleyn, that she was a common prostitute,[2] was not altogether lacking in foundation. As early as 1529 the French ambassador had suspected that Anne was then living with the king,[3] and at the end of 1531 there were rumours, which reached Rome, that she had miscarried.[4] More than once the pope had taken note of the rumours and written to Henry requiring him to remove the scandal.[5] But whatever may have been the truth with regard to any particular rumour, there could be no doubt as to the nature of the king's relations with Anne Boleyn.

The problem of how to bring to an end the king's marriage with Catherine was still to be solved, but the old policy of intimidating the pope was not abandoned. There can be little doubt that this was the principal motive that induced Henry to seek a meeting with the king of France in the second half of 1532. Preparations for the meeting were under way by the late summer, and in August inquiries were being made in the Cinque Ports to discover how many days notice would be required for the assembly of sufficient transports to carry the king and his train to Calais.[6] The project was not one that commended itself to the

---

[1] Deposition taken on 1 Aug. 1532 (*L. & P.*, v, 1209).
[2] cf. the gossip repeated by the abbot of Whitby to the effect that Anne Boleyn was a 'common stewed whore'; see p. 198.
[3] See p. 9, note 5.
[4] Ortiz to Charles V, Rome, 30 Dec. 1531 (*L. & P.*, v, 615); see p. 178.
[5] Clement VII to Henry VIII, 25 Jan. 1532 (Le Grand, iii, 560; Pocock, ii, 166; *L. & P.*, v, 750); Clement VII to Henry VIII, 15 Nov. 1532 (Le Grand, iii, 558; Pocock, ii, 378; *L. & P.*, v, 1545).
[6] Sir Edward Guildford to Cromwell, 16 Aug. 1532 (*L. & P.*, v, 1231). Sir Edward Guildford was constable at Dover, warden of the Cinque Ports, and master of the Armoury. On 18 Aug. a warrant was issued to Sir Thomas

council, and the duke of Suffolk was so outspoken in his opposition that he was several times insulted by the king at the council board. In the end the matter was settled privately between the king, Anne Boleyn and the French ambassador.[1]

The meeting took place in the following October. Accompanied by Anne Boleyn and by 140 lords and knights clad in velvet, and with a company of 600 horse, Henry left Calais on Monday 21 October to meet Francis I who was attended by the king of Navarre, the cardinal of Lorraine and the duke of Vendôme, together with a suitable retinue. They met at Sandingfield hospital near Calais, where, after embracing each other five or six time on horseback, the two kings rode hand in hand for a mile towards Boulogne. As they approached the town they were joined by the dauphin, the duke of Orleans, the count of Angoulême, and four cardinals; guns were shot off, and the streets of Boulogne were lined with soldiers as they passed. On the following Friday Francis I paid a return visit to Henry at Calais and was greeted with salvoes of artillery. Francis remained at Calais for several days and was entertained with bear baiting, bull baiting and dancing. The festivities came to an end on 29 October when the French king left for Paris. As a spectacular demonstration, for the pope's benefit, of the close political ties linking the kings of England and France, the meeting achieved its purpose,

---

[1] Chapuys to Charles V, 1532 (*L. & P.*, v, 1292); cf. [Langeais?] to —, 10 Sept. 1532 (*L. & P.*, v, 1308); Chapuys to Charles V, 15 Sept. 1532 (*L. & P.*, v, 1316); imperial ambassador in France to Charles V, 22 Sept. 1532 (*L. & P.*, v, 1337); Mai to Charles V, 27 Sept. 1532 (*L. & P.*, v, 1353); Chapuys to Charles V, 1 Oct. 1532 (*L. & P.*, v, 1377); Mai to Charles V, 6 Oct. 1532 (*L. & P.*, v, 1397). News of the meeting reached Rome on 10 Sept. (Benet to Cranmer, 15 Sept. 1532; *State Papers*, vii, 378; *L. & P.*, v, 1315). The pope deferred action in the marriage suit until he knew what the outcome of the meeting might be (see Ortiz to Charles V, 18 Sept. 1532; *L. & P.*, v, 1324; Ortiz to the empress, 30 Sept. 1532; *L. & P.*, v, 1364); he was hoping that the meeting would increase the differences between the two kings (see cardinal of Siguenza to de los Cobos, 9 Oct. 1532; *L. & P.*, v, 1405), but he was displeased that he had not received a formal intimation of the meeting (Benet to duke of Norfolk, 15 Oct. 1532; *State Papers*, vii, 381; *L. & P.*, v, 1431). For the proclamation (dated sometime before 11 Oct. 1532) announcing the appointment of a council of state during the king's absence, see *T.R.P.*, i, 204.

Wriothesley, garter king-of-arms, to be ready at Canterbury on 26 Sept. to attend the king at his interview with the French king at Calais in October (*L. & P.*, v, 1232). A chapter of the order of the Garter was held at Calais on 27 Oct. (*L. & P.*, v, 1474).

and Wynkyn de Worde was required to print an official report of the proceedings.[1]

As a result of the meeting at Calais, Francis I sent cardinals Grammont and Tournon to the pope. They were instructed to inform his holiness that the English and French kings, at their recent meeting, were so closely united that their interests were the same; great damage might, therefore, ensue if the pope provoked them into undertaking any action against him. The cardinals were to tell the pope that at one time the two kings had actually considered taking action against him but had decided to seek reparation first; however, should there be delay in making reparation, which would be regarded as a refusal, they would demand a general council and if the pope refused to summon a council they would do so themselves. The pope was also to be told that if he used censures and the king of England were forced to go to Rome for absolution, he would go so well accompanied that the pope would be very glad to absolve him. The cardinals were to represent to the pope the state of christendom and urge upon him the evils that would result if failure to obtain justice should separate the two kings from the church.[2]

It seems possible that Henry had intended to solve his matrimonial problem by contracting marriage while he was in France, with the support of Francis I, and that this was the reason why he was accompanied by Anne Boleyn. At any rate, almost immediately after the king's return to England rumours began to circulate that he had gone to France in order to marry Anne Boleyn but had found it necessary to postpone such a step.[3] Whatever the truth of the king's intentions may have been, it is likely that Francis I, anti-papalist though he was, would have recoiled from a proposal that not only outraged morals but affronted the emperor.

These were not the only rumours concerning the matrimonial plans of the king. In August, when preparations for the king's visit to France were under way, it was surmised that the probable purpose of the interview was to arrange a marriage between Henry and the elder daughter of

---

[1] The official report ('The maner of the tryumphe at Caleys and Bulleyn') is calendared at *L. & P.*, v, 1484. See also *L. & P.*, v, 1373, 1374, 1485, 1492, 1494, 1511, 1600; Chapuys to Charles V, 14 Oct. 1532 (*L. & P.*, v, 1429); J. Hannart to the empress, 6 Nov. 1532 (*L. & P.*, v, 1523).
[2] Instructions from Francis I to cardinals Tournon and Grammont, Amiens, 13 Nov. 1532 (*L. & P.*, v, 1541).
[3] Captain Thouard to M. d'Yre, 12 Nov. 1532 (*L. & P.*, v, 1538); Ortiz to the empress, 19 Dec. 1532 (*L. & P.*, v, 1642).

the French king;[1] and when, in September, Anne Boleyn was created marchioness of Pembroke with an annuity for life of £1,000,[2] it was taken as a sign that Henry was tiring of her and was proposing to marry her to someone else.[3]

Although the imperial agents at Rome were disturbed by these rumours, they were not deceived by their variety and remained convinced that the king intended to marry Anne Boleyn. The persistence of the rumours was sufficient, however, to send the imperial agents to the pope, to persuade him to write once more to the king, warning him, for the third time and in stronger terms than before, to take back Catherine and put away Anne Boleyn. Accordingly, on 15 November the pope, with some reluctance, wrote again to Henry. He began by expressing his grief that the king, who had always been a pious son to the pope and the holy see, had altered his conduct during the past two years without reasonable cause, although the pope had not changed his affection for him; and he hoped that when Henry's cloud of error had been dissipated he would return to his former attachment. The pope reminded Henry that he had committed the marriage case to the two legates in England, four years previously, at the king's own request, and it was only the queen's appeal that had caused him to commit it, not to the dominions of the queen's nephew or to other places where she might be favoured, but to Rome, to the auditory of the Rota, to be referred to himself and the college of cardinals. While the case was still proceeding the king ought not to have taken any new steps, yet he removed the queen from his company and publicly cohabited 'with a certain Anne'.[4] For this reason the pope had written to him the letter dated 25 January 1532,[5] and he was grieved to hear that the king was

---

[1] Chapuys to Charles V, 26 Aug. 1532 (*L. & P.*, v, 1256). The elder daughter of Francis I, Magdalen, subsequently married James V of Scotland.
[2] See *L. & P.*, v, 1274, 1370(1-3). She was created marchioness of Pembroke on 1 Sept. 1532.
[3] 'Relaciones de las cartas de Roma', 20 and 21 Oct. 1532 (*L. & P.*, v, 1459).
[4] '. . . quo pendente judicio, cum tu nihil innovare vel attentare in praejudicium litispendentiae debuisses, ecce nobis non solum ipsius Reginae lamentabili querela, verum etiam multorum literis & testimoniis affertur, te non expectata ulteriore nostra declaratione, ipsam Reginam a tua cohabitatione separasse, & quamdam Annam in tuum contubernium & cohabitationem publicam recepisse' (Le Grand, iii, 560).
[5] See p. 178.

still separated from Catherine and continued to cohabit with Anne. Again the pope exhorted him and warned him, on pain of excommunication, to take Catherine back as his queen, and to put away Anne, within one month of the presentation of the pope's present letter, until papal sentence be given. If the king should not do this the pope declared both him and Anne to be excommunicated at the expiry of the said month, and he forbade him to divorce himself from Catherine by his own authority and marry Anne or any other woman, for such a marriage would be invalid.[1]

The pope had despatched his letter to Henry with great reluctance. For two months the imperial agents had been vainly demanding the issue of such a letter, and it seems likely that it would never have been sent had it not been for the persistence of Dr Pedro Ortiz. In the middle of September he reminded the emperor that he had already reported that the pope had deferred sending the letter for fear of discouraging Henry from sending a mandate for his representation in the marriage suit in Rome; now Ortiz feared further delay as the pope wished

[1] Clement VII to Henry VIII, 15 Nov. 1532 (Le Grand, iii, 558; Pocock, ii, 378; *L. & P.*, v, 1545); cf. Ortiz to the empress, 19 Dec. 1532 (*L. & P.*, v, 1642). The last part of the pope's letter is as follows: 'Nos cum neque Dei honorem, nec nostrum officium, nec tuae animae salutem negligere debeamus, Te fili, sine tamen tutorum Jurium & causae pendentis praejudicio, iterum hortamur, ac sub excommunicationis poena monemus, ut si praedicta vera sint, eandem Catharinam Reginam apud te in reginali honore, ac solita cohabitatione habere, ipsam vero Annam a publica cohabitatione tua rejicere, intra unum mensem a die praesentationis praesentium tibi factae computandum debeas. Donec nostra sententia & declaratio inter vos fuerit subsequuta. Aliter enim nos dicto termino elapso, te & ipsam Annam excommunicationis poena innodatos, & ab omnibus publice evitandos esse, ex nunc prout ex tunc, & e contra authoritate Apostolica declaramus, & nihilominus tam etsi abhoret animus, talia de serenitate tua opinari, licetque id ipsum jam serenitati tuae a nobis nostroque Rotae auditorio & judice cui hujusmodi causa fuit commissa inhibitum fuerit, & ab amni tam humano quam divino jure, etiam prohibeatur, tamen permoti hominum fama, denuo serenitati tuae inhibemus, ne lite hujusmodi coram nobis, & dicto Rotae auditorio indecisa pendente, & sine sedis Apostolicae licentia speciali, Matrimonium cum dicta Catharina Regina Apostolica authoritate contractum, & prole subsequuta, tantoque temporis spacio confirmatum propria authoritate separare, aut divortium cum ea facere. Neve cum dicta Anna, aut quavis alia Matrimonium contrahere praesumas, irritum prout est denuo decernentes, si quid forsan attentari super hoc a tua serenitate, aut quovis alio, quavis authoritate contigerit, vel forsan hactenus fuerit attentatum, sicque a quibusvis judicibus tam extra Romanam Curiam, quam in ea, etiam S.R.E. Cardinalibus, & dicti Palatii auditoribus sententiari, dessiniri, judicari, & interpretari debere' (Le Grand, iii, 566-8).

to see what the French and English kings would conclude at Calais. Ortiz reported that Sir Gregory Casale had left Rome for England to express to Henry the pope's desire that the king should send a mandate, leave his concubine and restore the queen to her rightful place.[1] At the end of the month Ortiz wrote to the empress to say that the pope had postponed sending the letter until after the vacation, but he assured her that he would persevere in his demands.[2] Ten days later Ortiz told her that the pope had the letter ready, but would not allow it to be despatched until he had seen the emperor, as he was hindered by the meeting between the kings of England and France. Ortiz added that if he had been able to act on his own judgment he would have spoken to the pope with rigour, as he knew that his holiness feared the strength of his arguments; the emperor, however, had ordered him to defer to the opinions of the ambassador, Miguel Mai, and the ambassador would not allow him to have an interview with the pope, as he believed that Ortiz was trying to usurp his functions.[3]

On 16 November, two days before the pope left Rome, Ortiz asked to see the letter, which had been dated the previous day, and was told that the pope's secretary had orders in the matter; it was not until the next day that the imperial ambassador received a copy and was able to approve it; the actual letter was than handed to the ambassador who was required to promise that it should not be used until the nuncio had spoken with the king of England. In his letter to the empress telling her of these matters, Ortiz added that he was grieved at the delay as the letter would have been more effective had it been sent while the kings were meeting at Calais.[4] In the opinion of Chapuys, in England, the letter was of little use: the pope, he said, could have given sentence but, instead, had preferred to send the letter which, unlike the sentence, could be revoked at his pleasure.[5]

The greatest single influence in persuading the pope to despatch the letter to Henry seems to have been the prospect of a meeting with the

---

[1] Ortiz to Charles V, 18 Sept. 1532 (*L. & P.*, v, 1324); cf. Mai to de los Cobos, 4 Sept. 1532 (*L. & P.*, v, 1291), and Ortiz to de los Cobos, Sept. 1532 (*L. & P.*, v, 1325).
[2] Ortiz to the empress, 30 Sept. 1532 (*L. & P.*, v, 1364).
[3] Ortiz to the empress, 10 Nov. 1532 (*L. & P.*, v, 1532); cf. p. 176, note 1.
[4] Ortiz to the empress, 21 Nov. 1532 (*L. & P.*, v, 1567). The pope left Rome on 18 Nov. 1532 (Mai to de los Cobos, Nov. 21, 1532; *L. & P.*, v, 1566).
[5] Chapuys to Charles V, 27 Jan. 1533 (*L. & P.*, vi, 89 (p. 35)).

emperor. Charles V had not been slow to appreciate the need to counteract the effects of the meeting at Calais, and for this purpose he arranged a meeting between himself and the pope at Bologna. There were many important considerations which led him to take this step, and doubtless the promotion of his aunt's interests was not lost to sight.[1] Important though it might be, the question of Henry's divorce was of lesser moment to the emperor than the Turkish invasion of the empire, the spread of Lutheranism in Germany, and the proposed general council to be convened to redress the evils besetting christendom. Nevertheless, the overthrow of heresy and the defence of christendom were intimately bound up with the maintenance of the authority of the church which was directly threatened by the matrimonial manoeuvres of the king of England; the emperor could very suitably demand justice for his aunt, the queen of England, when he came to discuss the affairs of Europe with the pope.[2]

The meeting at Bologna began in December 1532,[3] but it could not be expected to achieve great results. The pope's interests and objectives differed considerably from those of the emperor, whereas the English and French kings had had much in common; and, like Henry and Francis, the pope was anxious to avoid a meeting of a general council which the emperor was pressing him to convene. All this meant that the support of the French king for Henry in the matrimonial suit had an effect on the pope's mind which Charles V could do nothing to counteract; and in the promotion of Catherine's interests he could do little more than

---

[1] Catherine wrote to the emperor expressing her hopes of a successful outcome of the meeting: Catherine of Aragon to Charles V, 5 Nov. 1532 (Pocock, ii, 340).
[2] After the pope left Rome to go to Bologna, a citation against Henry was read on 28 Nov. 1532, at the instance of Catherine's proctor, before Capisucchi. Carne immediately consulted the king's agents to devise means to counter this move. They decided that if the matter were proceeded with, they would appeal, and several documents were prepared for that purpose; but no one appeared on behalf of the 'party adverse', so that an appeal became unnecessary (see Carne to Henry VIII, 7 Dec. 1532; *State Papers*, vii, 392; *L. & P.*, v, 1612. For the text of the enclosures in Carne's letter, see Pocock, ii, 344-53).
[3] cf. Augustine de Augustinis to Cromwell, 24 Dec. 1532 (Pocock, ii, 357; *L. & P.*, v, 1657); Bonner to Cromwell, 24 Dec. 1532 (*State Papers*, vii, 394; *L. & P.*, v, 1658); Benet to Henry VIII, 24 Dec. 1532 (*State Papers*, vii, 401; *L. & P.*, v, 1659); Hawkins to Henry VIII, 24 Dec. 1532 (*State Papers*, vii, 404; *L. & P.*, v, 1660); Hawkins to Cromwell, 24 Dec. 1532 (*State Papers*, vii, 406; *L. & P.*, v, 1661); Benet and G. Casale to Henry VIII, 24 Dec. 1532 (*State Papers*, vii, 397; *L. & P.*, v, 1662). All these letters were written from Bologna.

repeat the protests and requests already made by his agents. In the event, the results of the meeting were very meagre. Little seems to have been achieved except a decision to summon a general council which the emperor extracted from an unwilling pope.[1]

There was one other factor which contributed to the lack of success of the meeting at Bologna. Cardinals Grammont and Tournon, who had been sent to the pope by Francis I immediately after his meeting with Henry at Calais,[2] arrived at Bologna while the emperor was still there. They reached Bologna in January 1533 and their presence had a marked influence on the discussions proceeding between the pope and the emperor. The pope took heart and, on many points which he had been about to concede to the emperor, his attitude stiffened and he refused to yield, a *volte face* that was the principal reason for the meagre results of the meeting; but more important, as a result of the intervention of the French cardinals a secret agreement was reached for a meeting between the pope and Francis I that should take place at a convenient time after the emperor had left for Spain, and at which the pope hoped to be able to 'direct [Henry VIII's] cause to some good end'.[3] The cardinals left the pope optimistically believing that all the difficulties could be smoothed away at his proposed meeting with Francis I, and the English king's complicated matrimonial problem solved to Henry's satisfaction.[4]

---

[1] There were only two important points of agreement, so far as English affairs were concerned: (1) that in the event of an agreement between Clement VII and Francis I for the marriage of the pope's niece, Catherine de Medici, with a son of the French king, the pope would obtain an assurance that, in the matter of the divorce, Francis would let justice take its course; (2) the pope agreed that there should be no delay in the divorce proceedings and that he would not permit them to be carried on elsewhere than in Rome, and he agreed that no alteration should be made in the proceedings begun in Rome without the consent of queen Catherine and without affording her an opportunity to be heard (see Bulla secreta inter Papam Clementem et Carolum Imperatorem super concilio indicendo et celebrando et aliis rebus, 24 Feb. 1533; Ehses, 201; the calendared version at *L. & P.*, vi, 182, is unsatisfactory). The pope sent out letters announcing the proposed council and requesting the co-operation of the princes of Europe; see, e.g., Clement VII to Henry VIII, 2 Jan. 1533 (Pocock, ii, 365; *L. & P.*, vi, 11); Clement VII to Francis I, 2 Jan. 1533 (*L. & P.*, vi, 12). See also *L. & P.*, vi, 13.
[2] See p. 203.
[3] See Instructions from Francis I to the bailly of Troyes [Jean de Dinteville, French ambassador in England], 27 Jan. 1533 (*L. & P.*, vi, 91). See also Benet to Henry VIII, 14 Jan. 1533 (*State Papers*, vii, 407; *L. & P.*, vi, 38).
[4] Cardinal Tournon to Francis I, 27 Jan. 1533 (*L. & P.*. vi, 92).

The pope's brief to Henry, of 15 November 1532, had been handed to the imperial ambassador on condition that no use was made of it until after the nuncio had spoken with the king.[1] Unhappily there is no record of the interviews between Henry and baron de Borgho, the nuncio, and we have to rely upon what Chapuys heard from the nuncio and then reported to the emperor. To the disgust of Chapuys, de Borgho was not very forthcoming and the ambassador was unable to obtain from him a detailed account of what had transpired at his interviews with the king. He learned, however, that the nuncio had told Henry that the matter would not admit of delay and that, if the instructions and powers of the English ambassadors were not in proper form, the pope would be constrained to proceed to judgment; for this reason the nuncio said that it would be well if the king were to communicate the whole matter to him, but Henry would not agree. When the nuncio told him that if the agreement between the pope and the emperor took effect he would have to recall the queen and treat her more cordially, Henry replied that he had already given his answer on that matter; he had good reasons for not taking back the queen. During his talks with the ambassador the nuncio told Chapuys that for a whole year the English had been offering him bribes to favour the divorce. Chapuys, who was anxious that judgment should be pronounced in the marriage suit, formed the view that the nuncio was more interested in preventing matters reaching a crisis than in accelerating the matrimonial proceedings in Rome.

In the course of these conversations de Borgho informed Chapuys that he had been conferring with a member of the council whom he did not name. This councillor, said the nuncio, was eager to promote a compromise (although Chapuys suspected that the nuncio was the prime mover in the scheme), and had at first proposed that the further hearing of the suit, and the pronouncement of the judgment, should take place away from Rome; later the councillor had changed his mind and thought that judgment should be pronounced in Rome. As to the place for the hearing, the councillor did not favour Cambrai but he thought that some place in France would be suitable, and it was evident to Chapuys that only French judges would be accepted as neutral. It was all too clear to Chapuys that such schemes were only designed to produce delay, and this increased his irritation with the nuncio. One of

[1] See p. 206.

the reasons why he suspected that de Borgho himself was at the back of the councillor's scheme was his knowledge of the nuncio's efforts to find means for having the suit decided away from Rome; the nuncio had been telling the king that the pope had a greater desire to be released from the suit than had Henry himself, and would do anything to free himself from the burden. Chapuys noted that this kind of talk by the nuncio made the king persist more obstinately in his efforts to ensure that the suit was not heard in Rome, as Henry believed that the pope would do his utmost to assist him in such a course.[1]

Henry had some reason for his belief. He had learned of the projected meeting between the pope and Francis I, and he had been informed that Clement VII had asked the French king to invite Henry to send to the meeting 'some honourable personages, most fully instruct of your highness' mind and said cause'.[2] Henry also knew that the pope was again considering a suggestion that the matrimonial suit should be tried in some neutral place. This suggestion had been put forward in May 1531 by cardinal Grammont;[3] it was now put forward once more by Sir Gregory Casale as a means of removing difficulties and, doubtless due to the influence of the cardinal, the pope showed himself willing to entertain the idea as a proposal from Henry himself. The pope's overtures in this matter were, however, hard to reconcile with the undertakings that he had given to the emperor;[4] but Henry responded with some warmth. He informed his ambassadors in Rome that he understood that the pope, 'favouring the justice of our great cause', was willing to consent to the following terms: that if the king would send a mandate for the remission of the cause to a neutral place, the pope would send to such a place a legate and two auditors, reserving judgment to himself; or, if Henry agreed and the French king were induced to accept a general truce for three or four years, that the pope would convene a general council to which the cause could be remitted by his holiness. Henry told his ambassadors that these proposals had been put to him verbally by the nuncio, and also by letter, as if they had been proposed to his

[1] Chapuys to Charles V, 27 Jan. 1533 (*L. & P.*, vi, 89); Chapuys to Charles V, 9 Feb. 1533 (*L. & P.*, vi, 142).
[2] cf. Benet to Henry VIII, 14 Jan. 1533 (*State Papers*, vii, 407; *L. & P.*, vi, 38); see p. 208.
[3] See Ortiz to Charles V, 25 May 1531 (*L. & P.*, v, 255), and Relacion de las cartas de Muxetula, May 1531 (*L. & P.*, v, 275); see p. 164.
[4] See p. 208, note 1.

holiness by Sir Gregory Casale in the king's name, and agreed to by the pope for his satisfaction. Henry said that he had never given Casale any authority to make such proposals, but, since he now had better hope than before that the pope, 'deeply pondering the justice of our said cause, will now take more respect to put us in more quietness therein than we had any expectation heretofore', he instructed his ambassadors that they were to tell the pope discreetly that he took these overtures in good part, and to thank him for them. As to the general truce, the ambassadors were to say that although Henry was much inclined to it, two things compelled him to withhold his consent: that he could not renew peace with others until 'we may be satisfied, and have pure and sincere peace with our own heart', and that his friendship with the French king prevented his consent until he had obtained the agreement of Francis I. As regards the general council, the pope was to be told that Henry saw many reasons to think it necessary at that time, and he had no doubt that his cause, if referred to it, would be determined in his favour; however, since he was now in hope that the pope would either 'admit the excusatory' or remit the whole matter for final decision in England, he must suspend his consent to the summoning of a general council since its assembly must depend upon the consent of the French king and other princes, and because the summoning of a council was only solicited by the emperor in consequence of 'the importunity of the Germans and the Lutheran sect'. Finally, the pope was to be informed that the king could not agree to send 'a mandate to require that the cause might be heard in an indifferent place', for this would be a submission to a foreign juris-diction and such a submission was contrary to his royal prerogatives and the privileges of his realm.[1]

Shortly afterwards the French ambassador, Montpesat,[2] was sent for by the duke of Norfolk. They discussed recent messages from the pope which, the duke said, contained good offers, but the ambassador was asked to inform Francis that nothing would induce the king of England to consent to them for he had too little trust in his holiness. Norfolk told Montpesat that the king never spoke to him without assuring him

---

[1] Henry VIII to his ambassadors at Rome, Jan. 1533 (Pocock, ii, 434; Pocock-Burnet, vi, 69; *L. & P.*, vi, 102). Pocock printed this document from a draft carefully corrected throughout by the king's own hand.
[2] Antoine de Prez, sieur de Montpesat, was French ambassador from Nov. 1532, to 13 Feb. 1533.

of his friendship for Francis, but he proposed to entertain the pope with fair words until he saw how his holiness would conclude his affair.[1] Henry was prepared to humour the pope until his new archbishop should be consecrated.

3

Meanwhile Henry had been making urgent moves to secure the appointment of Warham's successor. His choice surprised many of his contemporaries; for the new archbishop was Thomas Cranmer, who had first attracted the king's notice by his skill as a propagandist for the divorce.[2] Cranmer had recently been employed on diplomatic business in Italy and in January 1532 had been appointed resident ambassador at the emperor's court. On 1 October, before he met Francis I, the king wrote to recall him, and soon afterwards his successor as ambassador, Nicholas Hawkins, archdeacon of Ely, left England.[3] The king's letter does not appear to have reached its destination until the middle of November because of the movements of the imperial court.[4] During the summer the emperor had been assembling a large army with which he was ready to take the field against the Turkish invaders of the empire; the movements of this army took Charles V out of Germany to Vienna and on into Italy, and he reached Mantua on 6 November; it was there that Cranmer received Henry's letter. Hawkins reached Mantua about a week after the arrival of the imperial court, and on 16 November Cranmer had an audience at which he took leave of the emperor. On 19 November he left Mantua for England.[5]

Despite the haste with which he left Mantua, Cranmer travelled

[1] Montpesat to Francis I, 3 Feb. 1533 (*L. & P.*, vi, 110).
[2] cf. p. 122.
[3] cf. Henry VIII to the king of Hungary, 1 Oct. 1532 (Pocock, ii, 327; *L. & P.*, v, 1380); Henry VIII to Frederick count Palatine, 2 Oct. 1532 (*L. & P.*, v, 1381); for similar letters, dated 27 Sept. 1532, to other personages, see *L. & P.*, v, 1352. On 1 Oct. Chapuys reported that Norfolk had told him that Cranmer had been recalled and that his successor was Nicholas Hawkins (Chapuys to Charles V, 1 Oct. 1532 (*L. & P.*, v, 1377). For Hawkins's credentials, see Pocock, ii, 325.
[4] Charles V to Henry VIII, 18 Nov. 1532, Mantua (*L. & P.*, v, 1551).
[5] Hawkins to Henry VIII, 21 Nov. 1532 (*State Papers*, vii, 386; *L. & P.*, v, 1564). On 18 Nov. 1532, the emperor acknowledged the receipt of Henry's letter of 1 Oct. recalling Cranmer and announcing Hawkins as his successor (Charles V to Henry VIII, 18 Nov. 1532; *L. & P.*, v, 1551).

slowly; he was an exceedingly good horseman, yet he took seven weeks to accomplish a journey that Hawkins had done, without hurry, in six.[1] It is true that in December 1532 a severe frost had made the roads of France icy and dangerous, but the weather can provide only a partial explanation of Cranmer's leisurely pace; no doubt he dawdled because doubts about the future caused him to hesitate. But Henry had urgent need of Cranmer's presence in England and Cromwell sent Stephen Vaughan to France to hurry him on his way.[2]

Cranmer was now forty-three years old and until he had attracted the notice of the king he had pursued an undistinguished career as a fellow of Jesus College, Cambridge, where he was professor of divinity. His theological views were close to those of the continental reformers and he frequented the secret meetings at the White Horse Inn at Cambridge. He was much influenced by the humanistic approach to theology, and for some ten years had been, at heart, a heretic. Although he held preferment in the church[3] and had been appointed by the pope to be grand penitentiary for England, he did not scruple, while in Germany on diplomatic business, to marry secretly the niece of the wife of the reformer, Andreas Osiander; but when recalled by Henry he prudently left his wife in Germany.[4] When he reached England early in January 1533,[5] he learned that the king had chosen him to be archbishop of Canterbury and, perhaps with some trepidation, he accepted the honour.[6]

[1] Cranmer stated, at his trial, that the journey took seven weeks (see Foxe, *Acts and Monuments*, viii, 55), so that he arrived in London about 10 Jan. 1533. For Hawkins' journey, see Hawkins to Henry VIII, 21 Nov. 1532 (*State Papers*, vii, 386; *L. & P.*, v, 1564). In Jan. 1533, Bonner travelled from Bologna to Westminster in sixteen days (Bonner to Benet, 31 Jan. 1533; *State Papers*, vii, 410; *L. & P.*, vi, 101), and in Feb., 1533, Chapuys' messenger, riding post, travelled from London to Bologna in thirteen days (cf. Ortiz to the empress, 22 Feb. 1533; *L. & P.*, vi, 178).
[2] Vaughan to Cromwell, 9 Dec. 1532 (*L. & P.*, v, 1620). Vaughan found the roads dangerous and had a bad fall from his horse at Amiens.
[3] Hitherto, his highest dignity had been that of archdeacon.
[4] Such a marriage, contracted by a man in holy orders, was canonically invalid, whatever may have been the intention of the parties. Cranmer's wife came to England and he continued to live with her as well as his circumstances permitted. The famous story that when Cranmer travelled about he carried her with him, hidden in a chest, appears to be an invention; cf. Ridley, *Thomas Cranmer*, 148-51. [5] See note 1, above.
[6] Harpsfield (*A Treatise on the Pretended Divorce between Henry VIII and Catherine of Aragon*, Camden Soc. 1878, p. 290) has a story that Henry

Once the king had obtained Cranmer's acceptance, matters moved speedily. Benet was told that Dr Cranmer, elect of Canterbury, 'a man . . . of singular good learning, virtue, experience and all good parts', was sending to Rome for his bulls; he was told, too, that it was advisable to ensure that Cranmer was 'favourably handled' in respect of the charges for the bulls, especially the annates, for otherwise 'the matter of the annates . . . should be with all celerity called upon, and things attempted therein and otherwise, that should be not a little prejudicial to the court of Rome'. Benet was also told that the ambassadors were to make every effort to ensure that the king's matter was committed to England; the king was of opinion that this could be achieved if the pope were well handled.[1] Behind this request for the issue of the necessary bulls without a demand for the payment of annates lay the recently passed statute, prohibiting the payment of annates, which was to be brought into force by the king's letters patent. This veiled threat caused some consternation among the assembly of pope and cardinals, who were then at Bologna, for the annates of Canterbury amounted to 10,000 ducats, and Hawkins reported that 'they have been sore cumbered with debating of this matter, whether they should remit anything or no'.[2] In order to hasten matters Henry signed a warrant on 6 February authorizing Cromwell to pay a thousand pounds to Cranmer, and this sum was stated to have been 'advanced to him by way of prest and loan'.[3] On 11 February the king signed a further warrant authorizing Cromwell to pay one thousand pounds to the Italian merchant Antonio Bonvisi, for transfer to Benet in Rome.[4]

At this time the emperor was with the pope at Bologna, and Chapuys wrote to Charles urging him to intervene with his holiness to prevent the issue of the bulls until sentence in the marriage suit had been

---

[1] Bonner to Benet, 31 Jan. 1533 (*State Papers*, vii, 410; *L. & P.*, vi, 101).
[2] Hawkins to Henry VIII, Bologna, 22 Feb. 1533 (*State Papers*, vii, 424, at p. 425; *L. & P.*, vi, 177).
[3] Warrant dated 6 Feb. 1533 (*L. & P.*, vi, 131).
[4] Warrant dated 11 Feb. 1533 (*L. & P.*, vi, 149). Antonio Bonvisi was an Italian merchant of Lucca then resident in England; he was an old friend of Sir Thomas More.

---

appointed Cranmer archbishop at a bear-baiting, and a rumour to the same effect was current in Kent in 1534 (Articles against Winchelsea; *L. & P.*, vii, 1608); it may be that when Cranmer arrived at court the king was watching a bear-baiting and left immediately to see him.

pronounced in Rome, or to secure the insertion in the bulls of a clause requiring Cranmer to take an oath not to interfere in the suit.[1] However, on 21 February 1533, in consistory, Campeggio 'proponed' the vacation of the see, the pope provided Cranmer to the vacancy on the supplication of the king, and the necessary bulls were issued.[2] On the following day Hawkins reported that the whole matter was virtually settled for the modest outlay of 1,500 ducats paid as a 'propina' to Campeggio; there only remained, he said, the payment of smaller sums, amounting in all to some 3,000 to 4,000 ducats, to minor papal officials, but a sum of at least 1,000 ducats would be needed at the next consistory to obtain for Cranmer his pallium.[3] When the bulls reached England Cranmer was consecrated at Westminster on 30 March by the bishop of Lincoln, John Longland, with John Veysey of Exeter and Henry Standish of St Asaph as assistants.[4]

The consecration of the archbishop was accompanied by an extraordinary transaction. Cranmer had long been a dependant of the Boleyn family and was devoted to the will of his sovereign. Henry and Anne Boleyn must have congratulated themselves upon the choice of such a man, who was to be the means for annulling Henry's marriage with Catherine to enable him to marry Anne. But if archbishop Cranmer was to bring the marriage to an end he must, so far as outward forms could make it, be every whit as much a catholic archbishop as was archbishop Warham who had performed the marriage ceremony; the same authority that brought the marriage into existence must be the authority to bring it to an end. Accordingly Cranmer lost no time in seeking from the pope the pallium, the symbol of full archiepiscopal authority without which no catholic would regard him as archbishop. For this purpose, although Cranmer was already resolved to act in opposition to papal authority

---

[1] Chapuys to Charles V, 9 Feb. 1533 (*L. & P.*, vi, 142; see p. 65).
[2] Ehses, 214 (Acta consistorialia): 'Bononiae de veneris XXI februarii 1533. Ecclesiae Cantuariensi ad supplicationem regis Angliae provisum fuit de persona Thomae Cranmar.' There were no less than eleven bulls.
[3] Hawkins to Henry VIII, 22 Feb. 1533 (*State Papers*, vii, 424; *L. & P.*, vi, 177).
[4] Chapuys reported from London to the emperor that 'All people here cry "murder" against the pope for his procrastination in this affair [of the divorce], and likewise for his not having delayed the expedition of the Canterbury bulls until after the final sentence, since he was duly warned of the imminent danger pending therefrom' (Chapuys to Charles V, 31 Mar. 1533; *Span. Cal.*, iv, pt. 2(2), 1057 (p. 625); *L. & P.*, vi, 296).

his proctors in Rome swore, on his behalf, the oaths of spiritual allegiance to the pope and received the pallium for him on 3 March.[1]

For his consecration similar oaths would be required. But on the day of his consecration, by order of the king, the archbishop elect repaired to St Stephen's chapel in Westminster and there, in the presence of four witnesses, declared on oath that by the oath of obedience to the pope, which he was about to take for form's sake only, he did not intend to bind himself to anything contrary to the law of God, or prejudicial to the rights of the king, or prohibitory of such reforms as he might judge useful to the church of England.[2] From St Stephen's chapel he went to his consecration and there swore his oaths of allegiance and obedience to the pope.[3] Cranmer thus began his public life as archbishop of Canterbury with perjury; no wonder cardinal Reginald Pole later observed, 'Other perjurers be wont to break their oath after they have sworn it; you brake it before'.[4] After his consecration he took his oath of allegiance to the king, for the temporalities of his see, but in this oath, by a newly introduced variant, he acknowledged himself 'to take and hold the said archbishopric immediately and only' of the king 'and of none other'.[5]

[1] Ehses, 214 (Acta consistorialia): 'Bononiae die lunae III martii 1533. Mandavit (S.D.N.) tradi pallium ecclesiae Cantuariensi.' cf. Hawkins to Henry VIII, 22 Feb. 1533 (*State Papers*, vii, 424; *L. & P.*, vi, 177) (Nicholas Hawkins, archdeacon of Ely, was ambassador to the emperor; see p. 212, note 3).
[2] For the text of this sworn declaration, see Wilkins, *Concilia*, iii, 757 (*L. & P.*, vi, 291(1)).
[3] A year before, these oaths had greatly shocked the king; see p. 191.
[4] cf. Lingard, *History of England* (ed. 1826 Paris), vi, 213, 214: 'I will only observe that oaths cease to offer any security, if their meaning may be qualified by previous protestations, made without the knowledge of the party who is principally interested.' cf. the cross-examination of Cranmer by Thomas Martin, at his trial for heresy in Sept. 1555, in Foxe, *Acts and Monuments*, viii, 54 et seq. (the passage is printed in Ridley, *Thomas Cranmer*, 373). It is, perhaps, worth noting that, in the so called Bishops' Book of 1537, Cranmer subscribed to the statement that it was a transgression of the third commandment if men 'swear to do that thing which they intended not to do'.
[5] Strype, *Cranmer*, 685; *L. & P.*, vi, 291(3). Cranmer received the temporalities of his see on 19 April 1533; the grant was dated 9 April and delivered on 19 April (see Rymer, *Foedera*, xiv, 456; *L. & P.*, vi, 417(27)). In his recent book, *Thomas Cranmer* (Oxford 1962), Mr Jasper Ridley advances the thesis that Cranmer was not a time-server because he consistently acted in accordance with a principle. Mr Ridley wrote (p. 12): 'He believed that his primary duty as a Christian was to strengthen the power of the King, and was prepared if necessary to sacrifice all his other doctrines to accomplish this. There was only one

circumstance in which he considered that he was justified in opposing the royal policy—if he were ordered to sin. Then he must refuse to obey, as God must be served rather than man. When Cranmer was ordered to support a religious policy of which he disapproved, he had to decide, on this basis, whether to obey or resist. In the twentieth century, few people will deny that men are influenced by unconscious motives; and Cranmer, when he repeatedly faced this problem in Henry's reign, was obviously aware that obedience meant continued residence at Lambeth, and that resistance would bring him to the stake. But this is not the same thing as deliberate time-serving'. With respect, the present writer is unable to find a valid distinction between adherence to Cranmer's 'principle' and time-serving.

XIII

The Breach with Rome

The prorogued parliament[1] re-assembled at Westminster on 4 February 1533.[2] Among the 'bills depending in the common house since the last prorogation' was the bill relating to *primer seisin*, but despite two readings it failed to pass.[3] The most important work of this session was the passing of the act in restraint of appeals to Rome. The bill for this act had been some time in preparation and during the process its scope had been considerably enlarged.[4] It seems that the original intention had been the passing of an act dealing only with the king's case; there is in existence the draft of a bill, in the hand of Thomas Audley, that dealt with the 'king's matter' only, but this came to nothing.[5] Then Cromwell took a hand and his appears to be the predominating influence that determined the final form of the bill. That the intended legislation was not to be confined to the case of the king is indicated by the title endorsed on the first of Cromwell's drafts: 'Concerning the king's matter and other that none shall sue appeals hereafter to Rome but only within this realm.'[6]

[1] See p. 193.
[2] cf. Rolls of Parliament (*L. & P.*, vi, 119). The speaker of the house of commons was Humphrey Wingfield, a barrister of Gray's Inn (cf. Hall, *Chronicle*, ii, 223). Shortly before the re-assembly of parliament, on 26 Jan. 1533, Thomas Audley, then lord keeper, was appointed lord chancellor: at about 3 p.m., in a chamber near the oratory at Greenwich, in the presence of the duke of Norfolk, Thomas Cranmer, elect of Canterbury, the earl of Wiltshire, Thomas Cromwell, and others, 'the king took the great seal from the custody of Thomas Audley, and, after holding it a quarter of an hour, returned it to the custody of the said Thomas Audley, appointing him Chancellor of England' (*L. & P.*, vi, 73; Rymer, *Foedera*, xiv, 446; cf. Hall, *Chronicle*, ii, 222).
[3] cf. *L. & P.*, vi, 120.
[4] For a study (from the original drafts) of the preparation of the bill, see Elton, 'The Evolution of a Reformation Statute', in *E.H.R.*, lxiv (1949), 174-97.
[5] cf. Elton, op. cit., *E.H.R.*, lxiv, 177. Catherine's friends seem to have suspected that there was a move on foot to enable the divorce to be settled in England and to exclude papal intervention; cf. Chapuys to Charles V, 27 Jan. 1533 (*L. & P.*, vi, 89); Chapuys to Charles V, 9 Feb. 1533 (*L. & P.*, vi, 142).
[6] Elton, op. cit., *E.H.R.*, lxiv, 177. The various drafts are calendared at *L. & P.*, vi, 120(6-9) and *L. & P.*, vii, 1611(2); the latter is a fragment and in the calendar is wrongly attributed to another statute.

The earliest drafts betray traces of governmental uncertainty, but as the work of preparation progressed these traces disappeared. The most interesting instance of this process was provided by a long statement in the draft of the preamble which, on the ground that it was feared that 'evil interpretors . . . of the laws ensuing' might accuse the makers thereof of heresy, asserted the true Catholic faith of the king and the people and set forth a defence to the charge in anticipation of its being made. This passage was struck out at an early stage, but was subsequently reinstated, probably at the command of the king. Cromwell's views, however, prevailed; the fear of a charge of heresy and its accompanying hesitancy disappeared and the whole passage was finally deleted.[1]

When the bill was judged ready for parliament it was considered, on 5 February, by a gathering of selected churchmen who had been summoned to discuss, with the principal councillors of the king, the means by which Henry might achieve his matrimonial purpose.[2] It seems likely that the assembled churchmen voiced some opposition to the draft bill as it then stood; at all events, the introduction of the bill into parliament was delayed and further amendments were made, presumably for the purpose of removing objections made at the meeting of 5 February in order to secure a smoother passage for the bill when it reached the house of lords. Hitherto the preamble to the bill had contained a number of statements, claiming a royal origin for the law administered in the courts spiritual, which were excessive and incapable of being substantiated; and in the system of appeals devised in the bill for spiritual causes the ultimate appeal lay to a commission of ecclesiastical lawyers

[1] cf. Elton, op. cit., *E.H.R.*, lxiv, 182-4
[2] Chapuys to Charles V, 9 Feb. 1533 (*L. & P.*, vi, 142 (p. 65)): 'She [queen Catherine] has also heard that four days ago one of the king's chief councillors had assembled several doctors, both clerical and lay, and had proposed to them, on behalf of the King, that the opinion of all theologians was that if the first marriage was consummated, the second was null; and that to prove the consummation, besides the presumption the King had found an instrument, which he showed them, containing an assertion thereof by the King Catholic and the King's father. Having seen this, the whole company said that it only remained for the king to proceed to his purpose by the authority of the archbishop of Canterbury.' Those summoned appear to have been the archbishop of Canterbury (Cranmer), the bishops of Winchester, Lincoln and St Asaph, the abbots of Hyde and Burton, the king's almoner (Edward Foxe), doctors Oliver, Tregonwell, Lee and Gwent, and 'the fryer Carmelytane' who was, most probably, the provincial of the White Friars (cf. Cromwell's Remembrances, *L. & P.*, vi, 150). See, generally, Elton, op. cit., *E.H.R.*, lxiv, 189-92.

appointed under the great seal, and in the king's causes to the upper house of convocation. The first of these matters was deleted, and the second was changed so as to deprive the king of the last word. Both these matters related to the high claims of the 'imperial crown' then being put forward, and it seems certain that Cromwell would not have made either of these alterations without pressure from others; those others must have been the ecclesiastical lawyers, who would most readily detect the falsity of the claims made with regard to the origins of canon law, and the bishops, who were anxious to retain full control over all causes in the ecclesiastical courts and to preserve the prerogatives of the see of Canterbury.[1]

The bill was eventually introduced into the commons on 14 March when it was read a first time; Eustache Chapuys reported that it surprised many people.[2] The introduction of a bill directed against the papacy could scarcely have surprised anyone, and the public reaction was, no doubt, due to the sweeping nature of its provisions. In the commons the bill met with strong opposition which persisted for a fortnight or more. This opposition appears to have been grounded upon economic considerations. The principal argument of those opposing the bill was, according to Chapuys, that if the pope, being aggrieved at the passage of the bill, should induce other Christian princes to regard England as schismatic, those princes would refuse to trade with her and there would be a serious interruption of the wool trade, the chief prop of England's economy, which might well provoke rebellion and civil war. To that argument the government spokesmen replied that there was no such danger, because neighbouring princes would be only too glad to follow the king's example.[3] Nevertheless, Catherine was not without her champions. A group of members, instigated by a friend of Chapuys, who sat for the City of London, proposed that if Henry agreed to submit the decision of the marriage question to a general council, a grant of £200,000 should be made to the king. In reporting this proposal Chapuys observed that there was no chance that the king would agree to the matter being disposed of otherwise than by the archbishop of Canterbury, 'of whom he

---

[1] cf. Elton, op. cit., *E.H.R.*, lxiv, 189.
[2] Chapuys to Charles V, 15 Mar. 1533 (*L. & P.*, vi, 235 (p. 110)): 'Yesterday and today it was proposed in Parliament to make a statute declaring the Pope had no authority in this kingdom; which many people have found very strange'.
[3] Chapuys to Charles V, 31 Mar. 1533 (*L. & P.*, vi, 296).

The Breach with Rome

is perfectly assured'.[1] Chapuys' comment was well justified. The government were not then in financial difficulty and no grant of money, however large, would have deterred the king and his councillors from their purpose; and neither king nor pope had any desire for a general council.[2] However, the bill eventually passed the commons in the first week of April; it had an uneventful passage through the lords, and accordingly became law. The session ended almost immediately, on 7 April.

The Act in Restraint of Appeals of 1533 was perhaps the most important statute of the sixteenth century.[3] The preamble began by asserting the ancient power and pre-eminence of the kings of England and referred to the power and learning of the spiritual body, usually called the English Church:

Where by divers sundry old authentic histories and chronicles it is manifestly declared and expressed that this realm of England is an empire,[4] and so hath been accepted in the world, governed by one supreme head and king having the dignity and royal estate of the imperial crown of the same, unto whom a

[1] Chapuys to Charles V, 10 April 1533 (*L. & P.*, vi, 324).
[2] The sum of £200,000 was about twice the annual revenues of the crown at that time; and the unreality of the proposal induces some doubt whether it was ever actually put forward in the house (although some such thing may well have been discussed privately); cf. Elton, op. cit., *E.H.R.*, lxiv, 193.
[3] 24 Hen. VIII, c. 12 (printed in *Statutes of the Realm*, iii, 427; Pocock, ii, 460; *G. & H.*, 187); its full title is, 'An Acte that the appeles in suche cases as have ben used to be pursued to the see of Rome shall not be from hensforth had ne used but wythin this realme.' The act was modified by the Submission of the Clergy Act of 1534 (25 Hen. VIII, c. 19), and in 1554, together with several other Henrician statutes, was repealed by 1 & 2 Phil. & Mary, c. 8; that act was in turn repealed by 1 Eliz. I, c. 1, which also provided that the statute 24 Hen. VIII, c. 12 (and others) 'shall be revived and shall stand and be in full force and strength, to all intents, constructions and purposes'. The Act in Restraint of Appeals of 1533 is still in force (although repealed as to Northern Ireland by the Statute Law Revision Act 1950) and was given the short title, 'The Ecclesiastical Appeals Act 1532', by the Statute Law Revision Act 1948; parts of ss. 3 and 4 were repealed by the Ecclesiastical Jurisdiction Measure, 1963, which came into force on 1 Mar. 1965.
[4] The term 'empire' usually denotes, nowadays, an entity that has been built up by outward expansion (e.g. the Roman Empire and the British Empire), but Henry's 'empire' was produced by the reverse process; it was a nation state that had contracted itself upon its insularity. The preamble put forward Henry's statute merely as a logical development of the statutes of provisors and praemunire, and in doing so employed the term 'empire' which was a familiar concept to the canonists of the Roman curia; as sovereign of an empire Henry was entitled to all imperial prerogatives and rights, and *rex est imperator in regno suo*.

221

body politic, compact of all sorts and degrees of people divided in terms and by names of spirituality and temporalty, be bounden and owe to bear next to God a natural and humble obedience; he being also institute and furnished by the goodness and sufferance of Almighty God with plenary, whole, and entire power, pre-eminence, authority, prerogative, and jurisdiction to render and yield justice and final determination to all manner of folk resiants [residents] or subjects within this his realm, in all causes, matters, debates, and contentions happening to occur, insurge, or begin within the limits thereof, without restraint or provocation to any foreign princes or potentates of the world: the body spiritual whereof having power when any cause of the law divine happened to come in question or of spiritual learning, then it was declared, interpreted and shewed by that part of the said body politic called the spirituality, now being usually called the English Church, which always hath been reputed and also found of that sort that both for knowledge, integrity, and sufficiency of number, it hath been always thought and is also at this hour sufficient and meet of itself, without the intermeddling of any exterior person or persons, to declare and determine all such doubts and to administer all such offices and duties as to their rooms spiritual doth appertain; . . .

The preamble went on to declare the form of government of the estate temporal and then asserted that, for the spirituality and temporalty, 'both their authorities and jurisdictions do conjoin together in the due administration of justice the one to help the other'.

The preamble then referred to the statutes, such as those of provisors and praemunire, made in time past to prevent encroachments of the see of Rome[1] or other foreign power, and declared that notwithstanding them, dangers unprovided for therein had arisen by reason of appeals to the see of Rome; such appeals delayed justice and were inconvenient by reason of distance. It was then enacted that 'all causes testamentary, causes of matrimony and divorces, rights of tithes, oblations and obventions, the knowledge whereof by the goodness of princes of this realm and by the laws and customs of the same appertaineth to the spiritual jurisdiction of this realm' were to be determined in the king's courts, temporal or spiritual, any foreign inhibition or the like notwithstanding. It was further provided that only sentences pronounced in the king's courts should take effect, and that the clergy were to administer the sacraments to the subjects of the realm notwithstanding any interdict or suspension from the see of Rome; if any spiritual person failed to do so

[1] In early drafts of the bill, the draftsman had referred to 'the see apostolic'; Cromwell changed this phrase to 'the see of Rome', but, by inadvertence, failed to make the change in one or two places when revising the second draft; see Elton, op. cit., *E.H.R.*, lxiv, 181.

he should suffer one year s imprisonment and pay a fine and ransom at the king's pleasure. It was also provided that any attempt to procure an interdict from, or to appeal to the see of Rome should incur 'the same pains, penalties and forfeitures, ordained and provided by the statute of provision and praemunire made in the sixteenth year of the reign of the right noble prince King Richard the Second'.[1]

The act then provided that all appeals were to be determined within the realm, and prescribed the courts by which they were to be heard: from the court of the archdeacon an appeal lay to the diocesan bishop and thence to the archbishop of the province; and it was laid down that such an appeal should be made within fifteen days after the judgment or sentence had been given. Suits commenced before an archbishop were to be determined by him without further appeal; and the act contained a saving for the prerogative of the archbishop and church of Canterbury. Special provision was made for appeals in causes touching the king; in such cases appeal lay 'to the spiritual prelates and other abbots and priors of the upper house assembled and convocate by the king's writ in the convocation being or next ensuing within the province or provinces where the same matter of contention is or shall be begun', and every such appeal was to be made within fifteen days. Finally, the act provided that every person, and his aiders and abettors, who did not observe the provisions of the act should incur the penalties of the statute of praemunire of 1393.

Thus in one single measure the whole of the pope's jurisdiction over English laymen was completely abolished, so that henceforth, in matters of religion and conscience, they lay at the mercy of their sovereign and parliament. This masterpiece of Cromwellian statute making was the main foundation upon which Henry and Cromwell erected the statutory structure that removed England from the Catholic communion and which made possible the fundamental religious changes of later years. The preamble of the act, the first of many such expositions of policy, deserves special notice, since it embodied Cromwell's political thought and marked his emergence as the dominating influence in the councils of the king. It professed to base the provisions of the act on uncertain traditions and from that dubious historical platform went on to enunciate, as accepted fact, a new doctrine that the king was supreme head of a realm which was a sovereign state free from all foreign authority.

[1] i.e. the Statute of Praemunire, 1393 (16 Ric. II, c. 5).

In setting out a novel yet developed theory of the state, the preamble was a remarkable essay in conservative revolution that rested squarely on constitutional forms and practice. Whatever it might assert, the view expressed of the relationship between church and state had little in common with the concept of that relationship generally held in the Middle Ages. It argued that the total abolition of the papal jurisdiction brought about by the act was but the logical development of the statutes of provisors and praemunire. Those statutes limited the pope's jurisdiction in certain matters, it is true, but they did not deny that jurisdiction; yet the act in restraint of appeals, by destroying that jurisdiction altogether, implicitly denied it, and the change that was thereby brought about was so great and of so fundamental a nature that it can scarcely be regarded as the development of a process already begun but rather as the beginning of a totally new process.[1]

[1] In this connection the words of an eminent modern academic lawyer, Sir William Holdsworth, may be quoted: 'Henry VIII often inserted in the preambles to his statutes reasoned arguments designed to prove the wisdom of the particular statute. And, in drawing up these arguments he never hesitated to colour facts and events to suit his purpose. But the preamble to this Statute of Appeals is remarkable, partly because it manufactures history upon an unprecedented scale, but chiefly because it has operated from that day to this as a powerful incentive to its manufacture by others upon similar lines. Nor is the reason for this phenomenon difficult to discover. The Tudor settlement of the relations of Church and State was a characteristically skilful instance of the Tudor genius for creating a modern institution with a medieval form. But, in order to create the illusion that the new Anglican church was indeed the same institution as the mediaeval church, it was necessary to prove the historical continuity of these two very different institutions; and obviously this could only be done by an historical argument. When this argument had been put forward in a statutory form it became a good statutory root of title for the continuity and catholicity of this essentially modern institution. But a merely statutory title gave an obvious handle to its opponents, and could hardly be expected to satisfy its supporters. It is not therefore surprising that lawyers, theologians, and ecclesiastical historians soon began, from their different points of view, to amplify and illustrate this historical argument, in order to prove that it rested upon a solid basis of historical truth. Two great professions thus have had and still have a direct professional interest in maintaining this thesis. The lawyers are tied to it by their statutes and cases: the ecclesiastics by the tradition and the authoritative declarations of their church. Naturally, therefore, its truth is still believed and maintained by a long array of imposing names. It was not till an historian [F. W. Maitland] arose who, besides the greatest historian of this century, was both a consummate lawyer and a dissenter from the Anglican as well as from other churches, that the historical worthlessness of Henry's theory was finally demonstrated' (Holdsworth, *History of English Law*, i (7th ed. 1956), 590, 591).

While parliament was still debating the act, convocation was induced to define the christian theology of marriage in terms that would prepare the way for the judicial activities that Cranmer was about to undertake. When convocation assembled in St Paul's on 26 March they turned first to consider proceedings that had been commenced against Hugh Latimer concerning a sermon which he had preached at Bristol relating to the veneration of saints and pilgrimages to their images. Convocation then turned to the question of the divorce. The presiding prelate, the bishop of London, produced, for the information of those present, certain books containing the statements and depositions of witnesses in the cause; he also produced a treaty between Henry VII and Ferdinand of Spain, and a transumpt of the apostolic brief sent to Spain,[1] together with copies of the determinations of certain foreign universities, the originals of which he promised to produce. When it was questioned whether convocation might lawfully discuss such a matter, now that it was before the pope for decision, the bishop of London produced the transumpt of a further apostolic brief in which, he said, the pope had desired everyone freely to declare his opinion. At the next session, on 28 March, the bishop of London fulfilled his promise and produced the sealed originals of the opinions of the universities of Paris, Orleans, Bologna, Passau, Bourges and Toulouse, which were publicly read.

The king was insistently demanding a decision,[2] and after much discussion, in which several prelates expressed the opinion that the matter was extremely difficult and of great moment, two questions were propounded. The first question, which was to be answered by the theologians, was whether the prohibition forbidding a man to marry the widow of his deceased brother, when the first marriage had been consummated,

---

[1] Transumpt (*transumptum*) is a term of canon law signifying a judicially authenticated copy of a document or judicial process; cf. *Codex Juris Canonici*, can. 2054.

[2] Chapuys to Charles V, 31 Mar. 1533 (*L. & P.*, vi, 296): '. . . the King was only waiting for the bulls of the archbishopric of Canterbury, in order to proceed to the decision of his marriage; which having arrived these five days, to the great regret of everybody, the King was extremely urgent with the synod here for the determination of his said affair, . . . so that those present could scarcely eat or drink, and using such terms to them that no one dared open his mouth to contradict, except the good bishop of Rochester [Fisher]. But his single voice cannot avail against the majority, so that the queen and he now consider her cause desperate.'

were of divine law and not dispensable by the pope;[1] the second question, to be answered by the canonists, was whether the consummation of the marriage between prince Arthur and queen Catherine were sufficiently proved from the matters exhibited.[2] To each of these questions an answer favourable to the king was carried by a large majority.[3] Although the long discussions had taken place in his absence, the new archbishop appeared in convocation on 5 April to receive the votes of the theologians and canonists in answer to the questions put to them; and when the results were announced, Dr John Tregonwell appeared on behalf of the king and requested that the proceedings of convocation be reduced into writing and published. On 8 April Dr Clayborne exhibited a writ from the king proroguing convocation to 7 June, and it was ultimately prorogued to 31 March 1534.[4]

[1] 'An ducere uxorem cognitam a fratre decendente sine prole, sit prohibitio juris divini indispensabilis a papa?'
[2] 'An carnalis copula inter illustrissimum principem Arthurum et serenissimam dominam Catherinam reginam, ex propositis, exhibitis, deductis, et allegatis sit sufficienter probata?'
[3] On the first question, there were 253 ayes and 19 noes; of these 75 votes were given in person (59 ayes and 16 noes) and the remainder were given by proxy. On the second question, there were 41 ayes and 6 noes; of these, 44 votes were given in person (38 ayes and 6 noes) and the remainder were given by proxy.
[4] For the proceedings of convocation, see Pocock, ii, 442-59 (for the notarial record of the determination on the two questions, see pp. 446-9).

XIV

The Trial at Dunstable

I

While these momentous events were going forward Henry had been mindful of public opinion. Whatever the general body of his subjects may have thought of the king's treatment of queen Catherine, no one could have anticipated the crisis that was approaching so swiftly. Henry had a cordial ally in Francis I and his friendly relations with the emperor had not been broken; moreover, to all outward appearance there did not seem to be any real dispute between himself and the pope. Henry was at pains to receive the nuncio at court with every honour; and although the nuncio's proposals were invariably met with delay or evasion, his continued presence in England and the honour done to him at court seemed sufficient guarantee to Englishmen that a rupture with the pope was impossible.

To foster this state of public opinion Henry invited the nuncio to be present at the opening of parliament at the beginning of February, and the pope's representative appeared in the house of lords, seated on the right of the king. Had the public suspected that the question of the divorce was placing a severe strain upon the relations between the king and pope, it is likely that there would have been an outburst of popular feeling highly disagreeable both to the king and to Anne Boleyn. It was therefore imperative to hide the strains that were increasing daily. The Spanish ambassador believed that the only remedy for a worsening situation was the pronouncement of a judgment in the cause, and he thought that the nuncio was of the same opinion.[1] But the prospect of a judgment was remote.

Soon afterwards the king again invited the nuncio to be present in parliament; this time to listen to the proceedings of the house of commons. The nuncio accepted this invitation reluctantly, believing that it was the king's intention that he should be present when the house discussed some measure derogatory of the holy see. He went in the

[1] Chapuys to Charles V, 9 Feb. 1533 (*L. & P.*, vi, 142).

company of the French ambassador, Montpesat, who was about to return to France, and of his successor, de Dinteville, who had just arrived. He was relieved to find the commons discussing nothing more menacing than a bill to deprive thieves of the right of sanctuary. He did not stay long, and after feasting with the ambassadors and some of the council, he sought an interview with the king for that afternoon; he was, however, put off until the following day. The duke of Norfolk told him frankly that the chief purpose in deferring the interview was to ensure that he might be seen more frequently at court so that all the world might be aware of the great friendship and good understanding the king had with the pope. The device was apparently successful, for Chapuys reported that the king and his council expected to reap some profit as regards the people and prelates who had hitherto supported the authority of the holy see, both in the divorce and in everything else; but he also reported that Fisher had said that such people did not dare utter a syllable for fear of going against the pope. Public opinion was becoming uncertain, and in this way the effect of the repeated papal monitions, which had been kept secret in England, had been largely nullified. Moreover, the king's ministers attempted to conceal the execution of the last monition in Flanders by threatening with severe penalties those who dared to speak of it.[1]

At the same time Anne Boleyn had announced more than once over the dinner table that she was certain that the king would marry her shortly; her father told the earl of Rutland that the king would not delay much longer but would complete the marriage with his daughter, and when once that was ratified by act of parliament, objectors could easily be pacified.[2] Towards the end of February a rumour was current that the new archbishop of Canterbury had married, or at least betrothed, the king to Anne Boleyn; and the rumour gained credibility from the fact that, since his election, Cranmer had stated openly that he would maintain, even on pain of being burned, that the king might take Anne Boleyn to wife. The belief was spreading that Henry was only waiting for Cranmer's bulls before publicly celebrating his new marriage; and there appeared to be no means of preventing such a scandal.[3] The clergy

[1] Chapuys to Charles V, 15 Feb. 1533 (*L. & P.*, vi, 160).
[2] Chapuys to Charles V, 15 Feb. 1533 (*L. & P.*, vi, 160).
[3] Chapuys to Charles V, 23 Feb. 1533 (*Span. Cal.*, iv, pt. 2(1), 1053; *L. & P.* vi. 180).

had been effectively constrained by statute and Catherine had been moved further from the court, while Anne Boleyn openly took her place and provided sumptuous entertainments for the king and nobility.[1]

Meanwhile, preparations had been going forward for the pope's meeting with Francis I, to which Henry had been invited to send representatives. Henry was minded to send either the duke of Norfolk or the earl of Wiltshire,[2] but Francis suggested that Norfolk would be preferable to Wiltshire as the latter was Anne Boleyn's father and 'it might be said that the affair touched him nearer than any other, and he would be suspected of prosecuting it with more passion, which might be a cause rather of retarding it'.[3] However, in the middle of March the king sent lord Rochford, Anne Boleyn's brother, to France. Rochford was instructed to tell the French king that Henry, in his desire to have male issue for the establishment of his kingdom, 'hath proceeded effectually to the accomplishment of his marriage', and that he trusted that Francis would assist and maintain him should he be excommunicated by the pope. Now that he was following the French king's advice, Henry hoped that Francis, as a true friend and brother, would devise whatever he could for the marriage, 'preventing any impediment to it, or of the succession, which please God will follow, and which, to all appearance, is in a state of advancement already'. Henry appears to have been unaware of the incongruity of announcing to his ally, in the same communication, both his own marriage and the expected birth of an heir. Rochford was also instructed to remind the French king of the dishonour which the pope had done to Henry's royal dignity by summoning him to appear in Rome and especially by refusing to admit the excusator, and he was to urge Francis to send an agent to the pope to resist any further process against the king and to inform his holiness that unless the excusator were admitted the French king would never agree to the proposed marriage between the duke of Orleans and the pope's niece. Finally, Rochford was to assure Francis that there was no prince upon whose support Henry relied so much, especially as he had vowed never to abandon Henry in his cause and to aid and maintain him in his

---

[1] cf. Chapuys to Charles V, 8 Mar. 1533 (*L. & P.*, vi, 212).
[2] Du Bellay, Beauvoys and de Dinteville to Francis I, 26 Feb. 1533 (*L. & P.*, vi, 184).
[3] Francis I to the bailly of Troyes, 28 Mar. 1533 (*L. & P.*, vi, 282). cf. Extract from letters dated 25 Feb. and 2 Mar. 1533, received by Francis I from cardinals Tournon and Grammont (*L. & P.*, vi, 201).

succession.[1] Rochford was also provided with the draft of a letter which the king proposed should be written by Francis to the pope, urging the grant of a divorce to Henry in order to quieten his scruples arising from his marriage with Catherine.[2]

Such an approach to Francis I placed a severe strain upon a friendship that was not vital to French interests. If the French king were to accede to all Henry's wishes the only results would be the cancellation of the impending meeting between Francis and the pope, the breaking off of the match between the duke of Orleans and the pope's niece, and the bringing about of a situation that would throw the pope into the arms of the emperor. Accordingly, Francis replied somewhat coolly to Rochford's approach. He told him that his coming interview with the pope had been determined upon by Henry's advice and he could not now go back upon what he had done. He also told Rochford that it would be very ill advised to send the proposed letter to the pope, as the emperor was then in Italy and the pope could have no better excuse than the letter for putting off the interview which had been arranged principally to serve Henry. Francis did, however, propose to send a letter to cardinals Tournon and Grammont, at Rome, asking them to urge the pope to admit the excusator, and to beg his holiness to take no final step in the cause until after his meeting with Francis.[3] Henry realized soon enough that he could expect no more of Francis than the letter to the cardinals in Rome, and he expressed his approval of its contents.[4]

As a result Francis instructed the cardinals to urge the pope to admit the excusator; if his holiness refused to do so they were to beg him not to take any step in the cause until after the coming meeting when the matter could be amply discussed. Should the pope appear disinclined to comply with these requests he should be reminded of the need for reflection before he displeased the king of England, for the kings of England and France were so united that Francis would take to heart any displeasure done to Henry as if it were done to himself; this was not the

[1] Instructions for lord Rochford, Mar. 1533 (*State Papers*, vii, 427; *L. & P.*, vi, 230(1)). The instructions are in French.
[2] Draft letter (*State Papers*, vii, 435; *L. & P.*, vi, 230(2)).
[3] Francis I to the bailly of Troyes, 20 Mar. 1533 (*L. & P.*, vi, 254). The Bailly of Troyes, Jean de Dinteville, was the new French ambassador in England.
[4] Francis I to the bailly of Troyes, 28 Mar. 1533 (*L. & P.*, vi, 282): 'Is glad that the king of England approves of his letter to the cardinals Tournon and Grammont. Expects him to send it back in a day or two, and will then despatch it.'

time to irritate the two kings or other princes who were the pope's friends.[1] After an interview with the pope Tournon reported that his holiness appeared determined to conduct the affair so dexterously that, when he and Francis met, nothing would be altered or marred; but his holiness would have to act in such a way that he did not show himself too partial to Henry, and he wished Francis discreetly to inform him of this.[2]

Meanwhile, in preparation for what was about to happen, Henry caused a priest to preach before him and Anne Boleyn a discourse to the effect that all the while the king had lived with the queen he had been guilty of adultery, and that all his good subjects ought to pray that God would pardon his offence and enlighten him to take another lady; the lords of the council should solicit and even constrain him to do so, without any regard to the censures or other provisions that the pope could make, for his holiness ought not to be obeyed in such a matter since he was commanding what was against God and reason. The sermon was preached with such warmth and vehemence that the queen's servants were scandalized, and the queen herself was again compelled to seek the assistance of the emperor.[3]

Henry now began to press on with his plans with increasing urgency. Cranmer's bulls arrived at the end of March,[4] and immediately Henry brought the question of the divorce before convocation.[5] Parliament was induced to abolish all ecclesiastical appeals to Rome which effectively prevented papal interference in the king's matrimonial projects.[6] But Henry's language and his menacing proceedings caused the nuncio to remonstrate with him, saying that the world would find it strange that he who had formerly written in favour of the pope's authority should now annul it against God, reason and the obedience he had given to the pope. Henry replied that what he did was for the preservation of his own authority and to protect himself against the injuries done to him at

---

[1] Francis I to cardinals Grammont and Tournon, [? March] 1533 (*L. & P.*, vi, 255); the version calendared is a draft.

[2] Cardinal Tournon to Francis I, [? Apr.] 1533 (*L. & P.*, vi, 301). For subsequent proceedings, see Francis I to cardinal Tournon, May 1533 (*L. & P.*, vi, 424); cardinal Tournon to Francis I, 4 May, 1533 (*L. & P.*, vi, 440); Francis I to the bailly of Troyes, 5 May 1533 (*L. & P.*, vi, 444).

[3] Chapuys to Charles V, 15 Mar. 1533 (*L. & P.*, vi, 235).

[4] See p. 215.

[5] See p. 225.

[6] See p. 221.

Rome. It was quite true, Henry said, that he had written books in favour of the pope, but now he had studied the question more deeply and found that the contrary of what he had written was true; yet if the pope complied with his wishes he might have occasion to study the matter even further and re-affirm what he had written.[1]

On 9 April the king sent a small deputation of nobles, including the dukes of Norfolk and Suffolk, to acquaint the queen that her case was virtually settled; she need not trouble herself any more about the matter nor attempt to return to him, because he was already married. Catherine was also informed that she must cease to use the title of queen and must assume that of princess dowager.[2] Only a few days previously Catherine's staunch champion among the clergy, John Fisher, bishop of Rochester, had been arrested, to ensure his silence while Henry completed his plans; and Anne Boleyn boasted that before long she would be queen and would have the princess Mary as her lady's maid.[3]

Easter was now approaching,[4] and almost a month had passed since Rochford had been instructed to inform the French king that Anne Boleyn was noticeably pregnant.[5] The secret could not be hidden from the public any longer. Accordingly, on Good Friday, 11 April, only twelve days after his consecration as archbishop, Cranmer wrote to the king a letter which Henry had carefully amended and approved, humbly begging leave 'to proceed to the examination, final determination, and judgment in the said great cause [of matrimony], touching your highness', since such was his office and duty as archbishop of Canterbury, because there was great bruit among the common people on the subject.[6]

---

[1] Chapuys to Charles V, 31 Mar. 1533 (*L. & P.*, vi, 296).
[2] Chapuys to Charles V, 10 April 1533 (*L. & P.*, vi, 324).
[3] Chapuys to Charles V, 10 April 1533 (*L. & P.*, vi, 324): 'Last Sunday, being Palm Sunday [6 April], the King made the bishop of Rochester prisoner, and put him under the charge of the bishop of Winchester; which is a very strange thing, as he is the most holy and learned prelate in Christendom. The King gave out in Parliament that this was done because he had insinuated that Rochford had gone to France with a commission to present an innumerable sum of money to the chancellor of France and the cardinal of Lorraine to persuade the pope by a bribe to ratify this new marriage, or at all events to overlook it, and not proceed further; which the King thought his Holiness would naturally do, seeing that the matter was already settled. . . . The real cause of the bishop's detention is his manly defence of the queen's cause.'
[4] Easter Sunday in 1533 was 13 April.   [5] See p. 229.
[6] Cranmer to Henry VIII, 11 April 1533 (*State Papers*, i, 390, 391; *L. & P.*, vi, 327). There are two letters, both dated 11 April, from Cranmer to the king. The

On the following day the king wrote a gracious reply to the archbishop, saying that he could not be displeased with Cranmer's zeal for justice and his desire to quieten the kingdom. The king went on to say that 'albeit we, being your king and sovereign, do recognize no superior in earth, but only God, and not being subject to the laws of any other earthly creature; yet because ye be, under us, by God's calling and ours, the most principal minister of our spiritual jurisdiction, within this our realm' the request could not be refused, and licence was accordingly given him to proceed in the cause.[1]

Anne Boleyn did not wait for Cranmer to bring his allotted task to a conclusion but at once and openly assumed the title of queen. On Easter eve she went to Mass in royal state, with a suite of sixty young ladies. The Spanish ambassador noted that 'all the world is astonished at it, for it looks like a dream, and even those who take her part know not

[1] Henry VIII to Cranmer, 12 April 1533 (*State Papers*, i, 392, 393; *L. & P.*, vi, 332).

---

first was evidently not entirely to the king's liking, and was returned to the archbishop for a more suitable one to be written. The two letters are almost identical for the first two-thirds of their length. The principal changes are as follows, where omissions are indicated by italics and additions are printed within square brackets: 'I, . . . am . . . most humblie to beseche Your most noble Grace, that wher *my office and duetie is* [the office and duetie of thArchbisshop of Canturbery], by your and your *predecessours* [progenitours] sufferaunce and grauntes, [is] to directe *and* ordre [judge, and determyn] causes spirituall, in this Your Graces realme, *according to the lawes of God and Holye Churche, and for relief of almaner greves and infirmities of the people, Goddes subjectes and yours, happening in the said spirituall causes, to provide suche remedie, as shalbe thought most convenient for their helpe and relief, in that behalf;* . . . it may please *the same to ascerteyn me of Your Graces pleasure in the premisses, to thentent that, the same knowen, I may procede for my discharge afore God, to thexecution of my saide office and duetie, according to his calling and yours. Beseching Your Hieghnes moost humbly, uppon my kneys, to pardon me of thes my bolde and rude letters, and the same to accepte and take in good sense and parte* [, therfore, Your most excellent Majestie (considerations had to the premisses, and to my moost bounden duetie towardes Your Hieghnes, your realme, succession, and posterite, and for thexoneration of my conscience towardes Almightie God) to licence me, according to myn office and duetie, to procede to the examination, fynall determynation, and judgement in the said grete cause, touching Your Hieghnes. Eftsones, as prostrate at the feete of Your Majestie, beseching the same to pardone me of thes my bolde and rude letters, and the same to accept and take in good sense and parte, as I do meane; which calling Our Lorde to recorde, is onlie for the zele that I have to the causes aforesaide, and for none other intent and purpose].

233

whether to laugh or to cry'.[1] The king watched with anxiety how she was received by the people, and he urged the lords to go and pay their respects to the new queen, whom he intended to have solemnly crowned after Easter.[2] The king had reason for his anxiety, as disparaging remarks continued to be made about Anne Boleyn. For example, round about St George's Day, 23 April, at King's Sutton in Warwickshire, a priest named Ralph Wendon remarked to another priest that 'the new queen was a whore and a harlot,' a remark that he was said to have made earlier to the bishop of Exeter, and proceedings against him were begun.[3] Preachers were not wanting to offer prayers for Anne Boleyn by the title of queen,[4] but their action did not always command popular approval. For example, when a city congregation heard Dr George Browne, the prior of the Austin Friars in London, in the course of his sermon, recommend his hearers to pray for queen Anne, they were much astonished and scandalized and almost everyone left the church, with murmuring and ill looks, without waiting for the remainder of the sermon. The king was greatly displeased when he heard of this incident and instructed the mayor to take order to prevent anything of the kind happening again. In his despatch, Chapuys reported that the mayor assembled the officers of the city companies and commanded them, upon pain of royal displeasure, not to murmur at the king's marriage and to prevent their apprentices from doing so and, 'what is worse and more difficult, their wives'.[5]

On receiving the king's licence to try the matrimonial cause, and in flagrant disregard of the papal bulls forbidding any court to entertain the case while it was pending in Rome,[6] Cranmer cited Catherine to appear before him at a court to be held in the priory of the Augustinian Canons at Dunstable.[7] This place was chosen as being remote from

[1] Chapuys to Charles V, 16 April 1533 (*L. & P.*, vi, 351 (p. 167)). cf. Hall, *Chronicle*, ii, 223: 'After the kyng perceiving his newe wife Quene Anne, to be greate with childe, caused all officers necessary, to bee appoynted to her, and so on Easter even, she went to her Closet [i.e. her pew in church] openly as Quene, . . .'
[2] Chapuys to Charles V, 16 April 1533 (*L. & P.*, vi, 351 (p. 168)).
[3] See Examination of Sir [Thomas] Gebons, priest, complainant, taken by Thomas Bedyll (*L. & P.*, vi, 733).
[4] Chapuys to Charles V, 16 April 1533 (*L. & P.*, vi, 351 (p. 167)).
[5] Chapuys to Charles V, 27 April 1533 (*L. & P.*, vi, 391).   [6] See p. 135.
[7] See *L. & P.*, vi, 737(7); cf. Knowles and Hadcock, *Medieval Religious Houses*, 136. The house was suppressed in 1540.

London so that the trial could be conducted in an inconspicuous manner; it was, however, within a few miles of Ampthill where the queen was then detained. On the advice of the Spanish ambassador, Catherine ignored the citation, and with the intention of safeguarding her interests, Chapuys drew up 'certain protestations', and, on 5 May, sent a written protest to the king.[1] On Saturday, 10 May, Cranmer, with the bishop of Lincoln as assessor, sat for the first time at Dunstable. The bishop of Winchester, Stephen Gardiner, and seven others appeared on behalf of the king, and evidence was given that the citation had been duly served upon Catherine; and since she had not appeared she was pronounced contumacious.[2] Catherine's failure to appear must have caused Cranmer some satisfaction, and in reporting the proceedings to the king, he observed that, being pronounced contumacious, she was precluded from further monition to appear, 'by reason whereof, I shall make more acceleration and expedition in my process than I thought I should'.[3] A hint of the methods adopted to obtain the desired result may be gleaned from Bedyll's remark, in one of his letters to Cromwell, that 'my lord of Winchester, and all others that be here, as of the king's grace's council, studieth, as diligently as they can possibly, to cause everything to be handled, so as it may be most consonant to the law, *as far as the matter will suffer*'.[4]

After two further sittings Cranmer intended to pronounce sentence on Friday 23 May.[5] On 17 May he wrote to the king:

Your grace's great matter is now brought to a final sentence, to be given upon

---

[1] Chapuys to Charles V, 27 April 1533 (*L. & P.*, vi, 391); Chapuys to Charles V, 10 May 1533 (*L. & P.*, vi, 465), in which he set out verbatim the text of the protest which he had written to the king.
[2] Bedyll to Cromwell, 10 May 1533 (Pocock, ii, 473); Cranmer to Henry VIII, 12 May 1533 (*State Papers*, i, 394; *L. & P.*, vi, 470); Bedyll to Cromwell, 12 May 1533 (*State Papers*, i, 394; *L. & P.*, vi, 469). Thomas Bedyll was clerk to the council and was present at Dunstable.
[3] Cranmer to Henry VIII, 12 May 1533 (*State Papers*, i, 394; *L. & P.*, vi, 470).
[4] Bedyll to Cromwell, 12 May 1533 (*State Papers*, i, 394, at p. 395; *L. & P.*, vi, 469; italics supplied). Bedyll was at Dunstable for the purpose of sending a daily report of the proceedings to Cromwell; see Bedyll to Cromwell, 10 May 1533 (Pocock, ii, 473; *L. & P.*, vi, 461); Bedyll to Cromwell, 12 May 1533 (*State Papers*, i, 394; *L. & P.*, vi, 469); Bedyll to Cromwell, 17 May 1533 (Pocock, ii, 475; *L. & P.*, vi, 497); Bedyll to Cromwell, 23 May 1533 (*L. & P.*, vi, 526); Bedyll to Cromwell, 23 May 1533 (Pocock, ii, 476; *L. & P.*, vi, 527).
[5] Cranmer to Henry VIII, 12 May 1533 (*State Papers*, i, 394; *L. & P.*, vi, 470); Bedyll to Cromwell, 17 May 1533 (Pocock, ii, 475; *L. & P.*, vi, 497).

Friday [May 23] now next ensuing. And because every day in the next week [the week preceding Whitsunday] shall be ferial, except Friday and Saturday, therefore I cannot assign any shorter time *ad audiendam sententiam*, than on the said Friday. At which time, I trust so to endeavour myself further in this behalf, as shall become me to do, to the pleasure of Almighty God, and the mere truth of the matter.[1]

The archbishop, however, was fearful lest wind of his intention should reach Catherine and induce her to intervene. He wished it to be kept a close secret, and, on the same day that he wrote to the king, he also wrote to Cromwell:

I pray you to make no relation thereof, as I know you will not, for if the noble lady Catherine should, by the bruit of this matter in the mouths of the inhabitants of the country, or by her friends or council hearing of this bruit, be moved, stirred, counselled or persuaded to appear afore me in the time or afore the time of sentence, I should be thereby greatly stayed and let in the process, and the king's grace's council here present shall be much uncertain what shall be then further done therein. For a great bruit and voice of the people in this behalf might move her to do that thing herein which per-adventure she would not do if she shall hear little of it; and therefore I desire you to speak as little of this matter as ye may, and to beseech the king's highness in likewise so to do for the considerations afore recited.[2]

Cranmer's apprehensions proved ill founded, for there was no inter-vention by Catherine to disturb the smoothness of the archbishop's proceedings. On 23 May Cranmer formally pronounced sentence declaring the marriage between Henry and Catherine to be invalid and void *ab initio*.[3] In sending his usual report of the proceedings to Crom-well, Thomas Bedyll observed that he thought 'the sentence will please the king's grace very well, for in very deed it is much better now than when it was first devised, and ye know who emended it very singularly'.[4] The effect of Cranmer's decision was to declare that Henry had never

---

[1] Cranmer to Henry VIII, 17 May 1533 (*State Papers*, i, 396; *L. & P.*, vi, 495).
[2] Cranmer to Cromwell, 17 May 1533 (*L. & P.*, vi, 496).
[3] John Tregonwell to Cromwell, 23 May 1533 (*L. & P.*, vi, 525); Bedyll to Cromwell, 23 May 1533 (*L. & P.*, vi, 526); Bedyll to Cromwell, 23 May 1533 (Pocock, ii, 476; *L. & P.*, vi, 527); Cranmer to Henry VIII, 23 May 1533 (*State Papers*, i, 396; *L. & P.*, vi, 528); and document relating to the divorce (*L. & P.*, vi, 529). For the text of Cranmer's sentence, see Rymer, *Foedera*, xiv, 462; Burnet, i, Coll. of Rec., p. 120. Cf. Inspeximus and exemplification of writ of *certiorari*, dated 30 May 1533, to Cranmer, and the return thereon, touching the sentence given by Cranmer in the marriage cause (*L. & P.*, vi, 737(7)).
[4] Bedyll to Cromwell, 23 May 1533 (Pocock, ii, 476; *L. & P.*, vi, 527).

been married to Catherine, and it followed from this that he had always been at liberty to marry Anne Boleyn. Nevertheless, in the circumstances of the case, with the mystery surrounding the precise nature of his relationship to Anne Boleyn, a further decision was necessary to affirm that the king's marriage with that lady, if marriage there had been, was valid and binding; for the king had already appointed Whitsunday, 1 June, as the day of her coronation.[1] The king was assured that the necessary judgment would be given with all speed. Writing to Henry to inform him of the sentence of divorce, Cranmer wrote:

And where I was, by the letters of Mr Thirlby,[2] your grace's chaplain, advertised of your grace's pleasure, that I should cause your grace's council to conceive a procuracy concerning the second matrimony [with Anne Boleyn], I have sent the said letters unto them, and required them to do according to the tenor thereof. Most humbly beseeching your highness, that I may know your grace's further pleasure concerning the same matrimony, as soon as your grace, with your council, shall be perfectly resolved therein. For the time of the coronation is so instant, and so near at hand, that the matter requireth good expedition to be had in the same.[3]

Cranmer pronounced sentence concerning the second matrimony on 28 May, 'in a certain well known high gallery' at Lambeth in the presence of a number of witnesses that included Thomas Cromwell. The nature of the proceedings on that day is shrouded in mystery and we do not even know their precise locality, for all we have is the vague reference to the 'high gallery'. We are likewise ignorant of the nature of the evidence, if any, that was produced, and the decree is careful not to set out any of the circumstances surrounding Cranmer's sentence. All that can be said for certain is that it was determined that the marriage contracted between the king and Anne Boleyn was lawful and valid.[4]

From the extraordinary nature of these proceedings it seems clear that the real circumstances of the king's marriage with Anne Boleyn

---

[1] cf. Henry VIII to Lady Cobham, 29 April 1533 (*L. & P.*, vi, 395), in which the king appointed Lady Cobham to attend on horseback at the coronation of 'the lady Anne our Queen', on the feast of Pentecost, at Westminster. See also, 'For the Quenes coronacion' (*L. & P.*, vi, 396).
[2] Thomas Thirlby was appointed bishop of Westminster in 1540, and was the only bishop of that shortlived diocese.
[3] Cranmer to Henry VIII, 23 May 1533 (*State Papers*, i, 396; *L. & P.*, vi, 528).
[4] Inspeximus and exemplification of a writ of *certiorari*, dated 30 May 1533, to Cranmer, touching the sentence given with regard to the validity of Henry's marriage with Anne Boleyn (*L. & P.*, vi, 737(7); whence the quotation in the text is taken). For the text of the record, see Rymer, *Foedera*, xiv, 467.

could not be allowed to see the light of day. Even the date of the marriage was so close a secret that not even Cranmer himself, the old friend and former chaplain of the Boleyn family, was aware of it. Some three weeks after his judgment on the marriage he wrote to Nicholas Hawkins, his successor as ambassador at the imperial court, to give him an account of the events leading up to the coronation of Anne Boleyn. He wrote his account to justify himself against the current rumour that the marriage had been solemnized by Cranmer himself, for it was outrageous that the archbishop should judicially determine the validity of a marriage that he had himself performed. In the course of his long letter, Cranmer wrote that the coronation of Anne Boleyn was not performed before her marriage which, he said, took place 'about' St Paul's Day (25 January, the feast of the conversion of St Paul), 'as the condition thereof doth well appear, by reason she is now somewhat big with child'. And Cranmer went on to assert that the report that he himself had performed the marriage ceremony was false, 'for I myself knew not thereof a fortnight after it was done'.[1]

Thus, the man who sat in judgment on the matter could give no more accurate date for the marriage than that it took place 'about' St Paul's day. It should, of course, be remembered that the marriage must have taken place, if it took place at all, before the invalidity of Henry's marriage to Catherine had been determined, with the result that the marriage to Anne Boleyn was uncanonical, if no worse; no self-respecting cleric would be anxious to confess his responsibility in such a matter, and it is not surprising that dark clouds should surround the marriage. Since the circumstances of the marriage could not be disclosed, the archiepiscopal court was required to produce a judgment to certify to the world that the king was actually and validly married to Anne Boleyn; that was done, in secrecy, but everything else connected with the marriage was kept out of sight, and even today it remains a dark mystery.

Another date was given for the marriage by Henry's ardent admirer, Edward Hall, who recorded that, 'The king after his return [from Calais], married privily the lady Anne Boleyn, on saint Erkenwald's day [14 November], which marriage was kept so secret, that very few knew it, till she was great with child, at Easter after.'[2] This date, 14 November 1532, if correct, would render less disreputable the birth of the princess

---

[1] Cranmer to Hawkins, 17 June 1533 (*L. & P.*, vi, 661).
[2] Hall, *Chronicle*, ii, 222.

Elizabeth who was born on 7 September 1533, but it is unlikely that it is the true date. Cranmer who, having sat in judgment on the marriage, was presumably in the best position to know, stated that it took place 'about' 25 January 1533; and Chapuys wrote to the emperor that 'the king's marriage was celebrated, as it is reported, on the day of the Conversion of St Paul [25 January]; and because at that time Dr Bonner had returned from Rome, and the nuncio of the pope was frequently at court, some suspect that the pope had given a tacit consent; which I cannot believe'.[1] The contemporary statements of Cranmer and Chapuys may probably be preferred to the later pronouncement of Edward Hall, more especially as, at 25 January, Bonner had just come from Rome with the news that the pope was hopeful that matters would be arranged according to Henry's satisfaction. But whatever may be the truth of the mystery of her marriage, Anne Boleyn was now queen.

2

Whatever of ceremonial was lacking at Anne Boleyn's marriage was more than made up by the splendour of her coronation, which took place on Whitsunday, 1 June 1533. On the preceding Thursday, 29 May, in the afternoon, she left Greenwich by barge and, accompanied by other craft and 'shalmes, shagbushes, and divers other instruments which continually made a goodly harmony', she came to the Tower, and, as she landed, 'there was a marvellous shot out of the Tower as ever was heard there'. She remained at the Tower throughout the next day, and on Saturday she rode through London in a great procession to Whitehall where, after changing her attire, she 'went into her barge secretly to the king to his manor of Westminster where she rested that night'. On Whitsunday she went in procession to her coronation in Westminster

[1] Chapuys to Charles V, 10 May 1533 (*L. & P.*, vi, 465); the quotation is taken from the calendar. The reference to the effect of the nuncio's frequent presence at court is an interesting example of the success of the device mentioned on p. 228. For the remarkable memorandum used as the basis of a discussion that took place in the emperor's council chamber when news was received of Henry's marriage to Anne Boleyn, see 'Lo se que consulto con su Majestad sobre la causa matrimonial de Ynglaterra para despachar a Rodrigo Davalos que partio de Barcelona a postrero de Mayo de DXXXIIJ', 31 May 1533 (*L. & P.*, vi, 568); and see p. 247.

Abbey; there, in the course of Mass, she was crowned queen by Cranmer and 'received of the archbishop the holy sacrament'. There followed a great banquet in Westminster Hall. At this banquet the new queen had at her feet two ladies seated under the table to serve her secretly with what she might need; and two others who were near her, one on each side, often raised a great linen cloth to hide her from view whenever she wished 's'ayser en quelque chose'.[1] The festivities concluded with jousting and tilting on Whit Monday.[2]

The prospect of these events undoubtedly caused Sir Thomas More anxiety and distress. His long continued endeavour to remain aloof from the king's great matter was now likely to receive a severe check, yet holding, as he did, the opinion that the king's marriage to queen Catherine was good and valid, he could not be present at Anne Boleyn's coronation without appearing publicly to approve and sanction what had been done. To those who thought as More did, the king's marriage to Anne Boleyn was canonically unlawful and was, indeed, bigamous; and More was aware that, as part of the ceremony, Anne Boleyn would receive Communion at the hands of the archbishop; this was something that went far beyond the realm of politics and may well have been regarded by More as blasphemous.

Nevertheless, More's old friends, Tunstall the bishop of Durham, John Clerk the bishop of Bath and Wells, and Stephen Gardiner the bishop of Winchester, asked him to bear them company at the coronation, and knowing his straitened means in his retirement, they sent him twenty pounds to buy a gown for the occasion. More accepted the money but remained at home. But when next he met them he

said merrily unto them: 'My lords, in the letters which you lately sent me, you required two things of me, the one whereof, since I was so well content to grant you, the other therefore I thought I might be the bolder to deny you. And like as the one, because I took you for no beggars, and myself I knew to be no rich man, I thought I might the rather fulfill, so the other did put me in remembrance of an emperor that had ordained a law that whosoever committed a certain offence (which I now remember not) except it were a virgin,

---

[1] Narrative of the entry and coronation of Anne Boleyn, queen of England, dated 2 June 1533 (*L. & P.*, vi, 584); cf. Hall, *Chronicle*, ii, 241: 'The Quene had at her seconde course xxiii dishes, and thirtie at the thirde course'.

[2] For descriptions of the festivities, see Hall, *Chronicle*, ii, 229-42, and *L. & P.*, vi, 561-3, 583-5. Of all Henry's wives, Anne Boleyn was the only one to be crowned.

should suffer the pains of death, such a reverence had he to virginity. Now so it happened that the first committer of that offence was indeed a virgin, whereof the emperor hearing was in no small perplexity, as he that by some example fain would have had that law to have been put in execution. Whereupon when his council had sat long, solemnly debating this case, suddenly arose there up one of his council, a good plain man, among them, and said: "Why make you so much ado, my lords, about so small a matter? Let her first be deflowered, and then after may she be devoured." And so though your lordships have in the matter of the matrimony hitherto kept yourselves pure virgins, yet take good heed, my lords, that you keep your virginity still. For some there be that by procuring your lordships first at the coronation to be present, and next to preach for the setting forth of it, and finally to write books to all the world in defence thereof, are desirous to deflower you; and when they have deflowered you, then will they not fail soon after to devour you. Now my lords,' quoth he, 'it lieth not in my power but that they may devour me; but God being my good lord, I will provide that they shall never deflower me.' [1]

Although More professed that he did not remember the details of his tale, he was almost certainly aware that it was, in substance, the story of the daughter of Aelius Sejanus, recounted by Tacitus.[2] But whether the reminiscence were conscious or not, the irony implicit in the comparison of the tyranny of Tiberius with Henry's proceedings is unmistakable. Another notable absentee from the coronation was the duchess of Norfolk, aunt of Anne Boleyn, whose husband had recently been sent by the king on a diplomatic mission; she stayed away because of 'the love she bore to the previous queen'.[3]

One thing still remained to be done in order to complete the coronation of Anne Boleyn as Henry's queen in its domestic aspect; the position of the former queen must be settled. Accordingly, lord Mountjoy and others were instructed to wait upon Catherine and declare to her the king's wishes with regard to herself.[4] They had to wait until 3 July, for she would not receive them sooner. On their arrival at Ampthill, they found Catherine 'lying upon her pallet' because she could not stand or walk on account of a slight accident to her foot; she was also much

[1] Roper, 58, 59.
[2] *Annals*, v, 9.
[3] Extracts from a manuscript account of the coronation, unfavourable to Anne Boleyn (*L. & P.*, vi, 585).
[4] See 'Instructions for the right honourable lord Mountjoye' (*L. & P.*, vi, 759). Lord Mountjoy was the chamberlain of Catherine's household; the others who accompanied Mountjoy were Sir Robert Dymok, her almoner, John Tyrrell, Griffith Richards, and Thomas Vaux.

troubled by a cough. She demanded that Mountjoy should summon as many of her servants as could be found so that they might hear what the deputation had to say. She then required Mountjoy to read what the deputation had prepared in writing, but when he referred to her as 'princess dowager' she immediately objected to the title, saying that she was the queen and the king's true wife. Then, answered by Catherine point by point, Mountjoy recited the king's actions, referring to the acquiescence of the lords spiritual and temporal and of the commons, and informed her that the king had been lawfully 'separated and divorced' from her and had married again. Consequently, since the king could not have two queens, she must now content herself with the title of 'princess dowager', or else the king would be obliged not only to punish her servants but to withdraw 'his fatherly love' from her daughter, the princess Mary. When Mountjoy had finished, Catherine asserted that 'she was the king's true wife; and so she would take herself, and never to relinquish the name of Queen, until such time as sentence definitive should be given to the contrary by our holy father the pope, the college of cardinals, and the court of the Rota, before whom her matter dependeth'. When the deputation had put into writing a report of their interview with Catherine, she demanded that it be shown to her; when it was brought 'she called for pen and ink, and in such places as she found the name of Princess Dowager, she, with her pen and ink, struck it out'.[1]

The king's new marriage was not much to the liking of his subjects. So great was the outcry that rewards were offered to those who should denounce any person speaking of it in a derogatory manner, and priests were forbidden to preach without the licence of the bishop of London who was favourable to the marriage.[2] In a memorandum in the hand of one of Cromwell's clerks, and presumably drawn up on his instructions or at his dictation, the popular discontent was mentioned, and it was stated that the general muttering was not against the king (for everyone said that he was the most gentle and upright prince that ever reigned) but against some of the prelates and especially the archbishop of Canterbury. The memorandum continued: 'Wherefore I think it were very

[1] Report of Lord Mountjoy, 4 July 1533 (*State Papers*, i, 397; *L. & P.*, vi, 760); Report of Lord Mountjoy, 4 July 1533 (*State Papers*, i, 402; *L. & P.*, vi, 765). For the text to the proclamation (dated 5 July 1533) announcing that Catherine had been deprived of her royal style and must thenceforth be known as Princess Dowager, see *T.R.P.*, i, 209.

[2] cf. Chapuys to Charles V, 26 May 1533 (*L. & P.*, vi, 541).

necessary for these considerations that the said archbishop should make out a book, not over long, to declare that it that he hath done is not only according to the law of God, but also for the great wealth and quietness of all this realm.'[1] But despite the precautions taken the muttering did not cease.[2]

[1] Memorandum on the king's marriage, June 1533 (Pocock, ii, 487; *L. & P.*, vi, 738).
[2] cf. Sir Richard Bulkeley to Henry VIII, 9 July 1533 (*L. & P.*, vi, 790); earl of Derby and Sir Henry Farryngton to Henry VIII, 10 Aug. 1533 (Pocock, ii, 566; *L. & P.*, vi, 964). See also the prophecies of Mistress Amadas, July 1533 (*L. & P.*, vi, 923).

R

XV

Excommunication

I

Henry's activities during the first half of 1533 had momentous consequences. Early in April, before Cranmer had opened his court at Dunstable and when Anne Boleyn was boasting that she would soon be
queen, Chapuys was urging the emperor to 'make an enterprise' against
England;[1] a month later Francis I was informed by cardinal Tournon
that Charles V had warned the pope of the likelihood of war with England
if Henry persisted in his designs to injure the emperor's aunt; but Tournon thought that the emperor would 'put his hand neither to his sword
nor into his purse'.[2] Tournon was right. When Charles V heard of
Henry's marriage with Anne Boleyn he described the injury done to the
queen as extreme, and he believed that there was little hope of bringing
Henry to reason; but, after careful consideration, he thought it best
merely to persist in his demand for justice at Rome, and he wrote to his
brother, Ferdinand of Hungary, and to the king of Portugal asking for
their support.[3] Chapuys, who was inclined to be bellicose, received
instructions to be moderate in his behaviour and speech, and in May
he informed the emperor of what he had done to comply with his orders
not to embitter Anglo-Spanish relations and especially not to threaten
war or the abatement of friendship. He told Charles V that whenever
Henry or his council asked if the emperor intended to make war on
account of the king's treatment of Catherine, he had protested that they
should not speak to him of such a matter; since the king had put his
cause to trial there was no occasion to speak of war. He added his hope
that, even though the king had taken a new wife, he would not on that
account contravene the decision of the holy see. By such means, said

---

[1] Chapuys to Charles V, 10 April 1533 (*L. & P.*, vi, 324).
[2] Cardinal Tournon to Francis I, 4 May 1533 (*L. & P.*, vi, 440).
[3] cf. Charles V to Ferdinand of Hungary, 23 May 1533 (*L. & P.*, vi, 523); and
see p. 247.

Chapuys, did he disentangle himself from the inquiries of the English about the prospects of war.[1]

Meanwhile the count of Cifuentes, who had replaced Mai as imperial ambassador at Rome,[2] was reporting the displeasure of the pope at the news of the marriage, but when the ambassador pressed the pope to give judgment his holiness replied that it was within the emperor's power to remedy matters. The ambassador suspected, however, that the pope's anxiety sprang not so much from the news of the marriage as from his desire to know whether the emperor would go to war.[3] Nevertheless, Cifuentes continued to press the pope for judgment.[4]

When Francis I heard of the pope's displeasure he made efforts to restrain Clement from violent action against Henry. He instructed Tournon to warn the pope not to think it strange that he supported the English king as the friendship between them was such that no man could separate them, and Francis looked upon Henry's affairs as his own. The pope was to be reminded of the place held by Henry in christendom and that it was more profitable for his holiness to have him as a friend and devout son of the church than to irritate him and drive him to disobedience. The pope was therefore to be asked not to take any step in the affair until after the coming meeting.[5] The French ambassador in England was informed that, in Francis's view, Henry should not display irritation with the pope but rather show that he wished his affair to be decided at the meeting between his holiness and Francis I, and would leave it entirely in the hands of the French king.[6] Francis was vexed by Henry's recent activities and afraid that they might prejudice his coming interview with the pope which had been arranged chiefly on Henry's account. He thought, for instance, that the statute in restraint

[1] Chapuys to Charles V, 26 May 1533 (*L. & P.*, vi, 541). See also Chapuys to Charles V, 18 May 1533 (*L. & P.*, vi, 508).
[2] Fernando de Silva, count of Cifuentes, was Grand Standard bearer of Castille and a member of the emperor's council; he succeeded Miguel Mai at Rome in March 1533. Mai returned to Spain as vice-chancellor of Aragon.
[3] Count of Cifuentes to Charles V, 7 May 1533 (*L. & P.*, vi, 454); cf. cardinal of Jaen [Gabriel Merino] to de los Cobos, 7 May 1533 (*L. & P.*, vi, 455).
[4] e.g. Count of Cifuentes to Charles V, 10 May 1533 (*L. & P.*, vi, 466); Instructions of Charles V to Cifuentes and Rodrigo d'Avalos [who was sent to assist Cifuentes], [? May] 1533 (*L. & P.*, vi, 570); Bonner to Henry VIII, 13 June 1533 (*State Papers*, vii, 466; *L. & P.*, vi, 637); Benet to Henry VIII, 14 June 1533 (*State Papers*, vii, 468; *L. & P.*, vi, 643). And see p. 249.
[5] Francis I to cardinal Tournon, May 1533 (*L. & P.*, vi, 424).
[6] Francis I to the bailly of Troyes, 5 May 1533 (*L. & P.*, vi, 424).

of appeals would render the meeting more difficult. Henry assured Francis that he had been forced to take such a step because of the unjust censures of the pope who had acted not as his judge but as his enemy; and Francis was told that the archbishop of Canterbury was at work on the king's affair to decide whether the queen were his wife or not. He added that he did not wish the pope to give any judgment, and it was important that the judgment of the archbishop of Canterbury should precede any judgment that the pope might give.[1] Francis's misgivings increased when he learned of Cranmer's judgment and the coronation of Anne Boleyn.[2]

At the same time the emperor intervened with Francis I; he instructed his ambassador in France to tell the French king that the people of England were scandalized by Henry's barbarous conduct, and to urge Francis, as a christian prince related to Catherine by marriage,[3] to denounce Henry's marriage with Anne Boleyn.[4] However, at a consistory in Rome on 22 May cardinal Tournon announced that Francis would support the English cause to the extent of begging the pope, at their coming meeting, not to proceed any further against Henry; but the cardinal added that if Henry were excommunicated the French king would be unable to maintain his friendship with Henry if it compelled him to act against the church.[5] Francis, it seems, although alarmed at the violence of Henry's actions, did not believe that in the last resort the English king would dare to bring about his own separation from the universal church. For some time Henry had been looking to the German princes for support and he wished to prepare them for the news of the coming meeting between Francis I and the pope. Accordingly he suggested to Francis that the Germans should be informed of the meeting lest they should suspect that something to their prejudice was

---

[1] The bailly of Troyes to Francis I, 23 May 1533 (*L. & P.*, vi, 524). Francis's fears arising from the statute in restraint of appeals were partially set at rest by cardinals Tournon and Grammont (Francis I to the bailly of Troyes, 7 June 1533; *L. & P.*, vi, 600).

[2] cf. the remarks of Francis I to Stephen Gardiner and others at Marseilles; see p. 265.

[3] Eleanor, the second wife of Francis I, was the sister of Charles V and the niece of Catherine of Aragon.

[4] Charles V to his ambassador in France, 24 May 1533 (*L. & P.*, vi, 534).

[5] Relacion de las cartas del Embaxador de Roma, 29 May 1533 [an account of the audience given to cardinal Tournon in the consistory on 22 May 1533] (*L. & P.*, vi, 557).

being arranged; Francis agreed to do so.[1] At the beginning of June, however, Henry heard that a declaration had been made, in open consistory at Rome, that Francis would use all his power to resist the Lutherans and even attack them, if necessary. Henry sent for the French ambassador and instructed him to inform Francis that he was very displeased by this news; he asserted that the French had acted in this manner in order to break his links with the Germans and to render them innocuous to the emperor and the pope. Henry insisted that Francis had been badly advised and was too anxious about his coming interview with Clement VII; this was a meeting, he said, which should be of greater moment to the pope than to the French king. The ambassador replied that the meeting had been sought by Francis chiefly on Henry's account, and he assured Henry that there had been no practices except about the marriage. In reporting the matter, the ambassador added that he had never seen Henry so angry.[2] Francis denied all knowledge of the declaration at Rome and did not believe that the report of it was true. He took the opportunity, however, of again assuring Henry that nothing prejudicial to the Germans should be done at his meeting with the pope.[3]

Meanwhile in Rome the imperial agents had been insistently demanding that the pope give judgment, a step which his holiness was reluctant to take.[4] At the end of May a council held by Charles V in Spain decided that these demands should be reinforced, and a further representative was sent to Rome to assist Cifuentes. The council had been convened to consider the action to be taken now that Henry had annulled his marriage with Catherine and married Anne Boleyn. Three possible courses of action were considered: the prosecution of the legal process at the pope's court in Rome, the use of force, and a combination of force and legal process. It was recognized that each course of action had its own difficulties. Recourse to law seemed fitting as the matter was a spiritual one and the proceedings at Rome had been begun; but Henry would not obey the process of the Roman court, and the pope was dilatory. Force was recognized as dangerous as it would imperil all christendom

[1] The bailly of Troyes to Francis I, 23 May 1533 (*L. & P.*, vi, 524); Francis I to the bailly of Troyes, 7 June 1533 (*L. & P.*, vi, 600).
[2] The bailly of Troyes to Jean du Bellay, bishop of Paris, 9 June 1533 (*L. & P.*, vi, 614).
[3] Francis I to the bailly of Troyes, 26 June 1533 (*L. & P.*, vi, 707).
[4] See p. 245, note 4.

and especially the emperor's dominions; although the emperor was closely bound to Catherine, her affair was a private matter and public considerations must be taken into account. Combining force with law could not be attempted until after the pope had given judgment, when all princes and good christians would be equally bound to help his holiness, and the pope should then act as head of any enterprise to be undertaken. Moreover the third course might lead to war or, at least, to a rupture of commerce between England and the emperor's dominions and it was therefore for consideration whether the action to be taken against Henry should be limited to ecclesiastical censures. A further matter for consideration was the answer to be given to the pope should he renew his inquiries about the action the emperor would take to ensure the execution of his judgment.[1]

As a result of this meeting Rodrigo d'Avalos was sent to Rome to assist Cifuentes and he was provided with fresh instructions for them both. D'Avalos was instructed to travel as quickly as possible, and he reached Rome on 14 June.[2] The emperor wrote to Cifuentes to inform him of what had taken place at the meeting of the council; he said that he wished an interdict to be regarded as the extreme penalty, and he cautiously observed that his subjects in the Netherlands would be injured by such a penalty as no commerce was allowed with a people under interdict. The new instructions carried by d'Avalos required him and Cifuentes to take immediate advice as to the best means of preserving the rights of queen Catherine and of obtaining the annulment of the marriage with Anne Boleyn. They were also to obtain advice on the best means of compelling Henry to put away his concubine and, in view of the recent statutes passed in England, they were to canvas the possibility of persuading the pope to deprive Henry of his kingdom, which he held of the holy see. They were reminded, however, that the publication of censures would disturb English commercial intercourse with Spain and Flanders, so that if the pope decided upon an interdict it should be limited to one diocese only or to the place where the king dwelt, so as to minimize its effect upon trade. If the pope, on being pressed to accelerate judgment in the principal cause, should inquire

---

[1] cf. 'Lo que se consulto con su Majestad sobre la causa matrimonial de Ynglaterra para despachar a Rodrigo Davalos que partio de Barcelona a postrero de Mayo de DXXXIIJ' (B.M., Add. MS. 28,585, f. 264; *L. & P.*, vi, 568).
[2] See Rodrigo d'Avalos to Charles V, 16 June 1533 (*L. & P.*, vi, 656).

what the emperor would do to ensure execution of the sentence, he was to be informed that he must do his duty, from which nothing could relieve him, and that publication of the sentence, with its penalties, must precede recourse to the secular arm; his holiness, however, might depend upon it that the emperor would not fail to support the judgment. Cifuentes and d'Avalos were told that Francis I had expressed great displeasure at Henry's marriage 'with his concubine' and had endeavoured to dissuade him from it; the emperor had, therefore, written to Francis urging him not to yield any point to the king of England which might interfere with justice. The emperor added that he had considered a proposal to send a special agent to England for the purpose of visiting and consoling the queen, but, in view of the language used by Henry to Chapuys, he thought that Henry would behave even more insolently to a person sent especially for the purpose.[1]

Before d'Avalos reached Rome the imperialists presented several petitions to the pope demanding judgment, as Bonner reported to Henry. Bonner informed the king that the English representatives had also presented various appeals in order that the pope might have some pretext to delay the matter, and he did not think that the pope would give any decision before the vacation. He thought it possible, however, that the pope might, in the ensuing term, 'pronounce the dispensation valeable [valid]. Wherein albeit he should do wrong unto your highness, considering the truth in the contrary and the manifest presumption of the law, yet his proceedings, after that sort, would have some colour and visage of justice.'[2] Both sides were active, the imperialists to bring about a decision and the English to secure delay; and the activities of Carne, the excusator, contributed to securing the delay the English wanted. Although the dean of the Rota, Capisucchi, had concluded his examination of the process and reported to the consistory by the middle of June, no one expected any decision before the vacation.[3]

[1] Charles V to his ambassador at Rome, May 1533 (*L. & P.*, vi, 569); Instructions to Cifuentes and Rodrigo d'Avalos (*L. & P.*, vi, 570).
[2] Bonner to Henry VIII, 13 June 1533 (*State Papers*, vii, 466; *L. & P.*, vi, 637).
[3] cf. Bonner to Cromwell, 14 June 1533 (*L. & P.*, vi, 642); cardinal of Jaen to Charles V, 14 June 1533 (*L. & P.*, vi, 647); Ortiz to Charles V, 16 June 1533 (*L. & P.*, vi, 654); Cifuentes to Charles V, 16 June 1533 (*L. & P.*, vi, 655); Rodrigo d'Avalos to Charles V, 16 June 1533 (*L. & P.*, vi, 656); Cifuentes to Charles V, 17 June 1533 (*L. & P.*, vi, 663); Rodrigo d'Avalos to Charles V, 24 June 1533 (*L. & P.*, vi, 699). Stephen Gabriel Merino was bishop of Jaen and archbishop of Bari, and a member of the emperor's council; he was created a

At the end of June Capisucchi's report was considered in consistory, and the pope ordered the Rota to examine the case and give their opinion to the consistory. Nevertheless d'Avalos was pessimistic. He foresaw further delays and he thought that Catherine's case had been mismanaged. He was, too, hampered by lack of money; advocates and others had not been paid, and although documents had to be copied he was unable to pay for this to be done.[1] Within a week, however, d'Avalos was much more cheerful, but he clung to his opinion that the pope wished to delay matters until after his interview with Francis I.[2]

The reports which Henry received of the proceedings in Rome caused him to fear that he might be in danger of excommunication. Early in June the duke of Norfolk, who was in France in readiness for the pope's meeting with Francis which had recently been postponed to September, wrote to the king for instructions how he should act if the pope were to proceed against Henry, and Norfolk expressed his fears that his holiness would be pressed to take action. Henry replied with complaints about the pope's behaviour and said that he was sorry to think that his good brother, Francis I, should be so eager to meet a man who seemed determined to do Henry an injury; and he hoped that Francis was not seeking the meeting on his account. Norfolk was instructed to request Francis to order cardinals Grammont and Tournon to call for the admission of the excusator. Francis was to be urged

to write unto his agents with the pope, to be continually sounded and blown into the pope's ears, that if . . . he will not admit our excusator . . . it shall not only occasion and move us . . . from time to time to devise enact and establish such laws, as whereby the pope's estimation being decayed and diminished, the obedience in small process of time may be clearly, in this our realm, withdrawn from that see,

but the example might encourage other princes to put their heads together for the preservation of their rights, by which a great part of christendom might be alienated from the holy see; and if that should

---

[1] Rodrigo d'Avalos to the Commendador Mayor of Leon, 30 June 1533 (*L. & P.*, vi, 725).
[2] Rodrigo d'Avalos to Charles V, 5 July 1533 (*L. & P.*, vi, 773); cf. 'Relacion de las cartas del Conde de Cifuentes de v de Jullio 1533' (*L. & P.*, vi, 774).

---

cardinal on 19 Feb. 1533. He came with the emperor to the meeting at Bologna and remained at the papal court. D'Avalos thought that Cifuentes was jealous of the cardinal.

happen the pope could 'thank no man of it, but himself'.[1] It was plain that papal censures were inevitable and Henry was anxious to neutralize their effects by defiance. A fortnight after sending his blustering instructions to Norfolk he executed a document appealing to a future general council should he be excommunicated by the pope on account of his divorce from Catherine of Aragon.[2] As a last resort Henry determined to put financial pressure on the pope and on 9 July he issued letters patent bringing into force the act forbidding the payment of annates to Rome.[3]

In July he realized, from Bonner's letters, that, following the arrival in Rome of 'a gentleman of Spain', the pope was likely to proceed to 'the execution of some extreme process' against him, and he wrote to Bonner telling him to banish the 'fear and timourousness, or rather despair' displayed in his letters and to keep constantly before his eyes the justice of the king's cause. Bonner was assured that he would be defended by the king against the malice of his adversaries, and he was therefore to lose no opportunity to persuade the pope to admit the excusator.[4] Now that he believed papal action against him to be inevitable, Henry could see little purpose in the meeting between Francis I and the pope. At the beginning of August he sent further instructions to Norfolk who was told to dissuade the French king from meeting his holiness. Norfolk was to explain to Francis that all Henry's actions 'had been grounded upon law, equity and reason', and had been undertaken with the advice and counsel of the French king. Norfolk was further instructed to tell Francis of Henry's fixed determination, and that he would not permit any interference with his marriage, the sentence of the archbishop of Canterbury, the statutes of the realm or the recent proclamation; Francis, therefore, should make no promise to the pope on any of these matters. Norfolk was told to do all in his power to dissuade Francis from the meeting, and if he were successful in doing so 'then our pleasure is ye, tarrying still with our good brother [Francis I], do enter communication with him how and by what ways and means we should

---

[1] Henry VIII to the duke of Norfolk, 14 June 1533 (*State Papers*, vii, 473; *L. & P.*, vi, 641).
[2] Appeal of Henry VIII, 29 June 1533 (Rymer, *Foedera*, xiv, 476; *L. & P.*, vi, 721). The document was executed at Greenwich before Edward Lee, archbishop of York, and witnessed by Dr Richard Sampson, Sir William Fitzwilliam and Thomas Cromwell.
[3] See *L. & P.*, vi, 793, and *Statutes of the Realm*, iii, 387, note; and cf. p. 186.
[4] Henry VIII to Bonner, [July] 1533 (*State Papers*, vii, 484; *L. & P.*, vi, 806).

annoy the pope'. If, on the other hand, Norfolk were unsuccessful, and Francis should insist upon the meeting because it was important to conclude the marriage of his son, the duke of Orleans, with the pope's niece, Catherine de Medici, the French king was to be told that Norfolk could do nothing to prevent the marriage and could only bewail the necessity of returning to England, for that was better than 'to be present at the interview, and to be compelled to look patiently upon [his] master's enemy'. He was then to tell Francis that Henry had commissioned Sir Francis Bryan and Sir John Wallop to go to the meeting, 'having nevertheless charge, never to present them self to the pope, nor to be in a place of any assembling, where they might appear to do the pope, on our part, any honour'. Finally, Norfolk was to say to Francis, on taking leave of him:

Sir, if that succeed not that were best, the next is then to be thought upon; and if your majesty will needs meet with the pope, then could there nothing acceptable be done to the king my master, unless the pope, at your intercession, would pronounce there, and give sentence that the matrimony between my master and the lady Catherine was and is nought; wherein the pope should do somewhat not to be refused. And necessary it were, that some such thing he did, for the conservation of the opinion of amity between you and my master; and in this only point he can do pleasure.[1]

2

While Henry was working up his defiance of the pope events in Rome had, unknown to the king, reached a climax. Cranmer's activities in the spring and early summer amounted to such a challenge to papal authority that not even Clement VII could ignore it, and the judgment at Dunstable, given in defiance of a papal admonition, roused his holiness to action at last.[2] The matter was considered by the pope and cardinals

[1] Henry VIII to the duke of Norfolk, 8 Aug. 1533 (*State Papers*, vii, 493; *L. & P.*, vi, 954). For an account of Norfolk's interview with Francis, as a result of which he returned to England, see Francis I to the bailly of Troyes, 27 Aug. 1533 (*L. & P.*, vi, 1038).

[2] cf. the remarks of Francis I to Stephen Gardiner, then ambassador in Paris: '. . . but if my brother [Henry VIII] thinketh it expedient for him to have the pope for him, as he told me himself he did, he may not think that the pope, holding his peace at a sentence given by the archbishop of Canterbury, will confess himself therein no pope, and be made such a fool as he will apply to lose his preeminence and authority by entreaty' (Gardiner and others to Henry VIII, ? Nov. 1533; *L. & P.*, vi, 1427). See p. 265.

in a secret consistory on 9 July, when the advocates for Catherine and the emperor demanded that sentence be pronounced in the matrimonial cause, but although the matter was debated from eleven o'clock in the morning until six o'clock in the evening, no decision was reached. The matter came before the consistory once more on 11 July when Henry's defiance of the pope, in divorcing himself from Catherine and marrying Anne Boleyn while the matrimonial suit was still pending before the pope, was the principal subject considered. At this consistory the pope declared the judgment of Cranmer to be null and void, since it had been pronounced while the marriage cause was pending before himself, and he declared that any issue Henry might have by Anne Boleyn would be illegitimate; he ordered Henry to separate from Anne Boleyn and to restore Catherine to her lawful place as wife and queen, and he declared that the king had incurred the greater excommunication and the other censures mentioned in the pope's earlier letters. However, his holiness professed himself anxious to deal mercifully with Henry and the excommunication and other censures were accordingly suspended until the end of September, by which time the king was required to comply with the papal commands.[1]

Bonner immediately wrote to Cromwell to inform him of the papal sentence, saying that he would be more fully informed by the joint letters which the ambassadors had sent to the king. After summarizing the sentence he added, 'God knoweth, we have few friends here, *etiam in justitia.*'[2] The pope took advantage of the departure from Rome of Rodrigo d'Avalos to send a letter to the emperor assuring him that, although the principal cause had not yet been concluded, the proceedings

---

[1] Diary of Blasius de Cesena for 9 and 11 July 1533 (Ehses, 227, 228); Bonner to Cromwell, Rome, 12 July 1533 (*State Papers*, vii, 480; *L. & P.*, vi, 810); 'Relacion de lo que ha pasado sobre la causa de la Serenisima Reyna de Yngla-terra' (*L. & P.*, vi, 808). cf. *L. & P.*, vi, App., 3. The sentence of Clement VII, 11 July 1533, is printed in Ehses, 212, 213, and Pocock, ii, 677, 678 (the calendared version, *L. & P.*, vi, 807, is misleading). cf. Carne to [Cromwell], 12 July 1533 (*L. & P.*, vi, 809). (See Charles V to Clement VII, Monçon, 17 Aug. 1533 Ehses, 224). The bull setting out the papal sentence was sealed and dated 13 Aug. 1533 (a similar bull, dated 8 Aug. 1533, is noted at *L. & P.*, vi, 953); an abstract was fixed to the doors of the church of St Eligius, Dunkirk, on 19 Nov. 1533, and of St Mary's Church, Bruges, on 21 Nov. 1533 (cf. *L. & P.*, vi, 1447). See also Cifuentes to Charles V, 7 Aug. 1533 (*L. & P.*, vi, 940). Biagio de Martinelli of Cesena, otherwise Blasius de Cesena, was papal master of ceremonies from 1518 to 1540.

[2] Bonner to Cromwell, 12 July 1533 (*State Papers*, vii, 480; *L. & P.*, vi, 810).

would continue and be brought to a due determination without fail.[1] On the other hand his holiness told cardinal Tournon that he was sorry he had been unable to do what Francis I had so often requested; it was the actions of the English king, he said, that had compelled him to pronounce the censures. Henry had not been content to defy the papal prohibitions, but had also passed laws which were very injurious to the holy see, and he had caused the archbishop of Canterbury to give judgment on his marriage with Catherine. Tournon, in reporting this conversation, told Francis I that the greater part of the cardinals would have been exasperated with the pope had his holiness acted in any other way.[2]

Henry learned of the papal sentence against him early in August. He replied by appealing to the next general council against the acts of the pope who had, contrary to his promise, pronounced his marriage with Anne Boleyn void and required him to take back Catherine as his wife.[3] At the same time he withdrew his ambassadors from Rome.[4] Cardinal Merino observed that the king seemed to desire a divorce not only from his wife but also from the church.[5]

Chapuys noticed that Henry's great affection for Anne Boleyn appeared to have cooled in consequence of the papal sentence, and that he seemed to have misgivings; but when Henry had consulted his lawyers, who told him that he was protected from any papal censures by his appeal to a general council, Chapuys found that he 'changed his sail and returned to his first course'. Chapuys believed that Henry was being encouraged by the duke of Norfolk who had written to the king telling him not to care a button for the sentence as he would not lack supporters to defend his rights with the sword.[6]

As August drew to a close Henry made ready for the birth of his heir. He was certain that the child would be a boy, and he was confirmed in

---

[1] Clement VII to Charles V, 17 July 1533 (*L. & P.*, vi, 853).

[2] Cardinal Tournon to Francis I, 17 Aug. 1533 (*L. & P.*, vi, 996).

[3] Henry VIII to Bonner, 18 Aug. 1533 (Pocock, ii, 679; *L. & P.*, vi, 998(1)), enclosing the appeal (*L. & P.*, vi, 998(2)). cf. Chapuys to Charles V, 23 Aug. 1533 (*L. & P.*, vi, 1018). On 13 Aug. Chapuys reported that he believed that an appeal to a future council was then being projected (see Chapuys to Charles V, 13 Aug. 1533; *L. & P.*, vi, 975).

[4] Cifuentes to Charles V, 14 Aug. 1533 (*L. & P.*, vi, 979); cardinal of Jaen to de los Cobos, 14 Aug. 1533 (*L. & P.*, vi, 980); cardinal Tournon to Francis I, 17 Aug. 1533 (*L. & P.*, vi, 996).

[5] Cardinal of Jaen to Charles V, 14 Aug. 1533 (*L. & P.*, vi, 980).

[6] Chapuys to Charles V, 23 Aug. 1533 (*L. & P.*, vi, 1018).

that belief by the reports of his physicians and by the prognostications of the astrologers whom he had consulted.[1] He inquired of de Dinteville, the French ambassador, whether he had received instructions from his master to hold the child at the font, who, he said, would be christened Edward or Henry. The ambassador replied that he had no instructions but would write to the French king about it; he thought, however, that Anne Boleyn would be delivered before he could receive an answer.[2] Before his letter could reach the French king, Francis wrote to give him leave to return to France, which he had wished for some time to do, and informed him that the sieur de Castillon would replace him.[3] When the ambassador's letter reached him, Francis wrote immediately to say that he would be happy to send some notable personage to be present at the baptism of the expected prince, but if Henry could not wait for the arrival of such a representative the ambassador might do it;[4] but when Francis wrote his letter the christening had been done a week.

The child was born at Greenwich on Sunday, 7 September 1533, and, to the great disappointment of the king, was a girl.[5] Chapuys reported the birth of the child, saying its sex was a great reproach to the physicians and astrologers who had affirmed that it would be a male child; and he added, with satisfaction, that the people were doubly glad that the child was a daughter rather than a son and mocked those who had put their faith in divinations.[6]

The child was born between three and four o'clock in the afternoon, and 'for the queen's good deliverance, *Te Deum* was sung incontinently'. Preparations for the christening were set on foot, and Henry was callous enough to demand that Catherine should send, for the occasion, the robe in which her daughter, Mary, had been christened; he received a tart

[1] Chapuys to Charles V, 3 Sept. 1533 (*L. & P.*, vi, 1069).
[2] The bailly of Troyes to Francis I, 3 Sept. 1533 (*L. & P.*, vi, 1070).
[3] Francis I to the bailly of Troyes, 6 Sept. 1533 (*L. & P.*, vi, 1086). Castillon did not reach England until Nov. 1533; cf. bailly of Troyes to [Montmorenci] the Grand Master, 7 Nov. 1533 (*L. & P.*, vi, 1404).
[4] Francis I to the bailly of Troyes, 17 Sept. 1533 (*L. & P.*, vi, 1135).
[5] Anne Boleyn wrote immediately to lord Cobham to tell him of 'the dely-veraunce and bringing furthe of a Princes'. The word 'princes' occurs twice in the letter and in each instance the final letter 's' has been added subsequently to the writing of the letter; evidently the letter was prepared before the birth of the child, in the confident expectation that it would be a boy; see Anne Boleyn to lord Cobham, 7 Sept. 1533 (*State Papers*, i, 407; *L. & P.*, vi, 1089).
[6] Chapuys to Charles V, 10 Sept. 1533 (*L. & P.*, vi, 1112).

answer. The christening took place at Greenwich in the afternoon of 10 September. The mayor and council, wearing scarlet robes and their gold collars, were rowed to Greenwich, accompanied by a number of citizens in another barge. All the walls between the royal palace and the church of the Franciscan Observants were hung with arras and the way was strewn with rushes. The church, too, was hung with arras and in the middle was a silver font standing on a plinth with three steps covered in fine cloth; and 'divers gentlemen with aprons, and towels about their necks, gave attendance about it'. The old duchess of Norfolk carried the child, wrapped in a mantle of purple velvet, and a canopy was carried by lord Rochford, lord Hussey, lord William Howard and lord Thomas Howard. The archbishop of Canterbury was godfather, and two widows, the duchess of Norfolk and the marchioness of Dorset, were godmothers. The bishop of London and other prelates met the child at the door, and, after escorting her to the font, they christened her Elizabeth. The christening done, Garter king of arms cried aloud, 'God of his infinite goodness, send prosperous life and long to the high and mighty princess of England Elizabeth'; and the trumpets were blown. After the child had been taken to the altar to receive her christening gifts, there were 'brought in wafers, comfits and hippocras in such plenty that every man had as much as he would desire'. After the company had satisfied their hunger, a procession was formed to escort the child from the church, and her christening gifts were borne before her. When the procession had left, the mayor and aldermen were thanked for their presence by the dukes of Norfolk and Suffolk in the king's name and then, after drinking in the cellar, they entered their barge to return to the city.[1] It was a brave show, but Chapuys sourly observed that the christening of 'the daughter of the lady' had been 'like her mother's coronation, very cold and disagreeable to the court and to the city'.[2]

The popular pleasure at the birth of a girl was not due solely to a perverse delight in the discomfiture of the astrologers; the sex of the child gave the king's subjects some ground for hoping that the princess Mary would not now be superseded in the succession as recent events had led them to fear.[3] Henry and his newly crowned queen, however, had other ideas. Less than a fortnight after the birth of Elizabeth lord

---

[1] Hall, *Chronicle*, ii, 242-4.
[2] Chapuys to Charles V, 15 Sept. 1533 (*L. & P.*, vi, 1125).
[3] cf. Chapuys to Charles V, 10 Sept. 1533 (*L. & P.*, vi, 1112).

Hussey was sent to Beaulieu, in Essex, where princess Mary was then staying, to inform her that it was the king's pleasure that her household should be diminished and that she should cease to use the title and dignity of princess. Mary was astonished at Hussey's message, more especially as it was delivered without the accompaniment of any commission or other writing from the king. She told Hussey that she was the king's lawful daughter and heir, and she refused to believe that the king intended 'to diminish her estate without a writing from him'. When Hussey told her servants of the king's commands they replied that they were always ready to obey the king, saving their conscience, but they regarded a merely verbal message as insufficient authority. Lord Hussey had, therefore, to report to the council that his mission had been a failure.[1] Letters written in the king's name by Sir William Paulet, the comptroller of the household, were no more successful. Three councillors, the earls of Oxford, Essex and Sussex, with the dean of the chapel, Dr Richard Sampson, were then given written instructions on the matter ('Articles to be proponed and showed on our behalf unto our daughter lady Mary and all other the officers and servants of her household'). They were instructed to remonstrate with the princess on her disobedience; she was to be informed that, in order to prevent the spread of her pernicious example, they had been commanded to declare to her the folly and danger of her conduct, and to explain to her how the king intended that she should conduct herself both as to her title and as to her household; she was to be told that she had deserved the king's high displeasure and punishment by law, but if she conformed to his will he might, of his fatherly pity, incline to promote her welfare.[2] The princess received this deputation with dignity and informed them (and subsequently wrote to her father) that she would be as obedient to the king's commands as any slave, but she had no right to renounce or derogate from the titles and prerogatives that God, nature and her parents had given her, and as she was the daughter of the king and the queen she had a right to be styled princess; her father might do as he pleased, but she would do nothing either expressly or tacitly in prejudice of her own legitimacy or the cause of her mother.[3]

Henry was not the man to accept such a rebuff from a girl of seventeen.

[1] Lord Hussey to [the council], 20 Sept. 1533 (*L. & P.*, vi, 1139).
[2] Instructions concerning the Lady Mary (*L. & P.*, vi, 1186).
[3] Chapuys to Charles V, 10 Oct. 1533 (*L. & P.*, vi, 1249).

In order to break her spirit he resolved that she should be deprived of all her servants and be compelled to perform the office of lady's maid to his newly born daughter, to whom Chapuys referred as 'this new bastard'. Rumours of the king's intention caused anxiety to Catherine and her daughter, and Mary sent secretly to Chapuys to ask for his advice. Chapuys sent her the draft of a protest, while he himself remonstrated with Cromwell on the indignity which the king had in mind for his daughter. Cromwell, however, took care to avoid Chapuys and the ambassador found that his opportunities of seeing Cromwell were greatly reduced on account of his 'numerous preoccupations'.[1] On 2 December it was decided, at a meeting of the council, that Elizabeth should be conveyed to Hatfield where a household was to be established for her; it was also decided that the households of Catherine and of Mary should be broken up. The king appointed the duke of Suffolk, the earl of Sussex, Sir William Paulet and Dr Richard Sampson to repair to the 'Princess Dowager', and the duke of Norfolk, the earl of Oxford and Edward Foxe, the almoner, to repair to 'the lady Mary' who was no longer referred to by her title of princess.[2] On 13 December Norfolk escorted the infant Elizabeth to Hatfield and then waited on Mary to tell her that, at her father's desire, she was to enter the service of 'the princess'. Mary replied that that title belonged to herself and to no other, but when she saw that there was no escape she returned to her room for half an hour and there wrote out and signed the protest with which she had been provided by Chapuys; she then placed herself under Norfolk's protection. On her arrival at Hatfield Norfolk asked her whether she would go and pay her respects to the princess; she replied that she knew of no princess in England except herself, and she retired weeping to her chamber.[3]

While Norfolk had been subjecting Mary to these humiliations, Suffolk was carrying out his orders with regard to the princess's mother. In the middle of December Suffolk and the others went to Buckden, where Catherine was then staying, to induce her to remove to Somersham

[1] Chapuys to Charles V, 3 Nov. 1533 (*L. & P.*, vi, 1392).
[2] Acta in Concilio Domini Regis, 2ᵈᵒ Decembris, [1533] (*State Papers*, i, 414, 415; *L. & P.*, vi, 1486); see p. 268.
[3] Chapuys to Charles V, 9 Dec. 1533 (*L. & P.*, vi, 1510); Chapuys to Charles V, 16 Dec. 1533 (*L. & P.*, vi, 1528); Chapuys to Charles V, 23 Dec. 1533 (*L. & P.*, vi, 1558). See also Chapuys to Charles V, 6 Dec. 1533 (*L. & P.*, vi, 1501).

in the Isle of Ely; Somersham was a lonely, decaying house in the fens, approached by only a single road, and reputed to be very unhealthy. They found her 'persisting in her great stomach and obstinacy'; she vigorously protested that she was Henry's queen and true wife, and she utterly refused either to be known as the Princess Dowager, or to go to Somersham because of the danger to her health. Her servants, who had been sworn to her as queen, were reluctant to take a new oath to her as Princess Dowager, and since Suffolk found that 'they continued a time stiffly in their opinions' he committed them to the custody of the porter where they were to remain without speaking to anyone until Henry's pleasure should be known; a few servants were willing to take the new oath but Catherine resolutely refused to have them in her service. After three days of fruitless endeavour Suffolk was perplexed to know what to do, and sought Henry's directions, since Catherine, as he said,

wilfully, and against all humanity and reason, continueth still in this opinion, saying that, although your grace have [*sic*] appointed her to remove to Somersham, she may, nor will, in any wise follow your grace's pleasure therein, unless we should bind her with ropes and violently enforce her thereunto.

Suffolk and his fellow commissioners remained at Buckden six days, hoping that their menaces, the loss of her servants and her own helplessness would induce Catherine to comply with the king's wishes; but they failed to change her mind. She locked herself in her room and told them, through a hole in the wall, that they would have to break down the doors if they wished to remove her; this they dare not do, for fear of reprisals from the local people, and they departed, leaving Catherine where she was but deprived of almost all her servants.[1]

3

A pamphlet was published towards the end of 1533, at the instance of the council, which, in nine articles, justified the king's marriage and attacked

[1] Duke of Suffolk and others to Henry VIII, 19 Dec. 1533 (*State Papers*, i, 415; *L. & P.*, vi, 1541); duke of Suffolk and others to duke of Norfolk, 19 Dec. 1533 (*State Papers*, i, 418; *L. & P.*, vi, 1542); duke of Suffolk and others to Cromwell, 19 Dec. 1533 (*L. & P.*, vi, 1543); Chapuys to Charles V, 23 Dec. 1533 (*L. & P.*, vi, 1558); Chapuys to Charles V, 27 Dec. 1533 (*L. & P.*, vi, 1571).

the pope.[1] In these *Articles* there re-appear the ideas, and sometimes the phraseology, of an earlier tract, *A Glasse of the Truthe*;[2] and the *Articles* provide us with the first real example of the use of the printing press to produce propaganda for the purpose of rousing public opinion and of imposing on men's minds an official version and interpretation of events. The purpose of the *Articles* was to deliver an attack upon the pope by degrading his jurisdiction to that of any other bishop so that men might be induced to believe that Henry was within his rights in divorcing Catherine and marrying Anne; the attack was, in reality, an attack upon papal supremacy.

The first Article asserted that 'the mere truth is, that no living creature of what estate, degree, or dignity so ever he be, hath power given him by God to dispense with God's laws or laws of nature'. Since this was so, the archbishop of Canterbury, authorized by act of parliament, had pronounced 'the first matrimony' to be unlawful and 'the second matrimony' to be lawful and perfect; and therefore all the king's subjects ought to support the king 'in his just and true matrimony'. The *Articles* then went on to assert that the pope, who was described as 'the usurper of God's law and infringer of general councils', had wrongfully detained at Rome the king's 'great and weighty cause', and, had not the king and his parliament otherwise provided, would have continued to detain it 'contrary to all right and conscience to the utter undoing of this realm'. Consequently the king and his parliament had considered these matters, and having concluded 'that it were not meet that the inheritance of this realm should depend upon the bishop of Rome, or any other stranger's will', had made a law which rendered it impossible for the pope, by delaying justice, to keep men from their rights in matrimonial cases or to compel them to continue to live in unions that they knew to be incestuous. It was then asserted that by rejecting the king's excusator the

---

[1] 'Articles Divisid by the holle consent of the Kynges most honourable counsayle, his gracis licence opteined thereto, not only to exhort, but also to enfourme his louynge subiectis of the trouthe' (reprinted in Pocock, ii, 523-31).

[2] It is of interest to compare the *Articles* with the anonymous tract, *A Glasse of the Truthe* (*S.T.C.*, 11918, 11919), first printed by Thomas Berthelet in 1530; it is reprinted in Pocock, ii, 385-421, and is conveniently summarized in Hughes, *Reformation in England*, i, 248-52 (although Mgr Hughes's text implies that the *Glasse* was first published in 1533). The *Glasse of the Truthe* (in the composition of which Henry VIII appears to have had a hand) is very important as the source of much argument that later appeared in official and semi-official publications and in the work of such men as Foxe, Sampson, Gardiner and others.

pope had done the king a great injury which Henry's subjects would do well to ponder; the king would see to it that, unless that and other injuries were made good, he would 'revenge it to the uttermost of our power, and in so doing we do but our duty'.

The *Articles* declared that it was 'the right belief of all true christian people', that a general council was superior to all bishops, 'not excepting the bishop of Rome'.[1] This was followed by the astonishing assertion that 'by the law of nature' it was lawful to appeal from the bishop of Rome to the general council, which was 'most convenient for princes' and a thing which they should not neglect. It followed from this that once an appeal had been lawfully made to a general council, the 'bishop of Rome (which calleth himself Pope)' was bound by law 'neither to do, nor attempt any further process, in prejudice of the appellant, which if he do, by the foresaid laws, his doings cannot prejudice the appellant, and also it standeth void'. Since the king had appealed to a general council, 'all just and true christian men' would support him and any censures they might incur in so doing 'ought to be despised and manfully withstood, for they be nought indeed'. The sentence of excommunication against the king should be disregarded, and everyone should show themselves to be 'true and obedient subjects, not esteeming nor hanging upon any living creature, save only our prince and king', according to the old proverb, 'One God and one king.'

There followed a remarkable account of Cranmer's proceedings at Dunstable, in which it was said that 'our good bishop of Canterbury', realizing that the king was living in unlawful matrimony, 'meekly did admonish him, and . . . also reproved him, exhorting him to leave [the unlawful matrimony], or else he would do further his duty in it, so that at the last, according to God's laws he did separate his prince from that unlawful matrimony'. The final article was a diatribe against the papacy, in which resided, it was said, no greater jurisdiction than that in any other see; there was also a personal attack upon Clement VII, who was declared to be unlawfully occupying his usurped place, for he was a bastard who had reached his position by simony, and a heretic too.[2]

[1] This is the conciliar theory, which had been making head for some time; it was finally condemned by the bull *Pastor Aeternus*, of Julius II, which was read in the eleventh session of the fifth Lateran Council on 19 Dec. 1516 (see Mansi, xxxii, 967; Denzinger, no. 740).
[2] cf. 'The opinion of an anonymous writer on the point of Cranmer's instructing the clergy on the subject of the king's marriage and the abolition of the papal

Sir Thomas More was suspected of having written an answer to the *Articles*, which he was said to have given to his nephew, William Rastell, to print.[1] Rastell was examined before the council and denied any knowledge of the book, and More, learning of his nephew's examination, wrote a letter to Cromwell in which he, too, indignantly denied the charge.[2]

[1] William Rastell (1508-65) was the son of John Rastell, a lawyer in Coventry. At the age of seventeen he was assisting his father in his law practice, and he also learned printing and worked at his father's press. In 1529 he set up his own press. He was called to the Bar by Lincoln's Inn in 1539, and after a period in exile, he returned to England at the accession of Mary and became a judge in 1558.

[2] More to Thomas Cromwell, 1 Feb. 1534 (Rogers, 466).

---

supremacy, June 1533' (Pocock, ii, 487-9). The writer said that 'if the Pope be excluded out of this realm, the archbishop must be chief of all the clergy here, the which will not lightly be accepted in the people's hearts'; and he accordingly recommended that Cranmer should put out a book, 'not over long', to declare that what was done was 'not only according to the law of God, but also for the great wealth and quietness of all this realm'. The writer was sure that if Cranmer were to do this, he would 'by this mean greatly content the people's minds, and make them think that they be happy thus to be rid of the Pope's oppression, and that the archbishop is a perfect and a good bishop, and that he intendeth truly according to the word of God, and that he never did anything for the prince's pleasure so much to win him promotion, as he did for the truth's sake'. cf. pp. 242, 243.

XVI

The Royal Supremacy

I

The sentence of excommunication which the pope had reluctantly pronounced against Henry was followed by a breach between England and the papacy that appalled Clement. His policy of delay, pursued in order to postpone indefinitely a final decision in the hope that matters would solve themselves, had come to nothing. Henry's appeal to a general council was no doubt, little more than a gesture of defiance, for Henry had more reason than anyone to dread a general council, and Clement was aware that both Henry and his ally, Francis I, wished for a council as little as he did himself; but the appeal, following the sentence of excommunication, at last brought relations between king and pope to the breaking point.

Henry's recent proceedings, culminating in his marriage with Anne Boleyn, had also disturbed his relations with Francis I. For long Henry had received staunch support from Francis, and it was not long since the two kings had sought to win the friendship of the pope in opposition to the emperor, while the pope, for his part, had shown some signs of amiability. Francis had good reason to be hopeful of the outcome of his negotiations which were due to be brought to a conclusion at his meeting with Clement in the autumn. But Cranmer's decision and Henry's subsequent marriage were events to which Francis had not been made privy; when he met the pope he found that that part of his task relating to the marriage suit was no longer a subject for negotiation, and he was indignant to discover the extent to which he had been kept in ignorance.[1]

The pope had left Rome at the beginning of September; his departure was watched with exasperation by the emperor's agents, for the marriage

---

[1] In September Francis told Henry that at his coming interview with the pope he would employ himself in Henry's affair, both with the pope and elsewhere, so that Henry would see that he was as much concerned about it as about his own affairs; Francis I to Henry VIII, 8 Sept. 1533 (*L. & P.*, vi, 1101); cf. *L. & P.*, vi, 1572 (p. 635).

suit could not proceed in his absence. He took with him a summary of the whole process, and ordered Capisucchi, the dean of the Rota, and Simonetta, the auditor, to accompany him.[1] He landed near Marseilles on 1 October and made his solemn entry into the town on the following day.[2] Meanwhile Henry had sent the representatives whom he had nominated in place of the duke of Norfolk; they were sent to be 'witnesses and participators' in what should be done by Francis and the pope.[3] The deputation, headed by Sir Francis Bryan and Stephen Gardiner, travelled from England to join Sir John Wallop who was then Henry's resident ambassador at Paris; and Dr Edmund Bonner travelled independently from Rome.[4] As the papal sentence was due to take effect at the end of September, the Englishmen presented themselves before Francis I and requested him to write to cardinal Tournon with instructions to urge the pope to postpone the operation of the sentence of excommunication. Francis agreed to do so; his intervention was successful and the effective date was postponed.[5]

The meeting was doomed to failure. Francis soon found that the English representatives had no powers and were unable to commit Henry to any arrangement the French king might reach with the pope; and once the pope had discovered this he was not disposed to make concessions to Francis.[6] Even with these impediments some sort of accommodation might have been achieved had it not been for Henry's appeal to a general council, and the manner in which it was done made any progress with the marriage question impossible. Francis soon made plain to the Englishmen his indignation at Henry's behaviour which had not only left him uninformed of the course of events but had destroyed the founda-

[1] Ortiz to Charles V, 9 Sept. 1533 (*L. & P.*, vi, 1104).
[2] cf. *L. & P.*, vi, 1280; Gardiner, Bryan and Wallop to lord Lisle, 17 Oct. 1533 (*L. & P.*, vi, 1301). On 19 Oct. Jerome Ghinucci, the bishop of Worcester, wrote to the king informing him of his arrival at Marseilles with the pontifical court, and offering his services (Ghinucci to Henry VIII, 19 Oct. 1533; *State Papers*, vii, 515; *L. & P.*, vi, 1316). Cifuentes, the imperial ambassador in Rome, also travelled with the pontifical court.
[3] cf. 'Memoires pour le fait d'entre le Pape et le Roi d'Angleterre, auquel le Roi s'estoit entremis' (*L. & P.*, vi, 1572 (p. 635)); cf. p. 252.
[4] cf. Gardiner, Bryan and Wallop to lord Lisle, 5 Oct. 1533 (*L. & P.*, vi, 1218); Bonner to Henry VIII, 16 Oct. 1533 (*L. & P.*, vi, 1299).
[5] Francis I to the bailly of Troyes, 5 Oct. 1533 (*L. & P.*, vi, 1220); Ehses, 214 (Acta consistorialia, 26 Sept. 1533). cf. count of Cifuentes to Charles V, 6 Nov. 1533 (*L. & P.*, vi, 1403). Gardiner had left England on 3 Sept.
[6] Count of Cifuentes to Charles V, 6 Nov. 1533 (*L. & P.*, vi, 1403).

tions of his approaches to the pope. He spoke sharply to Gardiner, saying that

if my brother [Henry VIII] thinketh it expedient for him to have the pope for him, as he told me himself he did, he may not think that the pope, holding his peace at a sentence given by the archbishop of Canterbury, will confess himself therein no pope, and be made such a fool as he will apply to lose his preeminence and authority by entreaty.

Francis complained about Cranmer's judgment, saying that he 'was never made privy thereunto', and he went on to assert that

as fast I study to win the pope, ye study to lose him, and of such effect as in your intimation now made, yet to the worst purpose that could be devised, which, if I had known before, ye should never have done it. . . . I went to the pope to take a conclusion in your matters, and when I came there I found one making the intimation; which, when the pope had told me of what sort it was, I was greatly ashamed that I knew so little in it. . . . Ye require a general council, and that the emperor desireth, and I go about to bring the pope from the emperor, and you drive him to him. And can my brother call a council alone? Ye have clearly marred all.

Francis, in his exasperation, told Gardiner that he wished that he had never meddled in the matter of Henry's marriage.[1] The 'one making the intimation' to whom Francis had referred was Edmund Bonner. On 18 August Henry had written to Bonner ordering him to intimate to the pope that he appealed from the sentence of excommunication to the next general council.[2] On 7 November, accompanied by Gulielmo Penizzoni as witness, Bonner forced his way into the pope's presence; to use his own phrase, he 'succeeded after some resistance in getting access to the chamber, where he [the pope] stood between two cardinals'. Bonner waited for the pope to dismiss the cardinals and then, without more ado, he told his holiness of Henry's appeal to a general council and read to him the document. The pope was greatly incensed by this boorish behaviour and interrupted Bonner; Francis, however, happened to enter the room at that moment, and his holiness complained bitterly of the Englishman's lack of respect. The pope rejected Henry's appeal as frivolous, and Francis was not only indignant at finding himself fooled but deeply resentful that his hospitality should be so grossly abused by the agents of the king whom he was doing

---

[1] Gardiner [and others] to Henry VIII, Nov. 1533 (*L. & P.*, vi, 1427).
[2] Henry VIII to Bonner, 18 Aug. 1533 (Pocock, ii, 679; *L. & P.*, vi, 998); cf. Chapuys to Charles V, 23 Aug. 1533 (*L. & P.*, vi, 1018). See p. 254.

his best to assist.[1] The French king had good reason for his irritation with Henry. He remarked that he was surprised that Henry had gained a reputation for wisdom, and he shrewdly observed that the king was, in reality, working for the interest of Catherine, because by his appeal he had acknowledged the pope's jurisdiction.[2]

One result was achieved before the pope left for Italy on 12 November. Francis was anxious, for the well being of christendom, to prevent a complete rupture between Henry and the pope, and he busied himself to persuade Clement not to sever relations with Henry because of his recent behaviour. It was eventually agreed that Francis should send a representative to England to complain of the outrage done to the pope and to make friendly remonstrances while, at the same time, bringing about, if possible, a renewal of negotiations. The pope was aware that England might now be lost entirely to the holy see and readily agreed to this proposal, adding a promise that he would temporize and issue no fulminations from Rome, however much he might be urged to do so, in order to give Francis' representative time to carry out his task. Jean du Bellay, the bishop of Paris, was chosen to make this rather forlorn attempt, and he was charged to leave nothing undone that might tend to bring Henry to reason.

du Bellay set out at once and on his way he met de Dinteville returning from his post as ambassador in London. de Dinteville was riding post to inform Francis of the desperate state of affairs in England; it seemed, he said, that the English parliament was about to pass its final measures against the holy see. Francis was gravely disturbed by this news and induced Sir Francis Bryan to go with all speed to England for the purpose of dissuading Henry from taking any action until the arrival of du Bellay.[3]

[1] For Bonner's account of this interview, see Bonner to Henry VIII, 13 Nov. 1533 (Pocock-Burnet, vi, 56; *L. & P.*, vi, 1425); for du Bellay's account, see Friedman, *Anne Boleyn*, i, 253; cf. count of Cifuentes to Charles V, 9 Nov. 1533 (*L. & P.*, vi, 1409), and 'Memoires pour le fait d'entre le Pape et le Roi d'Angleterre, auquel le Roi s'estoit entremis' (*L. & P.*, vi, 1572).

[2] Count of Cifuentes to Charles V, 9 Nov. 1533 (*L. & P.*, vi, 1409).

[3] 'Memoires pour le fait d'entre le Pape et le Roi d'Angleterre, auquel le Roi s'estoit entremis' (*L. & P.*, vi, 1572); 'Memorial drawn up by M. de Polizy, bailly of Troyes, concerning certain conversations which the king of England has held with him' (*L. & P.*, vi, 1479); 'Memoires des points que M. du Bellay, evesque de Paris, aura a toucher au Roy d'Angleterre, pour imputer aux Ministres d'Angleterre, la rupture de la Negociation poursuivie par François Premier vers le Pape, pour le Roy d'Angleterre' (Le Grand, iii, 571; *L. & P.*, vi, 1426).

The circumstances in which du Bellay set out on his mission were anything but favourable. Henry had lost interest in the meeting at Marseilles, and now that he had obtained from Cranmer what he wanted he was only concerned to demonstrate that the pope and his censures were of little importance. Chapuys reported that Henry had forbidden all printers to print any description of the entry of the pope into Marseilles or of the obedience shown him by the king of France; such publications were regarded as contrary to Henry's statutes and to the statement put out by the king that Francis would adhere to his cause and would pass laws more prejudicial to papal authority than those of Henry himself.[1] Later the French ambassador told Chapuys that he had heard, several times, from the king and those about him that if Henry could get no other remedy he would throw off his allegiance to the holy see and that he repented of nothing more than of writing his book against Luther in which he had spoken in favour of the authority of the pope.[2] Henry told the French ambassador that, at the request of Francis and in the hope that something favourable to him would emerge from the meeting at Marseilles, he had ordered preachers to cease from preaching against the pope, but, now that the meeting had achieved nothing, he would set them on again and would issue books to reveal the abuses of the pope and churchmen in a way that had never been done before.[3]

Henry then turned once more to the German Lutherans. Early in December he wrote to Sir John Wallop to inform him of his intention to approach the German princes again. He said that he now had 'perfect advertisement and knowledge of the pope's indurate heart, and most obstinate and ungodly intent, purpose and disposition' towards him and his realm; and he had therefore resolved, after conferring with his council, to send to the princes of Germany and other in order to join himself in amity with them. Having regard to Henry's friendship with the French king, Wallop was instructed to inform Francis that the council, after considering the pope's violations of the laws of England and the privileges of the crown, had urged Henry that he should not only 'no longer suffer or endure these malicious attempts done by the pope . . . but should provide due remedy for the same, and . . . so to use the administration of our high authority within this our realm, as the same may

---

[1] Chapuys to Charles V, 12 Nov. 1533 (*L. & P.*, vi, 1419).
[2] i.e., *Assertio Septem Sacramentarum*, 1521; see p. 130.
[3] Chapuys to Charles V, 6 Dec. 1533 (*L. & P.*, vi, 1501).

redound to the utter abolition of the pope's authority'. Francis was therefore to be informed that Henry had 'already taken such order with our nobles and subjects, as we shall shortly be able to give unto the pope such a buffet as he never had heretofore'.[1]

Meanwhile Cranmer, in England, was enduring acute anxiety for what the pope might do as the result of his judgment at Dunstable, pronounced in defiance of the papal inhibition forbidding any person, under pain of excommunication, to entertain the marriage suit.[2] At the end of November he wrote to Bonner, telling him that he stood in dread lest the pope should make some process against him; he went on to say that, by the advice of the king and the council, he was appealing to the general council, and he enclosed his appeal, asking Bonner to consult with Gardiner as to the best method for proceeding with it.[3]

2

Unlike Francis, Henry was not concerned to maintain good relations with the pope; he knew well enough that the breach with Rome was incurable. No sooner had the pope left France than the king and his council began, by organized propaganda, to rouse the nation against the pope. The French ambassador reported, in the middle of November, that Henry was already cooling in his friendship towards Francis because of the poor results of the meeting at Marseilles; and the ambassador added that Henry was determined to withdraw himself and his country from obedience to the pope.[4] The council met on Tuesday, 2 December, and determined

First, to send for all the bishops of this realm, . . . and to examine them apart, whether they, by the law of God, can prove and justify, that he, that is now called the Pope of Rome, is above the General Council, or the General

---

[1] Henry VIII to Wallop, [Dec.] 1533 (*State Papers*, vii, 524; *L. & P.*, vi, 1491); this letter, the draft of which is not dated, must have been written within a day or two of the council meeting of 2 Dec. 1533 (see p. 270), since it was decided at that meeting that such a letter should be written.
[2] See p. 236.
[3] Cranmer to Bonner, 22 Nov. 1533 (Pocock-Burnet, vi, 68; *L. & P.*, vi, 1454).
[4] Castillon to the bishop of Paris, London, 17 Nov. 1533 (*L. & P.*, vi, 1435).

Council above him; or whether he hath given unto him, by the law of God any more authority within the realm, than any other foreign bishop.[1]

It was also determined that arrangements be concerted with the bishops

to set forth, preach and cause to be preached, to the king's people, that the said bishop of Rome, called the Pope, is not in authority above the General Council, but the General Council is above him, and all bishops; and he hath not, by God's law, any more jurisdiction within this realm, than any other foreign bishop, being of any other realm, hath; and that such authority, as he before this hath usurped within this realm,[2] is both against God's law, and also against the General Council's; which usurpation of authority only hath grown to him by the sufferance of princes of this realm, and by none authority from God.[3]

It was also resolved that this doctrine should be preached, every Sunday, at Paul's Cross and that the bishop of London should allow no one to preach there who would not set forth such doctrine; and the remainder of the bishops were to cause it to be preached throughout their dioceses.[4]

Arrangements were to be made with the provincials of the orders of

[1] Minutes for the Council, 2 Dec. 1533 (*State Papers*, i, 411, 412; *L. & P.*, vi, 1486, 1487), Item 1. Certain of the items of these minutes (B.M., MSS. Cott., Cleopatra, E, vi, f. 313) are annotated by Cromwell as to the action taken. According to the 'Acta in Concilio Domini Regis, 2ᵈᵒ Decembris' (*State Papers*, i, 414; *L. & P.*, vi, 1486) this proposal was committed to the care of Richard Sampson, dean of the chapel, Edward Foxe, the almoner, and other doctors, to report to the council upon the following Friday, 5 Dec., when the bishops of London, Lincoln and Bath were to be present. This was the council at which it was decided to take measures against Catherine of Aragon and her daughter, Mary; see p. 258.

[2] This is the first occasion on which it was asserted that the pope's jurisdiction in no way differed from that of any other bishop. It is also the first occasion that the pope's jurisdiction is said to be 'usurped', a statement that later became common form. cf. Pollard, *Cranmer*, 312, note: 'The acceptance of the theory of divine institution for the "powers that be" led to controversial dilemmas; for on that theory an authority once legitimate must be always legitimate, and it could never be abolished on such grounds as that it had ceased to perform its proper functions. Hence when Reformers wished to abolish an authority they were driven to maintain that it had always been a "usurped" authority, and this, of course, is always the reason put forward for the abolition of the Roman juris-diction, and not the real and historical reasons. Yet the primacy of Rome was as legitimate and natural a development as the Royal Supremacy; the one was no more usurped than the other'. cf. the book of *Articles*, p. 260.

[3] Minutes for the Council, 2 Dec. 1533 (*State Papers*, i, 411, at p. 412; *L. & P.*, vi, 1487), item 2.

[4] Ibid. items 3 and 4.

friars for the preaching of similar sermons. It seems that opposition from the Franciscan Observants was expected, for it was resolved 'to practice with all the Friars Observants of this realm, and to command them to preach in likewise; or else that they may be stayed, and not suffered to preach in no place of the realm'.[1] The heads of religious houses were to teach this doctrine to their brethren, and bishops were to order their clergy to preach it to their parishioners. Proclamations were to be made throughout the kingdom setting out the Act of Appeals,[2] and the act itself was to be 'impressed, transumed, and set up on every church door in England', so that no one might be ignorant of its provisions. Similar steps were to be taken to make it plain that the papal censures against the king were of no effect, and transumpts of the king's appeal to a general council were also to be fixed to every church door in the kingdom. Transumpts were also to be sent abroad, especially to Flanders, 'to the intent the falshood, iniquity, malice, and injustice of the bishop of Rome may thereby appear to all the world'.[3] It was also proposed that a letter from the lords, spiritual and temporal, should be sent to the pope setting out the 'wrongs, injuries and usurpations' done to the king and his realm; and spies were to be sent into Scotland 'to perceive their practices' and to discover whether the Scots intended to ally themselves with any foreign prince.[4] 'Certain discreet and grave persons' were to be sent to Germany to conclude a defensive league, while others were to go to Lübeck, Danzig, Hamburg, Brunswick and other cities of the Hanse, as well as Nuremburg and Augsburg.[5] Thus, while Henry attacked the pope at home there was to be organized a defensive league abroad from among the heretical princes of Germany.

Meanwhile, on 17 December, du Bellay arrived in London to make his attempt to bring Henry to reason, and with the additional purpose of justifying his master whom Henry, after the interview at Marseilles,

---

[1] Ibid. items 5 and 6.
[2] 24 Hen. VIII, c. 12; see p. 221.
[3] Minutes for the Council, 2 Dec. 1533 (*State Papers*, i, 411, at pp. 412, 413; *L. & P.*, vi, 1487), items 5 to 11; cf. Chapuys to Charles V, 9 Dec. 1533 (*L. & P.*, vi, 1510 (p. 611)).
[4] Ibid. items 12 and 13.
[5] Ibid. items 14, 15 and 16. As to these articles, it was ordered 'that letters shalbe, with all spede, devised and sent unto Mr Wallopp, to advertise the French King therof, before any of them shalbe put in execution'; it was in pursuance of this order that Henry's letter to Wallop was written (see p. 268).

had frequently accused of bad faith.[1] His mission was hopeless. The massive anti-papal propaganda was already under way. In a proclamation prepared by the council and couched in violent terms, Henry informed his subjects that he was not under the jurisdiction or power of any prince or potentate, and although the pope had promulgated certain decrees and sentences against him, he had appealed to 'the holy Council General now next to be holden'. If the sentences had any effect before his appeal, the fact that he had appealed robbed them of all force, 'so that neither these decrees and sentences nor their publication ought to be feared'.[2] Instructions had been given for the preaching of the sermons determined upon by the council,[3] and Henry had summoned the bishops and demanded their consent to the abrogation of papal authority in England. The king was anxious that the bishops should make their declaration before the arrival of du Bellay; but each had taken an oath of obedience to the pope on taking possession of his see, and it is to the credit of the bishops that, with the exception of Cranmer upon whom the obligations of an oath sat lightly, they refused.[4] Cranmer's acquiescence, however, appears to have been regarded as sufficient, and at the end of the year there was published the book of *Articles* justifying the king's marriage and attacking the pope.[5]

---

[1] For du Bellay's instructions, see Le Grand, iii, 571-88; *L. & P.*, vi, 1426. cf. Chapuys to Charles V, 22 Dec. 1533 (*L. & P.*, vi, 1558).
[2] cf. Preamble of a Proclamation (*L. & P.*, vii, 3).
[3] Order for preachers (*L. & P.*, vi, 464). cf. A sermon in defence of the conduct of Henry VIII in the divorce, commencing, 'If mortall creatures to theyr heddes souveraynes and naturell princes be chiefly bounde next unto God' (*L. & P.*, vii, 2); Cromwell's Remembrances: 'To remember devices for the bishops to set forth and preach the King's great cause, and also against the censures, and tha the Pope be no more prayed for at Paul's Cross or elsewhere' (*L. & P.*, vii, 48(2)).
[4] Chapuys to Charles V, 9 Dec. 1533 (*L. & P.*, vi, 1510 (p. 612)).
[5] See p. 260. At the beginning of January Chapuys reported that the book of *Articles* was only a 'preamble and prologue' to other, more important pamphlets about to be published. 'One is called *Defensorium Pacis* [see p. 146] . . . Formerly no one dared read it, for fear of being burnt, but now it is translated into English so that all the people may see and understand it. The other is entitled, "Concerning Royal and Priestly Authority", and proves that bishops ought to be equal to other priests, except in precedence and in the honour showed them in church, and that kings and princes ought to be sovereign over churchmen, according to the ancient law, which is the point most agreeable to the king, and have the administration of their temporal goods. The king will certainly try to put this last in execution, as well on account of his hatred for churchmen as from

Henry was now about to complete the work, begun with the Submission of the Clergy, the Act in restraint of Annates and the Act of Appeals, which would finally sever his subjects from their spiritual head, the pope. In so doing Henry had moved far along the road to heresy; and the king's heresy was not lost upon his subjects. The subprior of St John Baptist's, Colchester, a Benedictine abbey, declared that the king and his council were heretics because of the book of *Articles*.[1] Proceedings were taken against John Frances, a monk of the same monastery, who was accused of having said that those who had put forth the book of *Articles* were heretics, although previously he had said that they were but schismatics.[2] Again, in Essex, the town of Langham made a complaint against one, John Vigorouse, a 'questman', that he had molested them in the use of certain books put forth by the king's authority; and they also complained of his using unfit words at the preaching of a sermon by Mr Wade, calling it newfangledness; and they complained, too, that Vigorouse had asserted that if the king had made certain acts, he would be glad to pull them down again.[3] The nephew of Dr John London, the warden of New College, Oxford, deposed that after reading the book of *Articles* he was convinced that the supremacy of the pope (he referred to him as the bishop of Rome) was without foundation, and he had written 'a little declamation'. For that he was suspected; his papers were searched, and he was sent to Dr London who kept him in his garden for several hours and read him a lecture: 'Edward, you be my nephew . . . I have now sent for you only to give you counsel, that if God has endued you with any grace you may return to grace again.' The

[1] Dan Thomas Tye, monk of St John Baptist's, Colchester, to Cromwell, [?] Jan. 1534 (*L. & P.*, vii, 140).
[2] cf. *L. & P.*, vii, 454 (8 April 1534).
[3] Complaint relating to books issued by authority, [?] Jan. 1534 (*L. & P.*, vii, 145).

covetousness, and will be urged on by the Lady [Anne Boleyn] and his Council' (Chapuys to Charles V, 3 Jan. 1534; *L. & P.*, vii, 14). A month later, when reporting the propaganda then under way, Chapuys made an interesting comment: '. . . it would not be of much importance if it was only intended to revile the pope and the authority of the Holy See, for the people know that these writings proceed from malice and revenge, and do not put much faith in them, but are rather irritated; but the worst is that preachers inculcate the same things under the shadow of charity and devotion. All will be ruined unless an antidote is applied before the poison is rooted' (Chapuys to Charles V, 4 Feb. 1534; *L. & P.*, vii, 152).

warden then charged his nephew with writing many detestable heresies against the pope, which made the young man so pensive that he knew not what to say for shame or for the sake of his poor mother. Later when the warden's nephew was with the bishop of Winchester, the bishop rejoiced 'that this our university was so clear from all these new fashions and heresies', and he was grieved to learn that it was infected by one of his own college.[1]

Friar Charnock, a doctor of divinity, was called to account for writing a little book, in answer to the book of *Articles*, in which he gathered together authorities from the Fathers touching the primacy of the pope;[2] and an information was laid against the vicar of Newark who had told some friars that they could speak against the 'books issued *cum privilegio*' and had allowed a 'Schottesh frere' to preach in his church a sermon condemning the books as heresies.[3] So frequent were the adverse comments on the king's anti-papal activities that it was, for example, found necessary for the king to issue to the earl of Sussex a warrant to cause to be arrested and committed to ward, without bail or mainprise, seditious persons who spread, taught, preached or otherwise set forth pernicious opinions and doctrines, to the exaltation of the power of the bishop of Rome.[4] At court the vice-chamberlain, Sir John Gage, a wise and experienced soldier and a member of the council, resigned his office in order to enter a Charterhouse, intending, with the consent of his wife, to become a Carthusian. And John Longland, the bishop of Lincoln, who, as the king's confessor, had been one of the chief promoters of the divorce, openly expressed his regret, saying several times that he would rather be the poorest man in the world than ever to have been the king's councillor and confessor.[5] Even the duke of Norfolk told the French ambassador that neither he nor his friends would consent to the king casting off his obedience to the pope.[6] Many members of parliament privately informed the Spanish ambassador that they would oppose the king if they received promises of imperial support,[7] but there was no one

---

[1] Confession of Edward, nephew of Dr John London, [?] Jan. 1534 (*L. & P.*, vii, 146).
[2] Declaration of Friar Thomas Charnock, D.D. (*L. & P.*, vii, 259).
[3] *L. & P.*, vii, 261.
[4] Henry VIII to the earl of Sussex, 17 April 1534 (*L. & P.*, vii, 494).
[5] Chapuys to Charles V, 3 Jan. 1534 (*L. & P.*, vii, 14).
[6] Chapuys to Charles V, 7 Mar. 1534 (*L. & P.*, vii, 296).
[7] Chapuys to Charles V, 29 Jan. 1534 (*L. & P.*, vii, 121).

in parliament able to stand forth as a leader uncompromisingly opposed to the king.

These instances of disapproval can be multiplied many times, but mere numbers do not make them politically significant. Individual expressions of disapproval could only acquire political significance by organization and leadership, and there was no sign of either. Critics there might be, but nowhere did there exist that organized public opinion able to bring the king to a halt. Without leaders there could be no organization, and the potential leaders had already surrendered to the king; both houses of parliament, the landed interest and the traders supported Henry, and the mere consideration of royal displeasure had been sufficient to bring about the ignominious submission of the clergy. Moreover, the king now had at his disposal the political genius of Thomas Cromwell. At the beginning of 1534 Henry was secure, and he knew it. He had now little to fear from his subjects, and it only remained for him to consolidate his gains. Parliament was to be the instrument of that consolidation, and in the coming session it erected a system of repression that was characterized by personal oaths to vex honest minds and savage penalties to chastise recalcitrant bodies.

3

While this formidable body of anti-papal propaganda was being devised and put into effect, the prorogued parliament re-assembled at Westminster on 15 January 1534.[1] The chief work of this session, a vigorous onslaught against papal authority, had already been determined upon. There was, too, a matter relating to two bishoprics; in Cromwell's 'remembrances' there occurred the phrase, 'A bill to be made for the taking of the bishoprics of Salisbury and Worcester into the king's hands.'[2] The see of Salisbury had been conferred on cardinal Lorenzo Campeggio in 1524, at the request of the king who had given Worcester to Jerome Ghinucci in the previous year. Campeggio had been Wolsey's colleague in the legatine court and Ghinucci, as ambassador, had long been one of Henry's principal agents in the divorce; Henry had found it convenient to defray their expenses by means of the revenues of two

---

[1] Parliament (*L. & P.*, vii, 54, 55, 56).
[2] Cromwell's Remembrances (*L. & P.*, vii, 49).

English sees, but now the case was altered. A bill was introduced to deprive the Italians of the sees which they had held for ten years, on the grounds, as recited, that their appointments violated the laws prohibiting the farming of benefices of aliens and the sending abroad of the produce of English sees, and that their continued residence in Rome had evil effects. Parliament raised no objection and the bill was passed.[1] But these were secondary matters; the main business was the destruction of papal authority.

In order to reduce the clergy in England to absolute dependence on the crown, and to root out the last vestige of papal interference, five new bills were put before parliament when it re-assembled. The first of them was designed to extend and strengthen the Annates Act of 1532. It had been carefully considered by the council some time before parliament met,[2] and in the form in which it passed it provided that no person should be presented to the pope for appointment as bishop of a vacant see, and that no person should petition the pope for bulls of appointment nor pay to the pope any fees on his appointment. Provision was then made to regulate the manner in which vacant sees were to be filled. Deans and chapters were to elect the king's nominee in accordance with the royal *congé d'élire*, and if, after twelve days, they failed to do so the king might at once appoint his nominee by letters patent. It was also provided that a bishop elect should swear a new oath to the king, and that his election should be notified to the archbishop who was required to confirm the election and consecrate the elect with the customary rites; archbishops were to be consecrated by virtue of a royal commission. All this was to be done without reference to the pope, and penalties were imposed for infraction of these provisions.[3]

The second of the bills, which was the shortest of them all, gave the force of law to the Submission of the Clergy of 1532; the promises of 1532 were now transformed into statutory requirements enforced by the

---

[1] 25 Hen. VIII, c. 27. This act was repealed by the Statute Law Revision Act, 1948.
[2] At the beginning of the year, the Spanish ambassador had learned that, 'in order to encroach upon the sovereignty over the church, it has been proposed to give the archbishop of Canterbury the seal of the Chancery, and pass bulls, dispensations, and other provisions under it' (Chapuys to Charles V, 3 Jan. 1534; *L. & P.*, vii, 14).
[3] This was the bill that became the statute 25 Hen. VIII, c. 20 (*Statutes of the Realm*, iii, 462-4; *G. & H.*, 201-9).

T

penalties of praemunire. The Submission of the Clergy was confirmed; it was provided that the clergy should not enact any ordinances, constitutions or canons without the king's consent, that convocation should assemble only by the king's writ, and that no canons should be put in execution that were contrary to the king's prerogative or to the law. The bill then proceeded to develop and extend the provisions of the earlier Statute in Restraint of Appeals of 1533. It was provided that no appeals should be made to Rome, and that all appeals in causes of matrimony, tithes, oblations and obventions should be according to the statute of 1533.[1] But a further step was now taken and it was provided that all appeals from the archbishop's courts were to lie to the chancery, to be determined by commissioners appointed by the king, and that appeals from courts of abbots and other heads of exempt houses, which hitherto lay direct to Rome, were to be heard in the court of chancery. And the penalties of praemunire were provided for those who appealed to Rome or executed any process from thence.[2] These two bills were introduced into the house of commons where they appear to have had a slow but uneventful progress; they did not pass the commons until nearly mid February.[3]

The third bill related to papal dispensations and the payment of Peter's Pence. The bill was provided with a long preamble which, in the manner of many Henrician preambles, manufactured history to suit the purpose in hand. It began with a prayer from the commons against the exactions of Rome by which, it was said, large sums of money had been taken out of the realm, by means of fees for dispensations and the like and by payments for Peter's Pence, to the impoverishment of the king's subjects. It was recited that this realm was free from the operation of any law not devised within it, and that the power to dispense with, alter or annul the human laws of this realm belonged to the king and parliament. By way of remedy, the bill prohibited the payment to Rome of Peter's Pence and other impositions; but, despite the recited complaint that such payments had impoverished the king's subjects, the payment of fees was not abolished, and it was provided that they should be

---

[1] 24 Hen. VIII, c. 12; see p. 221.
[2] This bill became the statute 25 Hen. VIII, c. 19 (*Statutes of the Realm*, iii, 460, 461; *G. & H.*, 195-200); part of s. 4 and the whole of s. 6 were repealed by the Ecclesiastical Jurisdiction Measure 1963, which came into force on 1 Mar. 1965.
[3] Chapuys to Charles V, 11 Feb. 1534 (*L. & P.*, vii, 171).

received by the archbishop of Canterbury who was required to hand over the greater part of them to the king. It was further provided that no person, whether he be king or subject, should sue for any dispensation or licence at Rome; all such were to be had within the realm, and the archbishop of Canterbury was empowered to grant dispensations to the king and to the king's subjects.[1]

The fourth bill was designed to remove a practical difficulty in the way of the new anti-papal policy. Hitherto it had been heresy, for which a man might lose his life, to attack the pope or to use language that held him up to ridicule or contempt. It was impossible to carry out the heavy programme of anti-papal propaganda upon which Henry had now embarked, so long as the law remained unchanged, and accordingly the bill provided that

no manner of speaking . . . against the said bishop of Rome or his pretended power . . . nor . . . against any laws called spiritual laws made by authority of the see of Rome by the policy of men, which be repugnant or contrariant to the laws and statutes of this realm or the king's prerogative royal shall be deemed . . . heresy.[2]

The last of the five bills gave statutory approval to Henry's matrimonial position and settled the succession to the crown.[3] It was entitled 'An Acte for the establishment of the Kynges succession', and began with a long recital of the evils resulting from uncertainty in the title to the crown and the succession thereto.[4] It was then enacted that the marriage of the king and the Lady Catherine, widow of the king's elder

---

[1] This bill became the statute 25 Hen. VIII, c. 21 (printed in *Statutes of the Realm*, iii, 464-71; *G. & H.*, 209-32). The above summary omits many of the statute's detailed provisions.
[2] This bill became the statute 25 Hen. VIII, c. 14 (*Statutes of the Realm*, iii, 454-5.
[3] The Act is 25 Hen. VIII, c. 22 (*Statutes of the Realm*, iii, 471-4; *G. & H.*, 232-43). It was introduced into the house of lords on 21 Mar. 1534 (*Lords Journals*, i, 77).
[4] This recital contains phrases, characteristic of much of Henry VIII's legislation, such as 'the imperiall Crowne of [this realme],' and 'the lawfull Kynges and Emperours of this Realme', as well as an assertion that 'the Bisshop of Rome and See apostolike, contrary to the greate and invyolable grauntes of jurisdiccions geven by God ymmediately to Emperours Kynges and Prynces in succession to their heires, hath presumed in tymes past to investe who shulde please theym to inherite in other mennes Kyngdomes and Domynyons, which thynge we your most humble subjectes both Spirituall and temporall doo mooste abhorre and deteste'. With this may be compared Henry's earlier statement to More that 'we receaued from that Sea [of Rome] our crowne Imperiall' (Roper, 68).

brother, Prince Arthur (whose marriage to Catherine was declared to have been consummated, as appeared by the sufficient proof in the process before archbishop Cranmer), should be deemed to be against the laws of almighty God and void, and that the separation thereof made by Cranmer should be valid and effectual; and it was provided that Catherine should thenceforth be called only dowager to prince Arthur. This was followed by a declaration that the marriage between the king and Anne Boleyn, described in the statute as the king's 'most dear and entirely beloved wife Queen Anne', was valid according to the just judgment of Cranmer, the grounds of which had been confirmed by the whole clergy of the realm in both convocations, as well as by Oxford and Cambridge and many foreign universities and the private writings of many learned men. The act went on to ratify the marriage with Anne Boleyn as being 'good and consonant to the laws of Almighty God without error or default'.[1]

The statute then defined the prohibited degrees of kindred and declared that marriages within such degrees were plainly prohibited by God's law from which no one had power to dispense. There followed an enactment that no person should marry within the prohibited degrees, and that if any person had previously contracted such a marriage and had been 'separate from the bonds' of such marriage by a minister of the church of England, the separation should be permanent. It was further provided that a person already so married but not 'separate from the bonds' of the marriage, should be separated by sentence of the ordinary only, without any appeal to Rome.

The statute then declared that the king's issue by Anne Boleyn should be his lawful children.[1] Such children were declared capable of inheriting the crown according to the laws of the realm, and the limitation of the crown was then set out; that is to say, the crown should pass first to the king's sons in order of seniority and to their heirs, and in default of such sons, to the princess Elizabeth and the king's other issue female.

It was then provided that, before 1 May 1534, in all the shires of the kingdom proclamation should be made of the tenor and contents of the act. And it was further provided that any persons who should maliciously do anything by writing, printing or 'by any exterior act or deed', to the peril of the king or to the prejudice of his marriage with Anne Boleyn

---

[1] These provisions deliberately ignored the papal sentence of 11 July 1533 (see p. 253), which declared the 'divorce' at Dunstable to be null and void, and that any issue the king might have by Anne Boleyn should be illegitimate.

or to their issue capable of inheriting the crown under the act, should be guilty of high treason; any person so convicted, and their aiders and abettors, should 'suffer pains of death' and forfeit all their property, except such property as they might hold to uses. It was further provided that persons committing such offences by word should be guilty of misprision of treason.[1]

A further enactment provided that no such offender should have any privilege of sanctuary. It was then provided that upon the death of the king his male issue under the age of eighteen years and his unmarried female issue under the age of sixteen years should be under the guardianship of their mother and of a council appointed by the king; and it was enacted that any person who 'by writing or exterior deed or act' opposed such provisions should be guilty of high treason.

Then followed the enactment requiring all subjects to take an oath. This enactment, which was expressed to be 'for the more sure establishment of the succession of your most royal majesty according to the tenor and form of this Act', provided that

as well all the nobles of your realm spiritual and temporal, as all others your subjects now living or being or that hereafter shall be at their full ages, by the commandment of your majesty or of your heirs at all times hereafter from time to time when it shall please your highness or your heirs to appoint, shall make a corporal oath[2] in the presence of your highness or your heirs, or before such other as your majesty or your heirs will depute for the same, that they shall truly firmly and constantly without fraud or guile observe fulfill maintain defend and keep to their cunning wit and uttermost of their powers the whole effects and contents of this present act.

It was then enacted that any person suing livery, restitution or *ouster le main*,[3] or any person doing fealty by reason of tenure of land should swear a like oath. It was then provided that

[1] In the absence of special statutory provision, mere words would not have been held to be a sufficient overt act within the Treason Act 1351; see, e.g. Parmiter, 'The Indictment of St Thomas More', *Downside Review*, lxxv (1957), 149, at p. 152.

[2] A corporal oath was so called because it was ratified by corporally touching (e.g. by kissing) some sacred object such as a relic or a New Testament.

[3] Livery was the act of giving a person possession of land; restitution was the putting in possession of lands or tenements a person who had been unlawfully disseised of them; *ouster le main* was the livery of lands, out of the hands of a guardian, upon an heir attaining the age of twenty-one (it was abolished by 12 Car. II, c. 24), and the term was also used to signify the livery of land out of the sovereign's hands upon a judgment given for a person suing out a *monstrans de droit*.

if any person or persons, being commanded by authority of this act to take the said oath afore limited, obstinately refuse that to do in contempt of this act, that then every such person so doing to be taken and accepted for offender in misprision of high treason; and that every such refusal shall be deemed and adjudged misprision of high treason, and the offender therein to suffer such pains and imprisonment losses and forfeitures and also lose privileges of sanctuaries in like manner and form as is above mentioned[1] for the misprisions of treason afore limited by this act.[2]

The act concluded with a proviso that the prohibition of marriages within the degrees of kindred set out should be interpreted 'of such marriages where marriages were solemnized and carnal knowledge was had.'

These bills, and others, were not passed without some difficulty. One of the bills related to Elizabeth Barton, known as the Nun of Kent; she had been uttering 'prophecies' concerning that dangerous topic the king's marriage and had attracted a certain following. Eventually a bill for the attainder of the Nun and of those said to be implicated with her, including Sir Thomas More and John Fisher, was introduced, but the lords were reluctant to pass the bill until the king agreed to the omission of More's name; and much of the session was taken up by the discussion of a bill, little to the liking of the landed gentry, that sought to restrain those who, in their desire to increase their large flocks of sheep, turned tillage into pasture, bought up farms and ejected the tenants, raised rents and pulled down buildings.[3] A bill concerning the dowry of Catherine of Aragon was much amended during the debates and was not agreed until nearly the end of the session.[4] The bill regulating the succession was amended by reducing some of the offences created thereby from treason to misprision of treason; the bill relating to dispensations was

---

[1] That is, the provision whereby persons doing anything by words only to the prejudice of the king's marriage with Anne Boleyn were guilty of misprision of treason: 'every suche offence shalbe taken and adjudged for mesprision of treason; And that every person and persons . . . soo doing and offendyng, and being herof [therof, *in the original act*] lawfully convycte by presentment verdicte processe or confession, shall suffer imprisonment of theire bodyes at the Kynges wyll, and shall losse aswell all theire goods catallis [*scil.* chattels] and debts as all suche interesses and estates of freholde or for yeres which any such offenders shall have of or in any Lands Rents or Heredytaments what soo ever at the tyme of convyccion and attayndre of such offence' (*Statutes of the Realm*, iii, 474).
[2] *Statutes of the Realm*, iii, 474.
[3] See 25 Hen. VIII, c. 13.
[4] See 25 Hen. VIII, c. 28.

several times amended and the bill concerning heresy did not pass in the form proposed by the government.[1] The difficulties encountered with this legislation were great enough to cause the king to hold a long discussion with parliament; on 5 March 'the whole parliament were with the king at York Place for three hours, and afterwards all the lords went into the council house at Westminster, and sat there till ten at night'.[2] Ultimately all the legislation to which parliament had been induced to agree received the royal assent on the Monday in Holy Week, 30 March 1534, and since these acts were passed in a session which began on 15 January, they were effective as law from that date.[3] On the same day, 30 March, parliament was prorogued to 3 November.[4]

Meanwhile the bishop of Paris, du Bellay, who had arrived in London on 17 December 1533, had been pursuing his hopeless mission to restrain Henry.[5] The utmost that he had been able to obtain from the king was a statement that if the pope would grant before Easter what Henry demanded, without further process, he would not throw off his obedience to the holy see, but if he did not obtain the sentence he required within that time he would proclaim himself openly.[6] If this statement really represented Henry's mind, then time was short. Basing his hopes of success upon this slender foundation, du Bellay at once set out for

[1] cf. *Lords Journals*, i, 58-83; and see also Chapuys to Charles V, 26 Feb. 1534 (*L. & P.*, vii, 232); Chapuys to Charles V, 7 Mar. 1534 (*L. & P.*, vii, 296); John Rokewood to lord Lisle, 8 Mar. 1534 (*L. & P.*, vii, 304); Chapuys to Charles V, 25 Mar. 1534 (*L. & P.*, vii, 373); Chapuys to Charles V, 30 Mar. 1534 (*L. & P.*, vii, 393).
[2] John Rokewood to lord Lisle, 8 Mar. 1534 (*L. & P.*, vii, 304). Rokewood was the bailly of Marke, near Calais, but was then in England and wrote 'from the court'. Lord Lisle was deputy of Calais and vice-admiral of England.
[3] Before 1793 acts of parliament, unless the contrary were expressed therein, came into force as from the first day of the session in which they were passed because, by a legal fiction, a session of parliament, like an assize, was deemed to constitute a single day (see, e.g. *Panter* v. *Attorney-General* (1772), 6 Bro. Parl. Cas. 486; *R.* v. *Smith, R.* v. *Weston*, [1910] 1 K.B. 17, at p. 24). This led to a number of difficulties and to the extraordinary result that a man could be convicted of a crime which had not been created at the time it was committed. The Acts of Parliament (Commencement) Act 1793 (33 Geo. III, c. 13), provided that a statute should come into force on the day that it received the royal assent unless the statute otherwise provided.
[4] *L. & P.*, vii, 391. For the text of the proclamation (dated 9 June 1535) enforcing the statutes made for the abolition of papal authority in England, see *T.R.P.*, i, 229.
[5] See p. 266.
[6] Castillon to Francis I, 26 Mar. 1534 (*L. & P.*, vii, App., 13).

Rome, and arrived there on 2 February 1534 in company with the bishop of Mâcon, Charles de Hémard. As soon as he arrived he became aware of the great efforts then being made on behalf of Catherine to obtain from the pope a sentence in her favour, and he felt keenly the urgency of his mission. He at once declared to the pope the object of his presence in Rome, and his holiness, who was much perplexed, asked him to represent to the consistory the danger of schism in England. The cardinals were interested but they did not give du Bellay much cause for hope.[1]

Time was pressing and at the beginning of February du Bellay wrote to the French ambassador in England urging him to persuade Henry to delay any parliamentary action for a while.[2] He then proposed to the pope that the cause should be heard at Cambrai, and on the strength of some vague assurances on the point, he wrote again to the French ambassador in England suggesting that Henry be told that the pope was willing to send a cardinal to Cambrai, with assessors, to take cognizance of the matter up to, but short of, the definitive sentence.[3] The ambassador duly told Henry of this suggestion but found him unresponsive; matters had gone too far for Henry to be deflected from his course by such a proposal and the council, which included Cromwell, were unenthusiastic.[4]

Castillon in London, and du Bellay and de Hémard in Rome, continued their urgent activities, but it was of little use.[5] Henry was disinclined to listen, and Clement was angered by the king's defiance of the papacy and by the anti-papal propaganda in England.[6] On his return from Marseilles the pope had remarked to the imperial ambassador at Rome, the count of Cifuentes, that he had not troubled himself about the case since his arrival in Rome, but was very willing to do justice to the queen.[7] Towards the end of February the auditor, Simonetta,

---

[1] Bishops of Paris and Mâcon to Francis I, 18 Feb. 1534 (*L. & P.*, vii, App. 6).
[2] du Bellay to Castillon, 8 Feb. 1534 (*L. & P.*, vii, App. 7).
[3] du Bellay to Castillon, 22 Feb. 1534 (*L. & P.*, vii, App. 8). cf. bishops of Paris and Mâcon to Francis I, 24 Feb. 1534 (*L. & P.*, vii, App. 9).
[4] Castillon to Francis I, 6 Mar. 1534 (*L. & P.*, vii, App. 11).
[5] cf. Bishops of Paris and Mâcon to Francis I, 16 Mar. 1534 (*L. & P.*, vii, App. 12); Castillon to Francis I, 16 Mar. 1534 (*L. & P.*, vii, App. 13).
[6] Carnesecchi to Vergerio, 14 Feb. 1534 (printed in W. Friedensburg, *Nuntiaturberichte aus Deutschland, 1533-59*, i, 176, at pp. 180, 181; cf. Ehses, 229). Pietro Carnesecchi was secretary to Clement VII; Pietro Paulo Vergerio was the nuncio in Germany.
[7] 'Lo que escrive el conde de Cifuentes a xiij Diciembre', 13 Dec. 1533 (*L. & P.*, vi, 1520).

after much hard work, was ready to proceed with the marriage suit,[1] and the pope sought the emperor's assistance in enforcing the sentence to be pronounced, as he was of opinion that it would be detrimental to the holy see if a sentence were passed that could not be carried out.[2] The cause came before the consistory once more on 27 February, at the instance of Simonetta, and it was again discussed on 4 March. Three weeks later, on 23 March, while du Bellay was still writing hopeful letters to Castillon and Francis I, the pope, in a secret consistory and with the unanimous agreement of all the cardinals present, pronounced the final sentence in the marriage cause.[3] The sentence declared Henry's marriage with Catherine to be valid and canonical and imposed upon Henry perpetual silence as regards the question of the invalidity of the marriage; Henry was also ordered to pay the costs of the suit.[4]

On the day after the sentence had been pronounced, Dr Ortiz, the canonist who was one of the imperial agents at Rome, wrote to the emperor a letter in which he said,

Although both the Rota and the Consistory had determined last year [i.e. in July 1533] that the marriage was not unlawful in itself by divine or natural law, it was necessary to examine the same point again this year, of which some cardinals complained, saying that it was an insult to the previous decision of

---

[1] Ortiz to Charles V, 25 Feb. 1534 (*L. & P.*, vii, 230).

[2] Carnesecchi to Vergerio, 14 Feb. 1534, *ut supra*.

[3] Acta consistorialia (Ehses, 214, 215); diary of Blasius de Cesena (Ehses, 228); cf. *L. & P.*, vii, 362-4. The French ambassadors, who were annoyed at the turn of events, described the consistory of 23 Mar. as follows: 'In the other assemblies at 11 o'clock everyone will break and go to dinner. But then the obstination leaded them so to be nor hungry nor thirsty and to go not furth out till 5 of the clock' (The French ambassadors at Rome to Francis I, 1 April 1534; *L. & P.*, vii, 421).

[4] For the text of the papal sentence (*lata sententia*), see Ehses, 215. On 14 April Carne, from Bologna, wrote to the pope a letter of protest against the decision (Pocock, ii, 681; *L. & P.*, vii, 481). On 20 April 'executorial decrees' (*decretae executoriales*) were issued on behalf of Catherine (Acta consistorialia; Ehses, 216). Clement's irresolution persisted to the end. In February du Bellay wrote: 'I assure you the pope is as anxious to find the king's marriage good as he himself is; . . . I am no very great papist, but I declare I am sorry to see him in such pain how to express himself in favour of the king of England in full Consistory' (du Bellay to Castillon, Rome, 22 Feb. 1534; *L. & P.*, vii, App. 8 (p. 631)). In March the imperial ambassador wrote: 'The case is now in such a condition that he [i.e. the pope] cannot refuse to give a sentence, but I fear he will not do justice, for the usual reasons' (count of Cifuentes to Charles V, Rome, 10 Mar. 1534; *L. & P.*, vii, 311).

the Consistory, and therefore would not discuss it without referring to the previous deliberation. Campeggio said that if the case turned on the proofs of virginity contained in the *remissorias*, he would have great doubts of the justice of the queen's case; but as he considered it settled that the marriage was only unlawful by positive law, he had always been certain that she was in the right. The difficulties have been so great that the count of Cifuentes has had no hope of success, though he, as well as the advocate and proctor, has been very diligent. Formerly the sentence was deferred on the pretext that the king of England might return to obedience, and latterly they said there was no need of a sentence, as it could do no good. Now that it is given the pope says he fears he may have sinned, as the queen [Catherine] may be murdered in consequence of the sentence.[1]

Henry learned of the papal sentence a day or two after parliament had been prorogued.[2] His answer was the intensification of the anti-papal propaganda. The printing press, which had not been altogether success-ful,[3] was now to be powerfully reinforced by the pulpit, which was the

[1] Ortiz to Charles V, 24 Mar. 1534 (*L. & P.*, vii, 370). The quotation is from the calendar. In notes of a meeting of the council at Toledo on 12 April 1534, over which Charles V presided, the following occurs: 'Now that the sentence in favour of the Queen has been given, it must be considered what is to be done, as the Pope will persist in being assured of his majesty's intentions, and even if delay be not made here, the Queen will be ready to impute it to us beforehand. If the prosecution of the sentence is delayed the King [Henry VIII] will only become more insolent, and his subjects from despair will make up their minds to what has been done and his allies will become shameless. Those, also, who have abandoned the faith, with whom the King is treating for an alliance, will become hardened. Regard must be had to what the Emperor has always said, viz. that he will not fail in what is necessary for the execution of the sentence' (*L. & P.*, vii, 469). As matters turned out, however, nothing was done.
[2] Chapuys to Charles V, 4 April 1534 (*L. & P.*, vii, 434); Chapuys to Charles V, 12 April 1534 (*L. & P.*, vii, 469).
[3] cf. the proposal made in an undated letter, written some time in 1534, to Cromwell by John Rastell, More's versatile and eccentric brother-in-law, who was both barrister and printer, and was then near bankruptcy: 'Touching my book which is delivered to me to be reformed, give me a little leisure, as I intend to add more authorities to improve it. . . . I have spent four or five years in compiling books in furtherance of the King's causes and opposing the Pope, by which I have lost more than 100*l.* worth of my business and the profits I got by the law in pleading at Westminster, to the amount of 40 marks; . . . I have devised certain prayers in English to be put in primers of divers sorts at small price. Some are printed already in a little primer which I sent to the Court, intended to bring people from the haughty doctrine of the Pope. People are loth to buy any such books, and if they be given them they will scantly read them; but when the matter in English is put in primers, which they bring with them to Church, they shall, in a manner, be compelled to read them. If the king therefore

sole means of instruction for many of the middle and lower orders. It was necessary, not only to ensure an adequate number of sermons in favour of the king and hostile to the pope, but also to control and, if possible, stop those preachers who had been inveighing against the king's matrimonial proceedings or supporting the papal authority.[1] Accordingly, because certain persons 'under the pretence of preaching the word of God, minister to their audience matter of contention and debate', Cranmer, together with the bishops of London, Winchester and Lincoln, issued an inhibition forbidding all persons to preach by virtue of letters already granted and requiring them to obtain new letters; and curates who were authorized by law to preach in their parishes were required first to obtain a licence from Cranmer.[2] Besides ensuring that sermons should be preached, the council also prescribed the nature of those sermons, and there was issued 'An Order for preaching and bidding of the bedes in all sermons to be made within this realm'.[3] The preacher was to begin with the king's name and refer to him as 'our sovereign lord king Henry VIII, being immediately next under God the only and supreme head of this catholic church of England'. Every preacher was to preach once in the presence of his greatest audience against the power of the bishop of Rome; and for a year no sermon was to be preached either for or against the doctrine of purgatory, the honouring of saints, the marriage of priests, justification by faith, pilgrimages, miracles, and the like. Preachers were to declare, to the best of their ability, the justice of the king's second marriage, and to

[1] cf. one of Cromwell's Remembrances, written in April (*L. & P.*, vii, 420): 'To appoint the most assured and substantial gentlemen in every shire to be sworn of the King's Council, with orders to apprehend all who speak or preach in favor of the Pope's authority. To have substantial persons in every good town to discover all who speak or preach thus. To have the act of succession openly proclaimed, that the people may not make themselves ignorant thereof; whoever shall offend to be ordered according to the said statute.'

[2] Cranmer to —, April 1534 (*L. & P.*, vii, 463); the document is headed, 'The copy of an inhibition sent by my lord of Canterbury unto other for seditious preaching begun in Easter week concerning the King's grace's marriage in anno regni 25 Hen. VIII'.

[3] *L. & P.*, vii, 464; for the full text, see Pocock-Burnet, vi, 86-9.

would print 4,000 or 5,000, and give them away, it will bring the people to right belief and do as much good as preaching' (John Rastell to Cromwell, 1534; *L. & P.*, vii, 1073). The quotation is from the calendar; the full text is printed in Ellis, *Original Letters*, 3rd ser., ii, 309-12. The letter is interesting as giving a printer's opinion of the effect of the printed propaganda.

point out the injustice of the pope's actions from the beginning of the king's cause; in this connection they were to draw particular attention to the issue by the pope of a sentence of excommunication after the king's appeal, and to the pope's dealings with the French king during the interview at Marseilles.

So far as law and propaganda could do it, Henry's royal supremacy was now well established and the withdrawal of England from its traditional obedience to the holy see was almost complete. It only remained for parliament to add the finishing touches when it re-assembled in November; as Chapuys was informed, parliament was to re-assemble 'to complete the ruin of the churches and churchmen'.[1]

[1] Chapuys to Charles V, 4 April 1534 (*L. & P.*, vii, 434).

XVII

Conclusion

I

As soon as the Act of Succession had received the royal assent on 30 March, a proclamation was published, pursuant to the act, concerning Henry's matrimonial proceedings. It proclaimed the king's divorce from Catherine and his marriage to Anne Boleyn which, it was said, had taken place with the common assent of parliament and convocation; and it declared that any person doing anything in derogation of those proceedings should incur the penalties of the statutes of provisors and praemunire. The proclamation then announced that Catherine was not entitled to the name and dignity of queen of England but should be addressed as Princess Dowager, and it provided that any person obeying her by virtue of any warrant directed to them by the name of queen should incur the penalties already mentioned.[1] On the same day, before the members of parliament had dispersed to their homes, the king signed letters patent appointing commissioners to administer to them the oath required by the act. The commissioners so appointed were Thomas Cranmer, Thomas Audley, the duke of Norfolk and the duke of Suffolk, and they administered the oath set out in the letters patent to members of both houses of parliament.[2] In the ensuing weeks commissioners were also appointed to administer the oath throughout the kingdom.[3]

[1] For the text of the proclamation, see Pocock, ii, 502-4 (*L. & P.*, vii, 390).

[2] *Journals of the House of Lords*, i, 82. See the form of words appointing the commissioners, quoted in note 3, p. 288. See also the first two documents cited in the following note. Since John Fisher did not attend this session, the oath was not administered to him on this occasion.

[3] Unfortunately these commissions are no longer in existence. There are, however, preserved in the British Museum copies, of a later date, of three documents concerned with the administration of the oath. They are: B.M., Add. MS. 4,622, f. 298, gives a list of the lords present in parliament on 30 Mar. 1534, together with a note of the prorogation, and of the appointment of the chancellor, the archbishop of Canterbury and the dukes of Norfolk and Suffolk as commissioners to take the oaths of the lords spiritual and temporal (cf. *L. & P.*, vii, 391); B.M., Add. MS. 4,622, f. 297, is a later copy of the commission to Cranmer,

Although the members of both houses of parliament had taken the oath, the royal policy required that it should be taken without delay by the principal men of the kingdom who did not sit in parliament; without their sworn approval it was impossible to assert that not a single person of any consequence had failed to ratify the king's proceedings with his oath. Accordingly, within a fortnight of the act of succession becoming law, Sir Thomas More received a summons to attend commissioners at Lambeth in order to swear the oath. It is our misfortune that we do not possess the relevant commission nor the text of the oath that More was required to take, but there are good reasons for thinking that the text of that oath did not differ substantially from the text of the oath, taken by the members of parliament, which is recorded in the journals of the house of lords.[1] The text of that oath is as follows:[2]

Ye shall swear to bear your faith, truth and obedience alonely to the king's majesty, and to the heirs of his body, according to the limitation and rehearsal within this Statute of Succession above specified,[3] and not to any other

[1] For these reasons, see Parmiter, 'Saint Thomas More and the Oath', *Downside Review*, lxxviii, 1-13. It is stated in that article (p. 2) that 'there no longer exists any of the documents employed in the administration of the oath'; although this is true, reference should be made to the documents mentioned in note 3, p. 287. The text of the oath ni B.M., Add. MS. 4,622, f. 297, agrees exactly with the text of the oath in the *Journals of the House of Lords*. The text in B.M., Harl.MS. 7,571, f. 25 (the oath is upside down on the verso), agrees substantially with the text in the *Journals of the House of Lords;* there are, however, some variations which do not alter the effect of the oath.

[2] *Journals of the House of Lords*, i, 82.

[3] That is, specified in the letters patent appointing the commissioners, to which the form of oath was annexed: '. . . damus vobis Tribus, et Duobus Vestrum, plenam Potestatem et Auctoritatem capiend. et recipiend. Sacramentum et Fidelitatem omnium et singulorum Ducium, Comitum, Baronum, Episcoporum, Abbatum, Priorum, Militum, ac omnium et singulorum aliorum

Audley and the dukes of Norfolk and Suffolk, dated 30 Mar. 1534, to take the oaths of the king's subjects, to which the text of the oath is appended (cf. *L. & P.*, vii, 392); B.M., Harl. MS. 7,571, f. 25, is a later copy of a commission, dated 20 April 1534, to lord de la Warr, Sir William Fitzwilliam and others, to take the oaths of persons in Sussex, to which the text of the oath is appended (cf. *L. & P.*, vii, 518). In the Public Record Office there is a small vellum roll of three membranes joined together, which gives the names of those who took (or should have taken) the oath, in Waldingfield Parva, before Sir William Waldegrave, John Spryng and Robert Crane, commissioners in Suffolk. There are 87 names, of which 11 signed their names, one signed his initials, and 35 made their marks; against the remainder of the names there is nothing at all. The roll does not contain a copy of the oath (see P.R.O., Miscellanea of the Exchequer, E.163/10/23; cf. *L. & P.*, vii, 689).

within this realm, nor foreign authority, prince or potentate; and in case any oath be made, or hath been made, by you, to any other person or persons, that then you to repute the same as vain and annihilate; and that, to your cunning, wit, and uttermost of your power, without guile, fraud, or other undue means, ye shall observe, keep, maintain, and defend, this act above specified, and all the whole contents and effects thereof, and all other acts and statutes made since the beginning of this present parliament, in confirmation or for due execution of the same, or of anything therein contained; and thus ye shall do against all manner of persons, of what estate, dignity, degree, or condition soever they be, and in no wise do or attempt, nor to your power suffer to be done or attempted, directly or indirectly, any thing or things, privily or apertly, to the let, hindrance, damage, or derogation thereof, or of any part of the same, by any manner of means, for any manner of pretence or cause. So help you God and all saints.

It will be seen that this oath required those who swore it to 'observe, keep, maintain and defend [the act of succession] and all the whole contents and effects thereof'. Now the act[1] contained provisions to which no Catholic could assent without repudiating his faith. Examples are furnished by the provisions declaring Henry's marriage with Catherine to be against the law of God and invalid, those declaring the marriage with Anne Boleyn to be valid and in accordance with the law of God, and those declaring that no one, not even the pope, had power to dispense from the prohibition of marriage within certain degrees of kindred. Such points of conscience would have been apparent only to those who studied the oath in conjunction with the act of parliament; but the oath also required that those taking it should bear obedience only to the king of England and not to 'any foreign authority, prince or potentate'; the effect of such an oath was the denial of the papal authority and of a Catholic's spiritual allegiance to the pope. These are matters which should have been sufficient to deter any well instructed Catholic from taking the oath; the penalties for refusal, however, were sufficiently savage to ensure that it would be sworn by all but a few.

When the oath is compared with the act that authorized it, further difficulties become apparent; for the oath contained matter for which no

---

[1] See pp. 277, 280.

Legiorum et Subditorum Nostrorum, quorumcunque cujuscunque Gradus seu Conditionis fuerunt, juxta vim, formam et effectum, cujusdam Statuti, in presenti Parliamento Nostro, Securitatem, Statum et Successionem Nostram concernentem editi et provisi, ac juxta tenorem Sacramenti presentibus annexi . . .'

provision was made in the act. The oath begins with what is, in effect, an oath of allegiance to the king and his heirs as limited by the act, and although the act contains no specific provision requiring the taking of an oath of allegiance, it is probable that this part of the oath could be justified. The oath, however proceeds with the words 'and not to any other within this realm, nor foreign authority, prince or potentate'. For these words, which are wide enough to include the pope, no authority can be found in the statute and it was plainly illegal to require any man to take the oath while it contained such words. Moreover, the oath required any person taking it to repudiate any oath (the nature of which was not specified) made to any person other than the king.[1] The act did not require any such thing; and, having regard to their very wide ambit, the relevant words cannot even be justified on the ground that they were necessarily ancillary to the act. Finally, whereas the act required an oath that the king's subjects should 'observe, fulfill, maintain, defend and keep . . . the whole effects and contents of this present act',[2] the oath required the subject to 'observe, keep, maintain and defend this act above specified, and all the whole contents and effects thereof, *and all other acts and statutes made since the beginning of the present parliament, in confirmation of or for due execution of the same*'. It will readily be seen that there is no warrant for the words of the oath in italics which include, not only the act of succession, but any other act that might be passed confirming it or providing for its execution.[3] In other words, the oath as tendered was *ultra vires* the statute which authorized it, a point upon which More was quick to seize.

More appeared before the commissioners[4] at Lambeth on Monday, 13 April 1534, having received on the previous day, Low Sunday, a

---

[1] It seems clear that this part of the oath was chiefly directed at the oaths of obedience to the pope sworn by bishops at their consecration.

[2] See p. 279. It is desired to emphasize the words, 'of this present act'.

[3] The qualification at the end of the words in italics should be noted; the words in italics are not wide enough to include *all* acts passed since the beginning of the parliament, but only such acts as were 'in confirmation of or for due execution of' the act of succession. The phrase is not, therefore, wide enough to include such statutes as the Dispensations Act of 1534 (25 Hen. VIII, c. 21, which contained an unqualified statement that the king was the supreme head of the church in England), as has sometimes been supposed (e.g. Hughes, *Reformation in England*, i, 270, end of n. 1).

[4] According to Roper and Harpsfield, the commissioners on this occasion were Thomas Cranmer, Thomas Audley, and Thomas Cromwell (see Roper, 72;

summons to do so.[1] Several others, all clerics and including John Fisher, had also been summoned, but More, the only layman, was the first to be called before the commissioners. More and Fisher refused to swear the oath; it was again tendered to them a few days later, and when they again refused to swear they were committed to the Tower. Although More had refused to swear solely on conscientious grounds, he was well aware of the legal objection that could be taken to the oath in the form in which it was tendered to him. In a conversation with his daughter, Margaret, after he had been imprisoned in the Tower, More made a remark which was recorded by Margaret's husband, William Roper: 'I may tell thee, Meg, they that have committed me hither, for refusing of this oath not agreeable with the statute, are not by their own law able to justify my imprisonment.'[2] In saying this, More plainly meant that the oath contained matters to which the statute did not require him to swear, and he was, therefore, asserting that the oath was *ultra vires* the statute.[3] But, according to his own account, he did not raise this legal objection with the commissioners.[4]

[1] See Stapleton, 160. Stapleton recorded that the summons was served on More the previous day while he was at the house of John Clements after hearing the sermon at Paul's Cross in company with his son-in-law, William Roper. Stapleton mistakenly stated the day to be Palm Sunday instead of Low Sunday, writing *in palmis* instead of *in albis* (see Bridgett, 350 n.), a mistake that was repeated by 'Ro. Ba.' (see *The Lyfe of Syr Thomas More, by Ro. Ba.*, E.E.T.S. 1950, p. 189).
[2] Roper, 78. More added: 'And surely, daughter, it is greate pitye that any Christian prince should by a flexible Councell readyto followe his affections, and by a weake Cleargie lackinge grace constantly to stand to their learninge, with Flatterye be so shamefully abused.'
[3] See p. 290. See Roper, 77, 78: 'Whereas the oath confirminge the supremacye and matrimonie was by the first statute in fewe wordes comprised, the Lord Chauncelor and Master Secretary did of their owne heads adde more words vnto it, to make it appeare vnto the kinges eares more pleasaunt and plausible. And that oath, so amplified, caused they to be ministred to Sir Thomas Moore, and to all other throughout the realme.' See, also, the statement in the surviving fragments of the biography of More written by his nephew, William Rastell, who was a lawyer (Harpsfield, 228): '[Fisher, More and Dr Wilson] were wrongefully ymprisoned, bycause þe othe contaigned more thinges then were warranted by þe acte of succession'.
[4] For More's account of his appearance before the commissioners, see More to Margaret Roper, c. 17 April 1534 (Rogers, 501-7). The letter was written from the Tower of London.

Harpsfield, 166). But More, in a letter dated c. 17 April 1534, to his daughter, Margaret (Rogers, 506), expressly stated that the abbot of Westminster was also present and had endeavoured to persuade him to take the oath.

Meanwhile, commissioners were active throughout the country administering to Henry's subjects the oath that More and Fisher had refused. This work was done expeditiously and met with almost no resistance; and the surviving documents suggest that speed was important. Some idea of the manner in which the oath was administered may be gathered from the account which the bishop of Winchester, Stephen Gardiner, gave of his own activities as a commissioner. He was certainly not dilatory. He received his commission on Wednesday, 29 April, and on the following Monday, 4 May, he and some of his fellow commissioners assembled in the great hall of Winchester castle where there appeared before them

my lord Audley, a good number of gentlemen, all abbots, priors, wardens of friars and the governor of the friar observants at Hampton now in the absence of the warden with all the curates of all the other churches and chapels within the shire [i.e., Hampshire] the Isle of Wight only except, which all did take the said oath very obediently, as this bearer can signify unto you. And at the same time the abbots and priors and curates did according as I had ordered, viz. all of them, present unto us bills of all the names of the religious and servants in their houses and of the parishioners in their parishes menkind only which are above the age of fourteen.

Gardiner went on to say that if Cromwell wished for greater speed in the matter it would be well to put others in the commission, because, as he pointed out, taking the oaths was a lengthy process, especially if those of women were to be included.[1]

Throughout the rest of the country the work of taking oaths went equally smoothly. In London lord Lisle's agent reported to his master that 'this day most part of the city was sworn to the king and his legitimate issue by the queen's grace now had and hereafter to come'.[2] Sir George Lawson, the treasurer of Berwick, informed Cromwell that all went well in Yorkshire: 'the inhabitants of this county are most willing to take the oath according to the act of parliament and the king's commission; but the city of York, the wapentake of Ainsty, the town of Hull, and no commissioners are yet directed to them.'[3] Lawson was corroborated by the under-sheriff of Yorkshire who informed Cromwell that 'the king's subjects of Yorkshire have taken their oaths loyally under this

---

[1] Gardiner to Cromwell, 5 May 1534 (Pocock, ii, 536; *L. & P.*, vii, 610). There were twelve commissioners in this commission.
[2] John Husee to lord Lisle, 20 April 1534 (*L. & P.*, vii, 522).
[3] Lawson to Cromwell, 5 June 1534 (*L. & P.*, vii, App. 23).

commission'.[1] In Norfolk it was the same: 'I certify you of the diligence of the inhabitants of this city of Norwich concerning their oath to the king. Never were people more willing or diligent. . . . Such diligence as of those that were 16 and under never did man see. They would be sworn of free force, and I made 100 or 200 to kiss the book.'[2] Even in the smallest places the same readiness to swear was found. In the little village of Waldingfield Parva, in Suffolk, two priests and eighty-five others took the oath, of whom eleven signed their names, one his initials and thirty-five made their marks; the remainder did not sign at all.[3] Those unable to sign their names caused the commissioners some difficulty, and Cranmer wrote to the lord chancellor to seek advice. Cranmer said that he did not know how to order those who could not subscribe in writing. Hitherto, he said, he had caused one of his secretaries to subscribe for such persons, and had 'made them write their sheep mark, or some other mark as they can scribble', and he asked whether he should take their seals instead.[4]

Although the clergy, both secular and regular, were as docile as the laity,[5] there were some notable exceptions. The monks of the London

[1] William Maunsell to Cromwell, 5 June 1534 (*L. & P.*, vii, App. 24). cf. Sir William Gascoyne to Cromwell, 6 June 1534 (*L. & P.*, vii, App. 26): 'According to the commission, the people have taken their oaths like true subjects'.
[2] Reynold Lytylprow to Cromwell, 10 June 1534 (*L. & P.*, vii, App. 29).
[3] Oath to the Succession, 18 May 1534 (*L. & P.*, vii, 689); cf. p. 287, note 3. At the end of April, Latymer expressed some dissatisfaction at the progress made, saying that better results would be achieved 'if commissioners were always as mindful to advance the king's business as their own profit' (H. Latymer to Cromwell [end of April] 1534; *L. & P.*, vii, 578).
[4] Cranmer to the lord chancellor, n.d. [? May 1534] (*L. & P.*, vii, 702).
[5] cf. *L. & P.*, vii, 665, 865, 921, 1024, 1025, 1121, 1216, 1347, 1594 (acknowledgments of the royal supremacy). See also the oath taken by Thomas Goodrich on 2 April 1534, on becoming bishop of Ely, which acknowledged the king as supreme head of the church; the paper is headed 'This is the oath that every person elected or presented to any archbishopric or bishopric within this realm, or within any other the king's dominions, shall swear to the king's majesty' (*L. & P.*, vii, 427). In April Dr George Brown, prior of the Austin Friars in London and prior provincial of his order, and Dr John Hilsey, prior of the Black Friars at Bristol and also prior provincial of his order, were appointed by the king to visit all the houses of friars in the kingdom to reform what needed reformation and to administer the oath to the inmates. In June Hilsey reported to Cromwell: 'Although I have laboured in my progress, I have not found any religious persons who have utterly refused the oath of obedience. Some have sworn to it with an evil will and slenderly taken the oath, of whom I will show you more at my coming' (Friar John Hilsey to Cromwell, 21 June 1534; *L. & P.*, vii, 869).

Charterhouse could be induced to swear only by trickery and a show of force,[1] and the Bridgettines of Syon called Robert Rygote a wretch and a heretic when he prayed for the king as supreme head of the church.[2] In June it was found necessary to suppress all the houses of the Observant Franciscans who had caused so much trouble by their continued and determined opposition to the divorce and the king's marriage with Anne Boleyn. Nearly all the friars were arrested and imprisoned, some in the Tower and other prisons and the remainder in friaries of other orders; they were subjected to brutal treatment, and out of some one hundred and forty friars, thirty-one soon died from torture, hardship and starvation.[3]

2

Parliament, which had been prorogued on 30 March, re-assembled on Tuesday 3 November, 1534.[4] Its principal task during the coming short session of six weeks was the completion of the religious revolution which it had begun in the spring. Parliament had then given the king authority to appoint bishops without reference to the pope, and power to control all ecclesiastical legislation, to grant dispensations and to receive ecclesiastical fees, and had abolished the ecclesiastical jurisdiction in England of the pope who was, to Henry's satisfaction, reduced to the status of bishop of an Italian diocese. The spring legislation had given Henry almost complete power over the church, and all that remained for parliament to do was to provide the king with a legal right to the headship of the church and to enact more stringent penalties against those who might seek to attack the new religious organization.

Within a fortnight of the re-assembly of parliament, both houses had passed a bill to declare the king supreme head of the church, and the act which this bill became is usually known as the Act of Supremacy of 1534. The act was a very short one and was provided with a preamble

[1] cf. Knowles, *Religious Orders in England*, iii, 229, 230.
[2] When Rygote, a priest of Syon, sought Henry's help to leave that house, he assured the king that 'I have prayed for your majesty as supreme head of the Church of England, next under Christ, and for so doing have been called wretch and heretic' (Robert Rygote to Henry VIII [? Aug. 1534]; *L. & P.*, vii, 1092).
[3] cf. Knowles, op. cit. iii, 206-11.
[4] See p. 281; cf. *L. & P.*, vii, 1377.

designed to show that the statute did not bring about any change but merely recognized the restoration of the traditional state of affairs. After reciting that

albeit the king's majesty justly and rightfully is and oweth [i.e. ought] to be the supreme head of the Church of England, and so is recognized by the clergy of this realm in their convocations; yet nevertheless for corroboration and confirmation thereof, and for increase of virtue in Christ's religion within this realm of England,

it was enacted that

the king our sovereign lord his heirs and successors kings of this realm shall be taken accepted and reputed the only supreme head in earth of the Church of England called Anglicana Ecclesia, and shall have and enjoy annexed and united to the imperial crown of this realm as well the title and style thereof.

The act then conferred on the king power to make ecclesiastical visitations and to reform ecclesiastical abuses.[1]

Having thus disposed of the king's ecclesiastical pre-eminence, parliament then turned its attention to the oath which commissioners had been administering throughout the country during the summer and autumn. It will be recalled that More had formed the opinion that the oath was *ultra vires* the statute and illegal,[2] since it contained matter for which the act provided no authority; according to William Roper the amplification of the oath was the work of Audley and Cromwell.[3] However that may be, it seems clear that doubts were felt as to the legality of the oath in the form in which it was being administered, and the council took steps to put matters right. A bill was introduced which was passed as 'An Act ratifying the oath that every of the King's subjects hath taken and shall hereafter be bound to take for due observation of the Act made for the surety of the succession of the King's Highness in the Crown of the Realm.'[4] This second act recited the oath of obedience to the king and his heirs by Anne Boleyn required by the former act and it then recited

[1] 26 Hen. VIII, c. 1 (printed in *Statutes of the Realm*, iii, 492; G. & H., 243, 244). cf. Chapuys to Charles V, 17 Nov. 1534 (*L. & P.*, vii, 1437). At the same time drafts were prepared of a new coronation oath, in which the king was to swear to maintain the rights of the church only in so far as they were not prejudicial to his jurisdiction, and of a form of oath of supremacy to be taken by every bishop and archbishop; see *L. & P.*, vii, 1378, 1379.
[2] See pp. 290, 291.
[3] Roper, 77, 78. See also the *Rastell Fragments* printed in Harpsfield, 228. See p. 291, note 3.
[4] 26 Hen. VIII, c. 2 (printed in *Statutes of the Realm*, iii, 492, 493; G. & H., 244-7.

that 'at the day of the last prorogation of this present parliament' the members of both houses of parliament had taken 'such oath as then was devised in writing', adding that it was 'meant and intended to mean at that time that every other the king's subjects should be bound to accept and take the same'. The tenor of the oath was then set out and it agrees with only minor verbal variations, with the oath printed earlier.[1] The recited oath was then declared to be valid and to be the oath intended by the Act of Succession. Finally it was provided that a certificate of any refusal to take the oath before commissioners should be taken as an indictment for such refusal and process had thereon.

This was followed by an act which must have taxed to the limit Cromwell's skill as a draftsman. This act appropriated to the king all first fruits and tenths,[2] but since the act of 1532,[3] in conditional restraint of annates, had prohibited the payment of these sums to the pope because they had become, it was said, 'intolerable and importable' and had 'risen, grown and increased by an uncharitable custom grounded upon no just or good title', their appropriation to the king placed Henry in a position of some delicacy; the preamble to this act may, therefore, be judged a triumph of verbal ingenuity.

Parliament was then asked to complete the statutory structure by providing stringent penalties against those who sought to interfere with Henry's religious settlement, and they passed the Treason Act.[4] This act had no logical connection with the Treason Act of 1351 but merely converted into crimes certain things that had no other characteristic than their heinousness in the eyes of the king; if a subject failed to follow his king in matters of religious belief then he was to be made a traitor. The act provided that a person committed treason if, after 1 February 1535, he should maliciously attempt, by words or writing, to do any bodily harm to the king, the queen or their heirs apparent, or to deprive them or any of them of any of their royal titles, or if he should maliciously publish by words or writing that the king was a heretic, schismatic, tyrant, infidel or usurper; and the act provided, rather incongruously, that a person should also be guilty of treason if he rebel-

---

[1] See p. 288.
[2] 26 Hen. VIII, c. 3 (printed in *Statutes of the Realm*, iii, 493).
[3] See p. 185.
[4] 26 Hen. VIII, c. 13 (printed in *Statutes of the Realm*, iii, 508, 509; *G. & H.*, 247-51).

liously detained or kept any of the king's ships, ammunition or artillery. No such traitor was to have benefit of sanctuary, and provision was made for inquiry as to treasons committed by residents abroad who, upon conviction, were to be outlawed. Any person convicted of treason under the act was to suffer death as was customary in cases of high treason and forfeiture of his lands. Since the Act of Supremacy conferred upon the king the title of supreme head of the Church of England, it will be seen that denial of the royal supremacy now became treason.

Henry had not obtained parliamentary assent to the Treason Act without difficulty.[1] The origins of the act are to be found in a draft bill that was prepared for the session of parliament that began in January 1531. It seems probable that no bill was then introduced, but the draft was used as the basis for a further bill for the session of January 1532; this draft was amended but was then abandoned.[2] The bill introduced in the second session of 1534 was based on the earlier drafts and was itself further amended. All these drafts were corrected by the same hand, that of Cromwell, and the final document is identical with the act as passed.[3]

The two drafts used in 1534 throw an interesting light on the assertion, frequently made by biographers of Sir Thomas More, that the commons could be induced to pass the Treason Act only by the insertion of the word 'maliciously'. This assertion is based on the statement of William Rastell in one of the extant fragments of his biography of More, to the effect that the commons refused to pass the bill unless its rigour were modified by the insertion of the word 'maliciously',[4] and on a statement

---

[1] For the history of the gestation of the Treason Act of 1534 see Thornley, 'The Treason Legislation of Henry VIII (1531-1534)', *Trans. Roy. Hist. Soc.*, 3rd ser., xi (1917), 87-123. Miss Thornley's paper should, however, be read with great circumspection, as it is erroneous in some places and misleading in others. In particular, her observations on 'treason by words' need modification.

[2] These drafts are calendared, respectively, at *L. & P.*, v, 52(1), 52(2), and *L. & P.*, vii, 1381(5). See Thornley, op. cit. 88 et seq.

[3] The drafts of 1534 are calendared at *L. & P.*, vii, 1381(4) and 1381(3).

[4] *Rastell Fragments*, printed in Harpsfield, 221, at p.229: 'Note diligently here þat þe bill was earnestly withstode, and coulde not be suffered to pass, vnlesse þe rigor of it were qalified with this worde "maliciusly"; and so not eueri spekinge againste þe supreamacey to be treason, but onlei maliciusly spekinge, and so, for more playne declaracion therof, þe word "maliciusly" was twise put into þe acte, . . .' Rastell was More's nephew and a lawyer; he wrote his lost *Life* of More some twenty-five years after More's death in 1535; the extant fragments relate chiefly to Fisher. cf. *Life of Fisher.* 101, 102.

made to John Fisher in the Tower by his brother, Robert, and reported by his servant, Richard Wilson, when interrogated in June 1535.[1] Each of the drafts of 1534, however, contained the word 'maliciously' as it appears in the act and the word thus seems to have been in the original bill that was first introduced into parliament in 1534.[2] If this is so, as seems probable, it is difficult to account for the stories of Rastell and Robert Fisher, although it is clear from the extensive amendments made in the drafts that the bill did not have an easy passage.

3

Henry's long battle with the pope was now over. The spiritual authority which had existed in England for many centuries had been totally eradicated; the ancient spiritual allegiance of Englishmen was no more and the king was now pope in his own realm. The long struggle had brought about a profound religious revolution that has lasted for centuries, but Henry's religious changes, despite their fundamental nature, were accepted with docility by the whole country with few (but notable) exceptions. The quiet acceptance of this revolution was ensured by the savage penalties provided by parliament for those who should question it, and there began a bloody tyranny that can only be equalled in our own day. Soon after parliament had completed the statutory structure supporting Henry's religious innovations, the executions began. The king found it intolerable that men who had earned the respect of the whole of England, and even of Europe, by the quality of their learning and the integrity of their lives, should refuse to acquiesce in the new religious arrangements and, by their refusal, proclaim their condemnation of them. In 1535 men of the greatest eminence were put to death: the Carthusian priors, and Richard Reynolds, John Fisher and Thomas More were ready to go to the barbarous deaths provided for them rather than compromise their consciences by a denial of their fundamental religious beliefs. Europe was aghast at the death of such men.

[1] See 'Answers by confession of Richard Wilson', 11 June 1535 (*L. & P.*, viii, 856 (p. 326)). Wilson said that Robert Fisher told the bishop: 'But there was never such a sticking at the passing of any Act in the Lower House as was at the passing of the same, said he; and that they stuck at the last to have one word in the same, and that was the word *maliciously*, . . .'
[2] cf. Thornley, op. cit. 123.

But what of Anne Boleyn who had been the cause of all the upheaval? Her time of triumph did not endure for long; less than eighteen months after her coronation Henry's affections were engaged elsewhere. In the late summer of 1534 it was known that Henry was in love with another woman whom Chapuys described as 'a very beautiful damsel [*demoiselle*] of the court'.[1] It seems that she had already acquired considerable influence with the king, at the expense of that of Anne Boleyn who was considerably put out by the king's infatuation; but Anne's attempts to induce Henry to get rid of his new favourite met with no success; she was reminded of her humble origins and told that she should be well satisfied with what the king had already done for her, since he would not do the same again if things were to begin anew. Anne Boleyn's sister-in-law, lady Rochford, had lent her aid in the attempt to drive the new favourite away and was banished from the court for her pains. The new turn of affairs was welcomed by the court, who had suffered from the insolence of the lady Anne. Meanwhile the newcomer enjoyed her increasing influence with the king and sent a message to princess Mary telling her to be of good cheer as her troubles would be over sooner than she supposed; the new favourite assured her that when an opportunity occurred she would show herself to be her true and devoted servant.[2]

Anne Boleyn survived this crisis in her affairs, but not for long. She gave birth to a stillborn child in January 1536, at a time when Henry had become attracted to Jane Seymour, a lady whom a group of the old nobility had coached in the art of capturing the king's affections. Almost coincidentally Catherine of Aragon died on 8 January 1536, and this event sealed the fate of Anne Boleyn; for, as Chapuys remarked, although the world at large would never recognize queen Anne as the king's wife, now that Catherine was dead it might be induced to recognize a new wife as queen. Charges of adultery were soon brought against Anne Boleyn, and on 15 May she was convicted of high treason and condemned

---

[1] The identity of the young lady is unknown. It is tempting to identify her with Jane Seymour, but it is likely that it was some other person.
[2] Chapuys to Charles V, 27 Sept. 1534 (*L. & P.*, vii, 1193); Chapuys to Charles V, 13 Oct. 1534 (*L. & P.*, vii, 1257); count of Cifuentes to Charles V, 18 Oct. 1534 (*L. & P.*, vii, 1279); Chapuys to Charles V, 24 Oct. 1534 (*L. & P.*, vii, 1297 (p. 498)). It is of interest to note that information concerning the new royal favourite reached Cifuentes in Rome from a French source a week before Chapuys first reported the matter to the emperor; see count of Cifuentes to Charles V, 20 Sept. 1534 (*L. & P.*, vii, 1174).

to death. Her execution had been fixed for 17 May but it was postponed for forty-eight hours to enable Cranmer, in a closed court at Lambeth, to give judgment declaring void the marriage between Henry and Anne which, three years earlier, he had declared to be valid; it need hardly be said that the grounds of the judgment were not stated. Anne Boleyn was executed on 19 May 1536.

Parliament, it will be recalled, had re-assembled on 3 November 1534,[1] to put the finishing touches to Henry's religious revolution. A few weeks earlier Henry's old enemy, Clement VII, died on 25 September 1534. It seemed, at first, that Henry would be presented with a favourable opportunity to make his peace with Rome; and several members of the council believed that with the election of a new pope Henry would resume his obedience to the church. When news of the pope's fatal illness reached England the duke of Norfolk and the marquis of Dorset suggested to him that he should make no difficulty in coming to an arrangement with the new pope. Henry was not pleased by this suggestion; no one, he said, should mock him by advising such a thing, for the regard that he would have for any pope in the world that might be chosen would be no greater than what he had for the meanest priest in his kingdom.[2] The breach with Rome was complete.

[1] See p. 294.
[2] Chapuys to Charles V, 13 Oct. 1534 (*L. & P.*, vii, 1257).

INDEX

Abell, Thomas, M.A. (chaplain to Catherine), 83

Accolti, Benedict de (cardinal of Ravenna; nephew of Pietro de Accolti; called 'the young man'), 178n

Accolti, Pietro de (cardinal of Ancona; bishop of Sabino; called 'the old man'), 139n, 178

Affinity, impediment of, its nature, 16n; arises from carnal knowledge, 74, 127; development of, 127, 128; second and third kinds of, 127n. Other reference, 75n

Ahab, 199

Aleander, Jerome (papal nuncio), 174

Alessandria, 36

Alexander III (pope), 127n.

Alexander VI (pope), 6, 128

Allen, John, 12

Alleyn, John, 201

Aloisio, Juan, 178

Amiens, 2

Ampthill, 200, 235, 241

Ancona, cardinal of. See Accolti, Pietro de

Angers, 124, 137

Angoulême, comte de, 202

Annates, their nature 185; an old grievance, 185n; bill regulating, 183; act in conditional restraint of, 183, 185, 186; act brought into force, 186n, 251; act in full restraint of, 275; appropriated to king, 296

Answer of the Ordinaries, 189, 190

Appeals, ecclesiastical, bill in restraint of, 218-224; effect of act, 223, 224; to Rome, prohibited, 276

Aquinas, St Thomas, 128, 129

Aracoeli, cardinal, 40

Arthur, prince (son of Henry VII), 5, 226, 278

Articles, The, 259-262, 269n, 271, 272, 273

Arundel, Thomas, 96

Assertio Septem Sacramentarum, 130, 131

Asti, 36

Astrologers, and birth of Elizabeth, 255

Audley, Sir Thomas (afterwards baron Audley of Walden), elected Speaker, 117; appointed lord keeper, 193; and bill in restraint of appeals, 218; appointed lord chancellor, 218n; commissioner for administering oath, 287; said to have amplified oath, 295; administers oath to More, 290n

Augsburg, 270

Augustinis, Augustine de, 171

Authority of pope 'usurped', 269

Avalos, Rodrigo d', sent to Rome, 248; his instructions, 248, 249; his difficulties, 250; leaves Rome, 253

Avignon, 16

Avocation of cause, fears of, 103, 105, 107n; requests for, 91, 93, 95, 105, 106, 107; Wolsey realizes it is inevitable, 108; decree for, 108, 109; effect of, 132. Other references, 84, 97, 106, 132

Babylonian Captivity of the Church, The, 130

Bangor, bishop of. See Skevington, Thomas

Barcelona, treaty of, 106, 133

Bardi, Francesco, 148

Barlow, John, 26, 30, 36, 54, 56

Barlow, William, D.D., 26n

Barnes, Robert, D.D. (Austin friar), 172

Barton, Elizabeth (Nun of Kent), 280

Bath and Wells, bishop of. See Clerk, John

Bath House, 63, 65

Beaulieu, 257

Index

Index

Henry VIII—*cont.*

finds him adamant, 84; impatient at slow progress, 85; threatens to throw off allegiance to pope, 86; angered by pessimism of ambassadors, 87; proposes appeal to true vicar of Christ, 97; his representatives at legatine court, 98; anxious about peace negotiations, 100; his private discussion with Campeggio, 101; his protest against marriage treaty read at trial, 104; present at last sitting of court, 104; informed by pope of avocation, 109, 110; his shock at avocation, 109; complains of avocation to pope, 110

Summons parliament, 113; his relations with parliament, 114, 115; and possible summons to Rome, 114, 115; hunts at Waltham, 120; learns of Cranmer's qualities, 122; instructs Cranmer to study divorce, 122; and papal dispensing power, 125, 128; changes his ground, 126; his dispensation only second of its kind, 128; his case discussed by Cajetan, 128-130; his indecision after avocation, 132; his need for delay, 132; sends Thomas Boleyn to emperor, 133; threatens settlement of marriage problem by parliament, 134; agrees to suspension of papal hearing, 135; summons notables to write to pope, 136; his letter of complaint to pope, 137, 138; rejects pope's suggestion of two wives, 138; forbids purchase of bulls, etc., 140; summons nuncio, 140; suggests appeal to general council, 140, 141; wishes English custom to be raised with pope, 141; his cause espoused by Francis I, 141; his perplexity increases, 143

His vacillation ends, 147; Cromwell suggests his headship of Church, 147; demands compliance of pope, 147, 148; sends Carne to Rome, 148; forbidden by pope to remarry, 149; demands £100,000 in praemunire proceedings, 155; refuses grant of Convocation, 156; demands title of head of church, 156; recognized as head by Convocation, 157; agrees to pardon of laity, 159; plans proceedings in court of Canterbury, 163; instructs Benet to delay cause in Rome, 164; puts pressure on Catherine, 164, 165; at Windsor, 166; his relations with Catherine reach crisis, 166; parts from Catherine, 167; dines at Ely House, 168n; instructs Benet to obtain remission of cause, 169; instructs ambassadors to leave Rome if sentence given against him, 170, 174; his concern with heresy, 170-172; angry with More, 171n; recalls Benet, 175; refuses to plead in Rome, 176; sends Benet back to Rome, 176; tells nuncio pope is unlearned and venial, 178; rumours of his cohabitation with Anne, 178; ordered by pope to dismiss Anne, 178

Receives Commons' Supplication, 185, 188; sends copy of Annates Act to Rome, 187; passes Supplication to Warham, 189; demands submission of Convocation, 190; delivers Answer of Ordinaries to Speaker, 191; receives Submission from bishops, 192; and pope's brief, 193; his treatment of Catherine, 194; receives pope's brief, 194; popular feeling against him, 197, 198; hears Peto's sermon, 189, 199; rebukes Peto, 199; arranges for sermon by Curwen, 199; demands degradation of Elstowe, 199, 200; prepares for meeting with Francis I, 202; rumour of his marriage to Anne in France, 203; rumour of his marriage to French princess, 203, 204; rumour that he was tiring of Anne, 204; forbidden by pope to divorce Catherine, 204, 205; receives pope's brief, 209; and meeting of pope and Francis I, 210, 229; and trial in neutral place, 210, 211; and

Index